❖ ENJOYING ROSES

Enjoying Roses

CREATED BY

THE EDITORIAL STAFF OF ORTHO BOOKS

PROJECT EDITOR

JANET GOLDENBERG

WRITER

ANN REILLY

PRINCIPAL PHOTOGRAPHER

SAXON HOLT

ILLUSTRATORS

CYNDIE C. H. WOOLEY
RON HILDEBRAND

DESIGNER

GARY HESPENHEIDE

Ortho Books

PUBLISHER
Richard E. Pile, Jr.

EDITORIAL DIRECTOR
Christine Jordan

PRODUCTION DIRECTOR
Ernie S. Tasaki

MANAGING EDITORS
Robert J. Beckstrom
Michael D. Smith
Sally W. Smith

SYSTEM MANAGER
Linda M. Bouchard

MARKETING SPECIALIST
Daniel Stage

SALES MANAGER
Thomas J. Leahy

DISTRIBUTION SPECIALIST
Barbara F. Steadham

TECHNICAL CONSULTANT
J. A. Crozier, Jr., Ph.D.

> This book is dedicated
> to the memory of
> Georgiann Wright

Address all inquiries to:
Ortho Books
Chevron Chemical Company
Consumer Products Division
Box 5047
San Ramon, CA 94583

Copyright © 1992
Chevron Chemical Company
All rights reserved under international and Pan-American copyright conventions.

1 2 3 4 5 6 7 8 9
92 93 94 95 96 97

ISBN 0-89721-242-8
Library of Congress Catalog Card
Number 92-70585

Chevron Chemical Company
6001 Bollinger Canyon Road, San Ramon, CA 94583

CONSULTANT
Don Ballin

PHOTO EDITOR
Judy Mason

PHOTO RESEARCHER
Sarah Bendersky

FOOD CONSULTANT
Terri P. Wuerthner

ASSOCIATE ILLUSTRATOR
Wayne Clark

COPY CHIEF
Melinda E. Levine

COPYEDITOR
David Sweet

EDITORIAL COORDINATOR
Cass Dempsey

PROOFREADER
Deborah Bruner

INDEXER
Trisha Feuerstein

COMPOSITION BY
Laurie A. Steele

LAYOUT & PRODUCTION BY
Studio 165

ASSOCIATE EDITOR
Sara Shopkow

SEPARATIONS BY
Color Tech Corp.

LITHOGRAPHED IN THE USA BY
Webcrafters, Inc.

PRINCIPAL PHOTO LOCATIONS
Berkeley Rose Garden; Berkeley, Calif.
Brooklyn Botanic Garden; Brooklyn, N.Y.
Empire Mine State Historical Park; Grass Valley, Calif.
Filoli House and Gardens; Woodside, Calif.
Heritage Rose Gardens; Fort Bragg, Calif.
Huntington Botanical Gardens; San Marino, Calif.
Korbel Champagne Cellars; Guerneville, Calif.
Miniature Plant Kingdom; Sebastopol, Calif.
Rose Acres; Diamond Springs, Calif.
Rose Hills Memorial Park; Whittier, Calif.
Miriam Wilkins garden; El Cerrito, Calif.

ADDITIONAL PHOTOGRAPHIC CREDITS APPEAR ON PAGE 352.

SPECIAL THANKS TO
Russell Battle, Berkeley Rose Garden; Berkeley, Calif.
Joe Burks, Cooperative Rose Growers; Tyler, Tex.
Nancy Butler, Jackson and Perkins Co.; Medford, Oreg.
Linda Coppolino, Caswell-Massey Co., Ltd.; Edison, N.J.
Joyce Dimits; Fort Bragg, Calif.
Vincent Gioia, Christie, Parker & Hale; Pasadena, Calif.
Muriel Humenick; Diamond Springs, Calif.
James Kish and Dave McGraw, Copy Service Center; San Francisco
Jean and Troy Kitchens; Napa, Calif.
Clair G. Martin III, Huntington Botanical Gardens; San Marino, Calif.
Dale and Dorothy Mecham; Richmond, Calif.
Barbara Pitschel, Helen Crocker Russell Library of Horticulture; San Francisco
Phillip Robinson, F. Korbel and Bros., Inc.; Guerneville, Calif.
Omer Schneider, DeVor Nurseries; Freedom, Calif.
Sara Slavin; San Francisco
Angie Slicker, Empire Mine State Historical Park; Grass Valley, Calif.
Gordon Smith, Bear Creek Production Co.; Wasco, Calif.
Carol Spiers, American Rose Society; Shreveport, La.
Freeland Tanner, Proscape Landscape Design; Napa, Calif.
Patty Vandenberghe; Danville, Calif.
Van Winden's Garden Center; Napa, Calif.
Miriam Wilkins; El Cerrito, Calif.

FRONT COVER
'Queen Elizabeth' grandiflora

BACK COVER
Left: Pink climbers on a stone fence
Center: 'Simplicity' floribundas
Right: Pruning miniature roses

CONTENTS

Roses evoke a romantic past at Sissinghurst Castle in England.

CHAPTER ONE

HISTORY AND LORE

he roses we grow in our gardens today have a complex and intriguing history. For thousands of years, people around the world have reserved a special place for these exquisite flowers—both in their gardens and in their art, literature, and lore. Thanks to the efforts of rose breeders through the centuries, roses now exist in a prodigious variety of colors and forms.

*T*hroughout history no flower has been so loved, revered, or renowned as the rose. It is older than the human hands that first cared for it, drew pictures of it, and celebrated it in music and lore. Forty million years ago, a rose left its imprint on a slate deposit at the Florissant Fossil Beds in Colorado, and fossils of roses from Oregon and Montana date back 35 million years, long before humans existed. Fossils have also been found in Germany and in Yugoslavia. Roses grow wild as far north as Norway and Alaska and as far south as Mexico and North Africa, but no wild roses have ever been found to grow below the equator.

HISTORY AND DEVELOPMENT OF THE ROSE

An 18th-century porcelain bowl from the Qing dynasty period depicts a stylized rose. The Chinese may have been the first to cultivate roses.

*T*he rose apparently originated in Central Asia about 60 to 70 million years ago, during the Eocene epoch, and spread over the entire Northern Hemisphere. Early civilizations, including the Chinese, the Egyptians, the Phoenicians, the Greeks, and the Romans, appreciated roses and grew them widely—as long as five thousand years ago.

About 500 B.C. Confucius wrote of roses growing in the Imperial Gardens and noted that the library of the Chinese emperor contained hundreds of books about roses. It is said that the rose gardeners of the Han dynasty (207 B.C.–A.D. 220) were so obsessed with this flower that their parks threatened to engulf land needed for producing food, and that the emperor ordered some rose gardens plowed under. Unfortunately, there is little surviving record of the evolution of the rose in Asia, although reference to it does appear in Asian art and literature.

The oldest rose we can identify today is *Rosa gallica,* also known as the French rose, which once bloomed wild throughout central and southern Europe and western Asia, and still survives there. Although the exact origin of *Rosa gallica* is unknown, traces of it appear as early as the twelfth century B.C., when the Persians considered it a symbol of love.

ROSES IN THE ANCIENT WORLD

Descending from *Rosa gallica* is *Rosa damascena,* the damask rose, whose well-known fragrance has been part of rose history since the rose first appeared in about 900 B.C. About 50 B.C. a North African variant called *Rosa damascena semperflorens,* the 'Autumn Damask', thrilled the Romans because it bloomed twice a year—a trait previously unknown to them. The 'Autumn Damask', which has been traced back to at least the fifth century B.C., is believed to be a cross between *Rosa gallica* and *Rosa moschata,* the musk rose. Until European merchants discovered the tea and China roses in the Orient many centuries later, this rose would be the only repeat bloomer known to the Western world.

Another important early rose was *Rosa alba,* the 'White Rose of York'. Made famous as the emblem of the House of York during the fifteenth-century Wars of the Roses, this five-petaled rose is actually far older, dating to before the second century A.D. It probably originated in the Caucasus and traveled west by way of Greece and Rome. *Rosa alba* and its relatives, known as albas, are believed to have descended from some combination of *Rosa gallica, Rosa damascena, Rosa canina,* and *Rosa corymbifera.*

The early Phoenicians, Greeks, and Romans all grew and traded in roses, which they brought with them as they traveled and conquered. As a result, roses spread throughout the Middle East and elsewhere in the Mediterranean.

The Greek scientist and writer Theophrastus, cataloging roses known about 300 B.C., described their flowers as having anywhere from five to one hundred petals. His was the first known detailed botanical description of a rose. Alexander the Great, king of Macedonia around this

time, grew roses in his garden and is credited for introducing cultivated roses into Europe. He may have had something to do with rose growing in Egypt, too.

In 1888 English archaeologist Sir Flinders Petrie, while excavating tombs in Upper Egypt, found the remains of rose garlands that had been used as a funeral wreath in the second century A.D. He identified the rose as *Rosa × richardii,* a cross of *Rosa gallica* and *Rosa phoenicia* known commonly as the 'Holy Rose of Abyssinia', or 'St. John's Rose'. The petals, though shriveled, had retained their pink color and, when soaked in water, were restored to a nearly lifelike state. Other researchers have found paintings of roses on the wall of the tomb of Thutmose IV, who died in the fourteenth century B.C. References to the rose have been deciphered in hieroglyphics.

In ancient Rome patricians tended rose gardens at their homes, and public rose gardens were a favorite place to pass a summer afternoon. Records show that there were two thousand public gardens

The 'Apothecary's Rose', Rosa gallica officinalis, is one of the oldest garden roses.

A Rose Family Tree

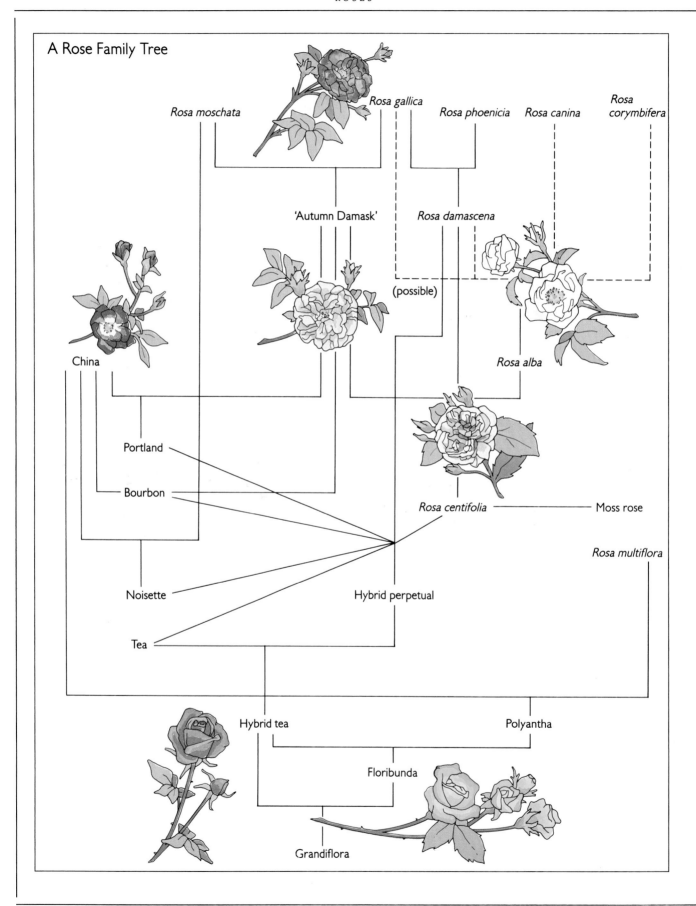

in Rome before its fall in A.D. 476. The poet and satirist Horace complained about the shortsightedness of the Roman government for allowing rose gardens to be planted where the land should have been used for wheat fields and orchards. However, he was not opposed to taking advantage of their abundance: He wrote that mixing rose petals in wine relieved hangovers.

MEDIEVAL ROSES

After the fall of the Roman Empire, as Europeans struggled to survive the on-slaught of armies and marauders, rose gardening became impossible for all but a few. Charlemagne (A.D. 742–814) grew roses on the palace grounds at Aix-la-Chapelle, but it was primarily the monks who kept roses alive, growing them and other plants for a variety of medicinal uses. Monasteries of the Benedictine or-der in particular became centers of botanical research.

As social conditions stabilized, about A.D. 1000, roses began to reappear in private gardens. During the twelfth and thirteenth centuries, soldiers returning from the Crusades in the Middle East brought back tales of extravagant rose gardens, as well as sample plants. Travel increased everywhere, and traders, diplo-mats, and scholars began to exchange roses and other plants. Interest in the rose was rekindled.

Early herbalists give testimony to the burgeoning knowledge of roses. John Gerard, an English herbalist who was also treasurer to Elizabeth I, wrote in his *Herball* in 1597 that 14 kinds of roses were known. By 1629, John Parkinson, the apothecary to James I, had reported 24 different roses in his herbal *Paradisus*. At the end of the 1700s, the English artist Mary Lawrance identified and illustrated some ninety different roses in a book titled *A Collection of Roses from Nature*— and there were only a small fraction of the roses then known.

Pink and coral climbers scale a weathered Italian wall. The descendants of many ancient roses still flourish around the Mediterranean.

With an amazing 100 petals, the cabbage rose created a sensation when introduced in 17th-century Europe. It was probably a hybrid of many ancient roses.

Captain John Smith wrote of the Indians of the James River Valley planting wild roses to beautify their villages, thus making roses one of the first North American native plants to be widely cultivated as an ornamental. Edward Winslow, a founder of the Plymouth Colony, reported that in 1621 the Pilgrims had planted "an abundance of roses, white, red, and damask, single but very sweete indeed."

When William Penn, the founder of Pennsylvania, lived in Europe in the late 1600s, he observed that roses enjoyed high favor in gardens as well as in the arts and sciences. Returning to America in 1699, he brought 18 rosebushes with him. He later discussed their beauty and medicinal virtue in a *Book of Physic* for the medical care of Pennsylvania settlers.

One marvel Penn had undoubtedly beheld in Europe (if he had not already seen it in the colonies) was *Rosa centifolia,* the cabbage rose. True to its botanical name, this rose has an astounding 100 petals, so densely arrayed that the flowers resemble small cabbages. Once thought to be ancient—perhaps the 100-petaled rose described by Pliny the Elder in the first century A.D.—the cabbage rose is now considered by many to be a product of late seventeenth-century Dutch rose growers. Others believe that it was imported from Asia in 1596. Whatever its history, the cabbage rose is probably a complex hybrid of many ancient roses, including the gallicas, damasks, and albas.

A famous sport (mutation) of the cabbage rose is *Rosa centifolia muscosa,* the moss rose, which appeared about 1700 and is still grown and used in hybridizing. It has tiny, highly fragrant, mosslike hairs along its stems and flower buds.

Although European hybridizers were busy during this period, they based their introductions on a limited gene pool, which made novelty hard to achieve. Moreover, the laws of heredity were poorly understood—a handicap that was

ROSES IN THE NEW WORLD

Across the Atlantic many separate strains of roses had arisen in the wilds of North America. Of some 200 rose species now known worldwide, 35 are indigenous to the United States, making the rose as much a native of North America as the bald eagle. These roses include *Rosa virginiana,* the first American species mentioned in European literature; *Rosa carolina,* the 'Pasture Rose'; *Rosa setigera,* the 'Prairie Rose'; *Rosa californica; Rosa woodsii;* and *Rosa palustris,* the 'Swamp Rose', named for the environment in which it grows best.

to persist until well after Gregor Mendel conducted his research in the mid-1800s. In addition, early breeders guarded their methods with paranoiac jealousy, worried that competitors would put them out of business. (Today's breeders are far more communicative, having learned that sharing knowledge benefits them all.)

ROSES FROM THE ORIENT

A revolution in rose breeding and growing took place in Europe in the eighteenth and nineteenth centuries when increased trade with the Orient brought *Rosa chinensis,* the China rose, to the attention of Europeans. 'Old Blush', the first variety of China rose to reach the West, was introduced into Sweden in 1752 and into the rest of Europe by 1793. *Rosa × odorata,* the tea rose, followed in 1808 or 1809. It was so named because of the tealike scent of its foliage.

Although the Chinese had grown these and other roses for centuries, their impact in Europe was truly phenomenal. Their most remarkable quality—continual repeat blooming—was completely unknown in Europe at the time and made them an instant sensation. Unlike the repeat-blooming 'Autumn Damask', which blooms briefly twice a year, continual repeat bloomers produce flowers over an extended period during the growing season. In addition to its flowering capabilities, the China rose possesses a foliage that is almost evergreen, and the tea rose a foliage that is resistant to mildew. European rose breeders were eager to marry these traits into existing rose lines. Indeed, the China and tea roses laid the genetic foundation for almost all modern roses. Unfortunately, they also passed on a lack of cold hardiness to many of their descendants.

The China rose had also been called the Bengal rose because it was imported to the West from Calcutta, the region's

New discoveries such as the American Rosa virginiana *(top), the European moss rose (center), and the China rose (bottom) expanded the horizons of Western rose fanciers.*

Left: The Chinese tea rose introduced mildew resistance and later became a parent of the hybrid tea. Shown here is 'Souvenir d'un Ami'.

Right: The Portland rose was one of the first good hybrids of European and Chinese roses. This is 'Comte de Chambord'.

capital. In the eighteenth century a large botanical garden flourished there, containing roses brought from China by merchants of the British East India Company. In 1789 a British sea captain took a plant home to England. Beginning in 1793, more specimens were shipped from Calcutta to many parts of Europe by Dr. William Roxburgh, the director of the company.

In the British colonies in America, rose commerce was active during the eighteenth century. Robert Prince opened the first American nursery in Flushing, Long Island, in 1737, and started to import a mounting assortment of new plants. By 1746 he advertised 1,600 varieties of roses—no doubt one of the largest collections in the world at that time. Prince's records show that in 1791, Thomas Jefferson ordered two centifolias, a 'Common Moss', a 'Rosa Mundi', an unidentified yellow, a musk rose, and, quite interestingly, a China rose. Since China roses did not reach most of Europe

until 1793, it is possible that the rose traveled directly from Asia, on a clipper ship that crossed the Pacific by way of Cape Horn.

Jefferson was not the only president interested in growing roses. George Washington, his predecessor, cultivated roses at Mount Vernon, and from his garden came the hybrid 'Mary Washington' rose. It is not known whether this rose was an accidental cross, or whether the nation's first president was also the nation's first hybridizer.

The Portlands were a class of rose that came into being about 1800, probably derived from a cross of the 'Autumn Damask' with the China rose and *Rosa gallica*. Named for the duchess of Portland, the Portlands were one of the first good garden hybrids to meld East and West, possessing the repeat-blooming ability of their China rose parent. Also called damask perpetuals, the Portlands were grown until the hybrid perpetual was introduced almost forty years later.

JOSEPHINE AND MALMAISON

No one did more to popularize the rose at the beginning of the 1800s than Empress Josephine, wife of Napoleon I. An ardent lover of the rose (one of her middle names was Rose), she started a "rose renaissance" by attempting to grow every known variety in her garden at Malmaison, near Paris.

In the 16 years between 1798, when she first started the garden, and 1814, when she died a month before her fifty-first birthday, she collected 250 rose specimens. To support her hobby, Napoleon ordered his captains to bring home any new rose they found blooming on foreign shores. So widely esteemed was her garden that the English, who were at war with the French, allowed plants for Josephine to cross blockades and permitted her head gardener to travel freely across the Channel. The reputation of Josephine's garden spread across Europe, igniting an interest in rose growing and hybridizing that would eventually lead to the birth of modern roses.

More than half of Josephine's roses were gallicas. The rest consisted of 27 centifolias, 22 Chinas, 9 damasks, 3 mosses, 11 species, 4 spinosissimas, 8 albas, 3 foetidas, and 1 musk. (Each of these rose classes is described in Chapter 2.) The empress's roses are a fair representation of those that were popular among all classes of Europeans during the Napoleonic era.

Because of the prestigious gardens at Malmaison, France became a leading grower and exporter of roses. In 1815 some 2,000 varieties of roses were available from French growers. That figure jumped to 5,000 varieties in only 10 years. French growers also exported roses to New Orleans and cities up the Mississippi River before the Civil War. Southern gardeners found the tender China and tea roses especially suited to their warm climate.

Napoleon presents his wife with roses in her legendary garden. Titled La Rose de la Malmaison, *this tribute by Jean-Louis Viger du Vigneau was painted about 50 years after Josephine's death.*

THE RISE OF THE HYBRID TEA

The Bourbon rose, *Rosa × borboniana*, was brought to France in 1817 from the island of Réunion (then called Île de Bourbon) near Madagascar in the Indian Ocean. Its background is unknown, but it is probably a natural hybrid of *Rosa chinensis* and the 'Autumn Damask', since both roses were grown as hedges on the island. The Bourbon rose quickly became one of the most popular roses of the early nineteenth century because of its recurrent bloom. Like the Portlands, it was one of the first to combine the best of the European and Oriental roses. The original Bourbon was bright pink; this rose is now lost, but among the many remaining hybrids of the Bourbon is one that was a primary source of red in today's roses.

Another product of a crossing of European and Oriental roses was the hybrid China class. These tall and somewhat unattractive plants did not repeat bloom well, and never became popular on their own. They were, however, among the ancestors of the hybrid perpetuals, polyanthas, floribundas, and hybrid teas.

In quest of roses and other plants, The Royal Horticultural Society of Great Britain sent a young Scot, Robert Fortune, to the Orient with 50 pounds sterling, a brace of shotguns, and instructions to bring back new plants of any kind. From 1843 to 1845, Fortune traveled to the major ports of China, which had recently been forced open to foreign trade. He returned to England with 190 rose varieties, 120 of which were new to Europe. Fortune made three more botanical forays to the Orient, during the last of which he gathered roses in Japan.

An American contribution to the history of the nineteenth-century rose was the noisette rose, *Rosa noisettiana*, the first rose known to be hybridized in America. (Although tradition has it that the American hybrid 'Mary Washington'

Top: The repeat-blooming Bourbon rose was brought to France from the isle of Bourbon (now Réunion) near Madagascar. This is 'La Reine Victoria', introduced in 1872.

Bottom: 'Mary Washington', a hybrid musk now classified as a noisette, is said to have originated in the garden of George Washington.

had appeared years before in George Washington's garden, it is not known whether this rose was created deliberately or accidentally.) The noisette rose was a cross between *Rosa moschata,* the musk rose, and *Rosa chinensis,* the China rose. It was hybridized in 1812 by a South Carolina rice grower named John Champneys, who called his creation 'Champneys' Pink Cluster'. But he lacked interest in marketing the rose, so he gave a cutting to his neighbor Philippe Noisette. Philippe, in turn, sent it to his brother Louis, a nurseryman in Paris. By crossing this low-growing rose with other, taller roses, Louis developed a tall new rose that he dubbed 'Blush Noisette'—uncharitably snubbing the original hybridizer.

In the 1840s explorer Captain John Charles Frémont wrote of the roses growing in virgin prairies 500 miles west of St. Louis: "Everywhere the rose is met with, and reminds us of cultivated gardens and civilization. It is scattered over the prairies in small bouquets, and, when glistening in the dew and swaying in the pleasant breeze of the early morning, is the most beautiful of the prairie flowers." When Frémont arrived in California, native roses awaited him there as well.

As pioneers crossed the United States, especially during the gold rush, they took with them frivolous things of beauty as well as essential things of life. Examples of the former were a hybrid of *Rosa foetida* called 'Harison's Yellow', now established in thickets across the country,

Old favorites such as the prolific 'Lady Banks' Rose' accompanied settlers as they crossed North America. Many such heirloom roses still survive in older gardens.

and *Rosa eglanteria,* with unique apple-scented foliage.

In the mid-1800s *Rosa rugosa,* well known as the rose of the seashore, came to the Western world from Japan. It does not hybridize well, and therefore has not contributed much to the history of roses. For over a thousand years, however, it has been valued for its crinkled foliage, single flowers, and copious production of hips, which are an excellent source of vitamin C.

The creation of modern roses was well under way by 1837, when most of the Chinese roses had traveled to Europe. That year saw the introduction of the hybrid perpetual, a complex French hybrid whose ancestors included the Bourbon, damask, China, Portland, cabbage, tea, and noisette roses. The hybrid perpetual was extremely hardy; its flowers were large and fragrant. Early varieties of hybrid perpetuals were pink, but when they were crossed with Bourbon roses, the Bourbons' red coloring entered the line.

Top: Hybrid perpetuals bloomed more often than other 19th-century roses and were very hardy. This is 'Baronne Prévost', introduced in 1842.

Bottom: Rosa rugosa came to the West from Japan. It thrives by the seashore.

The hybrid perpetual was not a true perpetual bloomer, but it did bloom more frequently than many other roses that were widely grown at the time.

The hybrid perpetuals remained popular until the turn of the century, when they were eclipsed by the superior hybrid tea. Unfortunately, most of them have been lost. Of the more than three thousand varieties hybridized during this golden age of roses—from the time of Josephine's garden at Malmaison through the assimilation of roses from the Orient—only about fifty varieties can be purchased today.

The result of a cross between a hybrid perpetual and a tea rose, the hybrid tea had a more compact growing habit and more dependable everblooming qualities than its hybrid perpetual parent. The first hybrid tea, 'La France', was introduced in 1867. The National Rose Society of Great Britain formally recognized the hybrid tea class in 1893. Since then it has been improved considerably, and it remains the most popular rose today.

The creation of the hybrid tea marked the start of a new era in rose breeding. All classes of roses in existence before 1867 were deemed old garden roses, whereas all new classes were to be called modern roses. These designations, subsequently endorsed by the American Rose Society, are still used.

By the end of the nineteenth century, many of the attributes of modern roses were in place except for one—the yellow to orange color range. Though appearing at times through genetic happenstance, yellow color had hitherto been a recessive trait that would always disappear under the dominant influence of pink.

In 1900, after 13 years of trying, French hybridizer Joseph Pernet-Ducher introduced 'Soleil d'Or', a cross between a red hybrid perpetual and 'Persian Yellow', *Rosa foetida persiana*, which had been brought from Persia to England by Sir Henry Willcock in 1837. This cross

created a yellow color that was able to survive interbreeding. Pernet-Ducher's 'Rayon d'Or', a golden yellow, soon followed. Thanks to these introductions, a range of colors never seen before in modern roses came into being: gold, copper, salmon, and apricot. Pernet-Ducher soon became known as the Wizard of Lyons, the town where he did his work. For the first 30 years of their existence, these roses formed a separate group called the Pernetianas. Later, for the sake of simplicity, they were merged with the hybrid tea class.

Unfortunately, 'Persian Yellow' and its fellow descendants of the Austrian rose, *Rosa foetida,* contributed not only their

'La France', the first hybrid tea, was more compact and repeated its bloom more dependably than its parents, a hybrid perpetual and a tea rose.

Top: 'Austrian Copper', an early bicolored rose, contributed yellow and orange coloring to modern roses.

Bottom: 'Soleil d'Or' was the first yellow hybrid tea whose coloring could be reliably inherited.

yellow color but also a susceptibility to black spot, a serious rose disease. Many of these roses were also not very hardy in winter, which is why most yellow roses today still do not survive cold winters without a great deal of care. One that did do well in the cold winters of colonial America was 'Austrian Copper', *Rosa foetida bicolor,* which had found its way from Asia Minor to Vienna before 1590.

Following soon after the yellow hybrid teas were modern roses with bicolored flowers. Several older roses (including 'Austrian Copper') had possessed this distinctive coloring, in which the inside and the outside of the petals have differ-ent hues, but none with the advantages of the hybrid tea. Combinations of red and yellow were the most prominent at first, but in time many other combina-tions emerged.

Hybrid tea roses resisted cold weather but were not vigorous growers, having spindly roots. In the late nineteenth century, nursery workers learned that these roses could be made to grow better if they were grafted onto the roots of *Rosa multiflora*, a vigorous plant with nondescript flowers. This practice continues today. Other roses onto whose roots modern roses are grafted include 'Dr. Huey', *Rosa × odorata,* and *Rosa manettii.*

On May 21, 1892, a dozen leading greenhouse rose growers in the United States signed a document creating the National Rose Society. Its goals were to stimulate and encourage the raising of new rose varieties in America, to establish rose exhibitions, and to rigorously classify roses. Membership was limited to professional rose growers; amateurs were not admitted. This rule was gradually relaxed, and today its successor, the American Rose Society, boasts some twenty thousand members, most of whom are amateurs.

TWENTIETH-CENTURY ROSES

At the beginning of the 1900s, Danish rose breeder Svend Poulsen hybridized many polyanthas. The polyantha was a new class of rose developed in the late nineteenth century by French nurseryman Jean Sisley, who crossed *Rosa multiflora* and a dwarf China rose. Polyanthas were low-growing bushes smothered in clusters of small flowers that bloomed repeatedly all summer. In much of his work, Poulsen used the East Asian species *Rosa wichuraiana,* which lent winter hardiness to its progeny.

In the 1920s Poulsen crossed the polyantha with the hybrid tea to produce the first floribundas: the pink 'Else Poulsen' and the red 'Kirsten Poulsen'. As its name implies, the floribunda has an abundance of flowers, a legacy of its polyantha parent. From its hybrid tea parent, the floribunda inherited plant height and long cutting stems.

Top: Polyantha roses, created in the late 1800s, were hardy, low-growing, prolific bloomers with small flowers. Shown here is 'The Fairy'.

Bottom: The free-flowering floribunda class was created by crossing a polyantha with a hybrid tea. This is 'Trumpeter'.

Left: Many climbers and ramblers descend from tall species roses. 'Tausendschön', shown here, is one of many ramblers that originated from Rosa multiflora.

Right: Semiclimbing kordesii shrub roses share a common ancestry with many climbers. This is the hybrid kordesii 'Dortmund'.

While the development of bush roses was unfolding, climbers were coming into being. Climbers have complex histories and lineages that are often difficult to trace. Many evolved from ramblers, the first of which was 'Crimson Rambler', an import from Japan in 1893. 'Crimson Rambler' was descended from *Rosa wichuraiana* and *Rosa multiflora*. Other climbing hybrids of *Rosa wichuraiana* are 'American Pillar', 'Blaze', 'Dr. W. Van Fleet', 'Dorothy Perkins', and 'New Dawn'. The large Bourbon roses also influenced climbers, as did the tall noisettes.

Other climbers are sports of bush roses that produced long, pliable canes; still others are descendants of large shrub roses. In recent years many have evolved from *Rosa kordesii*, a tall, semiclimbing shrub rose that resulted from a cross of

Rosa rugosa and *Rosa wichuraiana* in 1952. The hybrid musks, which are large shrubs or small climbers, were created in the 1920s from crosses between noisettes and *Rosa multiflora* ramblers.

Reimer Kordes, the twentieth-century German hybridizer who created *Rosa kordesii*, did a great deal of breeding using *Rosa spinosissima*, a rose that had existed since the Middle Ages or before. He crossed it with hybrid teas to develop a fine group of modern shrub roses called kordesii shrubs, including 'Frülingsgold' and 'Frülingsmorgen'. These are winter-hardy, low-maintenance plants, commonly found in public areas and along roadsides in Europe.

In 1930 an event took place that revolutionized the American plant world: the extension of U.S. patent law to include plants. Until that time, Americans had looked to Europe for most of their new rose varieties. Now that American cultivars could be protected by a 17-year patent, commercial hybridizers were freed from the fear of piracy, which had dampened their efforts in the past. The first plant of any type to receive a U.S. patent was a climbing rose called, appropriately, 'New Dawn'. Since 1930 thousands of American rose cultivars have received patents, placing the United States alongside Europe at the creative forefront of rose development.

The surge of innovation unleashed by the extended patent law presented a new dilemma for gardeners: how to choose from the many new varieties that now appeared each year. In 1938, determined to solve this problem, a group of U.S. rose producers and marketers formed the All-America Rose Selections (AARS). Its mission: to test and promote new varieties and to honor the most worthy with awards. Today, in more than two dozen

Top: Many new roses owe their existence to a 1930 patent law amendment that extended protection to plants. These roses have been cross-pollinated to produce new varieties for testing.

Bottom: The best new roses undergo a two-year trial at AARS test gardens around the country. This is the test garden at Washington Park in Portland, Oregon.

Top left: Many of today's miniatures descend from a species found in a Swiss window box around 1920. This miniature is 'Jeanne Lajoie'.

Top right: 'Tropicana' was the first orange-red hybrid tea.

Bottom: Grandifloras, such as 'Gold Medal', bloom in clusters like floribundas but have large flowers like hybrid teas.

test gardens around the country, new varieties undergo a two-year evaluation before the winners are decided. The AARS stamp of approval has become an important marketing tool for rose growers, and is the gardener's assurance that a rose will perform well in a range of soils and climates. A list of AARS winners appears on page 250. (The AARS, a nonprofit industry association, is not related to the American Rose Society [ARS].)

With the coming of World War II, the rose-hybridizing boom slowed down, especially in Europe, but resumed once the war ended. Despite the proliferation of forms and colors, one long-sought-after color range—pure orange to orange-red—was still lacking in modern roses. The floribunda 'Independence', introduced in 1951, was the first modern rose in this orange-red range. The key to its unique coloration was the pigment pelargonidin, which also gives geraniums their scarlet coloring. It was not until 1960, when the German hybridizing firm Rosen Tantau introduced 'Tropicana', that we had an orange-red hybrid tea.

In 1954 a new class of rose was created to accommodate the rose 'Queen Elizabeth'. Called grandiflora, this class resulted from crossing a hybrid tea with a floribunda. Its flowers resemble those of the hybrid tea, but they bloom in clusters like those of the floribunda.

Today, activity is high among growers of miniature roses, who are introducing many new varieties each year. The earliest known miniature was *Rosa chinensis minima*. Probably of Chinese origin, this rose inexplicably made its way to a botanical garden on the island of Mauritius in the Indian Ocean. An Englishman found it growing there and brought it home with him around 1815. For an unknown reason, it disappeared sometime afterward and was thought to be lost forever—until a Dr. Roulet, an officer in the Swiss reserves, found it growing in a window box in Switzerland around 1920. It was renamed *Rosa rouletii*.

California nurseryman Ralph Moore dedicated his life to breeding miniatures, and deserves much credit for their popularity. Instead of *Rosa rouletii*, he used 'Oakington Ruby', a 1933 miniature, to introduce dwarfness into his breeding line. Many other breeders, chief among them Harmon Saville of Rowley, Massachusetts, have also introduced large numbers of miniatures.

Today there are more than thirty thousand varieties of roses of all classes (some eleven thousand of these are hybrid teas). However, many of them, especially the older varieties, are no longer sold; they survive, if at all, only in private gardens. Sorting out their backgrounds and histories is frequently a difficult task. Some roses are natural hybrids, making their parentage virtually impossible to determine. Others are commercial hybrids whose lineage has been either lost or deliberately obscured in order to deter piracy. However, this has not stopped enthusiasts from attempting to reconstruct it. In growing numbers, they dedicate their spare time to combing old cemeteries and farmsteads, in search of forgotten roses that remain living links to the past.

ROSE LORE AND LEGEND

There are innumerable legends concerning roses—tales relating how, when, where, or why they came into being, or connecting them with historical persons or events. Roses also have many figurative associations: sensuality, romantic and erotic love, luxury, secrecy, and religious passion. Perhaps the contrast between the luxurious, fragrant flowers and their painful thorns is a reminder of the eternal truth that pleasure and pain exist together in the world. Whatever its inspiration, the lore of roses bears witness to the fascination these flowers have held for people throughout the ages.

EARLY MYTH AND HISTORY

Ancient history and legend are filled with references to the rose. It has been said, although certainly never proved, that roses grew in the Garden of Eden and the Hanging Gardens of Babylon. If Eden was

Cupid (Eros) rescues his lover Psyche from the clutches of Cupid's jealous mother, Venus (Aphrodite), in the 1871 painting Cupid Delivering Psyche *by Sir Edward Burne-Jones. Roses fall from the sky in token of their love.*

in Asia or the Middle East, as some scholars believe, the rose could well have grown there, because roses are known to predate the appearance of humans in the Northern Hemisphere. The Hanging Gardens were started about 1200 B.C. and continued through the time of King Nebuchadnezzar (605–562 B.C.). Because nearby gardens of the time are known to have included roses, it is very likely that roses grew among the plants in the Hanging Gardens as well.

Writings on clay tablets record that roses, grapes, and figs were part of the bounty won by King Sargon of Sumer in the Tigris-Euphrates valley between 2648 and 2630 B.C. Roses were probably included because they were important medicinally and because of their edible hips, or fruits.

The rose was the flower of Aphrodite, the Greek goddess of love. It was said that she embalmed the Trojan hero Hector, who was slain by Achilles, with rose oils. Another story relates that the goddess Cybele created roses so that there would be something on earth more beautiful than Aphrodite, her rival. The rose was also the emblem of Eros, the love god, and curiously the English word *rose* is an anagram of his name. Dionysus, the god of revelry, also took the rose as his symbol. The 'Autumn Damask' rose is reputed to have grown in the gardens of the mythical King Midas of Phrygia.

To date, there are still no blue roses, and a Roman myth explains why. Flora, the goddess of flowers, asked the gods to create a flower that all other flowers could use as a model of perfection. As part of her request she asked that there never be a blue rose, since the color blue was then associated with death.

History records that in ancient Greece and other countries the rose had a powerful mystique. The ancient city of Rhodes took its name and civic symbol from the Greek word *rhoden*, or rose.

Roses still grow there in abundance today. In the centuries before Rome conquered Rhodes in the first century B.C., roses appeared on more than a hundred Rhodian coins.

For the Romans the rose came to represent secrecy. When earlier citizens held clandestine political meetings, they placed a bouquet of roses over the door of the house where the meeting was taking place—hence the term *sub rosa* (under the rose). In a similar vein, a white rose was often placed over dining room doors to remind guests not to repeat things they heard inside. The Romans believed that the god Cupid had dedicated the rose to Harpocrates, god of silence, as an inducement for him to remain mute about the indiscretions of Venus, Cupid's mother. In accordance with this tale, Harpocrates was depicted as a young man holding a finger to his lips and a white rose in his other hand.

Cleopatra (69–30 B.C.) supposedly welcomed Mark Antony in a room filled with rose petals piled a cubit (20 inches) deep. The sails of her ship were soaked with rose water to perfume the breezes.

Legend has it that the emperor Nero (A.D. 37–68) once spent the equivalent of $450,000 in today's currency on roses for a party he held on the Gulf of Baiae. The roses were showered on guests from the ceiling. Still more hedonistic was the legend of Emperor Heliogabalus (A.D. 204–222), who was reputed to have had so many rose petals in one room that they suffocated his guests.

ROSES IN CHRISTIAN LORE

Christian legends had begun to include the rose by the fifth century. One legend maintained that roses did not have thorns until Adam sinned in the Garden of Eden. Nearly all roses possess thorns and probably always have, although their purpose is not known. It may be to trap moisture close to the stem, or to prevent the plant from being eaten by animals—although deer certainly find rose thorns no deterrent.

There still stands, in the German town of Hildesheim, a massive rosebush that is connected with Charlemagne's son Louis the Pious, who ruled his father's empire from 814 to 840. Louis was an avid hunter, and while out with a hunting party one day, he became separated from it and lost his horse. Frightened, he took a relic of the Holy Mother from around his neck and hung it on a nearby wild rose before falling asleep. After awakening he discovered that the ground around him was covered with snow, but that the area beyond was green and blooming—as was the rosebush, to which the relic was frozen.

Louis pledged to erect a chapel at the spot and was soon saved by his companions. The chapel was built, followed by a cathedral, and the rose continued to bloom alongside it. Although the cathedral was bombed during World War II, the rose survived, and today stands 30 feet high and 40 feet across—having lived for more than eleven hundred years. If this story is true, it is quite amazing, for rosebushes usually live only a few decades, although some old garden roses have survived for a century or more.

NORTH AMERICAN TALES

It is reported that Columbus, tired and discouraged, recorded in his log that he had picked up a rosebush floating in the Sargasso Sea, where his crew was becalmed. This sure sign that land was near gave him the hope and courage to continue. He sighted the West Indies the next day.

Native Americans tell several tales about the 'Cherokee Rose', *Rosa laevigata*, and its origins. One involves a warrior named Tsuwenahi, who returned from a hunting trip to find that his sweetheart,

Dowansa, had been turned into a rose. Complaining that thoughtless people now trampled on her, she begged for and received thorns. Native Americans also employed the Cherokee rose as a symbol of their patient and dignified endurance of the wrongs of white men. The very origin of the Cherokee rose is an enigma: Found growing wild in the Deep South by European explorers, it is actually native to China. How it reached the North American continent is a mystery that no one has been able to explain.

The Grant rose, which has a blood-red color and a heavy and unpleasant odor, is said to have sprung from the blood of a Mrs. Grant, a Florida pioneer who, with her husband and daughter, was killed during the 1835–1842 Seminole War.

WAR AND 'PEACE'

One of the most famous stories about roses is the account of the rose 'Peace'. The story is at least partly true, although undoubtedly some embellishments have crept in. Introduced in 1939 by French breeder Francis Meilland, this rose was an instant success for the size and longevity of its flowers. During the summer of 1939, Meilland sent buds to Germany, Italy, and the United States. War broke out on September 3 of that year, cutting off Meilland's communication with his distributors in other countries.

In Germany the rose became known as 'Gloria Dei' (Glory to God). In Italy it was named 'Gioia' (Joy). In the United States the Conard Pyle Company, Meilland's distributor, decided to name the rose 'Peace', embodying the hopes of the war-stricken world. By striking coincidence, the christening of the rose took place at the Pacific Rose Society exhibition in Pasadena, California, on April 29, 1945—the day Berlin fell.

Later that summer, Dr. Ray Allen, secretary of the American Rose Society, sent a single 'Peace' rose in a vase to each head of the 49 delegations to the United Nations, then convened in San Francisco. An accompanying note stated, "We hope the 'Peace' rose will influence men's thoughts for everlasting world peace."

There are other stories about the 'Peace' rose, some perhaps entirely apocryphal. Several biographers of Meilland state that as Hitler's armies were invading France, Meilland begged the American Consul in Lyons to smuggle propagation stock out of France and into the United States. This account does not appear in Meilland's memoirs and may not be true, but it is a marvelous tale nonetheless.

The Cherokee rose, a native of China, was found growing in the American South by early explorers. No one knows how it got there.

ROSES IN LITERATURE

*B*ecause of their many symbolic connections and their sheer sensuousness, roses have long been vehicles for metaphor and allegory in literature.

Literary reference to roses dates back to ancient times. In his *Iliad* Homer personifies the sunrise as "rosy-fingered dawn." He also mentions that a rose, the symbol of Aphrodite, adorned both the shield of Achilles and the helmet of his Trojan opponent Hector.

The Greek poet Sappho, in her "Ode to the Rose," was the first writer to refer to the rose as the "Queen of Flowers"—a sobriquet that has persisted to this day. The odes of Anacreon praise the rose as the most beautiful flower of all. Herodotus, in the fifth century B.C., described a double rose from Macedonia and remarked upon its fragrance. It is believed to have been the 'Autumn Damask'.

In his *Georgics* the Roman poet Vergil (70–19 B.C.) praises the roses of Paestum, a city south of Pompeii. He mentions that the roses bloomed twice a year, confirming that they were the 'Autumn Damask'—the only twice-blooming rose then known. In the second century A.D., the emperor and philosopher Marcus Aurelius wrote in his *Meditations*, "All that happens is as usual and familiar as the rose in spring and the crop in summer," reflecting his stoic philosophy and the prevalence of once-blooming roses.

The eleventh-century Persian poet and astronomer Omar Khayyám wrote of the rose in his *Rubáiyát,* which became famous in English-speaking lands through Edward FitzGerald's nineteenth-century translation. Exemplifying the work's world-weary tone are these famous lines:

Yet Ah, that Spring should vanish with the Rose!

Top: Introduced in Europe at the start of World War II, the hybrid tea 'Peace' was named officially on the day Berlin fell.

Bottom: The damask 'Omar Khayyám' is an offspring of a rose that grew at the Persian poet's grave.

That Youth's sweet-scented Manuscript
should close!

After FitzGerald died in 1883, seed from a rosebush at Omar Khayyám's grave in Nishapur was planted at Fitz-Gerald's grave in Suffolk, England. It was from a cutting of this plant that the damask rose 'Omar Khayyám' was propagated. Another rose named in tribute to the poet is the hybrid tea 'Rubaiyat'.

Sa'dī, a Persian poet of the thirteenth century, wrote a book called *Gulistan* (rose garden), which contains the thought that a rose may bloom for only four or five days, but a rose garden will bloom forever. His contemporary, the Persian poet Nezami, wrote, in *Treasure of Mysteries*, of a duel in which the victor kills his victim by casting a spell on a rose and giving it to the man to sniff.

THE ROMANCE OF THE ROSE

In Europe the rose became a symbol of courtly love and the subject of numerous songs of the troubadours. Reflecting this courtly tradition was the French *Roman de la Rose*, one of the most famous poems of the Middle Ages. In this elaborate allegory, a lover wandering in a rose garden tries to pluck a rosebud but is warned by Cupid that he must first prove his devotion by surmounting a series of dangers and trials. Chaucer's fourteenth-century translation, *The Romaunt of the Rose*, is resplendent with illuminations of these fabulous events.

William Shakespeare made figurative reference to roses in many plays and poems. In *Henry IV*, Hotspur offers this summary of the goal of Richard II's usurper, Henry Bolingbroke:

To put down Richard, that sweet lovely rose,
And plant this thorn, this canker,
*   Bolingbroke.*

In his thirty-fifth sonnet, Shakespeare again referred to roses metaphorically, in these lines about the virtues of forgiveness:

Roses have thorns, and silver fountains
*   mud;*
Clouds and eclipses stain both moon and
*   sun,*
And loathsome canker lives in the sweetest
*   bud.*
All men make faults. . . .

And in the famous lines from *Romeo and Juliet*, Juliet proclaims:

What's in a name? That which we call a rose
By any other name would smell as sweet.

That rose lovers of Shakespeare's day regarded these flowers more highly for their scent than for their beauty is confirmed in his fifty-fourth sonnet:

The rose looks fair, but fairer we it deem
For that sweet odour which doth in it live.

The association of roses with the fleetingness of beauty and youth was popular with poets of the time. In his sixteenth-century epic *The Faerie Queene*, Edmund Spenser wrote:

Gather therefore the Rose, whilst yet is
*   prime,*
For soon comes age, that will her pride
*   deflower:*
Gather the Rose of love, whilst yet is
*   time. . . .*

Amplifying these words in his "To the Virgins, to Make Much of Time," the seventeenth-century English love poet Robert Herrick wrote:

Gather ye rosebuds while ye may,
Old Time is still a-flying:
And this same flower that smiles today
To-morrow will be dying.

A 1908 illustration for Chaucer's The Romaunt of the Rose *shows the lover embracing a personified rosebud, the object of his courtly love.*

In addition to expressing the hedonism of their day, these poets remind us that continual bloomers were then unknown in Europe, and that apart from the 'Autumn Damask', which bloomed twice a year, roses flowered for only 6 to 8 weeks.

During the 1700s the poet Robert Burns made famous these lines, evoking the sentimentalism of the Scottish bards:

O, my Luve's like a red red rose
That's newly sprung in June:
O my Luve's like the melodie
That's sweetly play'd in tune.
As fair art thou, my bonie lass,
So deep in luve as I,
And I will luve thee still, my dear,
Till a' the seas gang dry.

For poets of the nineteenth century, the passionate, sensitive, mystical rose was the very soul of romanticism. Keats, Shelley, and their contemporaries all made poetic references to it. Robert Browning praised the rose as "This glory garland round my soul," while his wife, Elizabeth Barrett Browning, wrote, "O Rose, who dares to name thee?" And Thomas Moore's 1813 poem "'Tis the Last Rose of Summer" (later set to music in Flowtow's opera *Martha*) contained these equally dramatic lines:

You may break, you may shatter the vase,
    if you will,
But the scent of roses will hang round it
    still.

The rose appears in many children's stories of the time. In "Beauty and the Beast," as retold by the brothers Grimm, Beauty's father is captured by the Beast for cutting a rose from the Beast's garden. Offering herself as ransom, Beauty eventually grows to love the Beast, who turns into a handsome prince.

Roses also turn up in Lewis Carroll's *Alice's Adventures in Wonderland,* in which gardeners paint white roses red to please the Queen of Hearts. In *Through the Looking Glass,* roses and other flowers take on human qualities and talk to Alice.

Forsaking the flowery excesses of the Victorian era, poets of the early twentieth century tried to pare down their poems to the concrete essence of the words. Perhaps the most famous embodiment of this was Gertrude Stein's line "A rose is a rose is a rose is a rose," which she wrote in a circle to make it endlessly self-reinforcing. Just as the inherent beauty of the rose had been dulled by its symbolic associations, she felt, so too had we become separated from experience by unnecessary metaphor.

ROSES IN THE ARTS

*T*he earliest known painting of a rose was discovered by Sir Arthur Evans, excavating in Crete at the close of the nineteenth century in the palace of King Minos of Knossos. There he found frescoes of a rose grown during the Bronze Age, from around 1500 to 2000 B.C. Although the depictions are stylized, the rose is thought to be either a gallica or *Rosa foetida persiana,* the Persian rose.

Over the millennia, roses have been frequent subjects for artists. They were especially favored by the Persians, who often used roses symbolically in their art and literature, and who revered rosebushes in bloom. This reverence dates back at least as far as the ancient prophet Zoroaster. Legend says that as an infant he was thrown into a fire by Nimrod, king of Babylon, who feared him. The flames went out and the embers were changed into roses, on which the baby peacefully slept. The Louvre museum in Paris displays a thirteenth-century Persian dish decorated with roses, along with an ivory plaque depicting two warriors standing astride a rosebush. A painting of a fifteenth-century Persian prince shows him dressed in a coat patterned with roses,

Gardeners paint white roses red to avoid the wrath of the Queen of Hearts, in a John Tenniel illustration for Alice's Adventures in Wonderland.

holding a red rose in his hand. By the sixteenth century the Persians were weaving roses into their carpets, often picturing them with nightingales. There is a Persian saying that if you place a hundred handfuls of fragrant herbs and flowers before a nightingale, the bird will want only the sweet scent of the rose.

MEDIEVAL AND RENAISSANCE ART

In medieval Europe, early herbals, which were books containing botanical illustrations of plants, included woodcuts of roses. These woodcuts appeared in herbals through the fifteenth century, often beside figures from religious allegory. Italian artists made great use of the rose, often for its religious symbolism. In the sixteenth century, Bernardino Luini painted *Madonna with Roses.* Botticelli (1444–1510) frequently painted roses. His famous *The Birth of Venus* shows roses suspended in the air beside the unclothed goddess, no doubt a reference to her association with this flower. In *Coronation of the Virgin,* the air is filled with roses falling from heaven as symbols of the love of God.

Roses were also prevalent in the work of other Renaissance artists. The two roses most often portrayed are *Rosa gallica officinalis,* the 'Apothecary's Rose', and *Rosa alba,* both very popular in gardens of the time. In the sixteenth and early seventeenth centuries, the cabbage rose became known as the Rose of the Painters because it appeared in art so frequently.

During the Renaissance elaborate insets in the shape of a stylized rose were incorporated in the sounding boards of lutes and other similar instruments, and roses were painted on or carved into pianos and harpsichords.

In the sixteenth century Benvenuto Cellini fashioned rose jewelry of enamel, gold, and pearls. Elizabeth I was wooed

by the duc d'Alençon with jewels, among them a rose in white enamel with a butterfly of rubies and sapphires, and an enamel and ruby ornament of the White Rose of York and the Red Rose of Lancaster. (Elizabeth was the granddaughter of Henry VII, whose marriage united the warring families.) English pewter from this time was often stamped with a rose and a crown.

AFTER THE RENAISSANCE

Roses continued to appear in art of the seventeenth and eighteenth centuries. They are depicted in several paintings by the Dutch Masters. Jean-Honoré Fragonard painted a portrait of Madame de Pompadour, mistress of Louis XV and one of the greatest rose lovers of all time, reclining on a chaise longue in a dress adorned with roses. Madame du Barry,

Botticelli's paintings frequently pictured roses. In The Primavera, *the spirit of springtime dispenses roses from her gown while Chloris, Greek goddess of flowers, flees from Zephyr, god of the west wind.*

A watercolor by Pierre-Joseph Redouté depicts one of the cabbage roses that grew in Empress Josephine's garden.

English Jacobite glass made during the seventeenth and eighteenth centuries. Across the Atlantic, American glassmakers were imprinting roses on bottles. Later, in the 1800s, roses appear as a signature on a large number of paperweights made by the famed Clichy glass manufactory near Paris.

Pierre-Joseph Redouté, known as the Raphael of the Rose or the Raphael of Flowers, created exquisitely detailed watercolors of the roses in Empress Josephine's garden. His work *Les Roses,* which was first printed in 1817, is an unsurpassed reference still used today. Botanical descriptions were provided in *Les Roses* by a scientist named Claude Thory.

Contemporaries of Redouté include Mary Lawrance, who painted 90 color pieces for a book titled *A Collection of Roses from Nature,* and Paul de Longpre, who painted in California. De Longpre also wrote music, and many of the covers of his sheet music are decorated with his illustrations of roses.

The impressionistic era in art soon followed, and roses were again a favorite subject. Although Monet is better known for his water lilies, he also painted the roses in his garden. Renoir was a rose gardener, too, and he painted roses in several works including *Mme. Charpentier and Her Children,* which now hangs in the Metropolitan Museum of Art in New York. The postimpressionist Van Gogh included roses among his still-life paintings of flowers.

During the opulent Edwardian era, in the early 1900s, jeweler Carl Fabergé was the favorite of every European court. In 1907 he made one of his famous Easter eggs for Tsar Nicholas II of gold, diamonds, and enamel in a trellis design interspersed with pink roses. He also made animals, cigarette cases, and other pieces depicting roses. One piece, now owned by the queen of England, is a crystal vase holding an elaborate rose made of gold, enamel, and diamonds.

Louis's mistress after Madame de Pompadour, created a stir among interior decorators when she bedecked her bedroom at Versailles with rose-embroidered silk in the form of curtains, upholstery, and a canopy over the bed.

Several seventeenth-century Flemish tapestries portray the so-called Ceremony of the Rose, in which homage in the form of roses is paid to the English king in an annual parliamentary ritual. The background of these tapestries shows stripes in the colors of Charles II, whose rose emblem was woven into the design.

Snuff boxes from this era were often shaped in the form of roses, and roses appeared on Wedgwood, Spode, Sèvres, Worcester, and Bristol china. One of the earliest examples of roses on glass is the

ROSES AND ROYALTY

Left: A 19th-century Sèvres vase is decorated with cabbage roses.

Right: Lavish Fabergé eggs held gifts for the Russian Tsarina—in this case a stylized rosebud.

oses have long been associated with royalty, especially the English royal family. Edward I, who reigned from 1272 to 1307, was the first monarch to choose the rose as his badge, and his example has been followed for centuries. Each monarch after Edward I minted a new set of coins, and roses were often included on them. In fact, England has used roses on more of its coins than any other country.

In 1344 Edward III minted a gold coin known as the Rose Noble, adorned with a rose design. In 1465 Edward IV minted another Rose Noble depicting a ship adorned with a rose, to commemorate the rise of English sea power.

The rose attained even greater symbolic prominence in England after the Wars of the Roses (1455–1485). In those battles for the English throne, the House of Lancaster chose the red 'Apothecary's Rose' as its official badge, following the example of Henry IV, the first Lancastrian monarch. The opposing House of York chose the white alba rose as its emblem. In 1485 the two factions united upon the marriage of Henry Tudor (Henry VII) of Lancaster to Elizabeth of York. Legend has it that about this time

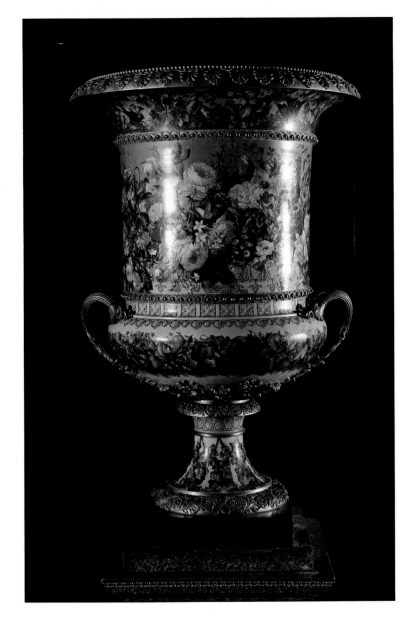

a bush bearing roses that were red, white, and red-and-white had been found growing in a country village, inspiring the opposing families to resolve the conflict. The pink-and-white damask 'York and Lancaster', *Rosa damascena versicolor*, is often said to be this rose; however, it could not have been, since 'York and Lancaster' was unknown in England until the seventeenth century.

After the union of the warring families, heraldic artists created the stylized Tudor rose, which was adopted as the floral emblem of England. The Tudor rose adorned many subsequent English coins, and royal heraldic devices often depicted several Tudor roses together, with some colored red and others colored white.

The rose 'York and Lancaster' is often confused with 'Rosa Mundi' (*Rosa gallica versicolor*), because of the striped pattern on its petals. 'Rosa Mundi' dates to 1581 and was originally called 'Rosamonde' after the mistress of Henry II, who ruled England from 1154 to 1189. For centuries after her death, Rosamonde was the subject of legends and ballads, as it was believed that she was murdered by Eleanor of Aquitaine, Henry's jealous wife.

Elizabeth I (1533–1603), the Virgin Queen, had a huge white rose embroidered on her banner, which was displayed wherever she went. Her coat of arms bore the motto A Rose Without a Thorn. When Elizabeth died, a rose was carved on the lid of her coffin.

In this legendary scene from the Wars of the Roses, members of the houses of York and Lancaster declare their opposition by plucking a white rose and a red rose, respectively.

Queen Anne, who reigned from 1702 to 1714, was an avid embroiderer and lace maker; a number of her pieces carried rose motifs and were known as rose point lace. Prince Charles Edward's Highlanders wore white roses when they marched into England in 1745, and the soldiers of George II wore white roses at the Battle of Minden in 1750.

The late Princess Grace of Monaco was an ardent lover of roses. Two roses have been named for her: 'Princesse de Monaco' and 'Grace de Monaco', in honor of her devotion to her favorite flower and to her rose garden at the royal palace. In 1976 she and Prince Rainier dedicated a rose garden at the Monaco National Museum in honor of Francis Meilland, hybridizer of the 'Peace' rose.

ROSES IN RELIGION

EARLY CHRISTIANS AND THE ROSE

*M*any plants and animals have been adopted as religious symbols, but perhaps none more fervently than the rose. The Christians in particular have found deep symbolism in this flower. The earliest Christians had shunned the rose, as it reminded them of the excesses of Rome and of the rose's association with sensuality. As Christianity began to grow and Roman decadence was forgotten, the rose took on important religious significance.

EARLY CHRISTIANS AND THE ROSE

At first, the early Christians used the rose secretly on catacomb walls as a code of their faith. Later, they used it openly. The rose was commonly displayed at funerals and cemeteries, a custom the Christians had adopted from the Greeks and the Romans. However, whereas the ancients considered the rose a symbol of grief at death, the Christians considered it a joyous symbol of the afterlife.

For medieval Christians the rose also symbolized the seal of confession, the guarantee that anything told to a priest during confession would be held in strictest confidence. Other examples of Christian symbolism include petals of a single rose for Christ's five wounds; red roses for the blood of the early martyrs; three roses for the Trinity; and white roses for the Virgin Mary.

The Catholic rosary, a circuit of beads fingered while reciting a series of prayers, may have taken its name from the custom of offering rose wreaths to the Virgin Mary. The rosary may also have been named after the crushed rose petals or rose hips that were used to make the first rosary beads.

A legend surrounds Saint Elizabeth of Hungary, who was feeding the poor during a thirteenth-century famine. When the king objected and demanded to see what she was carrying under her dress, the bread she had hidden there was turned into roses.

Saint Dorothea is painted with roses and apples to symbolize the good of

The pink-or-white damask 'York and Lancaster' is often identified as the flower that inspired the end of the Wars of the Roses in 1485. However, it was unknown in England until the seventeenth century.

Top: The infant Jesus
bestows a crown
of roses on Rose of
Lima, first saint
of the New World.

Bottom: The 13th-
century Cathedral of
Notre Dame in
Chartres is renowned
for its rose windows.

Christian life, for it is said that at the time she was martyred, an angel appeared carrying three roses and three apples. Theophilus, who had ordered her execution, was immediately converted to Christianity. Saint Francis of Assisi is painted with roses springing from his blood, because a legend says he fled from the temptation of Satan by rolling in a bramble of rose thorns. Saint Vincent is pictured as dying on a bed of roses.

CATHEDRALS AND GOLDEN ROSES

Rose patterns appear in church architecture, most spectacularly in the rose windows of Gothic cathedrals. These circular windows had rays of stylized stained-glass petals outlined in elaborate stone tracery. It is believed that the idea for the rose window was brought to Europe by returning Crusaders; the windows of the mosque of Ibn Touloun in Cairo are much like the medieval rose windows. The best-known rose windows are at the cathedrals of Lyons and Chartres in France, and of York, Westminster, and Lincoln in England. In Paris many people visit the thirteenth-century Cathedral of Notre Dame and the smaller but more spectacular Sainte Chapelle.

In 1049 Pope Leo IX began the unique papal custom of giving golden roses to royalty, churches, cities, and the like, and the pope's goldsmiths from that time on made many examples. It is possible, but not certain, that the custom may have started earlier when Constantine the Great, the first Roman emperor to become a Christian, placed a golden rose on the tomb of Saint Peter. Sovereigns of Catholic countries were often the recipients of the papal award; Henry VIII was the last English king to receive one.

Pope Pius IX sent a golden rose to Empress Eugenie, wife of Napoleon III, who ruled France during the second half of the nineteenth century. The rose was lost after the empire fell, but was anonymously returned years later.

The first papal golden roses were single flowers made of red-tinted gold, but the gifts became more elaborate over the years and were decorated with brilliant gems. The jewels, along with vestments and altar cloths, were blessed on what is now known as Rose Sunday, the fourth Sunday in Lent.

ROSES IN MEDICINE

As early as the fifth century B.C., the Greeks were making an ointment of rose petals with oils and fats for medicinal purposes. In the first century A.D., Dioscorides wrote an herbal that included several references to rose petals and rose hips. Because he drew from previous works, we know that roses were used medicinally for at least several centuries before Christ. One of the roses he cited is the dog rose, *Rosa canina,* so named because it was believed to be a cure for rabies. Pliny the Elder, who also wrote during the first century A.D., described several species of roses in his *Natural History.* In it he mentions 30 medicinal remedies made from roses.

During the second century the Greek physician Galen devised an ointment of waxes, fats, rose oil, and water that is still used today—and known as cold cream.

In the Middle Ages rose extracts were a valued component of medicines and ointments, and perhaps of seasonings and cosmetics. Rose oil was the treatment for eye ailments, and a rose conserve, made with rose petals and honey, was the treatment for lung and liver complaints. Rose vinegar was prescribed for curing nose bleeds, headaches, and upset stomachs. Sore-throat sufferers swallowed a hot mixture of crushed rose petals and peppercorns. The Crusaders treated battle wounds with a salve made from red roses. Ointments made from rose petals were thought to ease muscular aches and pains.

Medieval people made fires with aromatic wood, herbs, and roses and inhaled the smoke as a preventive measure against the dreaded plague. Those already afflicted placed pellets made from rose petals on their tongues.

The 'Apothecary's Rose' served as the basis for a thirteenth-century perfume industry in the town of Provins near Paris. By the nineteenth century, the streets of Provins were lined with apothecary shops, from which a large number of rose-based medications were shipped. The 'Apothecary's Rose' became the symbol of the British and U.S. pharmacopoeias.

John Gerard, in his *Herball* published in 1597, recommended eating the petals of musk roses, dressed like a salad with oil and vinegar, as a purge.

Like the poet Horace, John Heywood, the sixteenth-century dramatist whose book of sayings *Proverbs* is famous for the line "I pray thee let me and my fellow have a haire of the dog that bit us last night," recommended roses and wine for a hangover. He advised that roses could be used for eye strain, sore throats, bad gums, weak hearts, melancholia, rashes, eczema, ringworm, and liver and kidney problems.

The early American settlers, who regarded roses as a cure for almost every known malady, brought the flower with them as they crossed the country. As late as the mid-1800s, European and American doctors were still prescribing roses for indigestion, coughs, and colds. Medical researchers of the period reported that roses contained essential oils, potassium, and iron, all providing a sound basis for their inclusion in medications. By the late 1800s, however, the rose had disappeared from pharmacology, surpassed by newer patent medicines.

ROSES IN
DAILY LIFE

*S*ince at least the time of the Romans, roses have been a part of everyday life. The Romans used them in candy, wine, pudding, garlands, and rose water. Common people carried dried rose leaves in a pouch as an amulet against evil. Olive oil was scented with roses and applied as a lotion to bring youth to aging skin.

Throughout the history of Imperial Rome, roses were served as decorations for feasts, and rose festivals were common events. Roses crowned the heads of Roman revelers, and at memorial services for the dead, which were called Dies Rosationis, bereaved families decked the gravesides with roses. Pliny the Elder, in the first century A.D., described fountains running with rose water on special occasions.

Roses played a great part in the public games so loved by the Romans. Spectator boxes were looped and decorated with thousands of flowers, and the winners wore garlands of roses. In his oration against Verres, Cicero (106–43 B.C.) criticized the luxurious habits of this proconsul, who had toured Sicily on a seat made of roses.

When Romans said they slept upon a bed of roses, they meant it literally. Seneca (4 B.C.–A.D. 65), the Roman statesman and philosopher, wrote of a Sybarite named Smyrndiride who could not sleep properly if one of the petals in his rose bed was curled.

Roses have been used as cut flowers since ancient times. The Romans were excellent gardeners, and rose growing was a profitable industry in pre-Christian Italy near Paestum on the Gulf of Salerno, just south of Pompeii. The Romans learned to force roses into bloom in the winter by growing them in greenhouses and by watering them with warm water. Seneca wrote of the commercial rose industry, "Do not those live contrary to nature who require a rose in winter?" The Romans also imported many cut roses from Egypt. How the Egyptians kept roses fresh during shipment across the Mediterranean remains an unrecorded marvel, for the voyage took 20 days. In a plea to Romans to compete with Egypt in the cut-flower business, Vergil wrote, "Send us wheat, Egyptians, and we will send you roses."

The custom of presenting one's sweetheart with roses began in the Middle Ages. Before going off to battle, a knight presented his lady with a rose to signify his feelings. The rose became the flower of chivalry and love, and is now the most popular flower to give a loved one, especially on Saint Valentine's Day.

Although little is known about the types of roses grown in ancient Persia, the business of distilling rose water thrived there. This was, and still is, a major industry in the Middle East, where rose water is found in cosmetics and cooking. For centuries the rose water was shipped to foreign markets in wicker-covered bottles made of Syrian glass. The bottles were called *qarrabah*, source of the English word *carboy*. The carboy, filled with colored water, became the symbol of the pharmacy. The Persians were later traders in attar of roses, a fragrant oil distilled from rose petals.

Fourteenth-century Italians devised special ewers and basins for washing their hands with rose water before meals. For many centuries homes had "still" rooms where rose water was distilled and compounds made with plants from the herb garden.

Rose petals have been used for potpourri and the hips as a source of vitamin C. As recently as World War II, when citrus fruits were scarce in northern Europe, rose hips were harvested for their essential vitamin. British volunteers gathered

rose hips from the hedgerows for making a rose hip syrup, which was distributed by the Ministry of Health.

ROSES TODAY

Throughout the twentieth century roses have maintained their high visibility and status in popular culture. The 'American Beauty' rose, often referred to as the 'Million Dollar' rose because it was immensely profitable to grow, was the most popular cut flower of the 1890s. It became the floral emblem of the District of Columbia in 1925. Four states have also chosen a rose as their official flower: Georgia, the white 'Cherokee Rose'; Iowa, the wild rose; North Dakota, the 'Prairie Rose'; and New York, an unspecified "generic" rose. In 1986 the Congress of the United States officially declared the rose the national floral emblem, culminating 28 years of effort by rose fanciers and legislators.

Roses have been frequently depicted on modern postage stamps. In 1978 the first postage stamp in the United States to honor a rose was issued at the American Rose Center in Shreveport, Louisiana. Artist Mary Faulconer used as her models two roses, 'Medallion' and 'Red Masterpiece', hybridized by William A. Warriner of the Jackson and Perkins Company. In 1981 a block of four stamps commemorated the flowers of America, depicting the camellia, the dahlia, the lily, and the rose. In 1982 a rose adorned a U.S. stamp commemorating the fiftieth anniversary of the International Peace Garden on the North Dakota–Manitoba border. Several of the U.S. "Love" stamps have also pictured roses. Many other countries have issued stamps with roses on them, and, indeed, a philatelist could build a collection consisting entirely of rose stamps.

The prodigious history and lore of roses reflects cherished ideals—grace, beauty, dignity, strength, and pride. In reverence for the rose, daughters and cities have been named, and words and feelings for it exist in many cultures. Common though the rose has been in life and art, it has always transcended the commonplace. For if any flower can embody the wonder and poignancy of life, it is unquestionably the rose.

Left: A 1988 "Love" stamp features a pink rose.

Right: In a 1982 stamp, roses and maple leaves commemorate the 50th anniversary of the International Peace Garden on the U.S.–Canada border. The rose was declared the official flower of the United States in 1986.

*P*ublic gardens such as California's Berkeley Rose Garden are good places to observe a variety of roses.

SELECTING THE RIGHT ROSE

oses come in an astounding variety of
colors, scents, flower forms, and growth
habits—a selection so vast that the
beginning gardener may rightly feel
overwhelmed. Roses also range in their
tolerance of climate extremes and
their resistance to diseases. To help you
choose wisely, this chapter describes
the major classes of roses and their
characteristics.

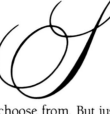

Roses satisfy a variety of landscaping needs. At New York's Brooklyn Botanic Garden, they fill formal beds and provide height on trellises and arbors.

Selecting the right roses for your garden may seem like a daunting task, since there are so many kinds to choose from. But just as avid travelers believe that half the fun is getting there, so do rose growers enjoy poring over books, leafing through catalogs, and visiting shows and gardens in quest of unfamiliar varieties. Although these activities are pleasurable in themselves, dedicated gardeners know that extra effort spent in making the right choice is the key to a long and happy relationship with plants.

Many of your decisions about which roses to plant will depend on your landscaping needs. Fences and trellises call for climbers; cutting gardens need hybrid teas and grandifloras; shrub borders should incorporate shrub roses and floribundas; small gardens look to miniatures; and low-maintenance gardens are fine homes for old garden roses. Chapter 3 addresses landscaping issues in detail.

In addition to choosing roses for their landscape value, you want to select those that grow well in your area, since many varieties have trouble in very cold or hot regions, or are susceptible to locally bothersome diseases such as black spot.

You should also consider the uses to which your roses will be put; for example, exhibiting or flower arranging. Certain rose varieties far surpass others in flower form, length of bloom, and other pertinent traits. See Chapter 7 for a discussion of these traits, and for lists of the best roses to grow for cutting and exhibiting.

Above all, plant what you love. If you love fragrant roses, or roses of a certain color, blooming pattern, or growth habit, be sure to include them in your garden.

CLASSIFICATION OF ROSES

The wide range of colors and forms exhibited by roses is the result of their ability to cross-pollinate freely, both in the wild and in cultivation. Complex hybridizing over thousands of years, along with the poor record keeping and once-secretive practices of hybridizers, has made it difficult to establish the lineage of many roses. As a result, their classification sometimes stymies even the experts.

All roses belong to the genus *Rosa,* of which there are some two hundred species and many thousands of hybrid varieties. Hybrids do not belong to a particular species and thus lack conventional botanical names; instead, they are identified by the variety names their hybridizers have assigned to them.

To help simplify matters, the American Rose Society has arranged all roses under two broad categories: old garden roses and modern roses. Old garden roses belong to classes that existed before 1867, the year the first hybrid tea was introduced. Modern roses consist of hybrid teas and other classes created after 1867.

A "class" of roses is not the same as the class category in taxonomy (kingdom, phylum, class, order, and so forth), but rather a grouping of species or hybrid varieties with similar characteristics and sometimes a common heritage. For example, hybrid teas are typically bushy plants with large, showy, solitary flowers; all descend from a nineteenth-century crossing of a tea rose with a hybrid perpetual. Climbers generally have large flowers and long canes; unlike hybrid teas, however, they represent various lineages. New classes of roses are continually emerging; any distinctive breakthrough in plant form, flower form, or blooming characteristic can serve as the basis for a new class.

In choosing a class of rose, you should look for one whose habits and requirements harmonize with those of your garden. The following are general descriptions of the rose classes that are commercially available. For details on individual plants, consult Chapter 10.

OLD GARDEN ROSES

Old garden roses consist of classes that existed before 1867, the year the hybrid tea class was introduced. Even if a variety was discovered or hybridized after 1867, it is considered an old garden rose if it belongs to a class that predates the hybrid tea.

In addition to their interesting histories, old garden roses have other characteristics that make them appealing. Most are long-lived, low-maintenance plants with good disease resistance; many are very winter hardy. They exhibit a wide range of plant sizes, flower forms, and flower colors.

The most common categories of old garden roses are described below.

ALBA   Albas are tall, dense, cold-hardy plants that resist many pests and diseases, making them especially useful in cold climates and low-maintenance gardens. They date to before the second century A.D. Leaves are blue-green, and the medium-sized blooms are either single or double. The flowers are in tones of pink or white, borne in clusters and usually deliciously fragrant. Albas bloom only once a year.

BOURBON   Bourbon roses are vigorous, shrubby plants that grow to about 6 feet high and have glossy, bright green leaves and clusters of small- to medium-sized, semidouble or double fragrant flowers of white, pink, red, and purple. The first Bourbon rose was discovered in the early nineteenth century on an island in the Indian Ocean that was known at that time as Île de Bourbon (now Réunion). Bourbons are moderately hardy and exhibit good repeat bloom. They reached the height of their popularity during the first half of the nineteenth century. Although the original Bourbon rose has been lost, many of its descendants remain. Some make good cut flowers, a trait rare among old garden roses.

CENTIFOLIA   Centifolias are the cabbage roses, so named because the hundred or more petals overlap and are closely packed like leaves of a cabbage. They are also called Provence roses after the section of France where they were once grown. Their origin is uncertain; they were once thought to be ancient, but they are now thought to be a product of seventeenth-century Dutch rose growers.
   The globular, sweetly fragrant, small- to medium-sized flowers are white to deep rose, appearing in clusters once a year on slender, arching branches with crinkled leaves. Plants are quite hardy, and small to medium sized, making them especially useful in smaller spaces.

CHINA   China roses (*R. chinensis* and its hybrids) have small, delicate, semidouble or double flowers and glossy, almost evergreen foliage on small- to medium-sized plants. They played an important

role in the development of today's hybrid roses, because they exhibited continual repeat bloom, something unknown when they were brought to Europe by way of China through India in the eighteenth century. They bloom reliably all season, typically producing pink, red, or crimson flowers with little fragrance. Unfortunately, they are extremely frost tender.

DAMASK   Best known for their fragrance, these roses are medium to large, with drooping or arching branches. They have long been grown in the Near East and Europe for the commercial production of attar of roses, a fragrant rose oil. Flowers are medium sized, semidouble or double, and appear in large clusters in shades of white or pink. They are very hardy and bloom only once a year, except for the 'Autumn Damask', *R. damascena semperflorens*, which blooms twice a year. Damask roses are descendants of *R. gallica* and have been known since 900 B.C.

EGLANTERIA   These roses are descendants of *R. eglanteria*, the 'Sweet Brier Rose'. They have a large, dense, thorny growth habit suitable for screening, and foliage that smells like apples, especially after a watering or rain. Flowers are small, single or semidouble, and pink, red, copper, or yellow. Blooms appear once a year on hardy plants and are followed by colorful hips.

GALLICA   The gallica, or French rose, is the class that contains the oldest identified rose. Gallicas have flowers of red, pink, or purple, and dark green foliage with a rough texture. The plants are hardy and compact, although they often look spindly and spread rapidly by underground runners, which are usually not found in roses. Flowers may be single or double and range in color from white to purple. Some varieties are richly fragrant; others have no scent at all.

Old roses such as this Bourbon have enjoyed a revival as gardeners rediscover their charms. Many are not only lovely but also hardy and carefree.

HYBRID FOETIDA   Most of the hybrids of the species *R. foetida* are pleasingly fragrant, unlike the parent species, which has an unpleasant, fetid odor. Hybrid foetidas are tall, vigorous plants that bloom only once a year. It is because of these roses that we have the color yellow in today's hybrids. Unfortunately, hybrid foetidas and their descendants are vulnerable to black spot disease. Flowers may be single or double.

HYBRID PERPETUAL   An immediate ancestor of the hybrid tea, which was the first modern rose, the hybrid perpetual is typically a tall, vigorous, hardy plant that blooms repeatedly all summer—although less prolifically than the hybrid tea, which has now eclipsed it. Flowers are large, double, fragrant, and white, pink, red, maroon, or mauve. Of the over three thousand varieties of hybrid perpetuals grown in the first half of the nineteenth century, only a few remain popular today.

HYBRID SPINOSISSIMA   The hybrids of *R. spinosissima* (the 'Scotch Rose', which dates to before A.D. 1600) are mostly twentieth-century additions to the list of good plants for the shrub border. Although these are often classified as shrub roses, they are technically old garden roses, because the class was in existence before 1867. They are large, vigorous, floriferous (abundantly flowering) plants, and among the thorniest roses, which makes them a good barrier plant. Some bloom only once a year; others repeat their bloom throughout the summer. Flowers are small to medium sized, may be single or double, and have various colors.

Anatomy of a Rose

Roses are classified by the form and color of their flowers, seed structures, leaves, and stems. As you study them, you'll find it useful to be familiar with these parts of their anatomy, since plant descriptions often refer to them. The illustration on the next page shows the significant parts of a typical rose.

Although *flower* is the term most often used for the showy portion of a rose plant, this structure is technically known as the corolla. The corolla is made up of petals, whose number determines whether the rose is classified as single, semidouble, double, or very double. A single flower has just one row of petals—usually 5 petals but as many as 12. A rose with 13 to about 25 petals in two or three rows is said to be semidouble. A rose with more than 25 petals, in three or more rows, is called double. A very full flower having more than 45 to 50 petals in numerous rows is known as very double.

You will sometimes see the term *quartered,* especially in reference to old garden roses. A quartered flower is one whose petals open in such a way that when viewed from above, the rose appears to be divided into distinct quadrants.

With some roses a solitary bloom appears at the top of the flowering stem; these are usually referred to as one-to-a-stem roses. When multiple flowers appear on a stem, the grouping is known as a spray or a cluster.

Flowers open from flower buds, which are initially covered by green leaflike sheaths known as sepals. Collectively, the sepals and the bulbous structure below them—the calyx tube—are known as the calyx. As a flower opens, the sepals turn down

and may eventually be hidden by the flower. Some sepals are small and plain; others are large and frilled.

When a flower has fully opened, thin filaments called stamens become visible in the center of the flower, which is called the disc. Stamens, the male reproductive portion of the flower, release pollen from parts at their tips called anthers. The stamens of roses are usually yellow, although sometimes they are red or maroon. The female portion of the flower, the pistil, is located at the center of the stamens. Only its topmost portion, the stigma, can be seen; hidden below it is the style, a slender tube that leads to the ovary, where seeds form if fertilization takes place. Seeds develop from ovules, egglike objects that are borne on structures called carpels within the ovary.

Once a rose has been pollinated—either by its own pollen or by pollen from another rose—the ovary swells and a seed-bearing fruit called the hip forms after the flowers fade. Although hips are found in some form on all roses, they are largest and most striking in old garden and shrub roses. The hips of these roses are often bright red or orange, with a characteristic pear, oval, or urn shape. So distinctive are the hips of many roses that experts can often identify the variety by its hips alone.

The main branches of rosebushes are known as canes. These arise from the crown, the point where the canes are joined to the root shank. (On roses that have been budded [grafted] to more vigorous root systems, the point where the canes are grafted to the roots is called the bud

union; the bud union functions as the crown.) A new cane that arises from the crown or the bud union is often called a basal break.

Stems are growths emanating from the canes and terminating in flowers. Roses produce stems of differing lengths, depending on their class. For example, most hybrid teas have longer-than-average stems, making them good for cutting.

Both canes and stems are usually covered by red or green thorns (also known as prickles), although some roses are thornless. Thorns vary in size, shape, and number. They can be so distinctive that they alone can be used to identify certain roses.

Roses have compound leaves, which are made up of several leaflets. Most modern roses have five-leaflet leaves except in the area near the flower, where three-leaflet leaves usually appear instead. Old garden roses may have seven, nine, or even more leaflets. The top leaflet, called the terminal leaflet, is attached to the rest by a small stem known as a petiole; the other leaflets have stalks known as petiolules. The base of a leaf has a winglike appendage known as the stipule; the tip of the stipule is known as the auricle.

New stem growth emanates from a bud eye in the leaf axil, the point at which a leaf joins the stem. The part of the stem between the highest leaf and the flower is known as the peduncle, sometimes referred to as the neck. Peduncles are generally thornless and soft wooded, and vary in length and thickness according to variety. Often, a small leaflike structure known as a bract appears partway down the peduncle.

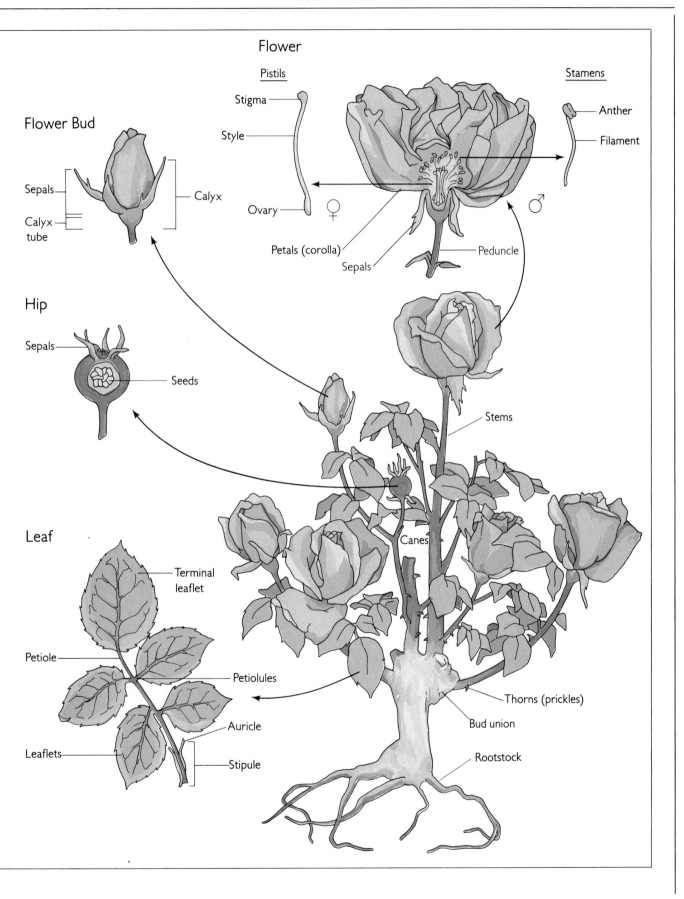

Flower

Pistils

Stigma

Style

Ovary ♀

Stamens

Anther

Filament

Petals (corolla)

Sepals

Peduncle

♂

Flower Bud

Sepals

Calyx tube

Calyx

Hip

Sepals

Seeds

Stems

Canes

Leaf

Terminal leaflet

Petiole

Petiolules

Auricle

Leaflets

Stipule

Thorns (prickles)

Bud union

Rootstock

MOSS   Moss roses are sports, or mutations, of centifolia roses. They are highly fragrant, the fragrance being emitted from small, hairy, sticky red or green glands that appear on the sepals and sometimes on the stem and leaves. These structures are unique to moss roses. Plants are hardy and usually medium sized, with large, double, globular flowers colored white, pink, red, or purple. Most bloom only once a season, with the blooms appearing later than those of other roses. Some produce a second, light bloom in the fall.

NOISETTE   The first hybrid group to originate in the United States, noisettes are a cross between the musk rose (*R. moschata*) and the China rose (*R. chinensis*), made in South Carolina in 1812. Noisettes are tall, bushy, tender plants that make good climbers, bearing fragrant clusters of white, pink, red, purple, or yellow double flowers throughout the season.

PORTLAND   This class includes sturdy, upright plants that have double, very fragrant flowers that bloom all summer. They are descendants of a China rose, the 'Autumn Damask', and *R. gallica*. They resemble Bourbon roses, to which they are closely related, but they generally have smaller (3-inch) flowers with brighter pink and red coloring. The Portlands were named for the first rose in the class, 'Duchess of Portland', which appeared about 1800. Soon surpassed by a vast new class of hybrid perpetuals, they were never very popular, and only a few varieties are still available.

SPECIES   The species roses are the wild and original roses, many of which are still grown and have a well-deserved spot in the garden. Most species roses have five-petaled single flowers, although some have double flowers, with 25 petals or more. Depending on the species, flowers may be white, pink, red, or yellow. Most are large, low-care plants; many can tolerate cold winters. Most species roses bloom only once in summer, although a few repeat their bloom. They are typically referred to by their botanical names; for example, *Rosa multiflora*.

TEA   Brought from China in the nineteenth century, tea roses are immediate ancestors of the modern hybrid tea. They are similar to the China roses, but have larger, fuller flowers up to 4 inches across. The double flowers are pastel pinks and yellows, with almost translucent petals and a fresh, tealike fragrance. The blooms repeat all season and have the classic, high-centered form that we regard today as perfection in the rose. (A high-centered rose has a center that is higher than the edges, giving the open flower a triangular shape when viewed from the side.) Tea roses are graceful but tender plants and were one of the first to have the long, pointed bud that has been passed on to modern hybrids.

MODERN ROSES

Since the modern classification of roses began in 1867, hybridizers have created many new classes and varieties of modern roses, expanding the color palette to bright colors, blends, and bicolors, and introducing more and more continually blooming varieties. Although some old garden roses showed repeat bloom (such as the 'Autumn Damask', which blooms twice a season), it was not until the China and tea roses were brought to Europe from the Orient that rose growers knew continual repeat bloom. This capacity for summerlong blooming has been passed on to modern roses. Modern roses include (in approximate order of popularity) the hybrid tea, floribunda, grandiflora, climber, miniature, polyantha, rambler, and shrub classes.

HYBRID TEA The classic, high-centered beauty of the rose flower is epitomized by the hybrid tea, which eclipses all other classes in popularity. As with other modern roses, there are varieties in every color except true blue and black, for which roses lack the necessary pigment. Many are fragrant, and almost all bloom repeatedly throughout the summer. Most hybrid teas are produced one to a stem, although some bloom in sprays. Most are double or semidouble, with the single, five-petaled 'Dainty Bess' a notable exception. With their large, splendid, long-lasting blooms and often long, strong stems, hybrid teas are excellent for cutting. Indeed, they are the mainstay of the cut-flower trade.

A cross between the hybrid perpetual and the tea rose, the hybrid tea surpasses both its parents in hardiness and repeat blooming, a decisive breakthrough that marked the beginning of modern roses. The first hybrid tea, 'La France', was introduced in 1867. The first yellow hybrid tea, 'Soleil d'Or', introduced in 1900, opened up a new world of color for hybridizers, since yellow was unknown in modern roses until that time. Six decades later, orange hybrid teas followed, and today an exceptionally wide color range is available.

The hybrid tea 'Perfect Moment' has yellow-based petals that are dramatically edged in red. Exotic color combinations are among the goals of modern rose breeders.

'Climbing Charlotte Armstrong' is a long-caned mutation of the hybrid tea 'Charlotte Armstrong'. Climbing sports of bush roses often have larger flowers.

GRANDIFLORA The grandiflora class began with the rose 'Queen Elizabeth', and grand it is. A cross between a hybrid tea and a floribunda, the grandiflora inherits the best characteristics of both parents. The hybrid tea side of the cross contributes high-centered flowers and long cutting stems. The floribunda side provides hardiness, continual flowering, and clustered blooms. Grandifloras are generally the tallest of the modern roses (except for climbers). This makes them most useful at the back of a border or as a screen.

CLIMBER It is difficult to trace the exact background of today's climbing roses. Many are derived from species and old garden roses that had long, arching canes—most important, the species rose *R. wichuraiana*. Some are descended from shrub roses, others from ramblers. The climbers of today are technically called large-flowered climbers, although in common practice they are referred to simply as climbers. Many are sports, or mutations, of bush roses; thus in books and catalogs you will see reference to climbing hybrid teas, climbing grandifloras, climbing floribundas, climbing miniatures, and others. One exception is 'Climbing Summer Snow'; in this case, the original plant was a climber, which sported to produce the lower-growing 'Summer Snow', a floribunda. Curiously, climbers that are sports of bush roses often have larger flowers.

Climbers are not vines; unlike climbing plants such as clematis and ivy, they lack tendrils to help them cling to walls or trellises and must be tied to their supports. Their long canes are sometimes pliable enough to be trained horizontally along a fence, a practice that forces them to produce more of the lateral branches on which flowers appear. Stiffer-caned climbers are excellent roses to train upright on a pillar or trellis, and thus are sometimes called pillar roses. Most

FLORIBUNDA As its name suggests, the floribunda has an abundance of flowers. It was crossed from a hybrid tea and a polyantha, and often has hybrid tea–type flowers, although not always. Some floribundas have single or semidouble flowers that are cup shaped or flat. Plants tend to be hardy and low growing, and produce flowers of varying size and color all summer in sprays. Floribundas are excellent plants for landscaping. Their low, bushy form makes them especially suitable for hedges, edgings, or mass plantings.

climbers produce flowers in clusters. Some bloom only once, in spring; others bloom on and off all summer.

MINIATURE Miniature roses are miniature in every sense of the word, with stems, leaves, and flowers all petite versions of those of full-sized plants. Miniature roses have become a special focus of hybridizers in the last few decades because their small size makes them easy to grow in any garden, indoors or out.

The miniature is descended from *R. chinensis minima* and reached Europe from the island of Mauritius in the Indian Ocean in 1815. It was thought to be lost, but was rediscovered growing in Switzerland in the 1920s. Plants range in height from 3 inches to 2 feet or more, and have flowers that range from less than 1 inch across to several inches across, in a wide range of colors. Although many miniatures resemble tiny hybrid teas or floribundas, they are a class unto themselves.

Top: Once a limited novelty, miniature roses now make up a large and varied class. This is 'Blue Peter'.

Bottom: 'May Queen' is one of the few ramblers that repeat their bloom.

popularity by floribundas, which have more attractive flowers and a wider color range, several are still popular and make excellent plants for hedges and edging. Polyantha flowers are white, pink, red, yellow, or orange.

RAMBLER   Ramblers were one of the forerunners of today's climbers, which have largely succeeded ramblers because of their more compact shape and larger flowers. Ramblers descended primarily from *R. multiflora* and *R. wichuraiana*. They are very large, rampant, hardy plants with pliable canes that generally bloom only once, in early summer. Although many varieties still survive in old cemeteries and around old cottage-style houses, most have disappeared from the marketplace.

SHRUB   Shrub roses are a class of hardy, easy-care plants that was created by the American Rose Society to encompass bushy roses that did not fit any other category. Some make good ground covers; others work well as hedges and screens. Some bloom only once a year; others bloom repeatedly, with single or double flowers in all colors.

The shrub class is divided into several major subclasses: hybrid moyesii, hybrid musks, hybrid rugosas, kordesii, and a catchall category whose members are known simply as shrubs.

Hybrid moyesii roses are tall, stiff plants with distinctively shaped and brightly colored red hips that follow the repeat bloom. Hybrid musks are partial descendants of *R. moschata*, the musk rose, and will tolerate less sun than other classes of rose. These hardy, disease-resistant, fairly tall plants bloom all season in large, heavily fragrant clusters; most have single flowers, although there are some with semidouble or double blooms. Hybrid rugosas are disease-resistant, dense, low-growing plants with wrinkled foliage and are descendants of

With its single flowers on tall, hardy plants, 'Francis E. Lester' is typical of the hybrid musk category of shrub roses.

POLYANTHA   The forerunners of floribundas, polyanthas are low-growing, compact, very hardy plants that flower continually. The origin of the class is clouded, but it is believed that the first polyantha descended from *R. multiflora* and *R. chinensis* in the late nineteenth century. The flowers grow in clusters and are small and decorative, opening flat. Foliage is fine and narrow. Although many polyanthas have been eclipsed in

R. rugosa. They can have single or double flowers, and their hips are a valued source of vitamin C. Among roses, hybrid rugosas are the most tolerant of wind and sea spray, and are therefore excellent for beach plantings.

Kordesii roses are twentieth-century hybrids of *R. kordesii,* a new species that arose in 1952 when the German hybridizer Reimer Kordes crossed *R. rugosa* and *R. wichuraiana.* They are shrubs or low-growing climbers with glossy foliage and exceptional hardiness. They come in a variety of flower forms and colors.

The remaining shrub roses, known simply as shrubs, are generally vigorous, hardy, and disease resistant. Some are tall upright plants excellent for hedges or inclusion in a mixed shrub border; others are low-growing, trailing plants useful as ground covers. Flowers can be single or double and of varying sizes and colors.

TREE ROSES   Tree roses are not a product of interbreeding but rather a plant form produced mechanically by grafting. A tree rose is usually a composite of three separate rose plants—one providing sturdy roots, another supplying a long straight stem, and a third grafted to the top to produce flowers and foliage. Any rose variety that might look pleasing atop a trunk can be grafted onto a stem to make a tree rose. The length of the stem depends on the variety to be grafted to it and the role the plant is destined to play in the garden. Some tree roses are stiff and stately; others have a graceful, weeping form created by grafting a pliable-caned variety to the top of the stem. Tree roses are the crowning glory of a formal rose garden, lending it an aristocratic air. Unfortunately, they are all very tender, even though the component plants may be hardy.

All tree roses are produced by grafting. Here, the climbing polyantha 'China Doll' has been grafted to a long, straight stem for a weeping effect.

CHOOSING ROSES FOR COLOR

Modern hybridizers have enlarged the palette of rose colors to an extent that would amaze the gardener of a hundred years ago. Whereas old garden roses were restricted mainly to stripes and solids in the white, pink, lavender, and red color range, today's modern hybrids come in vivid admixtures of every color except true blue and black—although genetic engineers may well achieve these colors in the future. (There is indeed a green rose, *R. chinensis viridiflora*.) Flowers may be solid-colored, bicolored (different colors on the insides and the outsides of the petals), or blends (two or more colors intermingled on each petal).

In this book and in other publications, you will see the colors of roses specified by letter codes, such as W for white or PB for pink blend. These codes refer to the color classes established by the American Rose Society and assigned to each new rose when it is registered. Knowing the color class makes it easy to identify a color when choosing varieties from a mail-order catalog; it is also essential to know when exhibiting roses, because many competitions require roses of a specific color. A complete list of these codes appears on page 280.

Flower color is among the most important factors in selecting roses for your garden, for the colors you choose project your personality and that of your home. A warm color scheme, made up of red, orange, gold, and yellow tones, is exciting, happy, and cheerful. It draws the eye to the garden and makes it look smaller than it is. However, such a color scheme also makes the garden seem hotter, so it would not be a good choice where temperatures scale high in the summer, especially if the roses are to be planted near outdoor living areas.

A cool color scheme, composed of violet, mauve, and purple, is soothing and refreshing. It is the best choice for a quiet garden meant for relaxing. It also makes a small garden look larger, and is a good color scheme to use when you want to hide an eyesore, since it does not draw attention to itself. Although they are technically not cool colors, whites, pastel yellows, and light pinks also have this same low-key effect.

When planning a garden, work within a limited color scheme to avoid a busy and distracting look. Start by choosing one color as the dominant hue, and add one or two other colors as subordinates. As you gain experience you will learn how to safely add more colors without creating discord.

To help you select color harmonies, use a color wheel such as the one on page 58, or buy one at an art supply store. Colors opposite each other on the wheel, such as purple and yellow, are called complementary. They make a strong and attractive harmony, yet may be too overpowering for a small garden. A useful compromise is split complementary harmony, in which one color is complemented by a color adjacent to its opposite on the wheel. An example of this type of harmony is yellow with red-violet or blue-violet.

Analagous harmony uses two or three colors that are adjacent on the color wheel; for example, yellow, yellow-orange, and orange. Putting two strongly colored roses with analagous harmony together, such as the pure orange 'Orangeade' with the red-orange 'Sarabande', creates drama.

Monochromatic harmony is a color scheme that uses shades and tones of a single hue. An example would be a garden using a variety of pinks, perhaps mixing light pink, medium pink, and deep pink roses.

Pink and white do not appear on the color wheel, yet are important colors in the garden. Pink, a tint of red, is used like red to complement colors such as yellow or mauve. Paler pinks tend to have a more cooling influence than darker, more saturated pinks or reds. White, the absence of pigment, can be used on its own as the dominant color, or as a buffer

Whites and pastels have a cooling, calming effect. They can make a garden seem larger.

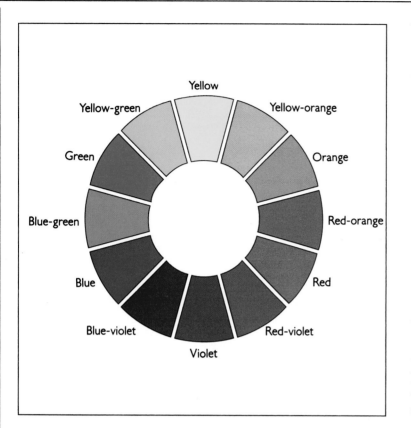

between bright colors. When used as an edging, white can have a unifying effect on a bed or border of multicolored roses behind it, because its brightness stands out as a vivid common denominator. For this reason, using white-flowered plants only here and there can make for a spotty look, so use white flowers only in contiguous masses or borders.

White, pink, and other light pastels are excellent tones for a garden that will be viewed at night, since dark colors fade into the background after sunset. Like cool colors, light colors are also good for camouflaging eyesores such as work sheds, gas tanks, and trash bins, since the eye is less drawn to them than it is to warm or dark colors.

Roses with strong colors like red or orange are good for accenting focal points, such as the end of a garden path, or a garden ornament, such as a bench, a statue, or a birdbath. Repeating the

Top: A color wheel is useful when planning the color scheme of a rose garden.

Bottom: White roses such as 'Iceberg' floribundas stand out awkwardly amid other colors and look best when planted in a mass.

accent color in a nearby bed carries the eye along through the garden.

Many rose growers like to grow as many different colors and varieties as possible, to afford themselves a large number of roses to study or exhibit. Unless thought is given to their arrangement, the result can be a visual jumble. Subtle tones, in particular, may go unappreciated in the absence of a unifying plan. If you want a wide palette of colors, try arranging them in a deliberate progression, or use different color schemes in different sections of the garden. To avoid a crazy-quilt effect, plant two or three roses of the same variety or color together, rather than scattering them throughout the garden.

In very large gardens, plantings have a more dramatic effect if masses of the same variety—or at least of the same color—are together. These masses give an impression of abundance. If you grow

Top: Avoid clashes in the garden by limiting the number of colors. Here, pink and white floribunda roses are combined with white and purple irises; a red climber adds dash in the background.

Bottom: Masses of a single color can look dramatic in a large garden. Roses on arbors repeat the bed colors, tying the garden together.

mass plantings of a single color, keep an extra plant or two growing in pots, in case disease or winterkill makes replacement necessary.

Bear in mind that solid-color roses can be more difficult to mix together than blends or bicolors, since they have no secondary tones to be picked up by a neighboring rose. However, placing too many blends together can cause the subtleties of their coloration to be lost. A good rule is to place solid colors next to blends, which makes the better qualities of each stand out.

Choosing colors for the garden is both a more complex and a less rigorous enterprise than choosing colors for the interior of a home, because a garden has so many variables. In a garden you must take into account the dappling of sunlight and shadow, the green of foliage or a nearby lawn, the brown of earth and branches, and the blue of the sky, all of which may change from hour to hour and from season to season. These natural elements, and the vastness of the outdoors, tend to relax even the strictest color scheme, allowing you to veer from the rules somewhat without creating visual discord.

Indeed, Mother Nature herself can be a source of inspiration, for she often combines colors in a striking manner. There are red-and-yellow gaillardias, violet asters with yellow centers, orange-and-gold marigolds, red-and-white impatiens. Borrow from these natural combinations to create an invigorating color scheme for your rose garden. Be wary of color clashes, though; for example, roses that have orange in them are likely to clash with pink or mauve roses.

The rules for choosing garden colors are more relaxed than those for interiors. Here, reds and pinks that might clash indoors look fine together in a dooryard garden.

The local climate may moderate your choice of colors, and even the colors themselves. For example, the heat and bright sunlight of warm climates can cause yellow roses to fade, and deep pink and red roses to develop darkened edges. In damp climates many yellow roses are exceptionally prone to black spot. Many white roses are prone to water spotting, so you may wish to avoid them in rainy climates, or where water will drip on them from eaves and trees.

Before making a final color selection, study the color of the house, fence, or wall against which your roses will be seen, and make sure that the juxtaposition is harmonious. A red or brick-colored structure looks best with yellow or white roses; a blue one with red, pink, white, or yellow. Against a white house, bright red and orange are dramatic. The grayed, weathered surface of an unpainted barn or a split-rail fence is complemented well by roses with soft pink, yellow, or apricot tones.

No one can tell you what color scheme is best for your garden; the preceding are only suggestions and guidelines. Response to color is a personal matter, a reflection of your tastes and temperament. Some like it hot; others don't. When selecting roses, choose the colors that are right for you.

CHOOSING ROSES FOR FRAGRANCE

What's the first thing most people do when they are handed a rose? They smell it. The fragrance of roses has been cherished for ages and is one of the main motivations for growing them. Fragrant rosebushes, placed under windows, along walkways, or near outdoor seating areas, fill the air with a wonderful scent that complements the beauty of the flower. If a fragrant garden is your goal, or if you want fragrant roses to use in potpourris or recipes, you need to choose from the most fragrant varieties available.

When selecting roses for landscaping, try to complement the colors of nearby structures. Here, pink roses warm the cool gray of a stone wall.

Like other sensory stimuli, fragrance is highly subjective. A scent that appeals to one person may repel another and be barely perceptible to a third. And a rose itself may have different degrees and types of fragrance at different times.

A rose is most fragrant when it is one-quarter to two-thirds open and has been slightly warmed by morning sun. This heating causes the rose to release droplets of fragrant oil from tiny scent emitters on its petals and, in some types of roses, from the leaves. However, too much sun or wind can quickly carry these oils away and leave the rose with a faint or disagreeable odor. On a sunny day fragrance declines by as much as 40 percent. On a cool or damp day, by contrast, a rose releases little or no fragrance,

and what fragrance is released may be masked by mildew.

Not all roses are fragrant, and the classic "rose" scent is just one of a variety of rose fragrances. Roses have seven basic fragrances: rose, nasturtium, violet, apple, lemon, clove, and tea. The traditional rose scent occurs only in red or pink roses—possibly for genetic reasons, although many red and pink roses are scentless. White and yellow roses tend to have tea, nasturtium, violet, or lemon scents. Orange roses usually smell of tea, nasturtium, violet, or clove. Eglanteria roses have an apple scent, which comes primarily from the leaves.

Rose breeders do not yet understand the genetics of rose fragrance, but they are aware that there are fewer fragrant

Fragrant roses such as 'Sheer Bliss' release the most scent when they are slightly warm and between one-quarter and two-thirds of the way open.

Fragrant Roses

Variety	Class	Color	Variety	Class	Color
Admiral Rodney	Hybrid tea	Pink blend	John F. Kennedy	Hybrid tea	White
Angel Face	Floribunda	Mauve blend	Keepsake	Hybrid tea	Pink blend
Apricot Nectar	Floribunda	Apricot blend	Kordes' Perfecta	Hybrid tea	Pink blend
Arizona	Grandiflora	Orange blend	La France	Hybrid tea	Light pink
Avandel	Miniature	Yellow blend	Little Jackie	Miniature	Orange blend
Beauty Secret	Miniature	Medium red	Miss All-American	Hybrid tea	Deep pink
Big Purple	Hybrid tea	Mauve blend	Beauty		
Blue Moon	Hybrid tea	Mauve	Mister Lincoln	Hybrid tea	Dark red
Broadway	Hybrid tea	Yellow blend	Papa Meilland	Hybrid tea	Dark red
Chrysler Imperial	Hybrid tea	Pink blend	Paradise	Hybrid tea	Mauve blend
Command	Hybrid tea	Orange-red	Pink Peace	Hybrid tea	Medium pink
Performance			Red Fountain	Climber	Dark red
Crimson Glory	Hybrid tea	Dark red	Royal Highness	Hybrid tea	Light pink
Dolly Parton	Hybrid tea	Orange-red	Saratoga	Floribunda	White
Don Juan	Climber	Dark red	Sheer Bliss	Hybrid tea	White
Double Delight	Hybrid tea	Red and white	Sonia	Grandiflora	Pink blend
Electron	Hybrid tea	Deep pink	Sparrieshoop	Shrub	Light pink
Folklore	Hybrid tea	Orange blend	Spartan	Floribunda	Orange-red
Fragrant Cloud	Hybrid tea	Orange-red	Sunsprite	Floribunda	Deep yellow
Fragrant Memory	Hybrid tea	Medium pink	Sutter's Gold	Hybrid tea	Yellow blend
Granada	Hybrid tea	Red blend	Sweet Surrender	Hybrid tea	Medium pink
Iceberg	Floribunda	White	Tiffany	Hybrid tea	Pink blend
Intrigue	Floribunda	Mauve blend	White Lightnin'	Grandiflora	White
Jennifer	Miniature	Pink blend			

modern roses than old garden roses. This may be because the primary goal of modern breeders is flower form, color, and disease resistance, with fragrance a somewhat lesser priority.

If fragrant roses are your goal, choose from the varieties in the list above. These roses are among the most fragrant available today. Some have been awarded the James Alexander Gamble Fragrance Award of the American Rose Society; a complete list of the winners of that award appears on page 249.

In addition, almost all alba, Bourbon, centifolia, damask, gallica, hybrid musk, hybrid perpetual, moss, noisette, Portland, and tea roses have fragrant flowers.

CHOOSING ROSES FOR THE CLIMATE

*A*lthough most roses will grow in a range of climates, many are susceptible to drought, dampness, heat, cold, and other extremes. If your climate is less than ideal, you can guard many sensitive roses by planting them in protected spots or by giving them extra care. But it is far better to choose varieties that can stand up to the worst your climate can inflict. Here are some guidelines for selecting the right ones.

In cool, humid, or rainy rose gardens, fungal diseases are often difficult to control. The ideal solution is to plant disease-resistant varieties.

DROUGHT AND DAMPNESS

Although no rose will thrive under drought conditions, *R. rugosa* and its hybrids do better than most, surviving without water for several weeks at a time once the plants are established. They will also tolerate the salt air and sandy soil that are found in beach zones.

At the other extreme, many roses are susceptible to the fungal diseases that prevail in damp climates. Yellow roses in particular are susceptible to black spot. If you live in a humid or rainy area, you need to pay strict attention to a program of preventive spraying (see Chapter 9). In these circumstances, choose a disease-resistant variety; see page 68 for a listing. In damp, cloudy regions you may wish to avoid roses with very double flowers,

which may not open properly if they are constantly moist or if they lack the heat of sunshine to open them before they start to fade.

HOT CLIMATES

Rose gardens in warmer climates, be they in subtropical, tropical, or desert areas, can be very successful if you select the right roses. Most modern roses will not live long in these climates, since they quickly exhaust themselves when denied winter dormancy. Two notable exceptions are the floribunda 'Iceberg' and the grandiflora 'Queen Elizabeth', which rose growers in subtropical Bermuda have found to be quite long-lived. In general, however, the best choices for hot climates are the old garden roses, especially Chinas, teas, hybrid perpetuals, and shrub roses. Yellow roses tend to fade in the heat, so this is a color you may want to avoid in such climates.

You may be able to coax a wider range of roses to grow in hot climates by taking some extra precautions. Keep the soil from drying out too quickly by working in extra organic matter and covering the surface with a mulch (see page 142). Keep the plants from drying out by sheltering them from the wind. Protect your roses against burning by placing them where they will be shielded from the glare of the afternoon sun.

COLD-WINTER CLIMATES

Gardeners who live in cold northern regions must face the fact that their climate is less than hospitable to some types of roses, which cannot adapt to cold weather. Although burying or covering these varieties will help many of them to survive the rigors of winter (see page 154), choosing roses with built-in hardiness can enable you to avoid this drudgery. This is a special boon to people whose time for gardening is limited.

Unfortunately, no one has ever tested each rose variety for winter hardiness in all of the 11 climate zones designated by the U.S. Department of Agriculture (see the map on pages 160 and 161). This is despite the fact that nearly every other garden plant has been assigned a hardiness rating. However, the roses in the list on page 66 can be expected to be hardy to Zone 6 (where average minimum temperatures range between -10° and 0° F) without winter protection. Some can withstand the colder winters of Zone 5 (between -20° and -10° F) and Zone 4 (between -30° and -20° F).

In addition to the plants listed, most ramblers are hardy to at least Zone 6, and many are hardy to Zone 5. Shrub roses other than those listed are hardy to at least Zone 6. Old garden roses, except for tender China, noisette, and tea roses, are hardy to Zone 6, and centifolias and damasks are hardy to Zone 5. See Chapter 10 for detailed descriptions of each variety.

SHADE

Most roses need full sun in order to grow and bloom successfully. However, a few can do with less sunlight than others. The roses that are most tolerant of shade are the hybrid teas 'Blue Moon', 'Christian Dior', 'Fred Edmunds', 'Garden Party', and 'Swarthmore'; the shrub rose 'Alchymist'; the rambler 'Etain'; and all

'Vogue' is a relatively cold-hardy floribunda.

Roses That Tolerate Cold

Variety	Class	Color	Variety	Class	Color
Admiral Rodney	Hybrid tea	Pink blend	Mary Marshall	Miniature	Orange blend
Aquarius*	Grandiflora	Pink blend	Maytime**	Shrub	Pink blend
Avandel*	Miniature	Yellow blend	Miss All-American Beauty*	Hybrid tea	Deep pink
Betty Prior*	Floribunda	Medium pink			
Big Purple	Hybrid tea	Mauve blend	Mister Lincoln	Hybrid tea	Dark red
Blaze*	Climber	Medium red	Mon Cheri	Hybrid tea	Red blend
Blue Moon*	Hybrid tea	Mauve	Music Maker**	Shrub	Light pink
Broadway	Hybrid tea	Yellow blend	New Year	Grandiflora	Orange blend
Camelot	Grandiflora	Medium pink	Olympiad	Hybrid tea	Medium red
Carefree Wonder*	Shrub	Pink blend	Paul's Scarlet Climber*	Climber	Medium red
Century Two	Hybrid tea	Medium pink			
Chicago Peace*	Hybrid tea	Pink blend	Peace	Hybrid tea	Yellow blend
Chrysler Imperial*	Hybrid tea	Dark red	Peaches 'n' Cream*	Miniature	Pink blend
Class Act	Floribunda	White	Permanent Wave*	Floribunda	Medium red
Dainty Bess	Hybrid tea	Light pink	Pink Parfait*	Grandiflora	Pink blend
Delicata**	Hybrid rugosa	Light pink	Pink Peace*	Hybrid tea	Medium pink
Dortmund*	Kordesii	Medium red	Polarstern	Hybrid tea	White
Electron	Hybrid tea	Deep pink	Popcorn	Miniature	White
Escapade	Floribunda	Mauve blend	Portrait*	Hybrid tea	Pink blend
Europeana	Floribunda	Dark red	Prairie Flower**	Shrub	Red blend
F. J. Grootendorst**	Hybrid rugosa	Medium red	Precious Platinum	Hybrid tea	Medium red
Flaming Beauty	Hybrid tea	Yellow blend	Queen Elizabeth	Grandiflora	Medium pink
Folklore	Hybrid tea	Orange blend	Rugosa Magnifica**	Hybrid rugosa	Mauve blend
Fragrant Cloud*	Hybrid tea	Orange-red	Saratoga	Floribunda	White
Garden Party*	Hybrid tea	White	Sheer Bliss	Hybrid tea	White
Gene Boerner*	Floribunda	Medium pink	Shreveport	Grandiflora	Orange blend
Golden Wings**	Shrub	Medium yellow	Simplicity*	Floribunda	Medium pink
Heidelberg*	Kordesii	Medium red	Starina	Miniature	Orange-red
Iceberg*	Floribunda	White	Sun Flare*	Floribunda	Medium yellow
Ingrid Bergman**	Hybrid tea	Dark red	Sunny June*	Shrub	Dark yellow
Keepsake	Hybrid tea	Pink blend	Sunsprite*	Floribunda	Deep yellow
Kordes' Perfecta	Hybrid tea	Pink blend	Swarthmore*	Hybrid tea	Pink blend
Las Vegas*	Hybrid tea	Orange blend	The Fairy	Polyantha	Light pink
Little Darling*	Floribunda	Yellow blend	Tournament of Roses	Grandiflora	Medium pink
Love	Grandiflora	Red blend			
Madame Violet	Hybrid tea	Mauve blend	Tropicana*	Hybrid tea	Orange-red
Magic Carrousel	Miniature	Red blend	Vogue*	Floribunda	Pink blend
Malaguena	Shrub	Medium pink	White Dawn	Climber	White

All roses hardy to Zone 6, except as noted.   * Hardy to Zone 5.   ** Hardy to Zone 4.

of the hybrid musks. In addition, many climbers and miniatures can grow in less sun than other roses.

However, no rose will thrive with fewer than four hours of bright sunshine per day. If your garden does not provide this, there are ways to compensate for the lack of light. See page 97 for suggestions.

CHOOSING ROSES FOR DISEASE RESISTANCE

*U*nfortunately, rosebushes are susceptible to attack by a number of diseases. Although good hygiene and preventive spraying can go a long way toward keeping these in check, you may find it preferable to plant roses with built-in disease resistance.

For example, if your climate is cool, humid, or rainy, you may find fungal diseases such as mildew especially difficult to control. Black spot, another fungal disease, is a significant problem in all regions of the United States except the Southwest. If you live in one of these areas and lack the time to spray as often as recommended, disease-resistant plants are almost a necessity.

The list on page 68 identifies the rose varieties that are the most resistant to all rose diseases. (Note, however, that no rose is completely invincible.) In addition to these, virtually all members of the shrub rose classification resist rose diseases. So do most alba and damask roses, and all species roses except those with yellow flowers.

Hybrid musks such as 'Ballerina' are hardy and disease resistant, and tolerate less sunlight than other roses.

Disease-Resistant Roses

Variety	Class	Color	Variety	Class	Color
Admiral Rodney	Hybrid tea	Pink blend	New Year	Grandiflora	Orange blend
Altissimo	Climber	Medium red	Osiria	Hybrid tea	Red blend
Aquarius	Grandiflora	Pink blend	Pacesetter	Miniature	White
Avandel	Miniature	Yellow blend	Paul's Scarlet Climber	Climber	Medium red
Big Purple	Hybrid tea	Mauve			
Black Jade	Miniature	Dark red	Peach Fuzz	Miniature	Apricot
Blue Moon	Hybrid tea	Mauve	Pink Peace	Hybrid tea	Medium pink
Bobby Charlton	Hybrid tea	Pink blend	Pleasure	Floribunda	Medium pink
Broadway	Hybrid tea	Yellow blend	Polarstern	Hybrid tea	White
Brown Velvet	Floribunda	Russet	Precious Platinum	Hybrid tea	Medium red
Camelot	Grandiflora	Medium pink	Prima Donna	Grandiflora	Deep pink
Centerpiece	Miniature	Medium red	Puppy Love	Miniature	Orange blend
Cherish	Floribunda	Medium pink	Queen Elizabeth	Grandiflora	Medium pink
Class Act	Floribunda	White	Red Flush	Miniature	Medium red
Color Magic	Hybrid tea	Pink blend	Ring of Fire	Miniature	Yellow blend
Debut	Miniature	Red blend	Royal Sunset	Climber	Apricot blend
Escapade	Floribunda	Mauve blend	Sea Pearl	Floribunda	Pink blend
Europeana	Floribunda	Dark red	Sheer Bliss	Hybrid tea	Blush white
First Edition	Floribunda	Orange blend	Sheer Elegance	Hybrid tea	Pink blend
Folklore	Hybrid tea	Orange blend	Shining Hour	Grandiflora	Deep yellow
Fragrant Cloud	Hybrid tea	Orange-red	Showbiz	Floribunda	Medium red
French Lace	Floribunda	White	Shreveport	Grandiflora	Orange blend
Graceland	Hybrid tea	Medium yellow	Starina	Miniature	Orange-red
Handel	Climber	Red blend	Sunbright	Hybrid tea	Medium yellow
Headliner	Hybrid tea	Pink blend	Sun Flare	Floribunda	Medium yellow
Holy Toledo	Miniature	Apricot blend	Sunsprite	Floribunda	Deep yellow
Impatient	Floribunda	Orange-red	Sweet Vivien	Floribunda	Pink blend
John F. Kennedy	Hybrid tea	White	Tempo	Climber	Dark red
Julie Ann	Miniature	Orange-red	The Fairy	Polyantha	Light pink
Little Darling	Floribunda	Yellow blend	Tournament of Roses	Grandiflora	Medium pink
Liverpool Echo	Floribunda	Orange blend			
Love	Grandiflora	Red blend	Tropicana	Hybrid tea	Orange-red
Magic Carrousel	Miniature	Red blend	Trumpeter	Floribunda	Orange-red
Mary Marshall	Miniature	Orange blend	Winsome	Miniature	Mauve blend
Mon Cheri	Hybrid tea	Red blend	Yellow Blaze	Climber	Medium yellow
New Beginning	Miniature	Orange blend			

LEARNING MORE ABOUT ROSES

*A*lthough it helps to know which varieties are most likely to survive in your garden, your final decision will most likely depend on what the rose looks like—the color of the flowers and the size and growth habit of the plant. There are a number of ways to study the physical characteristics of roses. You can look at books such as this one, browse through catalogs from mail-order nurseries (see page 340), and obtain useful publications from the American Rose Society. Although such printed information is handy, nothing beats seeing the roses themselves and talking with people who grow them. You can best do this by attending local rose shows and visiting public gardens.

THE AMERICAN ROSE SOCIETY

The American Rose Society (ARS) is the nation's largest organization of rose hobbyists, with nearly four hundred chapters across the United States. Membership is open to anyone, and attending its meetings and rose shows is an excellent way to learn more about the roses that grow best in your area.

At ARS-sponsored shows you will be able to observe the color and form of rose flowers at their best, and ask questions of the ARS members on hand. You can be sure that any rose you see at an ARS show has been rigorously identified and labeled, which is not always the case at garden club or state fair shows. By noting which varieties have been entered, you can quickly determine which roses grow best in your area. At many shows you can also pick up nursery catalogs, pamphlets on rose culture, and sometimes rose plants themselves.

Local newspapers and radio stations often publicize upcoming rose shows. If this information is not available, the American Rose Society can tell you the locations of rose shows near you. Telephone 318-938-5402, or write to the American Rose Society, Box 30,000, Shreveport, LA 71130. This is also the address to write to for information about becoming a member.

When you join the ARS you receive a number of worthwhile publications, including a monthly magazine and several annual directories. Perhaps the most useful of these is the *Handbook for Selecting Roses,* which lists all rose varieties that are available commercially in the United

Floribundas await judging at a rose show. ARS-sponsored shows are good places to gather expert advice.

States. It is sent free to ARS members; nonmembers can receive it by sending $1 and a self-addressed, stamped envelope to ARS headquarters. The booklet lists the classification of each rose, its color, awards it has won, and its official ARS rating—the latter a numerical index of performance compiled from nationwide surveys of ARS members.

Another directory published by the ARS is *Modern Roses,* considered the bible for serious rose growers. Updated every few years, it lists all roses currently in cultivation, along with roses of historical or botanical importance (even if they are no longer grown), and all roses registered with the ARS through the publication deadline. Later registrants are listed in the ARS's monthly magazine and in the *Combined Rose List,* an independent publication described on page 281. The alphabetical entries in *Modern Roses* provide a wealth of information about the flowering and growth habits of each rose, its parentage, hybridizer, color classification, year of introduction, and registration status with the ARS. Although the casual rose gardener may not need this level of detail, the book is essential to any serious grower, hybridizer, or exhibitor.

A boon to new rose gardeners is the ARS's Consulting Rosarian program, in which longtime ARS members make themselves available to local rose enthusiasts for support and advice. See page 199 for more information on this program, as well as more about the ARS and its many activities.

VISITING ROSE GARDENS

Even the best handbook or rating guide cannot anticipate everything about the performance of a particular rose variety. For example, a rose plant in a hot climate may produce paler blooms than expected, while rose flowers in a cool climate may not open as fully as those growing where it is warmer. Only by observing roses can you really know them.

There are a large number of private and public rose gardens across the country where you can study roses growing under conditions similar to yours. Many are in botanical gardens or parks; others exist in more unlikely places, such as shopping malls, airports, and the grounds of public buildings. Visiting one or more gardens can help you decide not only which roses you like, but also how to use them imaginatively in the landscape. You'll find a listing of prominent rose gardens on page 334.

The ARS Rating System

Every three years the American Rose Society surveys its members to obtain evaluations of the roses they grow. From this survey the ARS compiles official ratings for every commercially available rose and publishes them in its *Handbook for Selecting Roses,* a booklet sent free to members. These ratings are a national average based on overall performance, taking into account the variety's vigor, disease resistance, flower form, and quickness of repeat bloom. Because some roses grow better in certain regions than in others, you must keep this in mind when studying ratings. For example, in Shreveport, Louisiana, the rose 'Shreveport' would achieve a rating of Excellent to Outstanding. However, its official rating is Good, because its overall performance is less exemplary in other parts of the country.

Although it offers no guarantees, the ARS rating is a useful guideline for predicting the success of a rose. In general, the higher the rating, the more satisfactory the rose. If you wish to avoid disappointment, try not to purchase a rose rated lower than 7.0 unless the variety has some special virtue that offsets its low rating. Nursery catalogs rarely give ARS ratings, so it is helpful to obtain a copy of the handbook. The plant descriptions in Chapter 10 of this book also include ARS ratings.

ARS Ratings

10.0	Perfect (This rating has never been achieved.)
9.0 to 9.9	Outstanding
8.0 to 8.9	Excellent
7.0 to 7.9	Good
6.0 to 6.9	Fair
5.9 and lower	Of questionable value

HOW TO BUY A ROSE

merican gardeners purchase some sixty million rosebushes each year from garden centers and mail-order nurseries across the country. The vast majority of these are sold in one of two forms: bare root or in containers.

Bare-root roses are dormant plants whose soil has been removed from the roots to reduce the weight for shipping; they are sold by mail order and at some garden centers. Container roses are dormant or growing plants sold in small pots; garden centers and houseware stores offer them from early spring until the end of the planting season, or until the available stock sells out. If you buy your roses from a mail-order nursery, you will almost certainly receive bare-root roses. Miniature roses are the one exception; being lightweight, they are usually shipped in pots.

Many rose growers prefer to buy their roses by mail because the selection is greater and they can choose the varieties they want, rather than settle for those that are locally available. Rarer varieties of modern roses, as well as most varieties of old garden and shrub roses, are available only by mail. The biggest drawback to buying by mail is that you cannot inspect your purchases in advance. To avoid disappointment, deal only with reputable sources. Ask fellow rose gardeners for their recommendations, or refer to the list on page 340. Reputable firms usually guarantee the safe arrival and successful growth of everything they ship, and will replace any plants that are not satisfactory. Beware of advertisements touting "low-price specials"; if something sounds too good to be true, it probably is.

Even if you are buying locally, you may prefer to purchase bare-root plants rather than potted ones. The roots of bare-root plants are typically larger than those of potted plants, since they have not been cut to fit into a container. Stripped of soil, they are also easier to inspect for general vigor and signs of damage or disease. (To keep their roots moist, some bare-root

The Huntington Botanical Gardens in San Marino, California, contain one of the largest public rose gardens in the country. Visiting exemplary gardens can help you determine what roses to grow.

The best grades of potted roses are sold in 2-gallon containers. Choose plants with three or more canes and strong, healthy leaves.

roses are wrapped in damp sphagnum peat moss and placed inside a plastic bag. Although this prevents you from seeing the root system, you can usually feel it through the bag.) Where available, bare-root plants are sold only in early spring, because they must be planted before they start to grow. For information on planting bare-root roses, see page 112.

To ensure uniform quality in rose stock, the American Association of Nurserymen, a nonprofit trade association, has established a set of standards for bare-root and potted roses. If you buy only roses that conform to these standards, you'll be assured of receiving healthy plants that will grow and bloom satisfactorily.

To conform to the standards, bare-root roses should have three or more strong

canes. (An exception is polyanthas, which should have at least four canes.) The standards also specify that nurseries must allow at least two of the canes to reach a length of 18 inches, and the remaining cane or canes 13 inches, before pruning them in preparation for sale. There is no way you can know for sure that the canes actually reached these lengths, but if they extend at least 6 to 8 inches above the bud union and are about ½ inch thick, you can assume that the plant is probably a good one.

If these standards have been met, bare-root plants are known as Grade Number 1. This is sometimes marked on the plant's container or label, and is often listed in mail-order catalogs. Slightly smaller plants are known as Grade Number 1½. These are not as large or robust as Grade Number 1 plants, but can usually be grown quite successfully with a little extra care. Still smaller plants are sold as Grade Number 2; these are rarely satisfying to rose growers.

For potted roses, the standards permit the canes of Grade Number 1 to be cut to 4 inches above the bud union before the plant is placed in its container; this shorter length is allowed to provide for easier shipping. The container should be at least the 2-gallon size, measuring a minimum of 7 inches across the top and 7½ inches high. When buying potted roses that have already leafed out, look for three or more canes with strong, healthy leaves and additional growth buds in the area of the bud union.

With all roses, bare root or potted, the standards state that the canes should branch no more than 3 inches above the bud union. Plants should have a well-developed root system, and although the standards do not specify root size, you should choose a plant whose roots are in at least equal proportion to the above-ground portion of the plant.

The standards do not address the issue of insects and diseases, but obviously you should avoid plants that show signs of these; see Chapter 9 for more information.

IMPORTING ROSES

*M*any rose growers like to import roses that are not available in the United States, such as new European varieties. Before you can import roses from countries other than Canada, you must obtain permission from the U.S. Department of Agriculture. To begin the process, write to the USDA for the necessary permit forms (Permit Unit, USDA, PPQ, Federal Building, Room 638, Hyattsville, MD 20782).

After you fill out and return the forms, a USDA inspector will visit your garden to make sure that you have an area where you can grow the roses in quarantine; this area must be located at least 3 meters (about 10 feet) away from the rest of your rose garden.

After the inspector approves the forms, you will receive separate permit tickets to enclose with your rose orders. The vendors must attach these to the plants they ship to you. Once you have received and planted the roses, a USDA inspector will visit regularly to ensure that they are free of foreign insects and diseases. After two years, you will receive a Release from Postentry Quarantine notice, which allows you to move the roses to another area of your garden if you wish.

No permits are needed to import roses from Canada, though not all Canadian rose nurseries will ship to the United States. However, gardeners visiting Canada can drive to these nurseries and bring roses back with them.

Imports from certain other countries are banned from time to time. Check with the USDA for the latest list.

Bare-root roses are often shipped with padding around their roots. Remove the material upon arrival and make sure that the roots look healthy.

Climbing roses arch majestically over arbors at Elizabeth Park Rose Garden in West Hartford, Connecticut.

USING ROSES
IN THE LANDSCAPE

oses tend to be the focal points of a garden, so their selection and placement deserve special care. Although they are most often planted in beds, their many forms lend them to a variety of other applications—from hedges and ground covers to containerized accents for a deck or patio. By thoughtfully combining the forms and colors of your roses, you can create a spectrum of moods and effects.

ny garden spot that is bathed in at least six hours of sunlight each day can be a home for roses, even if only for one or two plants. Stationed by themselves or combined with other flowers, roses can be a rewarding part of any garden.

Fitting roses into your landscape is easier if you think in terms of the problems to be solved, and of the tone and feeling you want to achieve. Do you need to create a boundary? Brighten a dull expanse? Screen an eyesore? Accent an architectural feature? Enhance an outdoor living space? Grow flowers for cutting? Roses can do it all, evoking moods that can range from serenely majestic to passionately romantic to charming and demure. Perhaps more than any other type of garden, rose gardens are the gardens of dreams. Whether you are adding to an existing landscape or planning a new one, you can use roses to capture almost any garden fantasy.

Climbing and bush roses grow with informal abandon around the porch of a Victorian cottage.

FORMAL AND INFORMAL GARDENS

One of the greatest virtues of roses is that they are equally at home in formal and informal settings. Whether arrayed in dignified beds on a country estate or allowed to ramble over the eaves of a bungalow, they add an enchantment that no other flower can match.

If you are creating a new rose garden, you must first decide whether you want a formal or an informal design. Although to some extent this is a matter of taste, the design also depends on the style of your house and the size of your garden.

Formal gardens, with their symmetrically shaped beds filled with rigid rows of plants, best complement classical styles of architecture, such as French provincial, Georgian, and federal. In keeping with their stately tone, formal gardens usually demand ample space. They also require meticulous grooming, since overgrown edgings and unkempt beds can easily spoil the effect.

The shape of a formal garden is up to you; it may be round, oval, square, rectangular, or even triangular. A small formal garden can be limited to a single bed; a large one can encompass several beds that carry out a grand geometric scheme. The simpler you keep each bed, the more dramatic it will be. Edge it with tidy plants such as germander, boxwood, begonias, or miniature roses, and use a statue, pottery, a garden pool, a fountain, a sundial, or a tree rose as a focal point at the center. Formal rose gardens may also be bordered with fences or evergreens to set them apart from the rest of the plants in the garden.

Informal gardens strive for a look that is freeflowing and spontaneous, even though they are often carefully planned. Today's smaller gardens and modern styles of architecture are best enhanced by an informal design. In an informal garden, roses and other plants are arranged in asymmetrical groupings with wavy or indistinct edges, rather than planted in regimental rows. These groupings may line a walkway, hug a wall or a fence, or stand alone in the middle of a lawn. They may feature roses alone, or may include roses and other plants. Their shape is limited only by your taste and ingenuity, and the space available to you.

surrounded by lawn. If formal, it will have a geometric shape; if informal, its perimeter will have more graceful, flowing lines.

A border is the narrow area along a path, a wall, a fence, or other structure, accessible from three sides at most. Although some rose borders are only one plant deep (such as along a path or a foundation), they look fuller and more pleasing if they are two or three plants deep. Rose borders deeper than three plants are usually difficult to tend, since you may have trouble reaching the plants at the back. In a formal design, the rose border might be fitting for a straight pathway to the front door, perhaps accented by tree roses; in an informal design, the border could line a curved walkway and be interplanted with annuals or other garden flowers.

Large beds and borders composed of only one rose variety are known as mass plantings. Mass plantings of roses can be dramatic in both formal and informal settings. When selecting roses for a mass planting, choose from floriferous classes such as floribundas and miniatures to enhance the visual effect.

If you are laying out a network of beds or borders, be sure to leave enough space for paths, and make the paths wide enough so that garden equipment such as a lawn mower or a wheelbarrow can pass through easily. To allow for comfortable strolling, paths should be at least 2 feet wide; if you want two people to be able to walk side by side, construct the path 4 feet wide. Paths can be paved with brick, slate, gravel, or other construction material, or can be lined with grass. Set the roses far enough back from the path (about 2 feet back for most rosebushes) so that they do not entangle visitors in their thorns.

Plant height is an important consideration. In beds, the taller plants are usually grouped in the center and are framed by lower plants. In borders, the tallest plants are typically placed at the back.

Top: An edging of boxwood surrounds the beds of a formal cutting garden.

Bottom: Prolific 'Betty Prior' floribundas are ideal for borders.

BEDS AND BORDERS

Most formal gardens, and many informal ones, group plants within beds and borders. These groupings may contain plants of a single type, or may feature a wide variety. A bed is a planting area that is accessible from all sides and is usually

LANDSCAPING ROLES FOR ROSES

Thanks to their remarkable range of sizes and growth habits, roses lend themselves to a variety of applications outside traditional beds and borders. The following are some other landscaping roles for roses.

DEFINING A BOUNDARY

Living barriers can be beautiful when they are made of rosebushes. Instead of erecting a fence, plant a hedge of shrub roses. One of the thornier varieties, such as the hybrid rugosa 'F. J. Grootendorst', will also deter pets and intruders. Unlike constructed fences, living fences look equally pleasing from both sides. When using roses in this way, stick to a single variety for uniformity and visual appeal.

Low-growing floribundas or miniature roses can lend a fine finishing touch as an edging for a perennial or shrub border. They can also be used to line a path to a front door, to parallel a driveway, or to separate a patio from a lawn without creating a visual obstacle. For an informal look, plant roses in beds or borders with scalloped or gently curved edges. If the edging is two plants deep, you can choose a taller variety for the back and a lower-growing variety for the front. Roses for hedges and edgings should be planted up to 6 inches closer together than normal, to ensure dense, floriferous growth.

COVERING THE GROUND

A barren expanse or a bare slope can become a bank of color when roses are used as ground covers. Spreading, low-growing varieties can also prevent erosion and smother weeds. The best roses to use as ground covers are the hybrid rugosa 'Max Graf', the shrub rose 'Sea Foam', the miniature 'Red Cascade', or one of the several low-growing Meidiland shrub roses. Ramblers can also make good ground covers if allowed to grow along the ground instead of on supports. Many of these roses will take root along their canes as they sprawl, making them seem more like vines.

Evaluating Your Landscaping Needs

Before choosing roses for the garden, you should think carefully about your landscaping needs. Only when you have determined these can you select the varieties that will best accomplish your goals. Here are a few guidelines.

—Choose a garden style. Look at your house and grounds—their forms, colors, textures, and scale—and those of the surrounding neighborhood. What roles do they suggest for roses? Think of your favorite rose plantings. Are they formal or informal? Grand or humble? Public or private? You'll be happiest with a garden style that is close to your heart.

—Decide where you will place your roses. Do you want to fit them into the existing garden, or create new areas for them?

—Consider the practical factors, such as climate, drainage, and the distribution of shade. These can influence—and inspire—the design of a rose garden.

—Decide whether you need roses for special uses, such as hedges, fences, screens, fragrance, or cutting.

—Estimate how much time you can devote to the garden. This, too, can influence the design and the choice of plants.

—Set a budget. Quality plants and ornaments are an investment you may want to make over several years.

—Start with a simple plan. You will get quick results that you can enjoy immediately and elaborate upon later as time and money allow.

—Plan on paper. Use graph paper and colored pens to sketch out a plan. If you draw your plan to scale, you can use it to calculate the number of plants you'll need.

—Lay out beds and borders with string. This is an easy way to visualize how your plan will fit your gardening space.

SCREENING AN AREA

Almost every home has an eyesore such as a gas tank, a storage shed, or a trash receptacle that is in need of tasteful concealment. A rosy solution is to place a trellis in front of the area and let climbers do the screening. One or two large shrub or old garden roses will substitute nicely for climbers and will be just as appealing.

Tall privacy screens of roses can block out distracting street traffic, neighbors, or nearby buildings, and are more attractive than high fences.

Evergreen shrubs are usually the plants of choice to hide the unsightly foundations of houses because their foliage makes a year-round screen. But conifers do not flower, and broad-leaved evergreens flower mainly in spring. Mixing roses among these plants, or planting them in front of the evergreens, will add summer color without detracting too much from the winter beauty of the evergreens.

PROVIDING CUT FLOWERS

No cut flower is more esteemed than the rose. You can grow long-stemmed beauties for the home or office by dedicating a few plants as cutting material. If you plant a few rosebushes near the back door, it will be easy to reach out and snip a few blooms for the dining-room table.

A border of low-growing bush roses and perennials is backed by taller roses that have been trained to pillars to provide a sense of enclosure.

Rose beds devoted to cutting can also be laid out; such gardens are usually situated in an out-of-the-way place, with the roses aligned in functional rows. With their long stems and long-lasting, classically shaped flowers, hybrid teas and grandifloras are the best roses for cutting gardens. Some floribundas also make good cut flowers. See the list on page 192.

ADDING FRAGRANCE

Think of fragrance when planning locations for roses. Fragrant varieties are especially effective when planted near open windows, alongside a patio or a porch, or flanking a garden bench. If you have a fence with a gate, plant a fragrant rosebush at both sides of the gate to create a scented welcome for visitors. Many rose gardeners plant fragrant varieties exclusively, because they want to use the roses in potpourri or cooking. Lists of fragrant roses appear on pages 63 and 249.

Top left: Tree roses planted amid juniper shrubs provide summer color and winter greenery around a foundation.

Top right: A living fence of 'Simplicity' floribundas will keep out intruders with its thorns.

Bottom: Long-stemmed roses for cutting grow a few convenient steps from a back door.

Left: Planting roses by a window makes them easier to enjoy from indoors. This is the hybrid tea 'Talisman'.

Right: Brilliant red climbing roses surround a mailbox, bringing its drab colors to life.

ENHANCING THE VIEW FROM INDOORS

Roses can enhance not only the beauty of their outdoor setting but also the view from inside the house. If you place them within sight of a window, you can watch the buds unfold into exquisite flowers that glisten with morning dew, or enjoy your roses at day's end as they reflect the brilliance of the sunset. A many-windowed sun room or conservatory can make a brilliant vantage point for view-ing your roses. Roses in containers, placed near the windows, can make the room and its plants seem an extension of the garden.

FILLING SMALL SPACES

You don't need much room to grow roses; they can be effective even in small spaces. Look for pockets in the garden where roses will work—around the base of a flagpole, beside a rustic mailbox, or disguising an outdoor light. Rock gardens are ideal spots for small polyanthas, floribundas, and especially miniatures. Rock gardens are traditionally designed with more spring-blooming plants than summer-blooming ones, so using roses prolongs the attractiveness of the rock garden by several months.

A spot near where the driveway swings into the street is ideal for a welcoming burst of roses. Plant it with white or pastel roses, and it will stand out at night. A small brick wall in front or in back of the planting, and a spotlight to illuminate it, will complete the effect.

Miniature roses can play a very important role in a garden where space is especially limited. Plant them in accent spots or in drifts; use them in mass plantings instead of annuals. They are excellent for edging a bed or border, or in containers. If there are young children in your family, give them a few miniature roses to tend and watch them thrill at the appearance of tiny flowers, which they can present to friends, teachers, or grandmothers.

ADDING HEIGHT

A traditional rose arbor is a perfect addition to a sunny garden. Breezy and romantic, an arbor made of lath provides dappled shade if left unadorned, or becomes a focal point when embellished with climbers or ramblers. The top can be covered with coarsely woven shade cloth or a nonwoven material known as landscape fabric; both are available at hardware stores and garden centers. This will offer additional shade and protect the

Top: An arch of pink and white roses and purple clematis creates a magical gateway.

Bottom: Miniatures are ideal for lining borders and filling small spaces.

Top: A weathered
fence makes a perfect
foil for an effusive
pink-flowered
rambler.

Bottom left: A red-
flowered climber
wanders across the
window of a house,
creating a visual treat
for those indoors.

Bottom right: A tree
rose in a container
provides a colorful
accent beside a bench.

blooms growing under it from wind and hail, while letting rain drizzle through.

The uses of climbers and ramblers extend far beyond the rose arbor. Train them along split-rail or picket fences to brighten up the wood and add curving grace to the straight lines. A portico at the entrance to a house can be accented with climbing roses that are trained to grow up the sides and over the roof. If you have a porch, you can tie the garden and the house together by planting low-growing roses along the base of the porch or at the sides of its steps, and letting climbers sprawl from the ground to the porch roof or overhang.

Climbers can be espaliered (pruned and trained in two-dimensional patterns) against a stockade fence or the wall of a house. They can also cover eaves or outline windows and doors, adding graceful color to the outside of the home and softening hard edges. Climbing roses can ramble up posts, cover old tree stumps, grow high into trees, or spill over from the tops of stone walls. Darkly colored wooden retaining walls can be brightened by planting climbing roses atop them and letting the canes hang over the walls. Keep the canes in place by pegging them to the wall with hooks or clips; for summerlong color, be sure to select an everblooming variety of climber.

Some climbers, such as 'Don Juan' and 'Golden Showers', grow tall and erect since they have stiffer canes, and are perfect for trellises, arches, and pergolas. Large beds of roses or perennials can incorporate a freestanding pillar of climbing roses in the center to add height and break up the monotony. In large beds or borders, you can also install two posts or pillars and connect them with a chain. Plant a pliable-caned climber or rambler at each post or pillar, and train them to grow along the chain until they meet.

Tree roses, too, bring needed height and accent to the garden. They may be used as solitary specimens in a formal rose garden, or planted amid low-growing floribundas or annuals for a more informal look. If you plant them against a wall or fence of a contrasting color, the beauty and form of the tree rose will stand out even more. Tree roses are also effective in lining a walk. Standing straight and tall, they give direction to the path. To tone down their stiffness, try surrounding them with mounds of lower-growing roses, annuals, perennials, or a mixture of all three.

Roses for Every Purpose

Listed below are roses that work well in selected landscaping situations. The list is far from exhaustive; plants with similar growth habits can be substituted freely for these.

Arbors and trellises	City of York, Heidelberg, Red Fountain, most climbers and ramblers.
Pillars	Aloha, Don Juan, Dr. J. H. Nicolas, Golden Showers, Joseph's Coat, Piñata, other climbers with stiff canes.
Fences	Blaze, Handel, New Dawn, most ramblers.
Edgings	Any low-growing floribunda, polyantha, or miniature.
Ground covers	Max Graf, Ralph's Creeper, Red Cascade, Sea Foam, low-growing Meidiland shrubs.
Screening	Altissimo, Carefree Beauty, Carefree Wonder, Dortmund, Golden Wings.
Hedges	Betty Prior, Bloomin' Easy, Diamond Jubilee, F. J. Grootendorst, First Edition, Regensberg, Showbiz, Simplicity, Sun Flare.
Mass plantings	Apricot Nectar, Bonica '82, Europeana, Iceberg, Sarabande, Summer Snow, many miniatures.
Container plantings	Any low-growing floribundas, polyanthas, or miniatures.

COMBINING ROSES WITH OTHER PLANTS

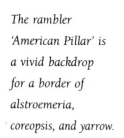

oses do not need a special place for themselves, but can be mixed with other plants throughout the landscape. Any plant—be it an annual, a bulb, a perennial, a shrub, or a small tree—can be combined with roses as long as it enjoys the same growing conditions. Roses and companion plants can complement one another in many ways, providing color harmony, filling in color between the other's blooming periods, providing greenery during the winter,

The rambler 'American Pillar' is a vivid backdrop for a border of alstroemeria, coreopsis, and yarrow.

and enriching the garden with a variety of heights and textures.

Roses are especially effective in border plantings because of the height and the color continuity they provide. Use shrub roses as a backdrop for lower-growing plants in a border. Try them, or floribundas, instead of other, more commonly used deciduous shrubs. You'll be pleased with their especially long season of bloom.

Roses can also be combined with other shrubs in a mixed border. Planted with spring-flowering azalea, forsythia, lilac, spirea, viburnum, and similar shrubs, they will extend the blooming period of the border substantially. When used with summer-flowering shrubs such as abelia, hydrangea, or rose-of-Sharon,

they provide a colorful complement. The roses can be placed either in an alternating pattern with other shrubs, or in rows in front of or behind them.

When rose borders and beds are bare in early spring, colorful borders of spring-flowering bulbs can add life to them. Try snowdrops, crocus, squill, chionodoxa, or early-blooming species tulips. Between rose plants grow clumps of daffodils to glisten in the sunshine just as the rose leaves start to unfurl. By the time the bulbs have finished blooming and their foliage begins to fade, the roses are ready to take over the limelight. As a bonus, you will find that the fertilizer you apply to your roses will make the bulb plants larger and more free flowering.

Many spring-flowering perennials, such as basket-of-gold, mountain pink, candytuft, primrose, and forget-me-not, bloom before the roses are ready, adding color to bare spots in the same way that bulbs can. Since their blooming period ends before the roses come into flower, you can use them without worrying about clashes with the color scheme of the roses. During their brief blooming seasons, perennials can also add exciting dashes of color to roses that are already in bloom.

For longer-lasting color harmony, roses can be mingled with low-growing annuals that bloom throughout the summer. Whether used as underplantings or planted in adjacent beds, annuals will not compete seriously with the roses for food or water.

Small, ornamental flowering trees, such as flowering cherry, dogwood, or magnolia, can be planted near roses as vertical accents, bringing color to the rose garden before it is in bloom. Miniature roses can be planted under the canopy of ornamental trees. However, take care that trees do not shade the roses, and that their roots are not so close that they contend with the roses for water and fertilizer.

CHOOSING COLOR FOR COMPANION PLANTINGS

Of all the qualities that companion plants impart to a garden, color has the greatest impact. In choosing color companions for your roses, you should try to complement them without overwhelming them, taking into account the hues of your roses and the color scheme you have established. Different companion colors have different roles to play.

Orange flowers bring warmth to a rose garden, blending best with dark red, yellow, or white roses. Good sources of orange are orange varieties of annual marigold, calendula, gazania, and portulaca;

Pink-tinged 'White Delight' and orange-red 'Fragrant Cloud' hybrid teas combine colorfully with shasta daisies, geraniums, 'Niobe' phlox, statice, and petunias.

Top: Blue cynoglossum makes a striking neighbor for pink 'Simplicity' floribundas. Because there are no blue roses, this color must be supplied by other flowers.

Bottom: The inner circles represent the major rose colors; surrounding segments are the flower colors that combine best with them.

Companion Colors

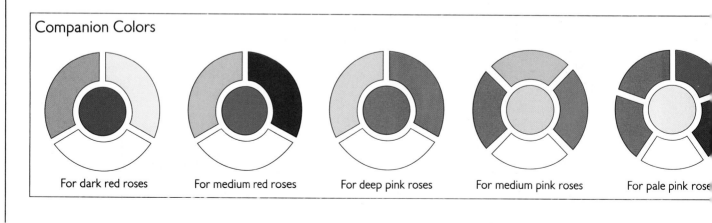

For dark red roses   For medium red roses   For deep pink roses   For medium pink roses   For pale pink rose

and perennial black-eyed-susan and day-lily. Yellow flowers, ranging from cream-colored annual zinnias to bright gold perennial coreopsis, add gaiety and a light touch. Use them with yellow roses of different tones and shades, or with almost any other rose.

Red is best used as an accent color because too much of it is overpowering, especially in small gardens. Red-flowered plants, such as annual petunia, salvia, geranium, verbena, phlox, begonia, and impatiens, look good either bordering or accenting white, soft yellow, or clear pink roses.

Pink companions go best with pink roses, and are most effective if they provide a contrast. With pale pink roses, use deep pink annual geraniums; with deep pink roses, choose light pink annual vinca. Pink annual petunias, snapdragons, begonias, phlox, impatiens, and zinnias blend well with red or yellow roses; select a tone and shade of pink that will best complement the color of the roses. Pink can also be used with mauve; put light colors next to dark colors for best effect. Next to white roses, pink companion plants look even pinker.

Blue is a popular companion color because there are no blue roses. Deep blue annual cornflowers or perennial anchusa blend well with soft yellow or red roses, whereas sky blue perennial delphiniums harmonize successfully with white, orange, or pale pink roses. Perennial bellflower and veronica, and annual ageratum, petunia, and verbena are also good sources of blue. Avoid planting blue-flowered companion plants alongside pale mauve roses, because they will make these roses look washed out.

Violet and purple, such as the colors found in perennial asters and heliotrope, and in annual petunias, sweet alyssum, nierembergia, and lobelia, blend best with pink, yellow, or white roses. However, they can clash with some oranges and orange-reds. But when orange and purple do work well together, the effect can be quite dramatic.

White is sometimes used in the garden as a buffer between strong colors, or as a unifying border. Try to plant white flowers in large groups, since too few scattered about can create a spotty effect. White companions can be used with almost any rose. Alongside brightly colored roses white has a softening effect; alongside pale roses it strengthens their color. Don't look just to flowers for color: Plants with silver or gray leaves, such as artemisia or dusty miller, can be planted in place of white-flowered annuals or perennials.

When choosing a companion for blended or bicolored roses, select a plant whose flower will complement or enhance either the main color of the rose or one of the colors in its shading. With these multicolored roses it is simplest and best to use solid-colored companions.

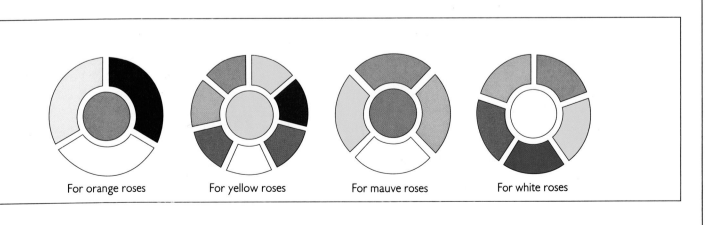

For orange roses For yellow roses For mauve roses For white roses

USING CONTAINERS
IN THE LANDSCAPE

*R*oses growing in portable planters can make a lively addition to the landscape, either out among the garden plants or on a deck or a patio. They are a perfect way to enhance small spaces, accent colorless expanses, or quickly change the look and mood of the garden.

Wide paths and walkways can be highlighted with tubs of roses placed along them at intervals. Steps leading to a doorway can be animated by a pot of roses on each tread.

A half-barrel of miniature roses provides a focal point in a bed of juniper.

Dress up window boxes with miniature roses. Rather than planting them directly into the box, fill it with individual flower pots. That way, the roses can easily be moved indoors in winter or replaced if something goes wrong.

Patios, decks, and terraces are favorite spots for relaxing and entertaining on warm summer evenings. Pots or planters of roses, teeming with color and fragrance, can add to the pleasure of these moments.

Wherever you have a spot to hang a basket, fill it with miniature roses for summerlong color. Suspend baskets from lampposts, tree limbs, gutters, overhangs, the porch roof, or brackets attached to fences or the house. In winter the baskets can be moved indoors. 'Red Cascade', with its long, graceful flowing canes, is one of the best miniature roses to use in baskets.

If you have room in an out-of-the-way place, you can grow extra containers of roses to hold in reserve as replacements. That way, when a container rose on display goes out of bloom, you can quickly replace it with another one.

Container gardening makes it possible to grow roses without a garden—on balconies, terraces, and rooftops high above city streets. The limited gardening space of many townhouses and condominiums can be augmented with planters.

When selecting roses for containers, limit your choice to floribundas, polyanthas, miniatures, and the shorter hybrid teas. When planted in pots, these types of roses look better than taller hybrid teas or grandifloras. Container-grown roses are best enjoyed when plants are low growing, enabling you to look down on an abundance of flowers as you walk by.

Tree roses, whether full size or the smaller type known as "patio" tree roses, are perfect for formal containers because the manicured look of tree roses meshes well with them. And since these types of roses are always tender, growing them

Planning Rose Gardens With Maintenance in Mind

If time is a factor in caring for your rose garden, you can make some planning decisions that will lighten maintenance chores and increase the attractiveness of your garden. If you live in a cold or damp climate where fungal diseases are common, or if you simply lack the time for regular spraying, choose disease-resistant varieties such as those listed on page 68. You can also lessen maintenance if you stick with shrub and old garden roses, which typically need less pruning and other care than do hybrid teas. In very cold climates select only cold-hardy varieties that need little or no winter protection; you'll find a list of these on page 66. If you do plant roses that need winter protection, try to place them in the backyard or in some other inconspicuous location, because roses under rose cones or other protective materials are not very attractive at the front of the house.

Top: A hanging basket of red miniatures brightens the weathered wall of a house. It can also be enjoyed from indoors.

Bottom: A tree rose adds color around the base of a larger tree. It, in turn, is underplanted with fragrant alyssum.

in containers makes it easy to move them indoors for the winter.

Containers for outdoor roses can be rounded or rectangular, but should be at least 18 inches across and deep (approximately 13 gallons) for good root growth of full-sized roses. Smaller 5- or 7-gallon pots (5-gallon pots are approximately 12 inches across and 15 inches deep; 7-gallon pots are approximately 15 inches across and 15 inches deep) can be used to grow excellent roses if watered properly and regularly, but the larger container is better. Miniatures can be grown satisfactorily in pots 6 to 8 inches across and deep. Containers can be made of plastic, clay, concrete, or wood. Metal

Freestanding tree roses and other container plants break up a lackluster expanse of brickwork.

containers should be avoided because they can get too hot, damaging the roots and hindering growth. Very heavy containers should be equipped with casters or set on a dolly so that they can be easily moved or rotated.

Longer planter boxes—either freestanding ones for a deck or smaller ones designed as window boxes—can also be good niches for roses. For best results with large plants, use a container that is 18 inches wide and deep (although with proper care, you can use a container as small as 12 inches wide and 15 inches deep). Miniatures will do nicely in containers measuring only 6 to 8 inches deep and wide. The length of the container should be a multiple of 2 feet for large plants or 1 foot for miniatures, depending on the number of plants you wish to grow in the container.

Instead of planting roses in containers to add interest to flower and shrub beds, try the opposite. Portable planters of annual marigolds, zinnias, geraniums, petunias, or phlox can add a contrast in color and texture to rose beds when placed alongside them.

GROWING ROSES IN RAISED BEDS

Raised beds are a landscaping feature that is often used to compensate for poor soil, bad drainage, or high pH. By elevating plants above the soil line and surrounding their roots with improved growing medium, raised beds enable roses to grow where they might otherwise not survive.

Raised beds are also attractive, drawing the eye to their contents. If the walls of the beds are made wide enough and are topped with wood or paving material, the edges of the beds can double as seating areas.

There are other, more practical advantages to raised beds. Rosebushes raised off the ground are easier to reach for pruning, watering, spraying, and other gardening chores. Should you choose to install an automatic watering system, you'll find it easy to do with raised beds. Moreover, in spring the beds will warm up faster than the surrounding soil, speeding growth. However, in regions where the soil freezes quickly, roses should be planted at least 2 feet in from the walls of the beds to insulate their roots from the cold.

Raised beds are usually made with wooden sides (redwood, cedar, pressure-treated pine, railroad ties, or landscape timbers), but can also be constructed of durable brick or stone. Regardless of the material used, a well-constructed bed will leak water from the sides or the bottom, making it impossible to overwater.

When deciding on a location for a raised bed, weigh all the factors you would when selecting a site for any rose garden. The foremost of these are sunlight and access to water. Another element to consider is the presence of any underground utility lines, such as electrical conduits, telephone cables, and water or sewage pipes. Although you can build over these, it is wiser not to, since you may some day have to dig them up for repair. Most utility companies will come to your house and mark the location of the lines for you without charge.

In finding a place for raised beds, you should take into account the natural flow of drainage on your property. Position the beds where water will flow away from them, and not where water will collect along their outer walls.

The size and shape of the raised beds are largely up to you, but there are a few practical points to consider. Be sure to design the beds so that you can easily walk around them or pass by with a lawn mower or other large garden tool. Make the beds narrow enough so that all the

plants are within easy reach of the sides, since walking on the soil of a raised bed compacts it too much. A good rule is to plant only two rows of large roses, and never more than three. Raised beds of miniature roses can have three to four rows of plants.

To allow proper depth for root growth, the bed should be tall enough to hold 10 to 15 inches of soil for miniature roses, or 18 to 24 inches for full-sized plants. Good drainage is important for roses; in a large bed, you may need to improve this by burying drainage pipe or tile in coarse gravel in trenches beneath the bed.

Raised beds can solve several problems at once. They compensate for poor soil or bad drainage, and their edges can be designed to provide seating.

A *doorway*
shelters a tender
noisette from wind
and cold.

CHAPTER FOUR

PLANTING ROSES

oses need a place where they can receive adequate sunshine, water, nutrition, and protection from chilling weather. Some roses are more demanding in these matters than others, but all thrive best if provided with optimum conditions. The roses you plant in your garden today may be with you for decades, so it pays to prepare for them properly.

Once you have decided what roses to grow and how they fit into your landscaping plan, the next step is to acquire and plant them. The advice that preparation is the key to success is nowhere more important than with rose planting. For no matter how much pampering you give your roses, they will never reach their potential unless they get a good start.

In this chapter you will learn the four steps to establishing successful roses outdoors: finding a suitable site, preparing the ground properly, improving the soil, and planting roses in it correctly.

SELECTING A SITE

The success of your roses depends a great deal on the conditions in which they are grown. Most roses need at least six hours of direct sunlight each day. They also need rich, fertile, moist but well-drained soil along with good air circulation, ample growing room, and protection from harsh elements. In addition, your caretaking tasks will be easier if you can locate the plants within easy reach of your water source and the place where you store tools and supplies.

Although you can do little to change the basic climate of your garden, the odds are that you can find or create a small area where roses can thrive. Even the harshest environment offers locations that are sheltered from prevailing conditions, thanks to differences in vegetation, variations in terrain, or the proximity of buildings and other structures. For example, the warm and sunny south wall of a house can harbor plants that would perish if placed in the middle of a chilly, windswept garden.

If a favorable site for rose growing does not exist in your garden, you may be able to create one through small modifications, such as building a fence to shelter plants from the wind or cutting back surrounding foliage to admit more air and light. Your roses will be your companions for years to come, so it is worth making the effort to provide them with the best possible surroundings.

If all else fails, you can still enjoy the beauty of roses by planting them in containers. That way, as conditions in your garden change (for example, as shaded areas receive more sunlight with the advance of spring), you can easily move your roses where they will do best. To give yourself and your roses a respite from winter, you can move small containers indoors for year-round flowers.

SUNSHINE

Roses need at least six hours of direct sun a day to grow and flower their best. It is better that the sunny hours occur in the morning than in the afternoon, since morning sun dries off the foliage early, reducing the chance of disease. Morning sun is also less likely than stronger afternoon sun to burn leaves and flowers, especially in hot climates.

Roses that are not receiving enough sunlight will show spindly growth and will have thin, weak canes. Leaves will be farther apart than normal and flower production will be poor. If these symptoms appear in your garden, you may be able to correct them by moving the plants, by trimming any nearby tree limbs that block the light, by painting an adjacent wall or fence white to reflect available light, or by using a light-colored mulch.

Some roses can grow in partial shade if you take some extra precautions. Locate your roses where they will not compete with other plants for food and water. Even though shaded roses do not grow as large as those grown in full sun, the

spacing of plants should be the same (see page 111). This ensures good air circulation—a necessity in shady areas, where disease organisms such as mildew can thrive. Before planting, work in extra compost or other organic matter to hold moisture and nutrients. But avoid the temptation to add extra fertilizer to compensate for the lack of light; since roses grow less profusely in reduced light, they need fewer nutrients. Overfertilizing is not only a waste of money, but can actually burn the roots and foliage. Regardless of the measures you take, however, there is no getting around the fact that roses grown in shade are usually leggier, and bloom less profusely, than roses grown in full sun.

Because the various classes of roses differ in their light requirements, you may get better results by planting another type. For example, if your garden is too shady for modern roses, try one of the hybrid musks, which can grow and bloom in less sun than other types. Hybrid musks need about four hours of direct sun a day. Miniature roses, too, tolerate a little more shade than some of their larger cousins, and are happy in four hours of direct sun or the daylong dappled shadow of an ornamental tree such as a magnolia or a flowering cherry. Many climbers also grow happily in the filtered shade of a tree. A list of roses that tolerate shadier-than-average conditions appears on page 65.

Roses in this woodsy garden are spaced well apart to admit maximum light. The white fence and light-colored gravel also reflect much-needed illumination.

Top: Terracing reduces erosion and makes roses on a hillside easier to care for.

Bottom: A morning misting adds humidity around roses in dry climates.

If you are planting roses on a hillside, terrace the slope with railroad ties, landscape timbers, bricks, or stones to retard runoff and to ensure that each plant receives enough water. Roses usually do not grow well in low areas where water collects and keeps the soil soggy. If you cannot avoid this type of planting site, take the steps described on pages 108 to 110.

HUMIDITY

When the air around roses is extremely humid, the incidence of disease rises, since the fungal spores that attack roses thrive in high-moisture conditions. For this reason you should select a site where air can move freely. But avoid a windy location, because rapid airflow can dry out roses and tear the flowers and foliage. In humid climates particularly, choose a spot where roses will not be closely surrounded by hedges, large plants, or walls that can constrict air movement. Where humidity is naturally low, you can raise it by reducing air motion, such as with a fence or other structure; by placing a coarse mulch on rose beds, which will evaporate a considerable amount of water into the air; or by watering often. Misting plants in the morning also raises the humidity around them.

SPACING

Because roses are demanding of sun, water, and nutrients, they should be placed where they will not be crowded by other plants. If possible, avoid positioning them at the bases of trees or where their roots will compete with those of other vegetation. If you must plant near a tree, locate your roses no closer than halfway between the trunk and the farthest spread of the tree limbs. Better still, place your rose completely outside the canopy of the tree. When planting roses near trees, prune away the lower tree limbs to improve air circulation and let in more light.

WATER

Although roses will survive with less than optimal watering, they will not fulfill their potential for lush growth and large, richly colored flowers with thick, firm petals unless they receive adequate moisture. A complete discussion of watering needs for roses begins on page 136. Be sure to locate your rose plants within reach of a garden hose or irrigation system, especially if you live where rainfall is unreliable.

Keep roses at least 3 feet away from the bases of other shrubs. If your garden is small and this is not possible, dig a hole that is 24 to 30 inches wide and 24 to 30 inches deep, and install an underground barrier around each rose. Ideally made of plastic or metal sheeting (such as vinyl siding, aluminum, or sheet metal, available at building supply stores), an underground barrier will prevent nearby shrub and tree roots from invading the territory around the rose. It is easiest, of course, to put one in at planting time. But if you don't, you can excavate the soil at a later date, cut out the invading roots, and then install the barrier. Be sure the barrier is as close as possible to the edges of the hole, so that the roots of your roses can grow to their fullest. Where a large rose bed is situated near competing plants, you will find it easier to install the barrier around the entire bed rather than around each plant.

An alternative to creating an underground barrier is to plant each rose in a large, well-drained plastic container (10 gallons or larger) and sink the container into the ground. These plants can stay in place for several years without repotting. When growth and flowering begin to slow down and disappoint you, it's time to replant. Dig up each container, replace the potting medium, and cut back any roots that have grown too large.

Roses can be interplanted with small shrubs, perennials, annuals, bulbs, and some ground covers, such as ajuga and periwinkle. Ivy, however, is usually too aggressive, growing into the rose plants and robbing them of fertilizer and water. Be aware that roses stationed among other plants need a little more fertilizer and water.

When planting roses near a building or a solid fence, set the plants out at least 18 inches from the structure to allow room for growth and air movement. In hot climates, try to avoid planting roses in front of a white wall or fence that can reflect

Top: These roses have been planted well away from trees and shrubs, which can compete for water and nutrients.

Bottom: Planting roses in sunken pots is another way to protect them from competition.

Spaces between rosebushes can be filled with lower-growing annuals, perennials, or shrubs, as long as they are not too aggressive.

burning light and heat. However, in cool climates or where light is low, planting near a reflective wall or fence can increase growth.

PROTECTION FROM WIND AND COLD

Although some roses can tolerate brisk conditions, most are warm-weather plants that thrive best when sheltered from wind and cold. If you find that an otherwise ideal spot is ravaged by winds, erect a barrier such as a fence or a hedge on the windward side. Make sure that the barrier is not so close that it casts shade. Solid barriers can actually magnify air turbulence as the wind flows over them and down the other side, so set them well away from your roses, ideally at a distance four to six times the height of the rose plants.

Just as water can accumulate in low spots where drainage is poor, cold air too can collect in low areas. Denser and heavier than warm air, cold air flows downhill and pools at the bottom of the depression if it has no outlet. Roses planted in such a site will be subject to colder, more stationary air—and thus more winter damage—than roses planted on a hillside.

If this is your situation, try to locate the plants in a part of the garden with a higher elevation. (But avoid hilltops, which are often exposed to chilling and drying winds.) If this is not possible, choose hardier roses, apply extra winter protection, or build a raised bed.

EASY ACCESS

An important consideration when planting roses is choosing a spot that you can

Top: Cold air can collect at the bottom of a depression, subjecting roses to more frigid conditions.

Bottom: Rosebushes should be set well away from fences, which can actually magnify wind turbulence.

Stepping-stones provide access to roses at the back of the garden, making maintenance easier.

easily get to and work in. The closer your garden is to tools, water, and supplies, the easier your work will be. If you are planting your roses against a wall or a fence, be sure you can reach the plants in the back row easily to spray, prune, or cut away flowers, since walking on the bed will compact the soil. If you're planting on a hill, plan so that you can get yourself and your equipment up and down easily. You may need to install steps and landings to make maintenance easier.

PREPARING THE SOIL

Although roses can grow in any reasonably good soil, they will thrive so much better in improved soil that it is worth making the effort to fine-tune it.

The best growing medium for roses is soil that is fertile, moisture retentive, rich in organic matter, and lose enough in texture to allow penetration by air and water. Soil of this type almost never occurs by itself; most often it is the product of careful tending over the years.

To create the best possible conditions for roses, you'll probably need to adjust your soil. To do this you must have a basic understanding of soil properties and how they are related to growth. The sections that follow discuss the most significant of these—soil texture, structure, and pH. You'll learn how to evaluate your soil and how to correct any deficiencies.

SOIL TEXTURE AND SOIL STRUCTURE

Soil is composed of particles of sand, silt, and clay, which exist in varying proportions. Sand particles are largest (0.2 to

0.05 mm), clay particles are smallest (0.002 mm or less), and silt falls in between (0.05 to 0.002 mm). The size of the soil particles determines what is known as soil texture; the arrangement of the particles is referred to as soil structure.

A soil that is too sandy cannot hold onto the water and the fertilizer you give it, so plants growing in sandy soil must be fed and watered frequently. On the positive side, the coarse texture of sandy soil provides the aeration needed for good root growth, and its fast-draining qualities help keep it relatively free of soil-borne diseases. On the negative side, fertilizer leaches through it rapidly and thus needs frequent replenishing.

Heavier clay soil holds water and nutrients well, but usually has poor drainage because the tiny spaces between its small particles do not let water through easily. Because of the compact nature of clay, aeration is also poor.

Silt, ranking between sand and clay in fineness, has both the good drainage of sand and the nutrient-holding capacity of clay. Silty soil is also extremely friable, or easy to work. It is almost as good as loam for growing roses, but like loam it rarely occurs naturally; it is usually mixed with sand and clay.

The best soil of all, called loam, is a mixture of 30 to 50 percent sand, 30 to 40 percent silt, and 8 to 28 percent clay (the total must naturally equal 100 percent). Like silt, loam drains well yet retains enough water to promote growth. It has good aeration, allowing roots to absorb oxygen and have room to grow, and it has excellent nutrient-retaining properties. Loose and friable, good loam is composed of 50 percent solid matter, 25 percent air, and 25 percent water.

SOIL TESTING

Since there is no way to be sure what kind of soil you have by looking at it, it's a good idea to have your soil tested every year or two. This can be done by a private soil-testing laboratory (check the yellow pages or advertisements in gardening magazines), or with inexpensive soil-test kits available at garden centers and agricultural supply stores. Many county agricultural extensions will also perform soil tests.

Soil-test kits usually measure only pH (see below) and thus may not reveal other, potentially serious defects of your soil. The tests done by laboratories are more complete, indicating not only pH, but also the soil texture, the amount of organic matter, the major and minor nutrients present, the level of plant toxins present, and often, the corrective measures you need to take.

The symptoms of excessively high or low pH are very similar: yellowing leaves, lack of proper growth and flowering, and in severe cases, the death of the plant. The only certain way to distinguish too-high from too-low pH is to test the soil.

An inexpensive pH test kit shows that this soil is mildly acidic—ideal for rose growing.

SOIL pH

The pH of a soil is the measure of its acidity or alkalinity—a characteristic that is independent of soil texture and structure but that is just as essential to good plant growth.

The pH of soil is expressed on a scale of 0 to 14, with lower numbers indicating acid soil and higher numbers indicating alkaline (basic) soil. A pH of 7.0 is neutral. Soil pH varies from region to region, depending on local soil chemistry, water table levels, and rainfall. In general, areas with high rainfall have acid soils in the 4.5 to 7.0 range, and arid regions have alkaline soils in the 7.0 to 8.0 range.

In a soil that is too acidic or too alkaline, plant nutrients become insoluble and cannot be absorbed by the roots of the plant. At the same time, toxic elements are more soluble, potentially killing the plants or severely damaging their roots. Moreover, beneficial soil bacteria will not grow in highly acid or alkaline soil.

Roses, along with many other plants, grow best at a pH of 6.0 to 6.5. In this slightly acid range, most of the nutrients roses need are readily available. Roses will tolerate a pH as low as 5.5 or as high as 7.8, but they will not grow as well as they could at the ideal pH.

*RAISING THE pH
OF ACID SOIL*

If a soil test indicates that the pH of your soil is too low, you can raise it by adding limestone (calcium carbonate). This is a powdery material, sold in bags at garden centers and agricultural supply stores. Ground dolomitic limestone (calcium magnesium carbonate) is the best type because it also contains magnesium, an element essential for plant growth. If this type is not available, use ground agricultural lime (calcium oxide), but stay away from hydrated lime (calcium hydroxide), which can burn plant roots. Apply limestone to the surface of the soil with a trowel, mix it with the top few inches of soil, and water it in. The pH should be corrected before roses are planted, and repeat treatments will undoubtedly be needed every few years, as confirmed by soil testing.

The following chart indicates how much limestone is needed per 100 square feet to raise the pH of different soils to 6.5. More is needed for silt or loam soil than for sandy soil, since the particles in silt and loam soils are finer and more numerous. However, you should apply no more than 5 pounds per 100 square feet at one time. If more is required, wait a month before making a second or third application. Be prudent when applying limestone, since too much can render trace elements insoluble and thus unavailable to plants.

Agricultural sulfur is added to alkaline soil to lower its pH. After spreading sulfur over the surface, dig it in to a depth of several inches, then water.

LOWERING THE pH OF ALKALINE SOIL

If your soil is too alkaline, you can lower its pH by adding agricultural sulfur. It is sold in powder form in bags, boxes, or cans at garden centers and agricultural supply stores. Spread agricultural sulfur over the soil, dig it into the top several inches, and then water it in.

Use a maximum of 2 pounds per 100 square feet per application. If a second or third application is needed, wait a month between applications.

Most humus (see below) and many fertilizers have a slight acidifying effect on soil, so if your soil is neutral or slightly alkaline its pH may not need any further adjustment. After applying one of these amendments, recheck the pH of your soil to determine whether the acidifying effect has been sufficient. If it has not, add sulfur as necessary.

Soil that is extremely alkaline is often difficult to correct. The best way to grow roses under these conditions is in raised beds that have been filled with imported soil, or in containers. See page 92 for a discussion on planting in raised beds; see page 90 to learn more about growing roses in containers.

SOIL AMENDMENTS

Because good loam rarely occurs naturally, your soil will probably need improvement with one or more soil amendments. These are organic or inorganic materials you can mix with the soil to improve its drainage, aeration, and nutrient and water retention. Many soil amendments also enhance soil structure, supply nutrients, and neutralize acidity or alkalinity.

ORGANIC MATTER Organic matter in the form of decomposed animal or plant material—often called humus—is the most valuable and versatile amendment

Reducing Soil Acidity

Pounds of limestone to apply (per 100 square feet) to raise pH to 6.5.

Original pH	Sandy Soil	Silt or Loam Soil	Clay Soil
4.5	10.0	11.0	12.0
5.0	7.0	7.7	8.4
5.5	5.0	5.5	6.0
6.0	3.5	3.8	4.2

Use a maximum of 5 pounds at one time. If more is called for, wait a month between applications.

Reducing Soil Alkalinity

Pounds of agricultural sulfur to apply (per 100 square feet) to lower pH to 6.5.

Original pH	Sandy Soil	Silt or Loam Soil	Clay Soil
8.0	2.2	4.0	6.0
7.5	1.5	2.0	2.5
7.0	0.7	1.5	2.0

Use a maximum of 2 pounds at one time. If more is called for, wait a month between applications.

you can apply to your soil. Added to clay soil, it makes the soil coarser and thus more airy and fast draining. Added to sandy soil, it helps retain moisture and nutrients. Although not a necessary component of loam, organic matter is added to soil to give it a more loamlike balance of solid matter, moisture, and air.

In addition to improving soil structure, organic matter helps supply the soil with nutrients by promoting the growth of microorganisms that convert soil nitrogen into a form roots can absorb. Organic matter can also supply nutrients in its own right—although usually at a level so low that additional fertilizer is needed. What's more, organic matter provides food for earthworms, which assist in

Top: Deadheaded blooms and other prunings can be composted and recycled as a soil amendment.

Bottom: Roses tolerate many soils, but thrive best in rich, friable loam.

aeration. Many forms of organic matter are acidic and help lower the pH as well.

There are many sources of organic matter for the garden. Among the most popular are sphagnum peat moss, leaf mold (shredded and composted leaves), shredded bark, dehydrated manure, and composted kitchen or garden waste. Some are sold at garden centers; others can be made inexpensively in a backyard compost pile. Any of these sources of organic matter is perfectly acceptable; your choice should be guided by local availability and cost.

The amount of organic matter to add to your soil depends on the condition it is in. Ideally, the solid portion of the soil should contain about 25 percent organic matter. Although it is impossible to determine the exact organic content of your soil simply by looking at it (only a soil test can tell you this for sure), organic soil is usually a rich dark brown or dark gray, and friable.

GYPSUM   Gypsum, or calcium sulfate, is an inorganic compound that is often used in soils with a high sodium content to improve the structure of heavy clay that does not drain well. Worked into the soil, it helps break up the sticky clay to allow air and water to penetrate the soil more efficiently. In addition to improving the soil structure, it forces toxic sodium in these soils to leach out. Since gypsum is a neutral salt, however, it will not change the pH of the soil, so you must add other amendments.

Gypsum is usually sold in 50-pound bags at garden centers and agricultural supply stores, in either granular or powdered form. Use 10 to 20 pounds per 100 square feet of garden, spreading it over the soil each spring and watering it in. When gypsum is added to individual holes as roses are planted, mix ⅓ to ½ pound of gypsum with the improved soil per hole.

SAND, PERLITE, VERMICULITE, AND PUMICE   Other amendments used to improve the structure of soil are coarse builder's sand, perlite, vermiculite, and pumice. They are helpful in clay soils with poor drainage and aeration. If their use is called for, they should be mixed with the soil when it is being improved for planting. Unlike gypsum, which reacts chemically with the soil, these amendments are sheerly mechanical in action—they add bulk and texture. The material to use will depend on the type of soil you have; check with your county agricultural extension or garden center to find the best solution for your region. Any of these amendments may be mixed into the soil so that up to 20 percent by volume of the final soil consists of one of the amendments.

Builder's sand is useful for coarsening fine clay soil to improve its drainage and aeration. It is available in bags or in bulk from building supply stores or from outlets that sell concrete and cement. Be sure to use only coarse sand; fine beach sand will not improve drainage and will actually do more harm than good because of its small particle size. The addition of sand will not affect the pH of the soil.

Perlite, vermiculite, and pumice are often added to soils to improve their structure without changing their pH; all are available in bags at garden centers. The one you choose will depend on the type of soil you have. Perlite, a grayish white granular material, is mined from volcanic lava flows and heat processed. Its lightweight, porous texture improves the drainage of heavy clay soils. However, it has no nutrient value.

Vermiculite, on the other hand, contains some magnesium and potassium and is an excellent retainer of other nutrients as well. This granular material is mined and then subjected to high heat, which makes it porous and capable of holding very large quantities of water and dissolved nutrients. It is therefore not recommended for heavy clay soils— which already retain water and nutrients effectively—but it will improve the performance of sandy soil.

Pumice is lightweight gray or white, chopped or powdered volcanic rock that is used to improve heavy clay soils because it does not absorb much water. It has no nutrient value.

In clay soils that are high in sodium, gypsum can be added to break the soil into clusters that air and water can penetrate.

IMPROVING THE SOIL

Once an inspection and a soil test have advised you of the deficiencies of your soil, the next task is to begin improving it. You should first decide whether to improve an entire planting bed or just the soil in individual planting holes. Preparing an entire bed is much more work, but in poor soil it is almost a necessity. If you don't prepare the entire bed, the roots of your roses will be trapped in pockets of ideal soil and surrounded by poor soil, which will damage them or retard their growth. If your soil is relatively good, however, you can normally get away with improving only the soil in each of the planting holes.

Whether you are improving a large bed or just the soil in individual holes, the procedure is the same. First, dig out the soil in the area to be planted, to a depth of 24 inches. Where soil cannot be dug that deep, dig as deep as possible but at least to 16 inches. Use a hoe to break up clods of earth. To this, add 25 percent by volume of organic matter such as peat moss, leaf mold, or compost. If you are preparing an entire bed, spread the organic matter over the area and work it in well, to the full depth you have dug. If you are digging individual holes, remove the soil from the hole and mix the organic matter with it. The final soil mixture will have a larger volume than it did previously. Do not add a complete granular fertilizer at this time unless you plan to leave the site unplanted for at least a month; this gives the fertilizer time to diffuse evenly through the soil so that the plant roots will not be burned. (For a complete discussion of fertilizing, see the section beginning on page 146.)

Do, however, add a source of phosphorus, such as bonemeal, rock phosphate, or superphosphate, at the rate of 3 to 4 pounds per 100 square feet, or about a half-cup per planting hole. Phosphorus, which is essential for good root growth, moves very slowly through the soil. If it is applied to the top of the soil, it may take several years to filter down to the root level where it is needed. The best way to get phosphorus to the root level is to put it there at the beginning.

Adjust the pH if necessary at this time. If there are any rocks, stones, root fragments, or other pieces of debris in the soil, remove them. Combine the soil, organic material, phosphorus source, fertilizer (if any), and any pH-adjusting materials, and mix them well; in large areas, a rotary tiller is helpful in breaking up large clods of soil and mixing in the soil-improving ingredients. Rake the soil level before planting if you are preparing a large bed.

It is best, although not always practical, to improve the soil one to six months before planting, as this allows the soil to mellow and settle and the pH to become properly adjusted. It also lessens the chance that fresh organic matter or fertilizers will burn the roots of new plants.

Soil should be improved only if it is in workable condition; that is, fairly dry and friable. Working with soil that is too wet will ruin its structure by binding its particles together. These will be difficult or impossible to break apart in the future. To test the workability of your soil, pick up a handful of it and squeeze it into a ball. If the soil sticks together, it is too wet. Wait several days and perform the test again. Soil is ready to be worked when it crumbles in your hand when you squeeze it.

DRAINAGE

Good soil drainage is essential for roses. If drainage is too slow, water will replace air in the soil, taking the place of oxygen that is vital for root growth, and leaving roots no room to develop. Ideally, the

Preparing the soil of an entire planting bed is much more work than improving just the individual planting holes. But doing only the latter may restrict the growth of your roses.

space between the particles in the soil should consist of one half water and one half air.

To test your drainage, dig a hole about a foot deep and wide. Fill it to the top with water and measure how long it takes for the water to drain. If the hole empties in an hour or less, your drainage is fine. But if water remains there longer, you need to take steps to improve the drainage. In many cases, mixing organic matter, gypsum, or one of the other soil amendments into the soil as described on page 108 will be sufficient to correct a drainage problem. After working this material into the soil, repeat the test. If your soil fails again, you need to take more serious steps.

One solution is to add several inches of coarse gravel to the bottom of each

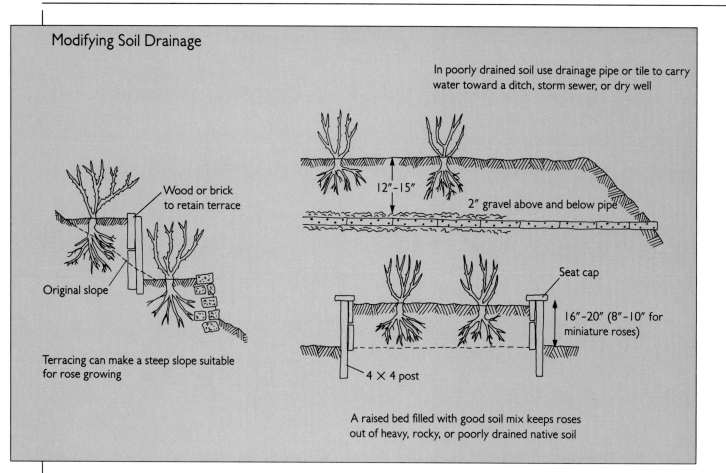

Modifying Soil Drainage

In poorly drained soil use drainage pipe or tile to carry water toward a ditch, storm sewer, or dry well

12"–15"

2" gravel above and below pipe

Wood or brick to retain terrace

Original slope

Terracing can make a steep slope suitable for rose growing

Seat cap

16"–20" (8"–10" for miniature roses)

4 × 4 post

A raised bed filled with good soil mix keeps roses out of heavy, rocky, or poorly drained native soil

planting hole. Alternatively, you can dig a large trench beneath the planting bed and install drainage pipe or tile at the bottom. The gravel, pipe, or tile should be slightly pitched to take the water to a lower spot where it can drain off or into a ditch, sewer, or dry well.

Another, attractive solution to poor drainage is a raised bed. This elevates your roses above the surrounding soil and allows extra water to drain out along the bottom or sides of the bed. Using wood, brick, or stone, construct a planting bed about 18 to 24 inches above ground level. Add an improved soil or purchase a high-quality topsoil or soilless mix and work it in with the soil below grade to a depth of 18 to 24 inches, adding other amendments as necessary to achieve proper soil structure and pH. For a discussion of landscaping considerations for raised beds, see page 92.

PLANTING

The old adage "Never place a $10 plant into a 10-cent hole" couldn't be truer with roses. The proper planting techniques will make both you and your roses happy for years to come.

WHEN TO PLANT

The proper time for planting roses depends on your climate and on whether you purchase bare-root or container roses. Bare-root roses are planted when they are still dormant and the ground is workable. In mild-winter climates where temperatures stay above freezing, bare-root roses are usually planted in late winter. In regions where winter temperatures do not fall below 0° F, roses can be set into the garden in early spring or late fall. Where winter temperatures drop below 0° F, it is wisest to plant only in the spring, as roses planted in fall may not have time to become well established before winter.

There are several advantages to fall planting if it is suitable for your climate. All commercially grown roses, whether they are sold bare root or in containers, are harvested in the fall and kept in cold storage for sale in the spring. Roses purchased just after the fall harvest are therefore fresher, and are often available in greater variety. Once in the soil their roots begin to grow, and continue growing as long as soil temperatures remain above 40° F. Such temperatures can persist into early winter, well after air temperatures drop below freezing. Although the stems remain dormant, the extra weeks of root growth help establish the plants and start them growing and blooming earlier than roses planted in spring. Another advantage to planting roses in the fall is that perennials and bulbs can be set out along with them, making it easier to lay out the garden.

If you live where it is too cold to plant in the fall, you can buy bare-root roses at that time and bury them in a trench over the winter. If drainage is good, dig the trench about 12 to 24 inches deep and bury the roses on their sides. If drainage is poor, dig the trench deep enough to bury the crowns 6 inches under the soil surface, and place a 12-inch-high mound of soil over the plants. To help you locate and remove the plants the following spring, tie a plastic or nylon cord around the canes and another around the shank between the crown and the roots. Let the ends of the cords extend well above the soil surface. When spring comes you can simply pull up your roses by the cords and plant them in the usual way.

Unfortunately, garden centers rarely sell freshly harvested roses in the fall, because the commercial growers who supply them do not ship roses until late winter and early spring. However, bare-root roses are available in fall through some mail-order nurseries, especially smaller ones that are willing to make this extra effort.

Container roses can be planted anytime from early spring through midfall. Follow the instructions on page 116.

When it is time to plant any type of rose, whether in spring, summer, fall, or winter, choose a day that is not windy—for your own comfort and for the plant's sake as well. Strong winds can be very drying to rose canes and exposed roots of bare-root plants. If you can, plant late in the afternoon or on a cloudy day, especially when planting bare-root roses that have been shipped by mail. Because these plants were shipped in a dark box, sudden exposure to bright sun can scald or dehydrate the canes. Planting late in the afternoon or on a cloudy day also lessens transplanting shock, as planting in full sun can cause the foliage to wilt. This is especially true with container plants already in leaf.

ROSE SPACING

In an ideally laid-out rose garden, plants are spaced closely enough that they fill out the beds attractively, yet far enough apart that they will not crowd one another's growth or foster disease. Optimum spacing between plants depends on your climate, the type of roses you are growing, and the visual effect you are trying to achieve.

In frigid or temperate regions, you should plant hybrid teas, floribundas, and grandifloras 24 inches apart (if floribundas have a spreading habit, plant them 30 inches apart). Plant polyanthas about 18 inches apart (larger polyanthas like 'The Fairy' require wider spacing). In warmer climates with little or no frost, add about six more inches between plants to allow room for more profuse growth. For a dense hedge or "living fence" effect, plant roses a little closer together.

Shrub and old garden roses vary widely in size, and their ideal spacing ranges accordingly. A good rule of thumb is to plant them as far apart as they will ultimately grow in height. In most cases, this will be about 4 to 6 feet apart. In warmer climates, add another 6 to 12 inches between plants. See Chapter 10 for dimensions of specific varieties.

Climbers to be trained horizontally on a fence in any climate should be planted 8 to 10 feet apart. Climbers to be trained vertically up and over an arbor, or on a trellis or a wall, can be planted as close as 3 feet to create a more solid cover.

Miniature roses, too, should be spaced in proportion with their ultimate size. Tiny minis that grow only 6 inches high should be planted about 6 inches apart. Tall minis that grow to 24 inches are best spaced 12 to 18 inches apart, as their growth is more vertical than horizontal. In warm climates add about another 3 inches to these spacing guidelines.

When laying out a new rose bed, plan it on paper first so that you will know how many plants to buy. Then use stakes to mark the spots where the plants will go in the garden. This helps guarantee that the visual effect will be what you want, and that the bed will be evenly filled with rose plants. You may find that you need to adjust planting distances to accommodate beds that are curved or ir-regularly shaped.

PLANTING BARE-ROOT ROSES

Bare-root roses are dormant plants with the soil washed away from the roots to re-duce the cost of shipping. Although they are most often sold by mail order, roses in this form can also be found at some gar-den centers and supermarkets. To keep them alive and from drying out, their roots are usually enveloped in moist sphagnum moss, sawdust, or newspaper in a plastic bag. It is important to plant them as soon as possible so that they do not dry out or start to push out new growth.

If for some reason you cannot plant your new bare-root roses immediately, keep them in a dark, cool (but frost-free) location so that they will not start to grow. If the nursery has not done so, wrap the roots in damp newspaper, sphagnum peat moss, sawdust, or burlap and wrap or cover them with plastic to prevent them from drying out.

If your new roses can't be planted for several weeks or more, bury the entire plants—roots and tops—on their sides in a trench about a foot deep and wide. The next best thing is to place plants side-by-side in a trench, either at a slant or standing upright, and "heel them in" by filling the trench with soil to cover just the roots. Choose a cool, shaded spot for either alternative. Remove the roses when you can plant them, but don't wait until the weather turns warm and the plants start to grow.

Immediately before planting, soak the roots of bare-root roses in a bucket of water or mud for 6 to 24 hours to restore lost moisture. Place the bucket where sunlight is good but not full. If you do not finish your planting chores on schedule and the roses have to soak for another day, no harm will be done. However, if you cannot plant them for several days or a week, remove the roots from the water, wrap them to keep them moist, and return the plants to their cool, dark storage area.

Dig a planting hole about 18 to 24 inches across and deep. If you have not yet adjusted the pH or the texture of the soil, do so now, following the directions on pages 102 to 110. Place a cone-shaped mound of improved soil in the bottom of the hole, high enough so that the bud union or the crown will be in the proper position after planting.

Top: To restore lost moisture to bare-root roses, soak their roots for 6 to 24 hours before planting.

Bottom: With the bud union or crown positioned at the proper height (see next page), splay roots around a mound of improved soil at the bottom of the hole.

Planting Bare-Root Roses

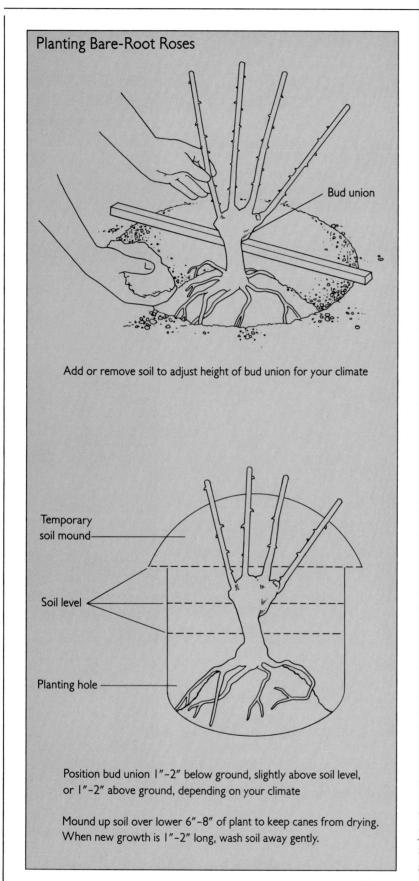

Bud union

Add or remove soil to adjust height of bud union for your climate

Temporary
soil mound

Soil level

Planting hole

Position bud union 1"–2" below ground, slightly above soil level, or 1"–2" above ground, depending on your climate

Mound up soil over lower 6"–8" of plant to keep canes from drying. When new growth is 1"–2" long, wash soil away gently.

The bud union is the point at which the rose variety was grafted, or budded, to more vigorous rootstock. Resembling a knobbed or knuckled joint on top of the root shank, it is the point from which the canes of the budded variety grow. Modern bush roses and climbers are budded, whereas most miniatures, species, and old garden roses are grown from cuttings, so they do not have a bud union. Instead, they have a crown, which is the point where the canes join the roots.

Most experts believe that exposure to sunlight encourages the crown or bud union to produce new canes, so it is a good idea not to cover this part of the plant unless absolutely necessary. In moderate climates where winter temperatures do not drop below 20° F, the bud union should be positioned so that it rests just above the soil surface. In frost-free areas, it can sit 1 to 2 inches above the soil level. Where winter temperatures drop below 20° F, the bud union should be placed 1 to 2 inches below the soil level to protect it from freezing. In summer the soil should be moved away to expose it to the sun. When planting into containers, position the bud union so that it rests just above the surface of the planting medium.

Floribundas are an exception to these rules. Many experts recommend planting the bud union of floribundas about 2 inches below the soil level, regardless of the climate. The theory is that deeply planted floribundas will send out their own roots, which are often stronger and more vigorous than the rootstock onto which they are grafted. (Most commercial rose growers make a practice of grafting all modern bush roses, whether or not they would grow successfully on their own roots.)

Because most miniatures have no bud union, plant them so that the crown is just at soil level. This recommendation should be followed for most species roses and old garden roses as well.

Before planting any type of bare-root rose, examine the roots for breaks or other damage. If you find any injured roots, cut them off with pruning shears. Also shorten any roots that are too long to fit easily into the planting hole without curling or twisting. Long roots that are simply shoved into the hole may become girdled, growing in a circular pattern rather than outward into the soil, thereby restricting the growth of the plant. If any stubs (short pieces of cane) are present on the bud union, cut them off flush with the bud union so they do not rot or hamper the development of new canes by blocking potential growing sites.

Set the plant on top of the cone of soil at the bottom of the planting hole, positioning the plant so that the bud union or the crown is at the proper level. You may need to add or remove soil to achieve this. Since newly prepared soil will settle after a brief time, set the bud union or the crown slightly higher than you eventually want it. Lay a broom or shovel handle or a wooden stake across the hole to serve as a reference for positioning the bud union or the crown correctly. When the plant is at the proper level, spread out the roots so that they radiate evenly from the center of the mound.

Holding the rose upright and in place with one hand, fill the planting hole with improved soil until the hole is about two-thirds full. Gently tap the soil around the roots with your hand and fill the hole with water to eliminate air pockets. After the water has drained, fill the hole to the top with improved soil. Make a catch basin for water by mounding a ring of soil in a circle around the perimeter of the plant, and water again.

Prune all new bare-root roses back by about one third, removing any weak, damaged, or dead wood at the same time (see page 124 for complete pruning instructions). Mound up soil around the bottom of the plant to cover the bud union and the lower 6 to 8 inches of the canes to prevent them from drying out in the sun or the wind. In all but frost-free climates, roses planted in fall need winter protection in addition to the mounding up of soil; see page 154 for information on winter protection.

If you are planting a new rose late in the spring, try placing a clear plastic bag over the entire plant as added protection against drying; remove the bag as soon as new growth starts. Propping a shingle or a piece of wood so that it shades the plant for about a week prevents the strong sun of late spring from scalding bare canes.

When new growth on the canes is 1 to 2 inches long, remove the soil or other protection. The best way to remove the soil mound is to wash it away with a gentle stream of water. Washing rather than digging soil away keeps new canes that have developed under the soil from being damaged.

Take a look at your newly planted roses at least once a week to make sure they are growing and healthy. A small amount of dieback, the blackening and dying of the cane tips, is to be expected and should be no cause for alarm.

Bare-root tree roses are planted in essentially the same way as other bare-root roses, but should be staked with a wooden, plastic, or bamboo pole to keep them upright and to support them against wind damage. The stake should be set at planting time so that roots will not be damaged.

New roses that have spindly root systems will benefit from being planted into containers with soilless growing medium before being permanently set into the ground (see page 172). The medium is better than soil for developing roots because of its high organic content, and the medium in containers will be warmer than ground soil if the container is placed in the sun, encouraging faster root growth. Once the plants are well established, they can be transplanted.

PLANTING CONTAINER-GROWN ROSES

Unlike bare-root roses, which can only be planted in the colder months when they are dormant, roses grown in containers can be transplanted at any time from spring through fall. This allows you to fill in a bare spot or add bits of color whenever you so fancy. You will have to expend a little extra effort when planting in the heat of summer, but it will be worth the effort.

Unfortunately, the selection of roses in containers is more limited than that of bare-root roses found in mail-order catalogs, and container roses are sometimes more expensive. If you cannot plant your container roses soon after you purchase them, keep them in a warm spot where they will receive adequate sunlight but are protected from the wind, which can dry them out or topple them over.

Because the soil in containers dries out quickly, it is very important to water the plants in them often. Many roses come in cardboard boxes with a protective cardboard covering over the soil around the base of the plant. It may be necessary to insert the end of a garden hose down through the hole in this covering to make sure that enough water will reach the soil underneath it.

Dig a hole about 6 inches deeper and wider than the container. Then fill the hole with enough improved soil to ensure that the bud union or crown will be at the proper level after planting. This level depends on the climate; see page 114.

The next, very important step is to remove the container, whether it is made of tar paper, metal, plastic, or less durable cardboard or compressed peat. Do this carefully to avoid disturbing the rootball. Even if instructions accompanying your plant state that the container may be planted, your new rose will grow more freely if its container is removed, since

containers can take several years to disintegrate.

To remove a container, first place the plant into the hole and adjust the depth of the hole until the bud union or the crown is at the desired level. Next, use a knife to cut the bottom out of the container and remove the bottom panel carefully so that you don't disturb the roots. Working from the bottom, slit the sides of the container three quarters of the way to the top. Then place the plant back into the hole and backfill to near the tops of the cuts.

With the soil now holding your plant in place, you can easily complete the cuts and gently pull the sides of the container up, bending them outward as you pull to avoid the canes and foliage.

Finish backfilling around the rootball, water thoroughly, and allow the backfill to settle. Add more soil and water until the desired level is attained. Finally, make a catch basin for water by mounding soil in a circle around the perimeter of the plant; then water the plant once again.

If you are planting in the heat of midsummer, any disturbance to the rootball can be very detrimental to the survival of the rose, since disturbed or damaged roots cannot take up enough water to prevent the plant from wilting. If the container is made of cardboard or peat, it is better to simply cut out the bottom so that the roots are displaced as little as possible. After doing this, use a knife to make several slits around the sides of the container. This will create openings for extra growth.

Containers made of metal, plastic, tar paper, or other durable materials must be removed completely, of course, but you should take extra care when doing so.

Roses planted from containers, especially during midsummer heat, need frequent watering and misting with a fine spray from a garden hose until they are well established. You should expect some wilting after planting, but it usually will not last more than five days to a week. If the wilting is prolonged, prune the plant back by about one third and remove all flowers and flower buds to force the plant to direct its energy into developing strong roots. Propping a shingle or a piece of wood next to the plant to shade it from the sun for about a week also helps to reduce wilting, as does an antidesiccant spray. Antidesiccant sprays are waxy liquids available in garden centers either in aerosol cans or as concentrates to be mixed with water. Sprayed once on the canes and leaves, they help prevent plants from transpiring water and therefore wilting.

RELOCATING ROSES

From time to time you may need to relocate one or more of your rosebushes—to give them more light, provide them with more growing space, or create better color harmony in the garden. The ideal time to do this is when the plant is dormant and the ground is workable—in other words, any time it is appropriate to plant bare-root roses. The day before transplanting, water the soil around the rosebush well to ease digging and ensure that the plant is turgid, or filled with water. A turgid plant experiences less transplanting shock.

When it is time to transplant, carefully lift the dormant plant from the ground with a shovel, a spade, or a garden fork, taking care to damage as few roots as possible. Perform the rest of the transplanting as you would if planting a bare-root rose. Take a careful look at the roots before planting to be sure you have pruned away any damaged or broken ones. Since you will undoubtedly lose some roots in the transplanting process, cut the plant top back by about one half to compensate for the root loss.

If the rose you are transplanting is very large or has been growing in the same

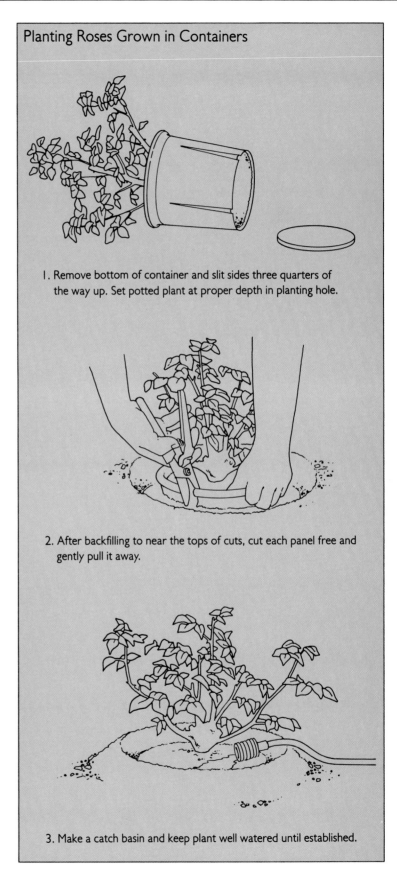

Planting Roses Grown in Containers

1. Remove bottom of container and slit sides three quarters of the way up. Set potted plant at proper depth in planting hole.

2. After backfilling to near the tops of cuts, cut each panel free and gently pull it away.

3. Make a catch basin and keep plant well watered until established.

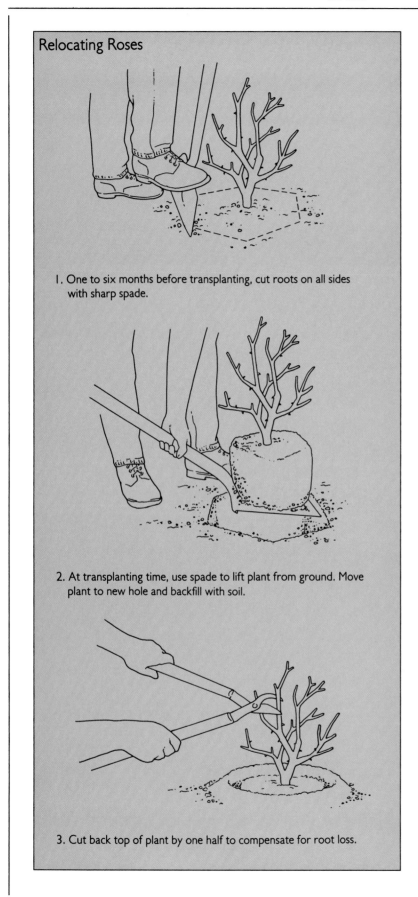

Relocating Roses

1. One to six months before transplanting, cut roots on all sides with sharp spade.

2. At transplanting time, use spade to lift plant from ground. Move plant to new hole and backfill with soil.

3. Cut back top of plant by one half to compensate for root loss.

spot for many years, it is a good idea to prune the roots while the plant is still in the ground; do this at least one month (and no longer than six months) before moving it. With a straight-edged spade, cut a circle into the soil in an 18- to 24-inch radius from the base of the plant. Your cuts should sever the roots to the depth of the spade's blade. Cutting off the outer roots in this way encourages new roots to develop closer to the base of the plant, enabling you to dig the plant up more easily. The plant will also recover more quickly after transplanting because it will have a more compact root system and there will be less root breakage in relocating it.

Larger plants, particularly shrub roses and old garden roses, can be unwieldy to move. To make the job easier, dig a narrow trench around the rootball and undercut the rootball with a spade. Tuck burlap underneath, wadding enough to pull through to the other side. Wrap and tie the burlap around the rootball to keep it intact, and lift the plant out of the hole.

Sometimes it is impossible to avoid transplanting roses that have already started to leaf out in the spring. In these cases a transplanted rose will most likely wilt as soon as it has been moved. To help the rose recover from the shock of transplanting, cut the canes back hard—by one half to two thirds—and keep the rose well watered and misted until it revives. An antidesiccant spray also helps prevent wilting.

It is possible, albeit difficult, to transplant a rose that has fully leafed out or is in bloom. Follow the directions above, taking extra care to treat the plant gently. In addition, remove all the flowers and flower buds to direct the energy of the plant into producing new roots.

Whether planting or transplanting, be on the lookout for any perennials and bulbs in the planting bed, and dig carefully so that you disturb their roots as little as possible. This may be trickier

A microminiature and a larger miniature bloom side by side in ceramic pots, lending personality to a bench.

than it sounds. If you are planting in the spring, the roots of many perennials will not yet have sent up telltale stems and leaves, and you may damage them severely before you realize they are there. Likewise in the fall, the foliage of most bulbs will have withered, making the bulbs hard to spot. One way to lessen any damage is to mark the location of the perennials and bulbs from the previous season with small labels or sticks.

PLANTING ROSES INTO CONTAINERS

Growing roses in containers is a practical way to make the most of your garden space, since you can display them when they are blooming and remove them when they are bare and severely pruned. Roses in containers can also add decorative touches around the garden or on the patio, porch, or deck. Roses, primarily

Planting Roses Into Containers

1. Place screening over drainage holes.

2. Add soil and set bud union at correct height. Pour in more soil, leaving 1″ watering space at top of container.

3. Pack soil to eliminate air pockets, then soak thoroughly.

miniatures, can also be grown in containers indoors; see Chapter 6 for more information.

Since roses grown in containers are showcase plants, choose varieties that are compact and free flowering for maximum visual appeal. You can plant either bareroot or container-grown roses, but the latter seem to get a better start because their roots are already growing in a confined space.

For full-sized rosebushes, the ideal container is at least 12 inches across and 15 inches deep, to provide roots with adequate growing space (although a container 18 inches across and deep is better). Containers for miniature roses should be 6 to 8 inches wide and 6 to 8 inches deep. Too little root space leads to stunted growth and poor flower production.

Containers can be made of a variety of materials, including wood, clay, cement, and plastic. Stay away from metal containers for outdoor growing, because they absorb too much heat and can stifle growth. Whatever type of container you use, be sure it has adequate drainage, since rose roots do not like to sit in water. Choose a container with drainage holes at the bottom, or on the sides near the bottom, and place wire or plastic screening over the holes to keep them from clogging.

If drainage holes are absent and cannot be drilled, plant the rose in a smaller container that has holes and set it inside the larger container. Place a layer of gravel at the bottom of the solid container to raise the inner container above the drainage water. Although you can grow a large rose in a container that lacks drainage holes by placing a deep layer of gravel and charcoal in the bottom, it is not advisable as you must take great care not to overwater.

If you are reusing a container, it is essential to clean the vessel thoroughly so that disease organisms will not be transmitted to the new plants. Scrub the pots with warm soapy water, and rinse well with clear water. Then rinse the container in a 10 percent solution of household bleach to disinfect it, and rinse with water again.

Because root space is so limited in a container, the quality of the growing medium is especially important. It is best to avoid garden soil, which is heavy and does not provide optimal drainage and aeration. Garden soil can also harbor harmful insects and diseases. Instead, use one of the all-purpose soilless mixes available in bags and packages at garden centers, or make your own mix by using half sphagnum peat moss or other organic material with half perlite or vermiculite. The formula for Cornell Mix, an excellent soilless mix for roses and other container plants, appears on page 172.

Set the plant in the container in the same way you would plant it into the ground, positioning the bud union or crown at soil level about 1 inch below the rim of the container. Water well and your instant decoration is ready.

Place the container where it will receive at least six hours of sun each day, turning it regularly if light does not strike it evenly. Avoid putting a container where it will become too hot, such as on an asphalt driveway or against a highly reflective light-colored wall.

When a rose outgrows its container, it needs to be repotted. Directions for repotting appear on page 174. You'll find other tips on container growing in Chapters 5 and 6.

LABELING

The final step in planting roses is labeling them. Whether you're a novice or an expert, you will want to keep track of the varieties in your garden for your own satisfaction and to share information with friends. Metal labels are durable and widely available, and can be written on

with waterproof ink or plastic labeling tape. Plastic labels can be used, but they break easily; wooden labels are also available, but the writing fades from them quickly.

Most roses come with name tags attached to them by wire. It is a good idea to remove these completely or reattach them with string, as the wire can cut into the cane.

It's also a good idea to keep a written record of the varieties you have planted. Write down their names, where they were purchased, and when and where they were planted. Labels can get lost outdoors, but a garden schematic is safe inside. It can also help when you want to add new varieties to your garden or share information with fellow rose growers.

Good drainage is essential for roses. These glazed containers have been placed on a bed of gravel to lift roots above the drainage water.

Roses in Portland's Washington Park frame a view of downtown and Mt. Hood.

CHAPTER FIVE

CARING FOR ROSES OUTDOORS

he care you give your roses on a daily basis has long-term effects on their health and flowering. Although roses make more demands than the average garden plant, they are not especially difficult to grow. All that is required is a basic command of a few simple techniques—namely pruning, watering, mulching, and fertilizing. This chapter describes them in detail.

he goal of every rose grower is a garden filled with healthy plants and large, colorful flowers. To achieve this goal, a rose grower must expend a certain amount of time and effort, but neither needs to be excessive. This chapter outlines the methods for proper pruning, watering, mulching, weeding, fertilizing, winter protection, and other routine care. These methods will enable you to grow roses that will reward you with dependable performance and matchless beauty.

True, roses are harder to grow than marigolds or petunias, or even most other shrubs, but rose lovers agree that this modest extra effort is more than repaid by the beauty it achieves. Also, some roses are easier to care for than others. For example, most old garden roses and shrubs require much less care than do hybrid teas and grandifloras, for they need less pruning and are not as prone to diseases. If you're concerned that you don't have time to tend a rose garden, start small; any garden can support even a few bushes. As you become experienced, you can add to your garden and increase your enjoyment of the Queen of Flowers.

An integral part of growing and enjoying beautiful roses is being able to identify and control any disease or insect problem that might occur. For complete information on this aspect of rose growing, see Chapter 9.

PRUNING

Many gardeners new to rose growing have no difficulty removing dead, damaged, diseased, or weak growth from a rosebush, but they do have trouble taking up pruning shears to cut away live, healthy growth. Experienced rose growers know, however, that pruning is essential to good growth and flowering. A rose that is not pruned well will soon grow tall and lanky, and its flower production will be poor. Pruning stimulates new growth, an important factor in flowering because many varieties produce flowers only on new canes.

Roses vary in their need for pruning. All hybrid teas, floribundas, grandifloras, and miniatures require heavy annual pruning to keep them in top shape. Climbers may need heavy pruning or only a light shaping, depending on the time of year and other circumstances, and many shrub and old garden roses may need only the annual light pruning you would give to other woody plants in the garden.

Pruning is the science of removing growth to achieve one or more goals: keeping the plant healthy, making it more productive, controlling its size, or encouraging it to grow in a particular shape or direction. The amount, type, and timing of pruning depends on the type of rose, the hardiness zone of the garden, the amount of winterkill, the condition of the plant, and what you want from your roses.

Watch an expert rose pruner at work and you will see several of these strategies in action. First, the pruner removes dead, damaged, or diseased canes (known among rose growers as the Three Ds) and any crossing canes, to enhance the appearance of the plant and prevent chafing. Next, the pruner tries to open up the center of the plant to improve air circulation and admit more light, which keeps down mildew and other diseases. Further cuts are made to encourage growth at desired points along the canes, or at the base of the plant, so that growth and flowering are stimulated. Still other cuts are made to give the plant an overall shape, or to ease the burden on a newly transplanted root system.

Like other skills, pruning is mastered with practice. Proper tools, good timing, and knowledge of your roses' growth habits are essential to perfecting this skill.

PRUNING TOOLS

Although a wide variety of pruning implements is sold at garden centers and hardware stores, you need just three types for pruning roses: pruning shears, lopping shears, and a pruning saw. It is wise to invest in the best tools you can afford. Well-made tools not only are a joy to own, but also last longer and make your work easier than do shoddy ones.

Pruning shears come in a range of forms for general and specialized uses. The best all-around shears for removing rose stems, flowers, and leaves are the hook-and-blade type (also known as

curved bypass shears), with two opposing curved blades. Choose the largest pair your hand can comfortably hold.

Anvil shears—a general-purpose type with a straight blade that strikes against a blunt surface—are less desirable because they can crush stems as they cut. This may cause the stems to die back or become prone to invasion by insects and diseases. The only task for which anvil shears can be used safely is removing dead wood. You may see other types of pruning shears for sale, including branch cutters, flower shears, fruit shears, and hedge shears. These specialized tools are not needed for rose pruning.

Lopping shears—heavy-duty, short-bladed shears with long handles—are used to cut out thick canes and to prune large old garden roses, shrubs, and climbers. If canes are too thick to cut with

Pruning is the art of shaping plants to promote pleasing form, good health, and robust flowering. This gardener is pruning away faded flowers to encourage faster reblooming.

lopping shears, use a special large-toothed pruning saw. The saws with a long, thin, curved blade are the easiest to handle. A pole saw or pole shears, the same types of tools but with extralong handles, may be necessary for pruning very tall bushes or climbers. Roses should never be trimmed with hedge clippers, even if they are grown as a hedge; these tools are designed for overall shearing rather than the selective pruning that roses require.

Be sure your pruning shears and saws are kept sharp. Dull shears and saws are not only hard to work with, but they also leave jagged cuts that heal slowly and admit insects and diseases. If your tools become dull, touch up the blades of pruning shears with a sharpening steel, hone saw blades with a file, or have both tools professionally sharpened. If necessary, you can buy a replacement blade for most saws.

Also make sure that your tools are kept clean, as contaminated shears and saws can spread disease. Rubbing alcohol is a good disinfectant for pruning tools, as is a solution of 1 part household bleach and 9 parts water. Using a clean cloth, you can wipe the tools with whichever disinfectant you choose, or you can dip the tools in a container holding the liquid.

In areas of high humidity, wipe shears and saws dry after each use and store them in plastic bags to retard rusting. Applying a thin coating of oil also helps prevent rust. The blades of teflon-coated pruning shears are not as likely to rust, but the bolt holding the blades together may be rust prone.

WHEN TO PRUNE

Roses are generally pruned according to the climate and the calendar; the ideal time to start is when growth buds swell in the spring. However, pruning rules vary somewhat with the type of rose.

Depending on your climate, pruning time for all types of roses is generally between midwinter and midspring. Look for forsythia to guide you: When you see its yellow flowers start to appear, you know it's rose-pruning time. If there is no forsythia in your area, prune when new growth buds start to appear along the canes. Also refer to the charts on pages 162 to 165 for timing guidelines.

Modern bush roses, such as hybrid teas, floribundas, grandifloras, and miniatures, should be pruned annually when growth buds begin to swell, but before they actually start to leaf out. In very warm climates where the roses may not lose their leaves, pruning should be done in mid to late winter. Since these roses bloom exclusively from new wood, pruning is essential to stimulate a good crop of new canes from which flowers can arise.

Climbers bloom on old wood—the previous year's canes. They should therefore not be pruned until after their first flush of bloom, or wood that will produce flower buds will be cut away. However, you can cut out dead, damaged, or diseased wood at any time, and if plants need shaping, you can do this in spring, or later in the season, as you wish.

It may not be necessary to prune old garden and shrub roses every year, since the need to prune them depends on their condition, size, and shape. If these plants are generally healthy and shapely, you may not have to prune them at all, except perhaps to remove dead, damaged, or diseased canes. If old garden or shrub roses are unshapely or too large, or have been transplanted, you should perform major pruning on them after the flowers fade. Exceptions to this are hybrid perpetuals, noisettes, Chinas, repeat-blooming damasks, hybrid musks, repeat-blooming Portlands, and moss roses—all of which are pruned in early spring (if they need it) in the same way that modern bush roses are. These old garden roses are pruned early because, unlike the other old garden roses, they bloom exclusively on new wood.

HOW TO PRUNE

The technique of pruning varies with the type of rose, whether it is growing in the ground or in a container, and the landscape purpose for which it was planted. Pruning can range from mild removal of unwanted buds to severe excising of canes. When a plant is properly pruned, growth at the buds closest to the cut will be stimulated and new flowering stems will be produced.

The first step in pruning any type of rose is to remove any dead, damaged, diseased, or weak and thin canes, cutting them off flush with the bud union, or in the case of own-root plants, flush with the crown. Any canes that are broken or wounded, or that have cankers (dark, sunken lesions caused by a fungus), should be pruned below the injury, at the highest point where the pith (the central portion of the cane) is healthy and white. Make the cut exactly ¼ inch above a growth bud. If the injury extends below that point, cut to a lower growth bud.

Next, remove canes that are growing into the center of the plant, or those that cross each other. Canes that grow inward keep light and air from the center of the plant and will eventually cross, chafing one another. These abrasions can become entry points for insects and diseases. Using shears, cut these canes down to their origin, whether that be another cane, the bud union, or the crown. It is important to keep the center of the plant open to let in sunshine and allow air to circulate freely.

Always prune to an outward-facing bud so that canes do not grow into the center of the plant. Prune close enough to the bud that no stub remains to die off and harbor insects or diseases, but far enough away that the bud will not die. A good distance is about ¼ inch above the growth bud. It is also important to cut at the proper angle, so that water runoff won't drip on the bud or collect in the cut and retard healing. The ideal angle is 45 degrees, slanted parallel to the direction of bud growth.

Left: A modern bush rose before pruning exhibits lopsided growth and a tangle of canes growing inward.

Right: Lopping shears are used to remove thick older canes.

Left: Thinner canes are shortened or removed with hand pruners.

Right: A pruning saw is used to cut away woody older growth.

Left: After a severe pruning, four short canes remain evenly spaced around the plant.

Right: A more moderate pruning has left a greater number of taller canes, which will produce higher, denser growth.

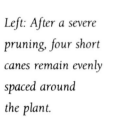

On hybrid teas, floribundas, and grandifloras, once you have pruned the diseased, damaged, weak, or excess canes, select three or four of the newest and healthiest remaining canes and cut off the rest flush with the bud union, using pruning shears or a saw if necessary. Next, prune the remaining canes of hybrid teas and floribundas to a height of 12 to 18 inches above the bud union, and those of grandifloras a few inches higher. Floribundas used as hedges can have five to six canes left on each plant, and can be pruned to 24 inches high so that they will grow denser and taller and produce more flowers.

Prune miniatures to about half their ultimate summer height. Up to six strong new canes can be left on the plants after pruning; the more canes you leave, the fuller the plants will be. Refer to page 181 for instructions on pruning miniature roses indoors.

Roses grown in decorative containers should be pruned so that they will be in proportion to the size of the container when they are in full bloom; this may mean shorter or higher pruning than is normally recommended. Since these are usually showcase plants, take care to prune them so that they are as symmetrical and pleasingly balanced as possible.

Because climbers bloom solely on old wood, they are pruned somewhat differently than bush roses. In early spring, while the plants are still dormant or have just started to grow, any dead or damaged canes can be removed, as can those that are too long or misshapen. However, leave all other pruning until after the plants first flower, so that you do not remove any flower buds. This is especially important with climbers that bloom only once a year. Those that repeat their bloom may actually be encouraged to have a heavier second bloom if they are properly pruned after the first bloom. The oldest canes should be removed to the bud union to leave room for new

growth. Thin out dense growth as well at this time. Removing flowers as soon as they fade encourages some climbers that would not otherwise flower again to repeat their bloom during the summer.

Because climbers flower only on lateral branches that grow from the main canes, they will bloom more heavily if they are trained along a fence or a trellis, and if the ends of the canes are directed to grow down toward the ground. This forces the plants to produce more laterals. As new canes of climbers grow, they must be trained into position and tied to their supports with cord, string, or twist-ties.

Shrub roses and old garden roses, including species roses, do not require severe pruning unless they are overgrown. In early spring, cut out weak, damaged, or dead wood, and prune only to shape the plant or control its size. Leave the plants as large and as natural looking as space permits. Perform heavy pruning either in early spring or after flowering,

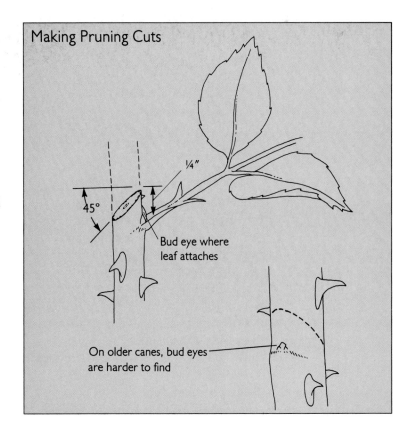

Making Pruning Cuts

45°

¼"

Bud eye where leaf attaches

On older canes, bud eyes are harder to find

Pruning Climbing Roses

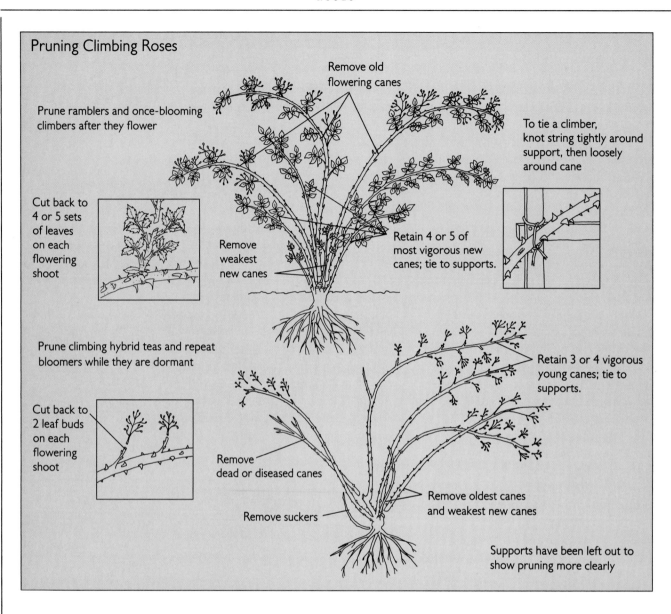

Remove old flowering canes

Prune ramblers and once-blooming climbers after they flower

To tie a climber, knot string tightly around support, then loosely around cane

Cut back to 4 or 5 sets of leaves on each flowering shoot

Remove weakest new canes

Retain 4 or 5 of most vigorous new canes; tie to supports.

Prune climbing hybrid teas and repeat bloomers while they are dormant

Retain 3 or 4 vigorous young canes; tie to supports.

Cut back to 2 leaf buds on each flowering shoot

Remove dead or diseased canes

Remove oldest canes and weakest new canes

Remove suckers

Supports have been left out to show pruning more clearly

depending on the type of plant (see above). Many old garden roses—albas, centifolias, and moss roses in particular—have long, supple canes that can be bent over and pinned to the ground. This practice makes these plants easier to control and gives them a bushier appearance. It also encourages the formation of new basal breaks (new canes that grow from the base of the plant), which will keep these plants constantly rejuvenated. The canes often root at the point where they were pegged to the ground, and new plants that form can be left in place or transplanted.

Polyanthas are hardy plants that, like many old garden and shrub roses, seldom suffer winterkill. They are therefore pruned more like old garden and species roses than like hybrid teas, floribundas, and grandifloras. If they are not overgrown, trim only to remove old, damaged, or diseased canes. If they are overgrown, prune them in early spring, to about half their former height, and remove the oldest canes. Leave them on the bushy side, as they are grown primarily for landscape effect.

Tree roses are pruned like modern bush roses, but to be most attractive they

Top: Climbing roses such as the climbing tea 'Sombreuil' will bloom more heavily if trained horizontally. This forces them to produce more of the lateral branches on which flowers grow.

Bottom: The long, supple canes of many old roses can be pegged to the ground to make them bushier and curb their tendency to sprawl. This is the hybrid perpetual 'John Hopper'.

must be as symmetrical and pleasingly balanced as possible. Prune canes to about 12 inches beyond the bud union at the top of the trunk and leave them as evenly spaced around the plant as possible. Leaving four to six canes on each tree rose will produce a full, attractive-looking plant.

In warm climates where rose plants grow quite large, pruning to the recommended height is not desirable, since it will remove too much of the plant. Instead, prune away about one half to two thirds of the plant each winter or early spring by removing the older canes and shortening the remaining canes. In cold climates where there is a great deal of winter damage, pruning heights may be determined for you by the amount of winterkill. Prune canes down to where there is no more winter damage, even if it is almost to the ground.

The higher a plant is pruned, the earlier it will flower—but don't jeopardize the health and vigor of the plant by pruning too high in pursuit of a few days' earlier bloom. On the other hand, there is little advantage to pruning your roses lower than the heights prescribed above; unlike disbudding (see page 133), it will probably not make the plants produce larger flowers.

Although black spot and other fungal diseases manifest themselves on leaves, their spores can overwinter on rose canes. If these diseases plagued your roses during the previous summer, you should prune them lower than recommended, as you will cut away and discard much of the source of the problem. Although you won't be able to see the spores on the canes, you can be assured that cutting off a few extra inches during spring pruning will reduce the number of spores somewhat. Never leave rose prunings on the ground. They not only look unsightly but can harbor diseases and pests that may potentially reinfect the plant or spread to others. Refer to Chapter 9 for other methods of controlling diseases.

Pruning cuts more than ¼ inch in diameter can be sealed with pruning compound, orange shellac, or grafting wax (available at garden centers or hardware stores) if boring insects are a problem in your area. Pruning compound and orange shellac are the easiest to use because they can be painted on. Otherwise, sealing is not necessary. Some types of white glue, which is sometimes used as a sealant, are water soluble and will wash away with the first rain or watering; they should therefore not be used.

Several weeks after you have pruned, take a second trip through the garden with your pruning shears. If you pruned early in the year, a late frost may have caused minor dieback on some of the canes. This dieback should be removed. Cankers that were not apparent at pruning time may be visible and should also be pruned away.

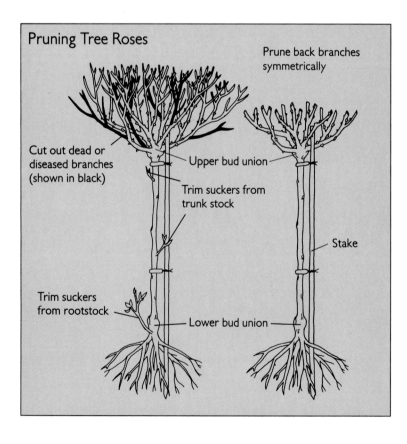

Pruning Tree Roses

Prune back branches symmetrically

Cut out dead or diseased branches (shown in black)

Upper bud union

Trim suckers from trunk stock

Stake

Trim suckers from rootstock

Lower bud union

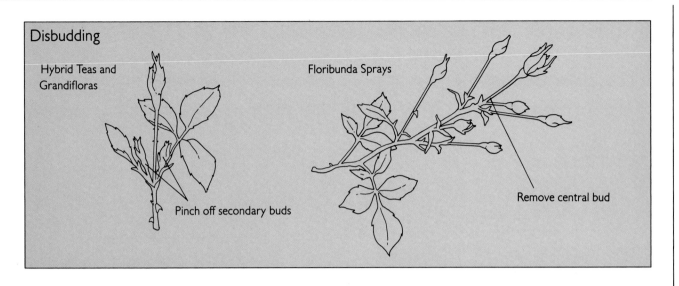

Disbudding

Hybrid Teas and
Grandifloras

Pinch off secondary buds

Floribunda Sprays

Remove central bud

Do not be too harsh when pruning young plants. Until plants are well established and have been growing robustly for two or three years, remove only weak, damaged, or dead wood, and shape and shorten the plants as recommended above without cutting away any of the older canes. In following years, old canes can be removed as new ones develop.

Pruning can be a scratchy job, so wear gloves and a long-sleeved shirt or jacket to protect your skin against thorns. Some kinds of fabric, such as the nylon used in windbreakers, catch easily on thorns and can tear.

New growth starts at the growing point immediately below a pruning cut. This is especially important to bear in mind when pruning back large, overgrown plants. If your ultimate goal is a plant 6 feet high or a climber trained to cover a section of fence 8 feet long, you must prune the plants shorter than the desired size in order to allow for new growth. For example, if your goal is a 6-foot-tall shrub rose, you should prune it to about 4 feet tall. Different plants have different growth rates, so gauge your pruning according to the past behavior of the plant.

Roots can be pruned as well. When you plant or transplant a rosebush, prune off any broken or damaged roots. You should remove about one third off the tops of the canes to compensate for this root loss. Before transplanting a large rosebush, it is a good idea to prune the roots with a spade by digging in a circle around the plant (see page 118 for instructions). Do this one to six months before the transplant so that the rootball will be more compact and easier to move.

DISBUDDING

Disbudding is a type of pruning aimed at producing a single, large flower at the top of the cane or forming a more uniform spray. To produce a single, large flower at the top of a cane, you remove all flower buds below the top one. This forces the plant to devote all its energy to growing one flower that can bloom twice as large. Disbudding is necessary for producing show-quality hybrid teas, grandifloras, and climbing hybrid teas, which must be exhibited with one flower per stem in order to qualify for the highest awards. (For more information on exhibiting and judging roses, see Chapter 7.) Even if you never dream of exhibiting your roses, disbudding will help you achieve the largest flowers possible.

As soon as small secondary buds are visible around and below the central flower bud, remove them by rubbing them away with your fingers or the point

Cutting Roses

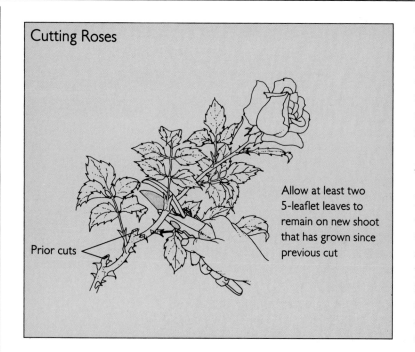

Prior cuts

Allow at least two 5-leaflet leaves to remain on new shoot that has grown since previous cut

of a small implement such as a toothpick. If you wait too long to disbud, and the flower bud is ¼ inch or more across, unsightly black scars will form and remain. Some roses naturally produce only one bloom per stem, and will not need to be disbudded.

Roses that bloom in sprays, such as floribundas, grandifloras, climbers, and some miniatures, naturally grow in such a way that the central flower bud opens first. As it fades, the surrounding flower buds open. When the faded central flower is cut away, a large gap remains in the center of the spray. To prevent this, remove the central flower bud as soon as it appears. The remaining flowers will fill in the gap, coming into bloom simultaneously for a prettier effect, although flower size will not increase. Although floribundas can be exhibited with one bloom per stem, they are usually shown as sprays, and the best floribunda in the show is almost always a spray. In the garden, allowing floribundas to bloom in sprays gives much more color and shows off their beauty more brilliantly.

Miniatures can be disbudded or not, depending on the effect you wish to

achieve and whether you want large flowers on single stems or uniform sprays. Polyanthas, climbers, shrub roses, and old garden roses are rarely disbudded, as this will destroy their natural appearance; their beauty rests in the large clusters of flowers they produce.

SUMMER PRUNING

Flowers are produced at the ends of secondary stems, which grow from the main cane. Though you may not think of it as such, gathering these flowers is a form of pruning. Whether you are cutting flowers for an arrangement or removing flowers that have faded (a technique known as deadheading), you follow the same rule: Cut the flower stem no shorter than just above the first five-leaflet leaf below the flower you are removing. This is the point from which the next stem will grow and, one hopes, bloom.

When removing flowers from tall and vigorous plants, you can take the opportunity to shorten and shape them. Cut the stems down as low as you want them, but leave at least two five-leaflet leaves per stem to contribute to food production. Do not remove more than 25 percent of the foliage; if you do, you will send the plant into shock and a short dormant period. First-year plants should be pruned only slightly when removing faded flowers, to encourage growth and foliage production.

Old blooms past their peak should be pruned away as soon as possible. This not only keeps the plant looking neat and the ground free of fallen petals, but also encourages the plant to send out new growth and flowers sooner.

Always remove a dead flower by taking a piece of the stem and cutting to just above a five-leaflet leaf. If you cut to a three-leaflet leaf instead, numerous small growth shoots will appear at the top of the stem but will never grow into sturdy, flower-producing stems.

possible, to encourage deep roots. In temperate climates a weekly watering is usually sufficent. Roses whose roots grow deeply will be stronger, healthier, and more drought resistant than those with shallow roots. It is also important to water early in the day so that the leaves do not stay wet through the night, as this fosters disease. Thus, if you are using an overhead watering system rather than a drip system (see the next section), water only in the morning. If the soil is heavy, apply water slowly so that it is absorbed rather than running off.

No matter what type of watering system you use, you must be certain that the water is getting down to the roots where it is needed. Using a trowel or a pipe, probe the soil to a depth of 12 to 18 inches, and bring up a column of soil. Do this right after you have finished watering. If the soil is moist to the lower level, you know that you have applied the right amount of water. If it is partly dry, you will need to apply more water for a longer period until your soil can pass the test.

To ensure that you are watering often enough, take another soil probe one week after you have watered. If the soil at the bottom of the probe has completely dried out, you need to water more than once a week. Try watering every five days, and see if the soil passes the test. If it does not pass, reduce the watering frequency until it does. If, however, the soil is still moist at the bottom of the probe when you first test it, an interval of 10 days might be better.

You also need to test how long you should run your watering system. If you are using sprinklers (see the next section), place an empty coffee can halfway between the sprinkler and its outermost reach and note how long it takes for 1 inch of water to collect in the can. You can then determine how long to run the sprinkler in a given spot to deliver 1 inch of water—assuming that your water pressure is constant. Under normal

conditions, it takes about 1 to 1½ hours for an average oscillating sprinkler to deliver an inch of water. You can keep track of the amount of rainfall with a rain gauge and adjust your watering accordingly. Combining this test with the soil-probe test tells you how long to run the sprinklers and how often to water. If you are using a drip irrigation system, a soil probe is the best way to gauge the proper amount, frequency, and duration of watering.

Adding organic matter such as compost or leaf mold to a sandy soil (see page 105) can help it hold moisture so that watering is not needed as frequently. A mulch of wood chips or other material applied to the top of the soil (page 142) not only holds moisture but also deters weeds, which are notorious water thieves. If your roses are planted near a large tree or shrub, you may need to compensate by giving the roses extra water; probe the

A rain gauge keeps track of precipitation so you know how much shortfall to make up for. Under normal conditions, roses need an inch of water a week.

Roses in containers need more frequent watering than those in the ground because they have less soil around them to hold moisture. A water wand makes the job easier.

soil around the roses as described above to determine whether more water is needed. Underground barriers (page 99) will help prevent neighboring plants from stealing water from the roses. In windy areas a windbreak such as a fence or a hedge helps slow evaporation. Refer to page 100 for a discussion of windbreaks.

One exception to the watering rule is newly planted roses. They should be watered daily for about a week and then every few days until new growth is evident. Then they can be watered in the same way as any other rose in the garden; if they show signs of wilting, you need to keep up the more frequent watering until they become established.

Roses growing in containers require more regular watering than the same plants growing in the ground. Water is quickly depleted from the limited growing space in a container, and can evaporate from the sides of porous pots. In hot or windy locations, container plants may need watering once a day or more, with smaller pots needing more frequent replenishing. Check the medium in the container every day, and water when the top becomes dry, applying water until it runs out of the drainage holes. Use a type of nozzle known as a bubbler or soaker head, which administers water in a soft flow to keep holes from being created in the planting medium. A water wand, which is a long tube with a nozzle at the end, is useful for reaching hanging baskets or out-of-reach containers. Roses can be watered with a watering can, but if you have many plants, this method is time consuming.

To help roses survive the winter, make sure that the plants are watered before the soil freezes. If it has not rained in the fall, apply a deep watering before draining the hoses and shutting down the watering system for the winter.

WATERING METHODS

There are a number of ways to supply water to rosebushes. The most traditional is with hoses and sprinklers, available at garden centers and hardware stores. The equipment for overhead watering with sprinklers is less expensive than that for drip irrigation, but overhead watering uses much more water and can promote fungal disease. Because of increasing concern about water conservation, many people are turning to drip irrigation, which is the most efficient way to water.

Drip irrigation uses less water than overhead watering since the water is applied only to the ground where it can be absorbed by the roots. Drip irrigation also prevents foliage and flowers from getting wet, thus protecting them from diseases and water damage.

There are two major kinds of drip systems: emitters and soaker hoses. An emitter system consists of a rigid main tubing interspersed with small holes from which flexible narrow tubes called emitters extend. The ends of the emitters are capped with small nozzles that emit water in a gentle drip or stream. These are placed wherever there is a plant to be watered; if there are no plants for a stretch of the main tubing, the holes can be plugged. Components of an emitter system can be purchased at garden centers or from irrigation supply stores.

An emitter system can be laid on the ground, buried, or hidden beneath a layer of mulch. It is better to bury the system because this keeps the ultraviolet rays of the sun from weakening the plastic hoses and insulates the system from winter freezing. It is also more attractive. In areas with cold winters, an aboveground system should be removed in autumn to prevent it from freezing and cracking. The holes in an emitter nozzle system are very small and can clog easily. To prevent clogging, install a filter at the water source and clean the filter once a month.

Top: In this variation on the typical emitter system, narrow tubes lead from a main hose to plastic drip rings around each plant.

Center: Micropore soaker hoses have spongelike sides through which water seeps into the ground.

Bottom: A moisture sensor installed at the proper depth can signal an irrigation system to water as needed.

beads of water "sweat" over the surface of the hose. These kinds of hoses are made from white plastic or recycled black rubber tires.

Like emitter systems, soaker hoses can be laid on the ground, but it is best to conceal them under mulch or bury them underground to protect them from the elements and prolong their life. The hoses are twined through the garden in such a way that each plant will receive water.

Any type of irrigation system can be set up to work automatically, using a moisture sensor or a watering timer to turn the water on and off. Moisture sensors, available at garden centers and irrigation supply stores, are probes placed in the ground to measure its moisture content. When the ground starts to dry out, they automatically turn on the water. Watering timers, available at the same places, are similar to the timers used to control household lights. They turn the water on and off on preset days at preset times. Moisture sensors are preferable to timers, since they deliver water to the garden only as needed and not by an imposed schedule.

Roses can be watered with sprinklers or other overhead methods if watering is done in the morning so that the foliage has time to dry out; leaves and canes that stay wet overnight can foster disease. For this and other reasons, it is far better to water with a drip irrigation system or with soaker hoses. But even if you have a drip irrigation system, occasional overhead watering every several weeks can help rid leaves of dust and spray residue, and can discourage spider mites, which thrive on foliage that is hot and dry.

Many types of sprinklers are available. Some oscillate, throwing water back and forth in a rectangular pattern. Others rotate, spraying water in a circle. A third type is the fixed sprinkler, which has no moving parts, and is usually used for watering small areas. It can be adjusted to spray water in a circular, rectangular,

A rotating sprinkler head helps keep water below leaf level, staving off mildew.

Like emitter systems, soaker hoses deliver water directly to the soil at the base of the plant. But unlike them, they exude water through pores or pinholes all along their length instead of at designated locations. The oldest kinds of soaker hoses are made of heavy canvas through which water seeps into the ground. Another type is made of flat plastic, punctured with pinprick-sized holes every few inches. The newest types are the tubular micropore hoses, which have a sponge-like network of tiny holes through which

or square pattern. The oscillating type is usually better than the rotating kind for large gardens, since its rectangular coverage results in less overlapping and thus less wasted water.

Sprinklers also come in different sizes to cover various square footages. Check packaging for specifications, and choose the sprinkler that best fits the size of your rose garden. Sprinklers are made of plastic or metal; both types work equally well, but the plastic sprinklers are not as likely as the metal sprinklers to corrode. Whichever sprinkler you choose, be sure to position it away from streets and driveways to prevent wasteful runoff. Never use an overhead sprinkler on a windy day, as the wind can waste water by carrying it away or causing it to evaporate before it reaches the ground.

Whatever type of watering system you use, shut it off and drain the lines after the final watering in the autumn. This prevents the water in the lines from freezing, thereby cracking the hoses and tubes.

Hoses, like sprinklers, come in various sizes. You should buy a hose that is long enough to reach across your garden, and preferably ⅝ inch in diameter (rather than the less common ½ inch) so that it can deliver more water. There are also hoses that are ¾ inch in diameter, but these work well only with very large sprinklers and do not work well unless the water pressure is very high. Hoses are made of plastic or rubber; those of rubber are less likely to kink, while those of plastic are more flexible. Plastic hoses do not work well in cold areas because they lose their flexibility and are likely to crack. Some hoses are reinforced with an internal mesh that protects them against bursting and kinking.

You can reduce kinking by coiling hoses when not in use. A wall-mounted hose hanger or a mobile hose reel makes this job easier. To keep hoses from dragging over low-growing plants, place guide stakes at the corners of the beds or in other strategic positions. Should your hose spring a leak, you can fix it with a repair kit from your garden center or hardware store. Be sure that the kit you buy will fit the diameter of the hose you are using.

Several types of nozzles are also available. Hand-held pistol nozzles can deliver water from a hard spray to a fine mist, as can nozzles with twist controls. The hard spray is for knocking aphids and other pests off plants; the intermediate spray is good for general watering; and the fine mist can be used to raise humidity. Fan-shaped nozzles give a wide, coarse spray that is useful for watering small rose beds. Soaker heads are good for watering containers or filling the catch basins of plants.

For adding water to the root area of a newly planted rose you need no nozzle at

A wall-mounted reel makes hose easy to unwind and keeps it from kinking.

all; simply place the end of the hose into the catch basin around the plant and let the water run gently until the catch basin is full.

Although many gardeners enjoy watering their roses by hand with a hose and nozzle, this method is time consuming, and there is a danger that the roses may not receive enough water. However, hand watering is sometimes necessary for roses in containers. Yet even for these, a drip irrigation system with emitters can be used to water plants easily and quickly. Allow the water to run until it flows out of the drainage holes; with high pressure, it should take about five minutes to water containers using this method.

To soak the roots of a newly planted or transplanted rose, run water gently until the catch basin is full.

MULCHING

A mulch is a layer of natural or synthetic material that is placed atop the soil to blanket it from the elements. Natural mulches include tree bark; leaf mold; compost; leaves such as pine needles; agricultural by-products such as buckwheat hulls, peanut hulls, and cocoa-bean hulls; gravel; and stones. Synthetic mulches include landscape fabric and black plastic.

The benefits of mulching are many. A good mulch keeps the soil evenly moist, insulates it from rapid temperature fluctuation, and reduces erosion by wind and water. Its protective covering keeps weeds down and helps prevent mud and disease organisms from splashing onto plants during watering. It also adds an attractive finish to the garden. Moreover, some mulches contribute organic matter and nutrients to the soil.

Once applied, mulches can be left in place permanently, and more mulch can be added as required. All mulches made of plant material can be worked into the soil once each season in spring or fall and then replaced, thereby doing extra duty as soil conditioners.

The selection of natural mulches that are available for sale varies from region to region. In the eastern and midwestern United States, many garden centers offer wood chips, bark chips, shredded pine bark, and cocoa-bean hulls. On the West Coast and in the Southwest, cedar chips, fir-bark chunks, peat moss, and redwood-bark chips are more commonly available. In the South, shredded fir bark, pine chips, bagasse, and cottonseed hulls are common. Leaf mold, grass clippings, and compost are seldom sold in stores; if you do not have these materials and cannot make your own, ask about local sources at nurseries or check classified ads in newspapers. Many communities

make leaf mold from the leaves collected in autumn and offer it to their residents without charge.

When shopping for a natural mulch, look for one that is permeable, attractive, and relatively slow to decompose. Your selection will also depend on price. Keep in mind that there is no panacea among mulches; each kind has trade-offs.

If you use buckwheat hulls, cocoa-bean hulls, or peanut hulls on your roses, pile the material to a depth of 2 to 4 inches. These mulches are moderately long lasting and do not need to be replaced for two to three years. Cocoa-bean hulls have the added advantage of supplying extra potassium, whereas peanut hulls have more fertilizer value than most other mulches. But if you purchase peanut hulls, be sure that they have not been salted and that they have been fumigated for nematodes (microscopic worms that infest the soil and can damage plants). Fir and pine bark and pine needles also make excellent mulch materials because

they decompose slowly and control weeds better than the others; apply them 2 to 3 inches thick. Bagasse, the chopped remains of processed sugar cane, sold primarily in sugar-producing areas, is slow to decompose and retains heavy amounts of water, which will assist in keeping the ground cool and moist. Apply it 1 to 2 inches thick.

Hay and straw make acceptable natural mulches but are less desirable than other types. Although inexpensive and moderately slow to decompose, they often carry weed seeds and make a good hiding place for rodents. They may also be a fire hazard, and being lightweight, will blow away easily. And they are not especially attractive. If you use hay or straw, pile it 3 to 4 inches deep to allow for settling. Grass clippings can be used if they are dried first; otherwise they will give off excessive heat and can become slimy. They also decompose rapidly.

Although compost and leaf mold are more often used as soil conditioners, they

Gravel lasts much longer than other mulches. It also slows wind or water erosion and reflects light in shady gardens.

A mulch of porous plastic landscape fabric is a barrier to weeds, yet allows water in and out. It can be hidden under a layer of bark or other natural mulch.

can also be applied as a mulch. Layer compost or leaf mold 2 to 3 inches thick. Their main disadvantages are that they decompose rapidly, within one year, and may not be readily available. On the plus side, if they are available, or if you can make your own, they are economical and add nutrients to the soil.

Sphagnum peat moss, though an excellent soil conditioner, makes a poor mulch because it actually pulls moisture from the soil. And as it dries out, it forms a thick crust that is very difficult to moisten again. Avoid sphagnum peat moss if you can. Sawdust can be used as mulch, but it will rob nutrition from your roses as it disintegrates if additional nitrogen is not added. If you use sawdust, apply a 1- to 2-inch layer and mix in 9 to 18 pounds of 5-10-5 fertilizer per 100 square feet to compensate. Wood chips must also be supplemented with nitrogen (use 5 pounds of 5-10-5 per 100 square feet), but they are superior to sawdust because they are slower to decompose. They are also heavier than

most other mulches and are thus less likely to blow away. Apply wood chips 2 inches thick.

Marble chips and gravel make excellent mulches where wind or water erosion is a problem. Their weight keeps them from blowing or washing away, and they last indefinitely. Their light color also makes them excellent reflectors of light and heat in shady gardens. Marble chips, actually a form of limestone, can raise the pH of the soil, which can be an advantage or a disadvantage. Gravel is a generic term for hard, crushed rock; its composition varies with the type of rock that is available locally. When gravel is made from granite, it is inert; when it is made from limestone, it can raise the pH of the soil the way marble chips do.

The most common synthetic mulches are landscape fabric and black plastic. Landscape fabric is a fine, woven or nonwoven gray or black material that water can penetrate but weeds cannot. It comes in sheets or rolls and can be laid on the ground. It is very effective at reducing weed growth and it warms the soil efficiently in cold climates, hastening growth. A cheaper alternative is black plastic, also sold in sheets or rolls. It is less desirable than landscape fabric because it seals in moisture, encouraging molds. If you use black plastic, be sure to poke holes in it so that water can pass through. Both black plastic and landscape fabric are more attractive if you cover them with a layer of natural mulch. Covered or not, both will need to be replaced in three to five years.

Timing is important when applying mulches. If you live where summers are hot, applying mulch in early spring will help moderate the buildup of heat in the soil, keeping the soil cooler, which roots prefer. In areas with short, cool growing seasons, it's better to hold off on mulching until the ground has warmed up in late spring; mulch applied too early will delay soil warming. Once the ground is warm and the mulch has been applied, the mulch will keep the ground warm.

You will often hear the term *winter mulch*. This is material used for winter protection. For more information on winter mulch and protecting roses during the winter, see page 154.

WEEDS

*W*eeds are simply plants out of place. Although they may not seem overtly harmful to your roses, they can thwart proper growth by robbing roses of sunlight, nutrients, and water; they may also harbor destructive insects and diseases. If they are not properly controlled, aggressive weeds can completely overrun a rose garden.

A rank growth of weeds is often an indicator of poor and compacted soil, improper pH, poor drainage, incorrect fertilization or watering, or insufficient light. The appearance of weeds is a sign not only that the weeds need to be removed, but that other corrective actions may have to be taken.

It is important to control weeds when they are young and actively growing, as this is the easiest time to eliminate them. If your rose garden is small or if weeds are few, simply pull them out by hand or with a hoe. Mulching helps reduce weed

Rampant weed growth may signal serious problems with the soil, the light level, or watering and fertilizing practices. If not controlled, weeds will soon take over the garden.

growth by smothering weeds and their seeds, and by keeping the soil cool, which will prevent the germination of crabgrass and other grassy seeds. The few weeds that may pop through can easily be removed.

In larger gardens weeds can be eradicated with a chemical herbicide. There are two classes of chemical herbicides: preemergent and postemergent.

Preemergent herbicides prevent seeds in the ground from germinating. You apply these herbicides to the soil beginning in early spring, depending on the weeds you want to control; see the product label for information. Some preemergent herbicides contain ingredients that may be harmful to your roses, so read the label carefully before using one of these products.

Postemergent herbicides kill weeds that are actively growing. Unfortunately, they may also kill or disfigure roses if not applied with extreme care. Thus they are not recommended for use in existing rose gardens.

If you are preparing a new rose bed, give your roses a good start by eliminating all weeds before planting—either by manually removing them or by treating them with an herbicide. If you are using a postemergent herbicide, apply it far enough in advance so that it will have time to decompose before you plant your roses; otherwise they may be harmed.

Preemergent herbicides that are labeled safe for roses can be applied either before or after planting, depending on the product, as some will not work if they are disturbed after they have been applied. Check the product label to be sure. Preemergent herbicides will not control weeds that have already sprouted.

A lawn that is allowed to grow into your rose beds can be just as troublesome as weeds. Metal, brick, or stone edgings around the rose beds will help keep the lawn at bay.

FERTILIZING

*L*ike other flowering plants, roses need food in order to grow and bloom successfully. Roses, however, have greater nutritional needs than do many other plants. Although small quantities of nutrients are available naturally in the soil and air, supplemental fertilizing is essential if you want your roses to perform their best. Your fertilizer must be not only of the right formulation for roses, but also applied in the right amounts at the right times. In this section you'll learn about the nutritional components of fertilizers, the different types, how and when to apply them, and how to recognize nutrient deficiencies.

FERTILIZER BASICS

Fertilizers contain three elements that are basic for plant growth: nitrogen, phosphorus, and potassium (abbreviated N, P, and K, respectively). Nitrogen promotes stem and leaf growth and deep green color, and stimulates early spring growth. Phosphorus encourages root growth and flower production and is necessary for photosynthesis. Potassium helps regulate the metabolism of the plant and contributes to hardiness, vigor, good flower color, and disease resistance. A fertilizer containing all three elements is said to be complete.

Because plants differ in their nutritional needs, fertilizers come with differing proportions of these three elements. A typical formulation is 5-10-5, containing 5 percent nitrogen, 10 percent phosphorus, and 5 percent potassium (the other 80 percent is inert material that helps distribute them evenly). These percentages always appear in the same order on product labels. Two other common formulations of rose fertilizers are 5-10-10 and 8-12-4.

Roses, like many other flowering shrubs, grow best when you use a fertilizer whose nitrogen, phosphorus, and potassium exist in approximately 1:2:1, 1:2:2, or 2:3:1 ratios. The relatively lower proportion of nitrogen keeps the plants from producing lush leaves at the expense of flowers.

Superphosphate (0-20-0) and triple superphosphate (0-45-0) are special fertilizers used at planting time to encourage root growth. They supply only phosphorus.

You often hear fertilizers referred to as organic or inorganic. Organic fertilizers contain carbon and may be either natural or synthetic. Natural organic fertilizers, such as bonemeal, cottonseed meal, and fish emulsion, are minimally processed animal or vegetable by-products. Synthetic organic fertilizers, such as IBDU (isobutylidene diurea) and sulfur-coated urea, are manufactured from organic materials by more elaborate methods. Organic fertilizers of both types take the form of particles, granules, powders, or liquids.

Inorganic fertilizers are synthetic products containing no organic materials. They are manufactured from mineral salts, typically potassium nitrate, ammonium nitrate, ammonium phosphate, ammonium sulfate, calcium nitrate, potassium chloride, and potassium sulfate. These fertilizers are solids in their pure form but are often sold in solution.

Although both organic and inorganic fertilizers supply plants with the same nutrients, each has its particular advantages and disadvantages. Inorganic fertilizers are highly water soluble and release nutrients to the plant quickly, but they leach through the soil rapidly and must be applied more often than organic fertilizers. Because they are very concentrated, they may burn plants if not diluted properly. Also, their component salts can accumulate in the soil over time.

Natural organic fertilizers are bulky, and many do not contain as a high a

concentration of nutrients as do inorganic or synthetic organic fertilizers. The exact proportions and amounts of nutrients may vary from batch to batch, and because most do not have the right proportions of nutrients on their own, they have to be combined or supplemented with other fertilizers. Some are difficult to obtain and are often more expensive, and a few have an objectionable odor. On the plus side, organic fertilizers are slower to leach from the soil, and they improve soil structure, encourage the buildup of beneficial soil organisms, and leave no residue of chemical salts. A few organic fertilizers, including seaweed and fish emulsion, are rich in trace elements (see page 153); seaweed also produces or stimulates plant-growth hormones. Dried banana peels, which are very high in potassium, have become popular lately among serious rose growers.

Because the nutrients in many natural fertilizers do not occur in ideal proportions—indeed, some nutrients may be

The natural organic fertilizers on the left are bulkier and slower acting than synthetics, but they last longer and help build up the soil. The synthetic fertilizer on the right has been supplemented with a systemic insecticide for convenience.

absent altogether—it is often useful to combine two or more of these fertilizers to achieve the right balance for rose growing. For example, a combination of blood meal, bonemeal, and wood ashes (dampened to extinguish smoldering) would give sufficient amounts of all three nutrients.

A more reliable solution is to buy a natural organic fertilizer that has been supplemented with an inorganic fertilizer. Often sold as "rose foods" at garden centers, these supply the best of both worlds—the precise formulation and quick action of inorganic fertilizers, and the long-lasting, soil-enhancing properties of natural organic fertilizers. By

law, the product label must specify the amount of organic and inorganic materials present.

Some organic and inorganic fertilizers are known as slow-release fertilizers because they release their nutrients over a long period, usually three to nine months. They are more convenient than the regular type because you don't need to apply them as often. Some slow-release fertilizers, for example, are applied only once per year in late winter or early spring, whereas regular fertilizers are applied more frequently (see the next section). The release is sometimes activated by soil moisture, and sometimes by high soil temperature.

A good way to determine whether a fertilizer is the slow-release type is to look on the label for the percentage of water insoluble nitrogen (abbreviated WIN). If the WIN number is 30 percent or more, the fertilizer is considered slow release.

The labels of some products also indicate the number of months they will last. If you only want to fertilize once a year choose a product that will remain active throughout your roses' growing cycle, whether it is four months, six months, or nine months. Note, however, that slow-release products lack the trace elements that are present in many other fertilizers, so supplemental applications of these elements may be needed.

Another important choice you face is whether to apply fertilizers in dry or liquid form. Although there are some natural organic liquid fertilizers, such as fish emulsion, the term *liquid fertilizer* is usually applied to dry or liquid concentrates of water-soluble inorganic fertilizers that are mixed with water before application. Typical formulations are 20-20-20 or 15-30-15. Because of their water solubility, they are fast acting, releasing their nutrients quickly. This is a special boon for container-grown roses, which must be watered frequently. Frequent watering

---

Choosing a Natural Fertilizer

Because the components of natural fertilizers often vary, it is impossible to predict the exact proportion of nutrients that are present in a given batch. However, the following analysis of common natural fertilizers shows the percentages of nitrogen (N), phosphorus (P), and potassium (K) that are typical of each. Among those listed below, the ones most commonly sold at garden centers are alfalfa; blood, bone, cottonseed, and fish meals; and processed sewage sludge. Dehydrated cow and horse manures are often sold; if you live near a farm or a stable, you can collect fresh manure and dry it yourself. Processed seaweed is becoming more widely available. Poultry manure is not readily available but can be obtained from farmers. You'll have to eat your own bananas to get the peels, and you or a friend will probably have to have a fireplace to get wood ashes.

Product	(N-P-K) Analysis
Alfalfa meal	2.5-5-.5
Banana peels	0-3-42
Blood meal	15-1-1
Bonemeal	3-16-0
Cow and horse manure	2.5-5-1.5
Cottonseed meal	7-2.5-1.5
Fish meal	8-13-4
Poultry manure	3.5-3-1.5
Seaweed	3-1-5
Sewage sludge	2-1.5-1
Wood ashes	0-1.5-7

can cause dry fertilizers to leach away before they have a chance to act.

Liquid fertilizers are less appropriate for roses growing in the ground, because they must be applied as often as once every two weeks. They are therefore not as convenient as dry fertilizers and are usually used only as a supplement. Rose growers who exhibit at shows often apply liquid fertilizer about 10 days before a show to give the plants a "boost," promoting deeper green foliage and larger, more colorful flowers. Liquid fertilizers can, however, be combined with fungicide and insecticide sprays for convenience; see Chapter 9 for a discussion on spraying.

When you are deciding on which fertilizer to use in the garden, choose a slow-release type if saving time is of the essence. Otherwise the best fertilizer to choose is one that combines organic and inorganic fertilizers. Use liquid fertilizer as a supplement if desired. For container-grown roses, liquid fertilizers are the best.

HOW AND WHEN TO FERTILIZE

Proper timing is essential when applying fertilizer, because nutrients must be present in the soil when the plants need them most. This critical time is when plants are at their most active stage of growth and flowering. This will vary with the climate, but it starts with the first signs of growth in late winter or early spring and lasts until cool fall weather slows growth. Fertilizer must also be applied in the proper amount, which depends on the type and size of the roses, the length of the growing season, possible competition from other plants, and the soil. A yearly soil test can tell you the nutrient content of your soil and what fertilizing regime is best for you.

Roses, being hungry plants, need to be fertilized often. Using a complete fertilizer or rose food whose N-P-K ratio is

1:2:1, 1:2:2, or 2:3:1, feed roses as soon as they are pruned, after the first flush of bloom, and about two months before the first fall frost. Gardeners who want to grow exhibition-size roses can feed them once a month from early spring to late summer or fall, depending on the length of the growing season. They can also use liquid fertilizers in advance of rose shows to produce better specimens.

If you have planted new roses correctly, there will be enough fertilizer in the soil to carry the plant through until its first bloom. At that time you should begin following the normal schedule.

A natural fertilizer combined with an inorganic fertilizer provides the best of both worlds. Be sure to pull away mulch before adding it to the soil.

Top: Spread fertilizer on moist soil above the root area, then work it in.

Bottom: Fertilizer solutions can be sprayed directly onto leaves, which absorb nutrients quickly. Iron deficiencies are often remedied in this way.

If the soil pH needs to be adjusted, it should be done about a month before fertilizing to create the optimum pH for roses, which is 6.5. The more efficient nutrient absorption at this pH will make your fertilizer go further. (For information on adjusting pH, see page 104.)

Slow-release fertilizers need to be applied less often, at a frequency that depends on the formulation. For example, a six-month formulation is applied only once in early spring in Zone 7, where the growing season is six months long. If a three-month formulation is used instead, it would be applied twice, in early spring and again in early summer. When applying slow-release fertilizers, it is best to move the mulch aside, lightly scratch the fertilizer into the ground with a hand-held cultivator, and then put the mulch back. Unless the fertilizer is in contact with the soil, it will not work properly.

Liquid fertilizers must be applied as often as every two weeks. Pour them over the ground with a watering can or a sprayer, or spray them on foliage with the same equipment. Leaves as well as roots can absorb nutrients; in fact, fertilizer applied directly to the foliage will be put to use more quickly. Do not apply any liquid fertilizers to foliage when the air temperature is over 90° F, since rapid evaporation at these temperatures makes the fertilizers more concentrated and thus more likely to burn the plants.

Many experts now recommend dormant feeding, which is the application of fertilizer during the late fall or winter when the plant tops are not growing. Since roots continue growing in fall and winter until the soil temperature falls below 40° F and start growing again in spring before top growth appears, they can absorb fertilizer supplied during the dormant period as soon as they are ready for it. If roses are dormant fed in fall or winter, an early spring application of fertilizer is not necessary. In warm areas, where roses grow all year, dormant feeding is not needed unless the plants are forced into dormancy to prolong their lives (page 184), or unless their growth slows significantly.

Always follow the directions on the label regarding the amount of fertilizer to apply, since this will vary with the formulation. It takes twice as much 5-10-5 fertilizer as 10-10-10 fertilizer to provide plants with the same amount of nitrogen and potassium. (The increased amount of phosphorus will not harm the plants since phosphorus moves slowly through the soil.)

Large shrub roses, old garden roses, and climbers need more fertilizer than hybrid teas—about twice as much per plant; miniatures need much less than any other rose—about half as much. Adjust your applications accordingly.

Since fertilizers leach more rapidly from sandy soils than they do from other types of soil, they may need to receive fertilizer more often. If you see signs of reduced growth from nutrient deficiency, either correct the soil or shorten the interval between fertilizer applications by about one third. When roses are growing near other plants, they may need about 20 percent more fertilizer if they show signs of reduced growth.

To keep from burning the roots, always apply any type of fertilizer to moist soil, spreading it over the entire area under which roots are growing. Generally this is the soil under the spread of the plant. Be careful not to spill fertilizer on the bud union; if you do so accidentally, wash the fertilizer off to avoid burning it. Work the fertilizer lightly into the top of the soil with a trowel or a hand-held cultivator and water again.

Fertilizing too late in the season can be detrimental to roses, since nitrogen encourages new growth that will not have time to adapt to the cold before winter chill can damage it. It is best to stop using complete fertilizers about two months before the first frost. However, a fertilizer that contains little or no nitrogen, but has phosphorous and potassium (such as bonemeal, superphosphate, or dried banana peels) can be applied in early fall. Phosphorus and potassium help the canes adapt to cold weather, lessening dieback and other winter injury.

Mixing many gallons of liquid fertilizer for a large garden can be a backbreaking and time-consuming job. An easy alternative is to make a concentrated solution of fertilizer and deliver it with a garden hose at the proper dilution, using a device called a siphon injector. Attached to the end of the hose, a siphon injector has a tube that siphons small amounts of concentrated fertilizer from a bucket to mix with outgoing water. Siphon injectors are sold at garden centers and come with instructions.

If rose foliage turns crisp and brown, it may be a sign of overfertilizing. Water the plants heavily to leach excess fertilizer out of the ground, and adjust the amount or concentration of future feedings to keep the problem from recurring. You can fine-tune this by trial and error, or better yet, by having your soil tested.

Diagnosing Nutrient Deficiencies

If your roses are not growing as well as you think they should, the cause may be a nutrient deficiency. The following table lists common symptoms that result from the lack of major and minor nutrients. The best way to confirm a suspected deficiency is with a complete soil analysis, available through your county agricultural extension or a private soil-testing laboratory. The analysis reveals not only the nutritional status of your soil, but also its pH, texture, and organic content. Many lab reports also tell you what corrective actions to take. If the report indicates no problems with the soil, but the plants are still growing poorly, take a step further to determine whether you have an environmental problem, an insect problem, or a disease problem. (See Chapter 4 for information about the growing needs of roses. Chapter 9 contains a complete discussion of insects and diseases.)

Nutrient	Symptoms of Deficiency
Boron	Young leaflets turn light green at their bases; leaflets are thick and roll up at the edges; terminal buds die back.
Calcium	Terminal buds die; young leaves have a light green edge; older leaves become dull and may curl at the margins; leaf margins turn brown.
Chlorine	This element is rarely if ever deficient, and its deficiency symptoms are not understood by soil and plant scientists.
Copper	Young leaflets wilt without yellowing; stem tips are weak.
Iron	Young leaflets are yellow except for main veins as they open; then entire leaves yellow but do not turn brown. Symptoms start at top of plant.
Magnesium	Yellowing occurs between veins of older lower leaflets, starting at the leaf tips and proceeding toward the middle, followed by browning and dying; leaflets are thick and brittle; roses are stunted and produce few basal breaks.
Manganese	Lighter green areas develop between veins in young leaves; brown, dry, dead areas appear on leaves.
Molybdenum	Similar to nitrogen deficiency; leaflets also tend to be narrow and elongated.
Nitrogen	Older lower leaves turn yellow, then brown, and die.
Phosphorus	Plant growth is stunted; foliage is dull with reddened undersides and small flowers.
Potassium	Leaves turn yellow at the tips and between veins; leaflets curl under; dry, black or brown dead spots develop in yellow areas.
Sulfur	Older leaves yellow without browning and dying; stems are elongated, slender, and weak.
Zinc	Older leaflets turn yellow in an irregular pattern, then turn bronze and eventually die.

TRACE ELEMENTS

In addition to nitrogen, phosphorus, and potassium, roses require small quantities of 10 other elements, called trace elements, for proper growth. These elements are boron, calcium, chlorine, copper, iron, magnesium, manganese, molybdenum, sulfur, and zinc. Most already exist in sufficient amounts in the soil, water, or air, but a few—namely calcium, magnesium, sulfur, and iron—may need to be supplemented occasionally because they are scarce in most environments. Sometimes they are present in fertilizer formulations; check the label to be sure. If not, you will have to purchase a supplemental source. Deficiencies of the other trace elements are possible but rare. Keep in mind that only a soil test can confirm any deficiencies for you. The chart on the opposite page outlines deficiency symptoms.

Roses use calcium for root growth as well as for the production of strong stems. Common sources are regular or dolomitic limestone, gypsum (also a source of sulfur), or crushed eggshells. You can purchase limestone and gypsum at garden centers, and collect eggshells in your own kitchen or from restaurants. Limestone and gypsum are used as soil amendments as well; limestone raises the pH of the soil, but gypsum is neutral. For more on soil amendments, see page 105.

In addition to containing calcium, dolomitic limestone also contains magnesium, the basic element in chlorophyll that enables plants to utilize other nutrients, especially phosphorus; magnesium is also essential for leaf production. If you are applying dolomitic limestone, follow the directions on the product label. If dolomitic limestone is not available, magnesium can be supplied with 1 to 2 ounces of Epsom salt (magnesium sulfate) per rosebush. Sprinkle the Epsom salt over the ground and work it into the soil. You can purchase Epsom salt at a drugstore.

Sulfur promotes root and top growth and helps maintain a dark green color. Sulfur, either pure or in some compounds, is also used to acidify the soil; see page 105 for more information. Sulfur is present in gypsum and Epsom salt, and in many inorganic fertilizers including those containing iron sulfate or ammonium sulfate. It is also possible to buy powdered agricultural sulfur at garden centers or agricultural supply stores. It is wise to check the soil pH after adding pure sulfur to make sure that it hasn't lowered the pH too much.

Iron is needed for the production of chlorophyll; if iron is lacking, leaves turn completely yellow or will stay green only

The leaves of roses suffering from iron deficiency turn completely yellow or stay green only along the veins. To remedy this, apply chelated iron and correct the soil pH.

153

Tie longer canes to a support to anchor them against winter wind.

all of the 10 trace elements. Garden centers and agricultural supply stores are sources of these. Follow the label for application rates and frequency of application.

WINTER PROTECTION

*I*n all but the mildest climates, most roses need some measure of winter protection. The degree of protection your roses need depends on how cold your area gets and on how hardy your roses are. The zone map on page 161 shows the distribution of average minimum temperatures within the continental United States.

Hardiness is the ability of a plant to maintain dormancy and not die during cold weather. When a plant is dormant, it is in a state of suspended animation, so to speak, with no growth occurring above or below ground. Tender plants are those that cannot adapt in this way to the cold.

Roses vary widely in their degree of hardiness. Although no one has ever compiled a zone-by-zone hardiness rating for each variety, some generalizations can be made. Typically, old garden roses, miniatures, and shrubs are inclined to be hardy, whereas many teas, Chinas, noisettes, and modern bush roses are tender. If you are fortunate enough to live in zones 9 to 11, where it rarely freezes, none of your roses will need winter protection. But if you live in zones 1 to 8, where freezing is common, some or all of your roses will need buffering against the cold, depending on the zone and the type of roses you are growing. See the chart on the opposite page.

The plant descriptions in Chapter 10 note the roses within each category that are exceptionally hardy or tender. But bear in mind that the survival of individual

along the veins. A solution of chelated iron, a powder or liquid sold at garden centers, can be sprayed onto plants if this yellowing, known as chlorosis, occurs. Also check the pH of the soil and correct it if necessary, since iron in alkaline soils is chemically unavailable to plant roots. Applying chelated iron to roses in alkaline soil is only first aid; adjust the pH to permanently correct the deficiency.

In addition to the special supplements already mentioned, many general-purpose fertilizers also supply trace elements. These elements are listed on the label and will probably be sufficient to cure all but extreme deficiencies. It is also possible to buy mixtures containing some or

plants will vary to some degree with the microclimate. For instance, a rose growing against a sunny southern wall may thrive without winter protection even if similar roses in your zone normally need it; or if you live by a lake, winter winds sweeping across it may make your roses more vulnerable to damage from the cold.

METHODS OF WINTER PROTECTION

Perhaps the best shelter against winter extremes is the one that nature provides—a thick blanket of snow. Snow keeps temperatures beneath it from dipping too far below freezing and from rising so high or so fast that plants are fooled into premature growth. Snow also blocks the wind, which can break branches and rob moisture from the canes and the soil. But snow can also be destructive, its weight breaking or deforming the branches of larger roses. After a snowfall, brush off branches that are sagging. If you live where heavy snowfall is common, you may want to tie large plants together with string to better support them against the weight of the snow.

In most areas snow is neither deep nor frequent enough to provide constant insulation, so you need to rely on additional means of winter protection. These

Roses Needing Winter Protection

The following classes of roses typically need protection in the zones indicated by dots. Note, though, that hardiness varies within each class and that roses in exposed locations may need extra protection.

ZONE	1	2	3	4	5	6	7	8	9	10	11
Centifolias	•	•	•	•							
Chinas	•	•	•	•	•	•	•	•			
Climbers	•	•	•	•	•	•					
Damasks	•	•	•	•							
Floribundas	•	•	•	•	•	•					
Grandifloras	•	•	•	•	•	•					
Hybrid teas	•	•	•	•	•	•					
Kordesii shrubs	•	•	•	•							
Miniatures	•	•	•	•	•	•					
Noisettes	•	•	•	•	•	•	•	•			
Old garden roses	•	•	•	•	•						
Polyanthas	•	•	•	•	•	•					
Shrub roses	•	•	•	•	•						
Teas	•	•	•	•	•	•	•	•			
Tender modern bush roses	•	•	•	•	•	•	•	•			
Tree roses	•	•	•	•	•	•	•				

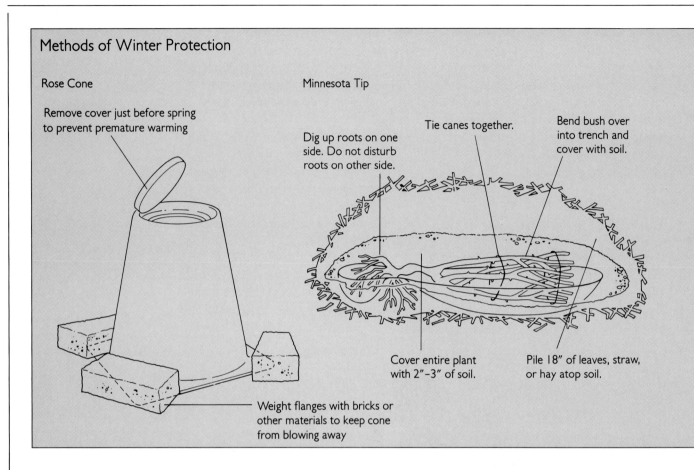

Methods of Winter Protection

Rose Cone

Remove cover just before spring to prevent premature warming

Weight flanges with bricks or other materials to keep cone from blowing away

Minnesota Tip

Dig up roots on one side. Do not disturb roots on other side.

Tie canes together.

Bend bush over into trench and cover with soil.

Cover entire plant with 2"–3" of soil.

Pile 18" of leaves, straw, or hay atop soil.

include covering plants with an insulating material, burying them partially or completely, or in the case of container-grown roses, moving them indoors before the frost. The time to apply winter protection to outdoor plants is in the fall, right after the first normal hard freeze has shocked them into dormancy. Any covering you apply should remain in place until spring, and should be removed gradually if possible as warming accelerates, to reduce potential losses from an unexpected late freeze. When removing a winter covering, be very careful to not break any new canes that may have emerged since you last saw the entire plant.

The traditional method of protecting roses over the winter is to mound soil over the bases of the canes, to a height of about 12 inches, to protect the frost-vulnerable bud union. It is important that the mounding soil be brought from another area of the garden, since removing soil from the immediate vicinity of the plant will expose its delicate feeder roots to the cold air, damaging or killing them.

Although highly effective, the mounding technique requires a lot of work, since you must move soil into the garden in the fall and remove it in the spring. A less arduous method is to apply to the same depth a layer of lightweight, non-absorbent organic material, sometimes called winter mulch. Good materials for winter mulch are shredded oak leaves, straw, or evergreen limbs from unsold or discarded Christmas trees that are available after the holidays. When spring comes you can either remove the mulch or work it into the soil to improve it. The main drawback of this method is that it will usually not provide enough protection in areas colder than Zone 6.

In zones 1 through 5, a useful technique is to cover roses with special caps known as rose cones, which are sold at

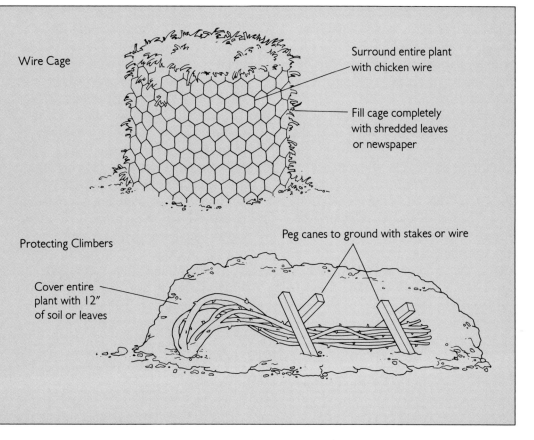

Wire Cage

Surround entire plant with chicken wire

Fill cage completely with shredded leaves or newspaper

Protecting Climbers

Peg canes to ground with stakes or wire

Cover entire plant with 12" of soil or leaves

Below: Protect the cold-sensitive bud union by mounding soil over the bases of the canes. To avoid exposing tender roots near the surface, do not take soil from around the plant.

larger garden centers and hardware stores. Made of thick-walled expandable polystyrene, most are rounded or multi-sided containers that taper toward the top and have flanges at the bottom that can be weighted or pinned to the soil. Some have solid tops; others have covers that can be removed on warm days to keep plants from breaking dormancy too soon. Venting the cones with holes provides additional air circulation that may reduce the growth of molds.

Rose cones come in two sizes: an economical 12-inch height and an 18-inch height for gardeners who don't want to prune their roses excessively to fit underneath. However, even with the taller cones, larger plants need to be cut back somewhat to fit. Tying rose canes together with string before applying the cones also helps them fit better. Rose cones can be stacked and stored over the summer and reused from year to year.

Another method for colder areas is to encase whole beds or individual plants in open-topped chicken-wire cages filled with organic material such as shredded oak leaves or shredded newspapers. Oak leaves are the best type of leaf to use as they don't mat down or become slimy.

In very cold areas, Zone 4 and colder, you can use a technique known as the Minnesota tip. First tie the canes of the plants together to make them easier to handle. Then dig a trench beside the rose. The trench should be as long, as deep, and as wide as the bush so that it can accommodate the entire plant. Next, use a spade to pry the plant from the ground on the side away from the trench. As you do so, take care not to break the plant's roots.

Leaving the remaining roots in the soil, carefully tip the plant over into the trench. Cover the whole plant with 2 to 3 inches of soil and then 18 inches of leaves, straw, or hay. Water the covering well enough to prevent it from catching fire and so that ice forms on it to help keep the plant at a constant temperature. In windy areas a covering of chicken wire will keep the leaves from blowing away.

Where climbers need protection, take the canes off their supports, lay them on the ground, peg them down with stakes or wire, and cover them with soil or leaves to a depth of 12 inches. In early spring remove the protection and tie the climbers back up. An alternative to this is to wrap the canes in burlap, but this method can be cumbersome.

Winter makes demands on both roses and gardeners. In cold climates, it may be easier to grow only cold-hardy varieties that can survive without special protection.

Roses grown in containers can be protected in several ways. You can dig a hole in the ground, set the container into the hole, and cover the plant with soil and mulch. You can also move the container into an unheated but not freezing garage or shed. Water the medium in the container before storage and wrap the entire plant in plastic. The plant can be unwrapped and moved outside about three to four weeks before the last anticipated spring frost. A third alternative is to remove the plants from the pots in which they are growing and wash the soil from their roots. This gives you a chance to inspect the roots for crown gall (a bacterial disease) or for other damage. Then bundle the plants together and bury them in a trench over the winter.

Tree roses are more difficult to protect, because the upper bud union is high above the ground and more susceptible to damage from cold and wind. They are also more difficult to insulate effectively. The easiest way to safeguard tree roses is to grow them in containers and move them indoors over the winter. Place them in an unheated (but not freezing) room such as a garage or sun room, watering them on arrival. The cool temperatures there will induce dormancy; you will not need to water again until you take them back outdoors in spring.

If you do grow tree roses in the ground, the entire plants can be wrapped in burlap, foam rubber, or special insulating wrap with a foil backing that is available in hardware or building supply stores;

Protecting Container Roses

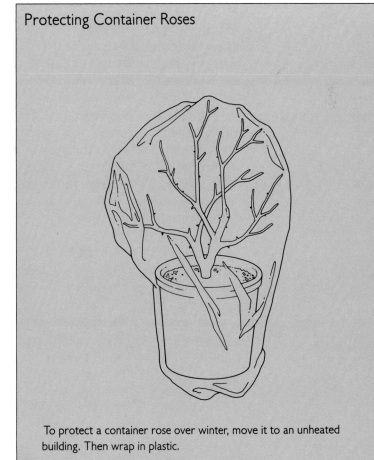

To protect a container rose over winter, move it to an unheated building. Then wrap in plastic.

however, these materials have only limited effectiveness. A better procedure is the Minnesota tip technique. Dig the tree rose from the ground enough to tip it over and bury it on its side under soil or leaves. Tree roses, except for the low-growing patio types, which are 18 inches high, are too large to fit underneath rose cones.

Ice that forms on roses for more than a few hours can damage rose plants and should be removed if the sun melts it enough to break it off. When melting ice on sidewalks or driveways, do not use salt, as it will damage nearby plants; use sand or a salt-free ice-melting compound instead. Roses growing close enough to the street risk being splashed with road salt and should be shielded with a snow fence made of narrow plastic or wooden slats, or a similar barrier. Snow fences are available at hardware stores and from distributors who supply to golf courses, parks, and beaches.

Roses die over the winter not only because it is too cold, but also because the ground alternately freezes and thaws, causing the plants to be heaved from the ground. During this process, roots break or are killed by exposure to cold, drying winds. Winter winds also break branches and rob moisture from canes and the soil surface. Soil that is frozen keeps moisture locked away from the roots, causing the plant to dry out and die.

There are several ways to lessen the effects of winter dehydration. If summer and fall rains have been scarce, give the soil a thorough soaking in the fall, before the ground freezes, so that the plant cells are filled with water and are less likely to become desiccated. Winter mulching not only helps keep soil temperature constant, but also retards moisture loss. You can also seal in moisture in the canes by applying an antidesiccant spray, available at garden centers.

A useful precaution against wind damage is to cut back long canes in the fall

Plant Hardiness Zones

The USDA Plant Hardiness Zone Map of the United States divides the United States into 11 zones, based on minimum winter temperature. This map, redrawn by the U.S. Department of Agriculture in 1990 to reflect climate changes that have occurred since the last revision in 1965, also adds an eleventh zone to more accurately show gradations in the warmest regions. As before, Zone 1 is the coldest, with winter temperatures dipping below −50° F. The new Zone 11 is the warmest; its winter minimums remain above 40° F. Remember, however, that colder or warmer microclimates that may exist within zones will affect the hardiness of local roses.

after the plants have lost their leaves. This reduces the chance of breakage. Windbreaks are another way to shelter roses from winter wind. If space allows, set up a snow fence or other temporary shield on the windward side of the plants, at a distance four to six times the average height of the plants.

If canes are damaged by cold or wind, do not prune them away until new growth buds start to swell in spring, as premature pruning can stimulate new growth that may not survive the chill of a late-spring frost.

Roses grown in zones 9 to 11 are seldom exposed to freezing and need no winter protection. But this is a mixed blessing, since the lack of deep cold keeps these plants from going dormant

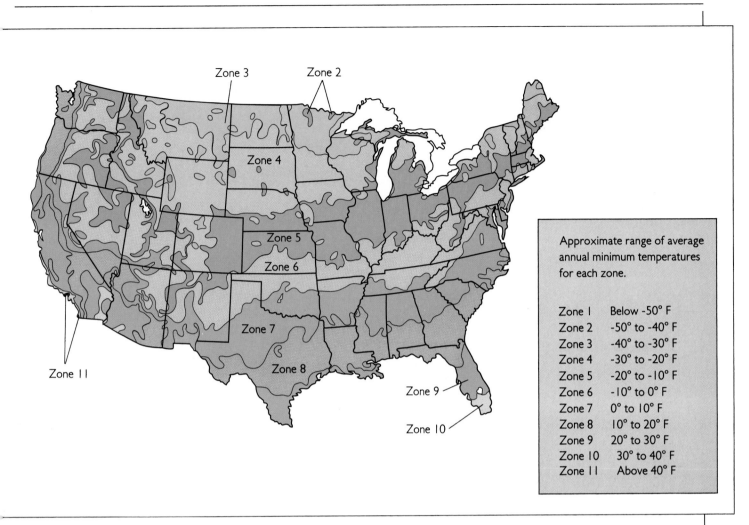

Approximate range of average annual minimum temperatures for each zone.

Zone 1	Below -50° F
Zone 2	-50° to -40° F
Zone 3	-40° to -30° F
Zone 4	-30° to -20° F
Zone 5	-20° to -10° F
Zone 6	-10° to 0° F
Zone 7	0° to 10° F
Zone 8	10° to 20° F
Zone 9	20° to 30° F
Zone 10	30° to 40° F
Zone 11	Above 40° F

and from getting the rest they need to live long and vigorous lives. The answer is to give roses in these zones an artificial respite by discouraging winter growth. To do this, withhold all fertilizer between September and January, and avoid supplemental watering during November and December. From mid-October until pruning time in January, do not deadhead winter blooms; instead, allow them to fade away naturally.

Wherever you live, keep in mind that rosebushes are more likely to survive winter successfully if they are healthy and well cared for. Giving your roses proper fertilizing, pruning, watering, and other care during the summer is an important way to gird them against the stresses of winter cold.

ROSE CARE MONTH BY MONTH

The calendars on the following pages outline month-by-month maintenance activities for roses in each climate zone. Their advice is for growing large, exhibition-type roses. If this is not your goal, apply fertilizer only half as often as is recommended for your zone (for example, every other month instead of every month); also eliminate supplemental fertilizing and disbudding. No matter what your level of aspiration, following these guidelines will help you create a showcase for your roses and a place of beauty for yourself and your neighbors.

Rose Care Month By Month

JANUARY ZONE	1	2	3	4	5	6	7	8	9	10	11
Study catalogs; order roses	•	•	•	•	•	•	•	•	•	•	•
Clean and sharpen tools	•	•	•	•	•	•	•	•	•	•	•
Test pH; adjust if necessary								•	•	•	•
Plant container roses									•	•	•
Plant bare-root roses									•	•	•
Transplant roses									•	•	•
Prune roses									•	•	•
Fertilize after pruning									•	•	•
Resume watering									•	•	•
Spray as needed									•	•	•

FEBRUARY ZONE	1	2	3	4	5	6	7	8	9	10	11
Study catalogs; order roses	•	•	•	•	•	•	•	•	•	•	•
Clean and sharpen tools	•	•	•	•	•	•	•	•			
Test pH; adjust if necessary								•	•	•	•
Plant container roses								•	•	•	•
Plant bare-root roses								•	•	•	•
Transplant roses								•	•	•	•
Prune roses								•			
Fertilize after pruning								•			
Apply summer mulch									•	•	•
Water as needed									•	•	•
Spray as needed									•	•	•

MARCH ZONE	1	2	3	4	5	6	7	8	9	10	11
Study catalogs; order roses	•	•	•	•	•						
Clean and sharpen tools	•	•	•	•	•						
Test pH; adjust if necessary						•	•				
Plant container roses						•	•	•	•	•	•
Plant bare-root roses						•	•				
Transplant roses						•	•				
Remove winter protection							•				
Prune roses							•				
Fertilize after pruning							•				
Fertilize roses								•	•	•	•
Apply supplemental liquid fertilizer								•	•	•	•
Weed rose beds							•				
Weed rose beds; apply preemergent herbicide								•	•	•	•
Apply summer mulch								•			
Begin regular spraying								•			
Continue regular spraying									•	•	•
Water as needed								•	•	•	•
Disbud for larger flowers								•	•	•	•
Deadhead faded flowers									•	•	•

Rose Care Month By Month

APRIL — ZONE	1	2	3	4	5	6	7	8	9	10	11
Test pH; adjust if necessary	•	•	•	•	•	•	•				
Plant container roses	•	•	•	•	•	•	•	•	•	•	•
Plant bare-root roses	•	•	•	•	•	•	•				
Transplant roses	•	•	•	•	•	•	•				
Remove winter protection	•	•	•	•	•	•					
Prune roses	•	•	•	•	•	•	•				
Fertilize after pruning	•	•	•	•	•	•	•				
Fertilize roses								•	•	•	•
Apply supplemental liquid fertilizer								•	•	•	•
Weed rose beds						•					
Weed rose beds; apply preemergent herbicide								•			
Apply summer mulch								•			
Continue regular spraying								•	•	•	•
Water as needed								•	•	•	•
Disbud for larger flowers								•	•	•	•
Deadhead faded flowers								•	•	•	•

MAY — ZONE	1	2	3	4	5	6	7	8	9	10	11
Plant container roses	•	•	•	•	•	•	•	•	•	•	•
Plant bare-root roses	•	•	•								
Fertilize roses	•	•	•	•	•	•	•	•	•	•	•
Apply supplemental liquid fertilizer								•	•	•	•
Weed rose beds								•	•	•	•
Weed rose beds; apply preemergent herbicide	•	•	•	•	•	•	•				
Apply summer mulch	•	•	•	•	•	•	•				
Begin regular spraying	•	•	•	•	•	•	•				
Continue regular spraying								•	•	•	•
Water as needed	•	•	•	•	•	•	•	•	•	•	•
Disbud for larger flowers	•	•	•	•	•	•	•	•	•	•	•
Deadhead faded flowers								•	•	•	•

JUNE — ZONE	1	2	3	4	5	6	7	8	9	10	11
Plant container roses	•	•	•	•	•	•	•	•	•	•	•
Fertilize roses	•	•	•	•	•	•	•	•	•	•	•
Apply supplemental liquid fertilizer	•	•	•	•	•	•	•	•	•	•	•
Weed rose beds								•	•	•	•
Weed rose beds; apply preemergent herbicide	•	•	•	•	•	•	•				
Apply summer mulch	•	•	•	•							
Continue regular spraying	•	•	•	•	•	•	•	•	•	•	•
Water as needed	•	•	•	•	•	•	•	•	•	•	•
Disbud for larger flowers	•	•	•	•	•	•	•	•	•	•	•
Deadhead faded flowers	•	•	•	•	•	•	•	•	•	•	•

Rose Care Month By Month

JULY

	ZONE	1	2	3	4	5	6	7	8	9	10	11
Plant container roses		•	•	•	•	•	•	•	•	•	•	•
Fertilize roses		•	•	•	•	•	•	•	•	•	•	•
Apply supplemental liquid fertilizer		•	•	•	•	•	•	•	•	•	•	•
Weed rose beds		•	•	•	•	•	•	•	•	•	•	•
Continue regular spraying		•	•	•	•	•	•	•	•	•	•	•
Water as needed		•	•	•	•	•	•	•	•	•	•	•
Disbud for larger flowers		•	•	•	•	•	•	•	•	•	•	•
Deadhead faded flowers		•	•	•	•	•	•	•	•	•	•	•

AUGUST

	ZONE	1	2	3	4	5	6	7	8	9	10	11
Plant container roses		•	•	•	•	•	•	•	•	•	•	•
Fertilize roses								•	•	•	•	•
Apply supplemental liquid fertilizer		•	•	•	•	•	•	•	•	•	•	•
Apply fertilizer for the last time		•	•	•	•	•	•	•				
Weed rose beds		•	•	•	•	•	•	•	•	•	•	•
Continue regular spraying		•	•	•	•	•	•	•	•	•	•	•
Water as needed		•	•	•	•	•	•	•	•	•	•	•
Disbud for larger flowers		•	•	•	•	•	•	•	•	•	•	•
Deadhead faded flowers		•	•	•	•	•	•	•	•	•	•	•

SEPTEMBER

	ZONE	1	2	3	4	5	6	7	8	9	10	11
Order roses for fall planting							•	•	•	•	•	•
Prepare soil for spring planting		•	•	•	•	•						
Plant container roses								•	•	•	•	•
Apply fertilizer for the last time									•	•	•	•
Weed rose beds						•	•	•	•	•	•	•
Continue regular spraying								•	•	•	•	•
Water as needed						•	•	•	•	•	•	•
Stop deadheading roses		•	•	•	•	•	•					

OCTOBER

	ZONE	1	2	3	4	5	6	7	8	9	10	11
Apply winter protection		•	•	•	•							
Order roses for fall planting							•	•	•	•	•	•
Prepare soil for spring planting						•						
Plant container roses								•	•	•	•	•
Transplant roses						•						
Weed rose beds							•	•	•	•	•	•
Continue regular spraying								•	•	•	•	•
Water as needed						•	•	•	•	•	•	•
Stop deadheading roses								•	•	•	•	•

Rose Care Month By Month

NOVEMBER ZONE	1	2	3	4	5	6	7	8	9	10	11
Apply winter protection					•	•	•				
Order roses for spring planting	•	•	•	•	•	•	•	•	•	•	•
Prepare soil for spring planting						•	•	•	•	•	•
Plant container roses								•	•	•	•
Plant bare-root roses						•	•	•	•	•	•
Transplant roses						•	•	•			
Spray as needed									•	•	•
Withhold water from established plants									•	•	•

DECEMBER ZONE	1	2	3	4	5	6	7	8	9	10	11
Order roses for spring planting	•	•	•	•	•	•	•	•	•	•	•
Prepare soil for spring planting								•	•	•	•
Plant container roses								•	•	•	•
Plant bare-root roses								•	•	•	•
Transplant roses								•	•	•	•
Spray as needed									•	•	•

Remove faded flowers until fall, then let them set hips. This slows growth, hardening the plant.

A miniature rosebush, grown indoors, makes a charming centerpiece.

CHAPTER SIX

GROWING ROSES INDOORS

*E*ach year, more gardeners discover the pleasures of growing roses indoors. In the space of a bright windowsill or a lighted shelf, you can have a dazzling assortment of miniature roses to cheer you while your outdoor garden is leafless and drab. If you are more ambitious, you can grow larger roses in your home or in a greenhouse. Whatever your preference, you will find that roses adapt readily to indoor life.

*R*oses are among the few plants that can be grown as successfully indoors as they can outdoors. Whereas most other garden plants need seasonal variation in order to thrive, roses can flourish readily in the unchanging conditions that prevail inside most homes. Even though they are cold hardy, they do not need to be subjected to cold winters to grow and flower, unlike many other hardy plants. The roses you grow indoors can be full-time residents, or they can be seasonal guests brought in to survive a freezing winter.

Although you can grow almost any type of rose indoors, practical considerations make miniatures the most rewarding varieties to grow. Their compact size, relative disease resistance, and comparatively modest need for sunlight (as measured against larger roses) make them ideal candidates for windowsill gardening. When winter winds keep you from tending your roses outside, you can be pampering dozens of delicate miniatures in the warmth and comfort of your home. Given enough light, miniature roses will bloom indoors all year long. Even when light is reduced in winter and their blooming may be slight or nonexistent, they will still retain their leaves and may continue to show some growth.

Whether you grow miniatures or their larger relatives, you apply the same basic principles to caring for roses indoors that you do for container roses outdoors. The biggest adjustments you must make are for drier, more uniform conditions that prevail in indoor settings. As with outdoor growing, your success indoors

Given enough light, indoor miniatures will bloom all winter while their outdoor cousins are dormant. Unlike larger roses, they do not need a winter rest period.

depends on starting with good plants, planting them right, and giving them what they need—light, temperature, humidity, water, fertilizer, insect and disease control, and grooming. The next few sections describe miniature-rose growing in a home setting. At the end of the chapter, you'll find instructions for growing larger roses in the house, and for growing various types of roses in a greenhouse.

BUYING ROSES FOR THE INDOOR GARDEN

*A*lthough some miniature roses are available all year at garden centers and nurseries, the largest selection is usually found in mail-order catalogs. See pages 340 and 341 for a list of mail-order nurseries and page 71 for advice on how to purchase plants by mail.

When buying miniature roses at a garden center, look for plants with healthy, deep green leaves that show no signs of insects or diseases. The plants need not be in bloom (unless you want to double-check flower color), but the presence of buds or other new growth is good assurance that the plant is healthy. However, plants in bud or in bloom may have more difficulty coping with the stress of transplanting.

Selecting miniature roses from mail-order catalogs vastly increases your choices of variety and flower color. Look through a number of catalogs before you order, because the range and quality of their offerings can vary. You may be tempted by large and exotic varieties, but usually the smaller, more compact varieties of miniatures will grow better indoors and make more attractive houseplants.

Unlike larger roses, which are usually shipped dormant in bare-root form, mail-order miniatures are almost always

shipped in full leaf—sometimes even in full bloom—in small, 2-inch pots. Note that in winter many vendors will not ship roses (even dormant ones) to regions where temperatures are severe. Should your mail-order roses arrive dead or damaged, contact the vendor immediately; a reputable nursery will replace them.

Help new miniatures adjust by clipping them back and covering them with plastic to raise the humidity around them.

Whether your plants come from a local source or from a mail-order nursery, it's a good idea to keep them separate from your other plants for a few days to make sure they are free of pests or diseases. New roses may take up to several weeks to adapt to their surroundings. Miniature roses that come from greenhouses are probably used to brighter light and higher humidity than are present in most homes, especially in winter. And roses shipped by mail have been in a dark box for several days, and may have been exposed to excessive heat or cold as well.

These environmental changes may cause your new plants to suffer a slight setback. Some leaves may wilt and fall, and the plant may appear to grow slowly—if at all—until it adjusts to conditions in your home. If you see these signs of stress, you can speed the adjustment by doing several things. First, water the plant well. Then, clip back each stem by up to one third and cover the entire plant with a clear plastic bag to raise the humidity around it. Place the plant in bright light but not direct sun. As the plant sends out new growth to replace the growth you trimmed away, punch a few holes in the bag and make more holes as growth continues. This allows the humid air inside the bag to mix gradually with the drier air of the house. Also check the plant frequently to see if it needs watering; if the top of the potting medium feels dry, the plant needs water. After a few weeks you can remove the bag completely and place the plant in direct sun.

Roses obtained from a greenhouse or a garden center were grown in direct light and can be placed immediately in a sunny window or under artificial lights. Mail-order roses should be placed in bright—but not direct—light to ease their transition from the darkness of the shipping box. After several days these plants can be moved into direct light and transplanted into containers.

CHOOSING A CONTAINER

Like other houseplants, miniature roses can be grown in containers made of plastic, metal, clay, or wood. There are pros and cons to each type of container, and even professional greenhouse growers can't agree on which is the best. You'll want to try a few of each and decide for yourself.

Plastic and metal pots, being nonporous, retain moisture longer than do clay and wooden pots, so roses growing in plastic and metal pots do not need to be watered as frequently. Plastic and metal pots are also easier to clean. In addition, plastic pots have more drainage holes than clay pots. On the minus side, metal pots can get too hot in direct sunlight, which will burn the roots. Metal and plastic pots, because they are nonporous, can promote root rots.

Clay and wooden containers allow the growing medium to "breathe" through their sides, providing better aeration than plastic or metal. However, the soil dries out more quickly in clay and wooden containers and needs extra watering. A white residue of accumulated salts from fertilizers and sometimes from water, as well as black or green, moldy growth, adheres more easily to clay and wooden containers than to plastic and metal, and will need to be washed off more often. Some people prefer clay and wooden containers because they are more attractive (when they are clean, of course).

Another consideration in choosing a pot is that it be in proportion to the size of the plant. Small, newly purchased miniature roses should be transferred to 4-inch pots. Pots of this size are best for root development because they allow just enough room for the roots to expand, yet not so much that there is a lot of unoccupied soil. Soil without roots growing in it

tends to stay too wet, promoting rot. As the roses grow, the pot size can be increased. See page 174 for information on when to transplant.

Perhaps the most critical requirement of all is that the pot provide good drainage, since rose roots should not sit in water. Plastic pots usually have four drainage holes at or near the bottom, whereas clay pots have only one—a disadvantage. The number of drainage holes in metal and wooden containers varies; if there aren't enough, you can drill more. Water should start to drain out of the bottom of the pot within seconds after it is applied, and should finish draining in two or three minutes. If it doesn't, the pot doesn't have enough drainage holes, or the drainage holes are blocked.

Even if your pot has no drainage holes and none can be drilled, you can still plant in it. First, place a 1-inch layer of coarse gravel on the bottom and then add the plant and the soil. The gravel serves as a drainage field. However, if you use pots without drainage holes, you must be extremely careful to avoid overwatering—a difficult feat with smaller pots. A safer approach is to use this pot as a decorative outer container; your rose, planted in a smaller, well-drained pot, can sit inside it. Layer gravel at the bottom of the outer container to raise the inner container above the drainage water. Make sure you do not allow water to collect on the bottom of the outside container; if it does, drain it off.

It is also critical that pots be kept clean. While plants are in them, wash the outsides with warm water whenever they become stained or dirty. Before reusing a container, be sure to wash it well with hot, soapy water. Scrub with a brush if necessary to remove any built-up salt or mold. Rinse the pot well with water, then with a disinfectant solution of 10 percent household bleach, and finally, again with plain water.

Even the experts don't agree on which material makes the best container for indoor miniatures. Choose one that drains well and is not too large for the plant.

POTTING MEDIUM

The limited growing space inside containers makes the choice of potting medium a crucial one. Soil that works well in a garden may be too finely textured to allow the good drainage and aeration that potted plants require; or it may be too coarse to hold enough moisture and nutrients. Garden soil may also harbor insects and diseases that could contaminate your indoor plants. For these reasons soil from the outdoor garden is not recommended for indoor rose growing.

The best medium for growing miniatures indoors is a soilless mixture consisting of half organic and half inorganic matter. The organic portion can be sphagnum peat moss, compost, leaf mold, or shredded bark; the inorganic portion can be perlite, vermiculite, pumice, or coarse builder's sand. These materials are described in full on page 107.

Premixed bags of soilless potting medium are sold at garden centers, supermarkets, and hardware stores in a range of sizes—from small bags holding enough medium for two or three containers to large bags providing several cubic feet of material for an extensive indoor garden. Look for a product containing organic and inorganic components in 50:50 proportion.

If you find a soilless medium whose label says it contains a wetting agent, so much the better. Wetting agents help spread moisture evenly throughout the medium. This is such a valuable feature that if the medium you buy lacks a wetting agent, you might consider adding one. Wetting agents are available at garden centers or from greenhouse supply stores.

Some potting mixes also contain a fertilizer, which will usually fulfill the nutritional needs of the plant for about six weeks.

Making Your Own Potting Medium

If your indoor rose garden will be large, you will find it more economical to make your own potting medium than to buy a ready-made mixture. A good basic recipe to follow is the so-called Cornell Mix, a general-purpose formula developed at Cornell University that is excellent for roses as well as for other houseplants. Composed mainly of sphagnum peat moss and vermiculite (from which comes its other name, peat-lite), the formula provides the excellent drainage and aeration that potted plants require. It also supplies soil conditioners and fertilizer. The following recipe for Cornell Mix, or peat-lite, makes 1 cubic foot.

1¼ bu (9¾ gal) sphagnum peat moss
1¼ bu (9¾ gal) vermiculite
½ lb ground limestone (preferably dolomitic)
¹/₁₀ lb superphosphate
¼–1¼ lb 5-10-5 fertilizer

First, premoisten the sphagnum peat moss. Then mix the materials thoroughly. Add about 3 gallons of water to thoroughly moisten the mix. Adding a wetting agent (follow directions on the label) will help wet the sphagnum peat moss evenly. The mix can be made in a large box or bucket, where it can also be stored.

Depending on what is available to you, you can alter this formula by replacing the sphagnum peat moss with a different organic material, such as compost or leaf mold, or by substituting perlite or coarse builder's sand for the vermiculite. However, most experts agree that the sphagnum peat moss/vermiculite combination provides the best drainage and aeration; and since both components are sterile, the combination also discourages soil-borne diseases. Ground limestone, which is sold in garden centers, is included in the mix to raise the pH of the medium to the proper level; dolomitic limestone is preferred because it also contains magnesium, an element essential for good plant growth. Superphosphate is sold in bags at garden centers; its high phosphorus content encourages heavy root growth, which is the reason for its inclusion in the formula. Any type of granular 5-10-5 fertilizer sold in garden centers and hardware stores is acceptable to provide the basic nutrients needed to get the plants off to a good start.

If you use the larger amount of fertilizer, plants will not need additional feeding for about six weeks. If you use the smaller amount, plants will need supplemental feeding (see page 180). Many growers prefer to use the smaller amount of granular fertilizer in their planting medium so that they can start fertilizing with soluble plant food sooner.

For large indoor gardens, you can save money by mixing your own potting medium. A popular blend is Cornell Mix; see the opposite page for ingredients.

PLANTING MINIATURE ROSES INDOORS

*O*nce you have a new miniature rose on hand, you will no doubt be eager to add it to your collection. If the plant is already in a 4-inch pot, no replanting is needed at this time. However, plants in smaller containers should be transferred to 4-inch pots as soon as they have adjusted to their new home, usually within a few weeks.

First, assemble your containers and potting medium (plan on a pint of potting medium for each 4-inch pot). If the container is made of wood or clay, soak it in water until it has absorbed as much as it will hold; otherwise it will draw moisture away from the potting medium and the plant roots. Even though you must water the roses after planting them, moisten the potting medium thoroughly before planting, if it is not newly made and already moist, since moistening the medium evenly after planting is difficult. You can do this by placing the medium in a bowl, plastic bag, or other container; 1½ cups of water should be sufficient to evenly and completely moisten 4 cups of dry medium. When it has absorbed all the water it can, strain off any excess.

To enhance drainage and prevent the planting medium from washing out through the drainage holes, place a piece of window screening in the bottom of the new container. On top of this add enough planting medium to raise the crown of the plant—the place where the stems join the roots—to a point about ½ inch below the rim of the pot. To estimate the amount of planting medium to place in the new pot, set the original pot inside it to see how much space needs to be filled.

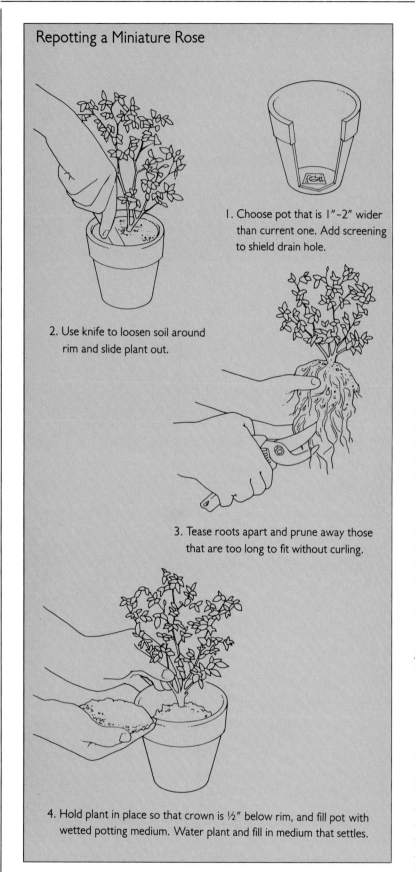

Repotting a Miniature Rose

1. Choose pot that is 1"–2" wider than current one. Add screening to shield drain hole.

2. Use knife to loosen soil around rim and slide plant out.

3. Tease roots apart and prune away those that are too long to fit without curling.

4. Hold plant in place so that crown is ½" below rim, and fill pot with wetted potting medium. Water plant and fill in medium that settles.

Before removing the rose from its original pot, water it well. Using a knife or similar implement to loosen the soil around the edges, carefully slide the plant out of the pot, taking care to disturb the roots as little as possible. If the roots are growing in a circle around the outside of the rootball—evidence that the plant is pot bound—use your fingers to carefully tease them apart and spread them out so that they will grow properly.

With one hand, position the plant over the new pot so that the crown is ½ inch below the rim. With the other hand, add potting medium around the roots, firming it gently in place with your fingers as you add it. Any roots that are so long that they would need to be curled around the bottom of the pot should be pruned away. After you have added all the medium, water it well to eliminate air pockets and to ensure that the roots are in contact with the planting medium. Keep the newly potted plant out of direct light for several days to allow it to recover from transplanting shock, and then move it to its permanent home.

Your miniature rose has outgrown its container when roots grow out of the bottom of the pot or when growth and flowering cease. When you see these signals, it is time to repot. Select a pot that is 1 inch larger than the current one (or up to 2 inches wider if the plant is very pot bound), and proceed with planting as explained above. Plants should not be jumped to a pot that is more than 1 to 2 inches larger than the current one, because the roots will not develop properly.

When repotting a pot-bound plant—one whose roots have completely filled the container—use your fingers to loosen the roots to ensure new, free root growth. If you choose not to move the plant into a larger container, prune the roots back by about one third and return the plant to its original pot. Prune back the top of the plant by about the same amount to compensate for the root loss.

There may be times when you will have a bare-root miniature rose to plant—because it arrived that way from the mail-order nursery or because you dug a dormant plant from the garden to move indoors. The technique for planting bare-root miniature roses in indoor containers is essentially the same as that for planting full-sized bare-root roses outdoors. Soak the roots in water for 6 to 24 hours before planting and, holding the plant in the proper position with its crown ½ inch below the rim of the pot, add growing medium around the roots. Even root growth is best obtained if a cone-shaped mound of medium is placed in the bottom of the pot and the roots evenly spaced around it, as is done with planting bare-root roses outdoors.

If you are moving a miniature rose indoors from an outdoor garden, you lessen injury and shock to the plant by waiting until it is dormant. Dig leafless plants in spring or fall, washing all the soil from the roots either with a hose or in a bucket. Prune away any broken or damaged roots, then proceed with planting.

PROVIDING ENOUGH LIGHT

Miniature roses need a lot of light to grow and bloom properly indoors. Although they will grow in four hours of direct sun outdoors, they need more hours of light inside because the light indoors is less intense. The light they need is the direct light of a curtainless windowsill, where the sun shines directly at least six hours each day. In winter, only south-facing windows supply direct light. During the rest of the year, east-, west-, and south-facing windows can supply it.

When placing a miniature rose on a windowsill, be sure that the window does not produce a draft, since this can chill and dry the plant and make it lose its leaves. Also make sure that the plant is as close to the window as possible without touching it, since direct contact with frigid glass can cause the rose to lose its foliage and possibly die. Growing roses

Place miniature roses close to the window to give them maximum light. Good air circulation is helpful, but avoid drafts and chills.

on a windowsill backed by a curtain is not recommended, since the curtain will hamper air circulation and block your view of the roses. Also avoid placing miniature roses on a windowsill directly above a radiator, since heat from the radiator will be too hot and drying.

If your windowsill roses show lopsided growth toward the light, rotate them frequently to keep them growing symmetrically.

USING ARTIFICIAL LIGHT

Miniatures bloom all year, provided that there is enough light. Though your windowsill may receive enough light for summertime blooming, it may not get enough to enable roses to bloom during the short and cloudy days of winter. The solution is to grow the plants under artificial light—either all year long or only during the days from midfall to midspring. Artificial lighting not only helps you maximize blooming during the darker months, but also permits you to grow roses anywhere in the house—even in the attic, the basement, or an empty closet. Indeed, by setting up your nursery in an out-of-the-way place, you can produce a steady supply of blooming plants to serve as showpieces throughout the house. As one miniature rosebush fades from bloom, you can replace it with another.

Equipment for gardening under lights can be as simple or as elaborate as you choose. For a small space with just a plant or two, an incandescent bulb designed for indoor gardening should provide enough light; place your plants as close to the bulb as you can, but not so close that they burn. Sold at hardware stores, these bulbs are convenient because they fit ordinary lamps.

For larger indoor gardens, fluorescent lights are preferable because they emit more light and less heat, while consuming less power. Garden centers sell decorative shelf units or plant stands with fluorescent light fixtures built in. You can also make your own by adding lights to existing furniture, or by installing fluorescent fixtures over the spot where you will be gardening; for instance, above a shelf over the kitchen sink. Utilitarian light shelves, usually made of metal and often adjustable, are perfect for a basement or a back room. Or you can simply hang fluorescent fixtures over a table, using chains or ropes.

The size of your fluorescent light garden is limited only by available space. Fluorescent fixtures, available in hardware and electrical supply stores, come in 1- to 4-foot lengths. You can install as many as space allows. If you have room, choose fixtures that hold two tubes—or better yet, four tubes—to provide maximum light for your roses.

Many types of fluorescent lights are available, but some are better for rose growing than others. Wide-spectrum fluorescent lights, or "grow lights," are designed specifically for indoor gardening, since they emulate the broad spectrum of wavelengths found in natural sunlight. Although ideal for rose growing, these lights tend to be expensive. A more economical approach is to combine two standard fluorescent tubes—one "cool white" type, which emits the shorter, blue-to-violet wavelengths required for foliage growth, and one "warm white" type, which emits the longer, red-to-yellow wavelengths needed for flowering. Although gardening books once recommended using regular incandescent lamps to provide the reddish wavelengths, this is no longer advisable for larger growing spaces, since incandescent bulbs waste energy and create too much heat.

Along with light of the proper wavelength, you must also provide your plants with light of the proper intensity. If your light supply is too dim, plant growth will be leggy, leaves will turn yellow, and flowering will be poor. If the light is too

bright, growth will be compact and the foliage may burn. You may need to experiment to adjust the light properly.

Ideally, plants and lights should be positioned so that the tops of the plants are almost touching the lights, since even a small extra distance between them decreases the light intensity dramatically. Shelves in adjustable units can be raised or lowered in order to achieve this. Shorter plants can be propped up with a brick or an overturned flowerpot to bring them closer to the light source.

If you find that your plants are still not getting enough light even though they are almost touching the lights, you can take a number of measures to increase light intensity. These include using fixtures with longer light tubes, installing more lights, or moving the lights closer together. Another way to boost intensity is to install aluminum foil or white reflectors above the lights, or to paint the surrounding walls white. Strange as it may seem, flat white paint is a better reflector

than glossy white paint. Note that light intensity is higher at the center of a fluorescent tube than at the ends. And be aware that older tubes—those that have been in service longer than a year—may have dimmed with age and should be replaced. This dimming may have occurred even though the lights seem as bright as ever. Alternatively, you can keep the lights on longer; this will not increase the intensity of the light, but rather the cumulative amount of light that reaches the plants.

To stimulate proper flowering, the lights above your miniature roses should shine on the plants for 14 to 16 hours each day. (Although roses grown in natural light require only 6 hours of direct sunlight, they also receive light when shaded—a total of about 15 hours per day at midsummer.) Avoid leaving the lights on continuously, since the plants need a dark period for respiration. An automatic timer will free you from the chore of turning the lights on and off.

Miniature roses thrive under fluorescent light. Position them as close to the light as possible.

TEMPERATURE

Miniature roses enjoy the same indoor temperatures that their human caretakers appreciate. Daytime temperatures of 70° to 72° F, and nighttime temperatures about 10 degrees cooler, are ideal. Plants should be kept out of drafts, away from radiators and air conditioners, and away from cold windows in winter.

WATERING

Indoor miniatures should receive enough water that their growing medium is constantly moist, yet not so much that it becomes soggy. Failure to maintain this fragile balance is one of the chief causes of problems with these plants. To maintain proper conditions, it is best not to water on a regular schedule, but rather when your plants actually need it—since temperature, light, and humidity in the environment can change from day to day. Plants need more water when the temperature is high or the humidity is low. If growing in natural light, they need less water in the short days of winter, when their metabolism slows, than they do while actively growing during the rest of the year. Plants in small containers need more water than identical plants in large containers, since they have less material around the roots to serve as a reservoir.

The best way to determine whether your miniature roses need watering is to feel the planting medium around the base of each plant. If the top has started to dry out, it's time to water. Use room-temperature water to avoid shocking the plant, and do not let it drip on leaves, since this can cause spotting and encourage disease. If the leaves do become wet

Top: A long-necked watering can is ideal for miniatures. Use room-temperature water and take care not to wet the leaves.

Bottom: Stiff white roots indicate that this miniature has received adequate watering.

accidentally, dry them off to discourage any problems. Do not use softened water for plants; it contains sodium, which is toxic to roots. If unsoftened tap water is not available, use distilled or natural bottled water, or collect rainwater.

Add water until the excess fluid flows out from the drainage holes of the pot. After the water has drained through, empty the saucer under the pot to keep the roots from sitting in water, which can cause rot. Although you can water your roses from the bottom by placing them in a water-filled sink or bucket, this is not the recommended method since it fails to leach out the damaging salts left by fertilizers.

Unfortunately, it is often difficult to distinguish between overwatering and underwatering by simply looking at the plant, because the symptoms of both are the same—yellowing foliage. If your roses show signs of yellowing, remove each plant from its pot and examine the roots. Roots should be stiff and white. If they are soggy or slimy and either black or brown, then you have overwatered. If the growing medium is dry or if the roots are so compacted that little growing medium is left in the pot, then you have under-watered. The latter case is a signal to re-pot the plant.

HUMIDITY

*T*he ideal relative humidity for indoor rose growing is about 50 to 60 percent. In most regions the air indoors contains adequate moisture during the warmer months (unless air conditioning is kept on continually), but in winter, central heating can promote almost desertlike dryness. If you want your roses to flower successfully during these months, you'll need to raise the humidity artificially. If you suspect that humidity is low, you can buy a hygrometer at a greenhouse supply store to measure humidity and see if an adjustment is needed.

There are a number of ways to humidify the air around indoor roses. The traditional method is to grow them on so-called pebble trays. To do this, place pebbles in the saucer under each pot, and fill the saucer almost to the top with water. (Just take care to keep the bottoms of the pots above the water.) As the water evaporates it increases the humidity around the plant—yet because the pot is raised above the water, the roots do not become waterlogged. Check the water level daily to see if it needs replenishing. The runoff from watering may be enough to fill the pebble tray; if not, add more. If you have many individual pots, you can save effort by placing them all atop a single pebble-filled tray.

Placing miniatures on pebbles above the drainage water raises the humidity around plants and keeps their roots from rotting.

179

Another way to raise humidity is to place a room humidifier in the area where roses are growing. The type that holds 6 gallons of water is the most practical, as it does not need frequent refilling. Position it anywhere in the room with your rose garden as long as the mist does not fall directly on the foliage. You can test the humidity in the room with a hygrometer (available at greenhouse supply stores) to determine when to turn the humidifier off. Alternatively, simply open some windows, since outside air is usually more humid than inside air, especially in winter. Just be careful not to create a draft, which can harm your roses. Misting is another method that is often recommended; however, its effectiveness is only short-lived and it can encourage disease.

Yet another technique for boosting humidity is to place plants close together so that they can add moisture to the air collectively as they transpire. If you do this, be sure to keep the plants about 1 inch apart so that air circulation is not restricted. Stagnant air can promote disease.

Because they never go dormant as outdoor roses do, indoor miniatures need only occasional pruning to maintain their size and shape.

FERTILIZING

Miniature roses need ample fertilizing in order to grow and bloom successfully indoors. Many ready-mixed growing media will provide enough fertilizer to see your new transplants through their first six weeks, as will the Cornell Mix described on page 172. After that, supplemental feeding should begin.

Because roses grown in containers need to be watered often, any fertilizer applied to the plant will leach out of the planting medium quickly. It is therefore essential that the type of fertilizer be a fast-acting, soluble one. For this reason granular fertilizers, which are excellent for outdoor use, are not recommended. Instead, use a powdered or liquid soluble fertilizer; 20-20-20, 15-30-15, or similar formulations are good ones. Although the labels for many of these products instruct you to use the liquid full strength and to apply it monthly, it is better to dilute the

fertilizer to one-quarter strength and apply it weekly. This frequent, low-dose feeding will promote more even growth.

Whatever instructions you follow, be sure to water your plants before fertilizing them, so that the fertilizer will not burn their roots. If you accidentally overfertilize, the foliage will become crisp and dry and its edges will turn brown. White or tan deposits may also be present at the edges of the soil. To remedy overfertilizing, flush the growing medium with water until the runoff is colorless instead of orange to brown—a sign that all harmful salts have leached out.

In the short days of winter, when plants stop growing and flowering, cut back on fertilizer completely, and resume fertilizing when plants start to grow in midspring. When plants are not growing and flowering in winter, they do not need fertilizer; indeed, adding it then will damage the plants. If you are growing roses under artificial light, there will be no seasonal dormancy period and fertilizing will be a year-round necessity. For more information about fertilizing, see Chapter 5.

OTHER HINTS

*I*n addition to providing proper temperature, moisture, and fertilizer, you can do several other things to keep your indoor miniatures thriving.

As soon as flowers have faded, cut back the stems with small scissors or pruning shears to at least the first five- or seven-leaflet leaf. This encourages new shoots to grow and flower. (If you want large flowers, follow the disbudding procedure described on page 133.) At the same time you can take the opportunity to shape the plants. Prune back any stem that is too long, so that the entire plant looks symmetrical.

Although most large roses need a dormancy period in order to live long, miniature roses grown indoors are rarely if ever forced into dormancy, since lack of dormancy does not have the same effect on them. Thus the annual pruning given to outdoor roses is not necessary for miniatures grown inside. However, whenever

Accumulated dust can block light from roses, slowing their growth. Remove it with a feather duster or immerse the leaves in water.

Take advantage of the warm weather and longer days of summer by moving miniatures outdoors.

from overfertilized ones by checking the color of the runoff water; if the runoff is brown to orange, fertilizer is the culprit.

The leaves of miniature roses may collect dust, which not only is unattractive but also prevents the leaves from making the most of available light. You can dust leaves individually with a feather duster, but the easiest remedy is to turn each plant upside down in a sink or a bucket full of water. Holding the plant carefully to keep it from falling out of the pot, either reach into the water and rub the leaves, or agitate the plant slightly so that the dust is completely removed. This immersion also helps rid the foliage of any insects, especially spider mites. After the leaves have been washed, dry them off, as wet leaves are prone to spotting and diseases.

Miniature roses will benefit from being moved outdoors for the summer so that they can grow in full sunlight. It's easiest to keep them in their original containers, and to place the containers either into the ground or where they will add a decorative accent—such as on steps, a porch, a patio, or a deck. Before moving the roses back indoors in early fall, inspect them carefully for signs of insects or diseases, and treat them if necessary. If heavy growth has occurred over the summer, you may have to repot the plants, or remove them from their pots, prune the roots, and return them to their original containers. For instructions on root pruning and repotting, see page 174.

It is easy to increase the size of your miniature-rose garden by propagating your own plants. Miniatures are easily rooted from stem cuttings; for instructions see page 237. You can grow more plants of the same variety, or swap cuttings with fellow rose fanciers to increase the scope of your collection. Be aware, though, that many patented varieties may not be reproduced without a license; any restrictions are usually printed on the plant label or package.

a plant becomes too large, you can prune it back using the same methods as for outdoor roses. For instructions, see the section beginning on page 124.

If foliage turns brown from hot or dry conditions, cut the stems back to below the point of damage, and adjust the environment to prevent further stress to the plants. You can distinguish dry leaves

PESTS AND DISEASES

Although miniature roses are not as prone to diseases indoors as they are outdoors, they can still be subject to attack by black spot and mildew—two of the most common diseases of outdoor roses. Similarly, fewer insects bother miniature roses indoors, but aphids can be troublesome and spider mites can be a special bane. Mites in particular thrive in the warm, dry conditions most homes provide. Keeping water off the leaves and providing good air circulation around the plants will stave off many diseases; however, avoid cold drafts. Washing and drying the foliage from time to time will lessen many insect problems.

If insects or diseases attack and the techniques above can't control them, stronger measures may be necessary. If the weather is warm and dry enough, take your plants to a shaded spot outside to spray fungicides, insecticides, or miticides, and return them once they have aired thoroughly.

If the weather is cold or rainy, you can treat your plants indoors by setting them on a table covered with newspaper, well away from other furniture, and spraying them with a houseplant spray designed for indoor use. You can also plunge plants into a bucket containing a solution of pesticide or fungicide that has been diluted at the rate recommended for a spray; consult the product label for instructions.

If the pest is lodged in the potting medium, plunge the entire plant in the bucket of solution. Be sure to rinse the bucket afterward with clear water. Always move an infested or infected plant away from others until the problem is corrected. For more about disease and insect control, see Chapter 9.

GROWING LARGER ROSES INDOORS

It is possible, but much more difficult, to grow full-sized roses indoors. These plants and their containers are usually too big to be handled easily, and they won't fit conveniently on the average windowsill. Large roses also require more light than miniatures, and the light indoors is rarely intense enough to satisfy them. However, if you have a very bright sun room, a skylight, or a fluorescent-light system, you may have some success. Making adjustments for scale, you can follow most of the instructions for growing miniature roses in containers.

There are a few differences, however. Unlike miniatures, which grow from their own roots, most large roses are grafted to a more vigorous understock. With these larger plants, the bud union (the knobbed joint where the two plants unite) should be placed just above the top of the planting medium when planted.

Roses of all sizes can be grown indoors if you have the space and can provide enough light.

Large roses will live for only a few years if they do not receive a winter dormancy period. If you want to extend the indoor life expectancy of these roses, remove all the leaves in the late fall to induce dormancy, and prune the plants back as with outdoor roses, as described on pages 124 to 136. Whether or not the plants are forced into dormancy, they may become so large that they still need an annual pruning in spring.

Large plants obviously cannot be plunged into a bucket of water to wash their leaves or rid them of insects and diseases. Instead, the leaves of the plants can be dusted or sponged off to keep the foliage clean.

GROWING ROSES IN A GREENHOUSE

Devoted gardeners who have the time and the money often turn to greenhouse gardening to extend the gardening season and increase the variety of plants that they can grow indoors. Greenhouses vary from expensive aluminum structures covered with glass to more economical wooden ones covered with plastic. For those who don't want to cope with a full-sized greenhouse, small window greenhouses are available. Complete information about greenhouse installation and maintenance is available in Ortho's book *Greenhouses*.

If you have a greenhouse, you can grow both miniatures and large bush roses with great success. All the growing requirements that roses have, especially direct light and high humidity, can be precisely controlled in a greenhouse. Greenhouses provide more light than conventional buildings, and can be kept humid more easily than today's centrally heated homes. A greenhouse can also be kept at temperatures that might be uncomfortable in a home.

Those who live in very cold climates find that having a greenhouse is the only way to grow tender varieties of roses. These roses, when grown in containers, can be moved to the greenhouse for the winter and returned outdoors for the summer. Greenhouses are also ideal places to root cuttings, sow seeds, and hybridize, since the environment can be more easily controlled than in the house or in the outdoor garden. Hybridizing in particular benefits from a greenhouse, where the chance of accidental pollination by wind or insects is eliminated and where cross-breeding can be conducted all year long.

Some varieties of modern bush roses that are typically grown outdoors can be grown in a greenhouse; others, however, will not bloom profusely, or may not bloom at all. Those garden varieties of roses that will grow best in a greenhouse are 'Catherine Mermet', 'Marina', 'Prima Donna', and 'Sonia'. Most old garden and shrub roses grow too large for a greenhouse, and since many old garden roses bloom only once a year, few gardeners would want to devote greenhouse space to them. Likewise, climbers are rarely grown in greenhouses because they take up so much space.

For maximum growth and blooming in a greenhouse, choose what are known as started eyes. These are the rose varieties that are grown in commercial greenhouses for the cut-flower trade and are genetically distinct from garden roses. They are available in bare-root form from several specialty firms, but since the minimum order is usually about two hundred and fifty plants, buying from them would be impractical for most amateur rose growers. The best way to obtain them is to find local greenhouse operators who are willing to order a few plants for you from their wholesale supplier.

Planting techniques for greenhouse roses are the same as for any other rose. Plant your selections in containers set on the greenhouse floor or on benches, or in built-in planting beds. If you choose containers, use vessels at least 12 inches across and 15 inches deep to allow room for root growth; containers 18 inches across and deep are better, however. If you prefer to plant in beds, construct them so that they are at least 24 inches deep. Beds are best constructed so that two rows of plants can be grown in them, set 24 inches apart. In either case, use a soilless growing medium such as the Cornell Mix described on page 172.

LIGHT INTENSITY

Roses should be placed in the sunniest part of the greenhouse to enhance their growth and blooming. If you measure the light intensity with a special kind of light meter that measures footcandles, as many professional greenhouse growers do, make sure the roses are receiving between 6,000 and 10,000 footcandles of light in the middle of the day. Light meters of this type are available from greenhouse supply stores, as well as from companies that sell scientific instruments and supplies. It is difficult, if not impossible, to determine light intensity by eye.

Greenhouse roses for the cut-flower market are grown through a grid of strings that provide support for their long, straight stems.

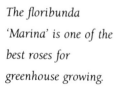

*The floribunda
'Marina' is one of the
best roses for
greenhouse growing.*

TEMPERATURE

Greenhouse roses have approximately the same temperature requirements as roses grown indoors. Daytime temperatures can range between 70° and 75° F (versus 70° to 72° F indoors). Nighttime temperatures for established roses should be set at 58° to 60° F (versus 60° to 62° F for indoor growing). Newly planted roses will benefit from a somewhat cooler nighttime temperature of 50° F for two weeks, until the roots become well established. To maintain these temperatures, you'll probably need a heating system for winter and a system of vents, fans, or both for hot summer days. During the winter ensure that plants do not touch the cold walls, which can damage them. In large greenhouses this problem is often solved by growing plants close to the center of the greenhouse and using the perimeter as a walkway.

Greenhouse supply stores can provide you with everything you need for your greenhouse, from the house itself to benches, timers, thermostats, heaters, fans, vents, pots, and irrigation equipment. Greenhouse manufacturers can also supply you with many of these items as well as advise you on the type of equipment you need. Completely computerized environmental controls can be purchased for greenhouses, but these are probably out of economic reach for most amateur growers with small greenhouses.

WATER AND FERTILIZER

Watering requirements are also similar to those for indoor rose growing. Apply water, preferably at room temperature, whenever the surface of the planting medium starts to dry out, so that the medium stays evenly moist but not soggy. You can water your roses with a can or a hose, or by drip irrigation (see page 139).

The ideal relative humidity for greenhouse roses is 50 to 60 percent—the

If the light exceeds 10,000 footcandles during the summer, when the sun is the most intense and highest in the sky, consider applying a liquid shading material to the greenhouse roof, or installing shade cloth over the plants, to prevent the foliage from burning. Shading materials and shade cloths are both available from greenhouse suppliers. If the light level drops below 6,000 footcandles in winter, you may wish to install fluorescent lights. See the section on artificial light beginning on page 176.

same as that for indoor growing. You can measure humidity with a hygrometer, available from greenhouse supply stores. Although pebble trays (see page 179) can increase the humidity around small plants, they are not practical for large ones. The easiest ways to raise humidity throughout the greenhouse are to let in moist outside air through doors and vents, or to frequently hose down the greenhouse floor; as water on the floor evaporates, humidity rises. If vents are opened during the day to allow fresh, humid air inside, be sure to close them at night if it is cold outside.

Roses in a greenhouse should be fertilized weekly (or when you water), using a quarter-strength solution of soluble liquid or powdered fertilizer, such as 20-20-20 or 15-30-15. If you water with a drip irrigation system, you can buy a fertilizer injector that automatically adds fertilizer solution to the irrigation water. These are available from greenhouse supply stores and garden centers. When growth slows in winter, cut back fertilizing to once a month. (If you use lights to supplement winter sunshine, however, you'll need to maintain weekly fertilizing.)

OTHER TIPS

Any roses that become quite tall can be staked to encourage straight stems; this is especially recommended if you are growing the roses for cutting. You can stake individual stems or the entire planting bed. To do the latter, place a stake 6 feet high at each corner of the bed and run parallel strands of wire or string around the bed at levels 6 inches apart. At each level, crisscross the bed with string to make a three-dimensional 6-inch grid. The stems will grow straight up through the spaces in the grid.

To encourage new growth and future blooming, cut off each flower as soon as possible after it fades, pruning back to at least the first five-leaflet leaf. As you remove the spent flowers, also take time to shape the plants and control their size.

Roses bloom more profusely if carbon dioxide is added to the air. Small canisters of carbon dioxide are available from greenhouse supply stores. Set one of these off inside a closed greenhouse every month or two to increase flowering. Although all plants release carbon dioxide during the night, this is not enough to encourage more profuse blooming, as they use the carbon dioxide during the day for photosynthesis.

Most greenhouse growers try to keep their roses from entering winter dormancy, since winter blooms are among the chief goals of greenhouse gardening. Gardeners do this by increasing light and continuing to water and fertilize. If you use this technique, be aware that roses denied their yearly rest period will have much shorter lives than those allowed to lapse into natural dormancy—typically 4 to 5 years versus 10 to 20. If you want to force your greenhouse roses into dormancy in winter, lower the temperature to 50° F, stop fertilizing, and provide only enough water to keep the soil barely moist.

Insect and disease control is essential in the closed environment of a greenhouse, where an unwelcome organism can quickly make the rounds. If you are growing miniature roses, you can plunge each plant into a bucket of insecticide or fungicide solution, diluted at the proper ratio. Or you can spray them. When spraying in a greenhouse, shut all doors and windows, apply the insecticide or fungicide while wearing protective clothing and a mask, and leave the greenhouse closed up overnight. Before going to work the next day, open the vents, turn on the fans, and air out the greenhouse thoroughly. Complete airing may be impossible in winter, so you may have to stay out of the greenhouse for several days while normal ventilation clears the air of pesticide residue; read the product label for instructions.

*Roses preserved
with a flower press
are enduring
mementos
of summer.*

CHAPTER SEVEN

THE PLEASURES
OF ROSES

*G*rowing roses can be a satisfying hobby,
but many rose lovers delight in finding
other ways to spend time with their
favorite flower. Arranging, exhibiting, and
photographing roses are a few of the
pastimes they enjoy. Roses can also be
preserved and included in recipes. Here is
a potpourri of ideas for enjoying roses,
both in and out of the garden.

The elation you feel as you walk through your rose garden, savoring its sights and fragrances, might seem to be pleasure enough. But your enjoyment of roses can go far beyond mere appreciation as you discover where else they can lead you. If you want to indulge your creative side, you can learn to use roses in arrangements. If you crave recognition for your gardening skills, you may wish to exhibit your roses. If your interest is cooking or crafts, you'll find roses quite accommodating. Many unusual recipes feature roses, and roses can be easily preserved in dried arrangements or fragrant potpourris. If you enjoy photography, you may want to combine this with your love of roses. And as you plan your vacation, you might consider heading for one of the rose festivals that take place annually around the country.

Whatever your interest, roses can take you in a lively and productive new direction. This chapter describes some of the many paths you can explore.

ROSES AS CUT FLOWERS

Many gardeners like to enjoy their roses twice—first in the garden, then indoors as cut flowers. By choosing the right roses, cutting them at the proper time of day, and conditioning them after cutting, you can enjoy your cut roses for the longest possible time—up to five days or more after cutting.

In general, the more petals a rose has, the slower it will open and the longer it will last. Thus the best roses to use as cut flowers are the fully double varieties. Flowers with fewer petals open quickly and need to be replaced more often. Old garden and shrub roses generally wilt rapidly because their petals lack the substance (thickness and sturdiness) of modern roses and therefore do not make good cut flowers.

In addition to the form of a rose, you should consider its blooming stage. A rose will last longer if it is cut when the sepals have separated from the bud and have turned downward, and when the bud has softened, but before the central stamens of the flower are visible. If you squeeze the bud and it is still hard, wait a day or two before cutting it, or it may not open after it is cut.

Roses should be cut from a well-watered plant, late in the afternoon when the sugar and nutrient content of the plant is highest. This provides the bloom with ample energy to develop and open normally, and to stay open longer without wilting. During hot weather, when there is chance that a flower may be somewhat dehydrated by late afternoon, be sure to water the plant well several hours before cutting.

Using pruning shears or flower-cutting shears, cut the stem at a 45-degree angle, no shorter than just above the first five-leaflet leaf below the flower; you may cut a stem as long as you like, provided that at least two sets of leaves are left on the main stem to act as food producers for future growth and flowering. Carry a bucket of water with you into the garden so that you can place the cut stems in the water immediately, as the flowers will last much longer if the uptake of water is not interrupted for too long and the stems do not dry out. It is all right to submerge the leaves temporarily, as they too will absorb moisture.

Although you will not harm a plant if you cut off all its flowers at one time, you may want to leave a few on the plant for garden color. Cutting roses, whether new or faded, will encourage the plants to grow and rebloom quickly.

After you have cut all your roses, recut the stems at a slant, underwater, to permit maximum water absorption. Place the bucket of water containing the cut roses in a cool, dark place such as the basement to allow the roses to become conditioned before arranging them in a vase. Conditioning roses allows them to get used to being detached from the plants and slows down the respiratory rate of the leaves. Leave them for at least several hours or preferably overnight.

You can condition cut flowers in a refrigerator, as long as the refrigerator is intended only for roses and not for food. Many types of fruit stored in a refrigerator release ethylene gas, a ripening agent that causes cut flowers to open prematurely.

Water for cut flowers is best if it is slightly acidic, as acid water breaks up air bubbles in water by neutralizing the carbon dioxide gas. Air bubbles may clog the capillaries in the stem and prevent water from reaching the flowers and foliage. Water also travels more quickly up a stem when the water is acidic. If you're not sure whether your water is acidic, ask your water company. If it is not acidic, add lemon juice to acidify it. You should not use artificially softened water, as it contains sodium, which is toxic to plants. In most circumstances, use cold water, as this slows down the respiratory rate of the leaves. However, if the flowers have wilted—because they have been out of water too long or because the stems were not cut underwater soon enough and the stem ends have become clogged—hot water will revive them faster than cold water because the stems absorb hot water more quickly.

Before placing the roses in a vase, remove any leaves and thorns that will be below the water after arranging, since these will quickly disintegrate, foul the water, and shorten the life of the cut flowers. Thorns can be snapped off by hand or with a special thorn-stripping tool sold by florist supply stores. Then

clean the remaining foliage with soap and water if necessary to remove dirt or spray residue, and make the leaves shine by rubbing them with a paper towel, a soft cloth, or a nylon stocking. If any of the leaves are ripped or chewed, they can be manicured with small scissors.

A further tip: If the roses you have picked are exceptionally fragrant, be sure to handle them gently. The petals of

Cut roses can last up to five days or more if properly conditioned.

fragrant roses have more scent-emitting glands than do those of less-fragrant kinds, and they therefore tend to bruise more easily.

To lengthen the life of your cut roses, always use a clean container for the flowers, and add a floral preservative to the water. Because they are acidic, contain sugar, and include a bacteria-retarding agent, floral preservatives provide some nutrients and restrain and prevent the growth of bacteria that will shorten the life of the flowers. These preservatives can be purchased at a flower shop. If you can't buy floral preservative, mix any clear citrus-based soft drink containing sugar with three parts water; or make a solution of 2 tablespoons lemon juice, 1 tablespoon sugar, and ½ teaspoon household bleach in one quart of water.

Keep the container filled with water to lessen the chance that it will evaporate or be consumed by the roses. If possible, change the water daily and recut the stems underwater each time you change it. If it is not possible to change the water, check the level every day and add fresh water as necessary. To prolong the life of cut roses as long as possible, keep them in a cool place away from drafts, air conditioners, radiators, and full sun.

ARRANGING ROSES

Arranging your roses is a matter of taste. An arrangement can be as simple as one long-stemmed rose in a bud vase or a large flower floating in a shallow bowl, or as elaborate as a massive arrangement of hundreds of flowers.

You can display your roses in all-rose arrangements or combine them with other flowers from the garden. Try asters, astilbe, chrysanthemums, delphinium, gladiolus, iris, lilies, peonies, snapdragons, stock, or veronica, depending on the season and the color harmony you wish to create. Foliage, too, can come from plants other than roses. For a tall, spiked look, use the leaves of iris, gladiolus, or canna. For more graceful, lower arrangements, use the variegated leaves of hosta. For a delicate look, snip a few fronds of ferns. Broad-leaved evergreen leaves can impart shininess, and for a silvery look, try a few stems of dusty miller or artemisia.

The flowers and foliage you combine with roses should be appropriate for the type of arrangement. For example, peonies and iris can be used in formal arrangements, whereas daisies look better in informal ones. Spiked foliage is often

Best Roses for Cutting

In a test conducted at Rose Hills Memorial Park in Whittier, California, the following double roses (listed in alphabetical order) fared best as cut flowers, lasting five or more days after cutting.

Variety	Class	Color
America	Climber	Coral-pink
Bewitched	Hybrid tea	Pink
Deep Purple	Floribunda	Purple
Duet	Hybrid tea	Pink
French Lace	Floribunda	White
Gingersnap	Floribunda	Orange
Gold Medal	Grandiflora	Yellow
Honor	Hybrid tea	White
Iceberg	Floribunda	White
Marina	Floribunda	Orange-red
Mister Lincoln	Hybrid tea	Red
New Day	Hybrid tea	Yellow
Olé	Grandiflora	Orange-red
Olympiad	Hybrid tea	Red
Paradise	Hybrid tea	Mauve blend
Pascali	Hybrid tea	White
Prominent	Grandiflora	Orange-red
Sonia	Grandiflora	Coral-pink
Touch of Class	Hybrid tea	Pink blend
Viva	Grandiflora	Red
Voodoo	Hybrid tea	Salmon

used in modern designs because of its strong lines. Similarly, curved branches of plants such as flowering cherries are often incorporated in oriental designs, with or without foliage. (See Elements of Design on page 194.)

CONTAINERS AND ACCESSORIES

When choosing a container for your arrangement, keep two things in mind. First, the container should be in proportion with the height of the roses: Long-stemmed roses call for a tall, elegant container, whereas roses with shorter stems are delightful in a low container, a rounded teapot, or a sugar bowl. Second, consider the material from which the container is made. Formal arrangements look more refined in china, silver, or glass containers, whereas informal arrangements are appealing in earthenware vessels or straw baskets. You can arrange miniature roses in any small container

you happen to have around—a thimble, a shot glass, a perfume bottle, or a seashell, for example.

Many arrangements are made without vases or containers and are instead placed in shallow trays, bowls, or other vessels. To anchor the flower and foliage stems and to provide them with a source of water, set them in either floral foam or pinholders; both are available from craft stores and florist supply stores.

Floral foam looks like soft Styrofoam; it is sold in blocks that can be cut with a knife to the correct size. In addition to holding the stems in place, it absorbs and stores water to supply them with moisture. If you use foam, be sure to soak it completely in water before plunging the stems into it. The disadvantage of foam is that it can be reused only once or twice.

A pinholder consists of a thicket of pointed pins sticking up from the bottom of a small receptacle that can hold water.

Floral foam and pinholders can be used with dried as well as fresh arrangements;

The icelike clarity of glass containers makes a refreshing contrast with the warm, dry tones of their background. These casual groupings include the miniatures 'Cinderella', 'Mary Marshall', 'Starina', and 'Over the Rainbow'.

in the case of dried arrangements, of course, you would not need to worry about watering.

When making an arrangement with foam, cut the foam to size according to the number of stems to be inserted into it, soak it in water, and fasten it to the container or vessel with floral tape. When using a pinholder, first anchor it to the vessel with floral clay before inserting stems. Both floral tape and floral clay are available at florist supply stores. Whichever anchoring device you use, be sure to keep the water supply steady by making sure the foam is always moist or the pinholder is filled with water frequently. Because foam and pinholders can dry out quickly, be sure to check the amount of water. If the container does not hide the anchoring device, conceal it with foliage, pebbles, marbles, shells, or other accessories.

Floral wire is thin and flexible and is often wrapped around stems to strengthen them or to give them a curved shape. Wire can also be used as a substitute for a stem if you dry flower heads only. (See Dried Flowers on page 208.) The wire can be wrapped in a self-adhesive green tape to camouflage it. Both wire and tape are available at flower shops and florist supply stores. To cut stems while making arrangements, you can use pruning shears or flower-cutting shears, and you can strip thorns off by hand or with a thorn-stripping tool.

ELEMENTS OF DESIGN

Although there are many styles of flower arranging, all employ the same basic elements to create an appealing result. These elements are space, line, form, pattern, texture, and color. A successful flower arranger builds with these elements to achieve inspiring balance, dominance, contrast, rhythm, scale, and proportion. Although a flower arranger may not be consciously aware of these

components, they are important ingredients in any harmonious and expressive arrangement.

Space refers to the area to be filled by the flowers and their container. Before creating an arrangement, imagine a picture frame around it and make the proportions of the frame fit the intended setting. For example, an arrangement for a serving table or atop a mantle should be horizontal, whereas one for a pedestal should be vertical. Space concerns itself only with filling two dimensions—length and width; the third dimension, height, is treated under form.

The line of an arrangement is the route your eyes follow from one part of it to another. The line may be long or short, straight or curved, delicate or bold, horizontal or vertical, but it must be there. A horizontal line imparts an air that is restful, tranquil, and static. A vertical line is dramatic and inspiring. Diagonal lines create a feeling of surprise or movement. Curved lines are graceful.

The form of an arrangement is the way it occupies three dimensions—length, width, and height. A flower arrangement is a kind of sculpture, and as such it must occupy its setting harmoniously. For example, an arrangement for the center of a table might have great depth, whereas one placed against a wall might be relatively flat. The form of an arrangement also depends on whether it will be viewed from all sides or seen only from the front.

Pattern is the organization of shapes and colors in an arrangement. A pattern is established by using the same color, size, or variety of flower in several places, or by placing the flowers of a small arrangement in a structured grouping.

Texture encompasses the tactile and visual qualities not only of your roses but also of the container, the foliage, and the other flowers that may be present. Textures can harmonize or contrast. For example, a delicate arrangement of pale roses with ferns harmonizes well with a fine porcelain vase, whereas a bold arrangement of brightly colored roses, black-eyed-susans, and coarse foliage contrasts well with a black metallic bowl.

Color is one of the most important elements of design because it engenders a strong emotional reaction. Red, hot pink, bright yellow, and orange are dazzling and exciting; mauve, pale pink and yellow, and white are more calming. Formal arrangements are best made with a single color or with closely related subtle colors; informal arrangements can use a kaleidoscope of brighter colors. An appealing technique is to combine complementary colors, such as violet with yellow, or blue with orange. The split complementary harmony of blue with red or pink is also

attractive. Try to fit the colors to the mood of the occasion.

If the arrangement is intended to be viewed from a distance, colors that reflect the most light are the best choices for it. These include bright red, yellow, orange, pink, and white. Blue and violet appear as shadows or voids from 15 feet or more away. Dusky and subdued colors, such as smoky whites, salmon, and dusty pinks, do not project well, as they absorb more light than they reflect.

Accomplished floral arrangers use the elements described above to achieve balance, dominance, contrast, rhythm, scale, and proportion. Balance is not necessarily symmetry; rather it is equilibrium, visual stability. To achieve balance, place buds at the top of the arrangement

A worn metal tub is a rustic complement for a mass of silken roses in a mannered bedside setting. This informal arrangement includes the hybrid tea 'Sweet Surrender' and the floribunda 'French Lace'.

and large, open flowers at the bottom. Use lighter colors at the top, and weight the bottom with darker colors. If the container has an irregular shape, the arrangement should be skewed in the same fashion.

Dominance is control of the design by one of its elements—space, line, form, pattern, texture, or color. A design that lacks dominance is nondescript; it makes no definitive statement. After you have decided on a theme for your arrangement, select one of its elements and emphasize it, making all of the other elements work with it.

Contrast is the placement of elements to emphasize their difference; for example, tight buds with open flowers, or tall stems with short ones.

A good design also has rhythm, a lively interaction of the parts. In a rhythmical arrangement the eye is constantly moving from element to element, savoring what it sees.

The finished arrangement should be in scale and proportion to the container and the space it occupies.

STYLES OF DESIGN

There are probably as many styles of flower arranging as there are people who arrange them. But over the years a number of traditional styles have evolved. The most common styles used by arrangers in the United States, and displayed at rose and flower shows, are mass, Williamsburg, Victorian, line, line-mass, Hogarth curve, modern, and oriental. These are described here as models that you can vary according to your taste, mood, and the materials you have to work with.

A mass arrangement, as its name implies, consists of a large number of flowers massed together in one container. It may be formal or informal. Large mass arrangements in fine china vases are generally seen at formal occasions and in formally decorated rooms, whereas smaller mass arrangements in low bowls are often a centerpiece in an informal setting. To achieve the correct balance and proportion, the height of a mass arrangement must be one and a half times the height and the width of the container added together. Otherwise the arrangement will look too "squat."

A mass design is symmetrical and takes a geometrical shape such as that of a fan, a pyramid, a globe, or an oval. To avoid a hodgepodge effect, have in mind a well-coordinated color scheme and a structured pattern.

A Williamsburg arrangement is a type of mass arrangement that originated in colonial times and can be seen extensively throughout the restored homes in Colonial Williamsburg, the historical district of Virginia's former capital. Williamsburg arrangements are usually large and are used in formal settings. The key to making a good Williamsburg arrangement is to use roses and containers that are in keeping with the colonial era; for example, orange hybrid teas would be out of place since these did not exist in colonial days. Old garden roses would naturally be more fitting, and you would likely see them in a pewter vase. Williamsburg arrangements can take the symmetrical shape of any mass arrangement, with oval or pyramidal shapes the most common. In addition to being symmetrical in form, the colors of one side mirror those on the other.

A Victorian mass arrangement, from Victorian England, is similar to a Williamsburg arrangement, but its colors are placed in asymmetrical drifts rather than in a mirrored pattern. Like a Williamsburg arrangement, it is formal in character, and any flowers other than roses should also be formal in appearance. Containers are ornate, such as highly decorated china vases or urns on pedestals, in keeping with the period.

When making any type of mass arrangement, first decide what shape and size it will take. Then place the flowers to form the outer perimeter of the design. Next, fill in the rest of the roses, other flowers, and foliage.

Line and line-mass arrangements are both distinguished chiefly by a strong, simple line. This is created by either plant material or accessories such as small statuettes. Line arrangements use only three to five flowers; line-mass arrangements may use many more. A line arrangement has very little depth and is placed against a wall rather than displayed as a centerpiece; a line-mass arrangement is somewhat deeper and can be used in either setting. The container should be small enough that it does not distract from the line; it can actually be a part of the line. Because only a few flowers may be used in either arrangment, it takes practice to learn how to position them in a graceful line rather than in a stilted row.

The Hogarth curve arrangement (named for the eighteenth-century English artist William Hogarth) is a type of line-mass arrangement that features an S-shaped curve. A typical container is a pedestaled vase, which allows the lower portion of the S-curve to extend below the container. It is usually placed against a wall rather than displayed as a centerpiece. Its swoop of line is exciting, emphasizing the fullest part of the design, usually where the stems emanate from the container. To create the curves necessary in this type of arrangement, you may need to wire some of the stems so that they can be bent to conform to the S-shape.

Modern, or abstract, twentieth-century designs are bold, strong, and interpretive of a mood or feeling. Depending on the size and shape of a modern design, it can range from a centerpiece to a large accent piece in a room. Empty space is a deliberate part of the design, so this type of arrangement typically uses very few flowers. Unlike more traditional styles, where pattern and color are the more dominant elements, modern designs are held

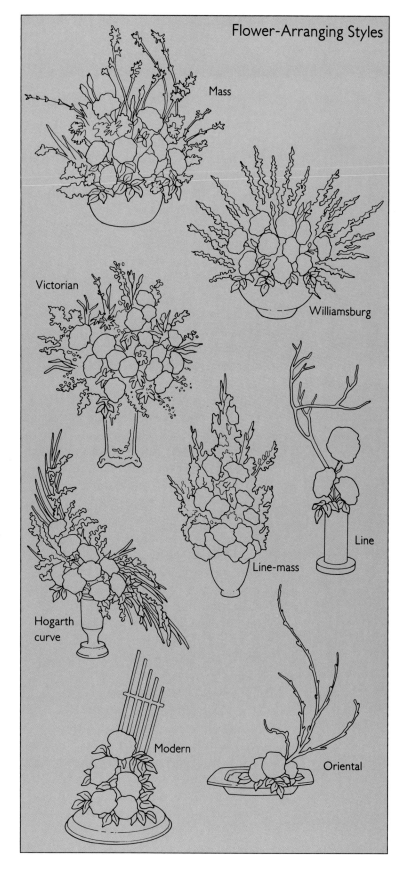

Flower-Arranging Styles

Mass

Williamsburg

Victorian

Hogarth curve

Line-mass

Line

Modern

Oriental

together more by their line. Containers match the theme of the design; for example, if the designer is creating an interpretation of motion, the containers could be hub caps or air filters.

Oriental designs come principally from the Japanese. There are several major styles, all employing asymmetrical line arrangements that are simple, symbolic, and clean. Quality is emphasized over quantity. Oriental designs usually consist of three or fewer flowers, although more can be added as long as there is an odd number. Containers are generally shallow bowls or dishes. Oriental designs can be placed against a wall, or can serve as an accent on a table.

The type of design you follow depends on your taste, the decor of the setting in which the arrangement will be placed, and the formality of the occasion. The color of the flowers should harmonize with the setting and fit the mood; for example, bright colors are appropriate for a child's birthday party, and subdued colors for formal dinner parties. In large mass arrangements, some flowers can be removed as they fade without disturbing the overall design, but as the majority of the flowers fade, the arrangement should be started anew.

Flower arranging is an art, not a science, even though structured principles are applied to it. Since the materials and the context can be so variable, improvisation is more important than following strict rules. With a little trial and error, you'll soon be making lovely arrangements for your home or to give to friends on special occasions.

An excellent way to learn about flower arranging is to study books on the subject, such as Ortho's *Arranging Cut Flowers.* You can also hone your skills by joining a garden club or taking one of the adult education courses available in many communities. There are also floral design schools, but these are geared mostly for professionals.

THE AMERICAN ROSE SOCIETY

People who enjoy the same hobby inevitably get together to discuss their activities, exchange information, and through their common bond enjoy their hobby even more. The American Rose Society (ARS) is a national organization with a membership of about 20,000. Founded in 1892 as an association of commercial rose growers, the ARS today is made up primarily of amateur rose enthusiasts. It is the only national rose association, and among flower-oriented groups its size is exceeded only by that of the American Orchid Society.

Joining the ARS is a step to becoming a better rose grower. As a member you receive a monthly magazine, *The American Rose,* which provides up-to-date information about rose care, new varieties, landscaping, and other topics. Yearly the magazine publishes the winning entries from its photographic slide contest.

Another important publication members receive is the *American Rose Annual,* a book that includes descriptions of all new roses that have been registered with the ARS during the past year, as well as articles on various aspects of rose growing. Each annual contains a section called "Roses in Review," a compilation of ratings and comments about new rose varieties from gardeners all over the country. This section's "show me" attitude makes it an invaluable guide in weighing the promotional claims of nursery catalogs.

Members also receive the yearly *Handbook for Selecting Roses,* a buyer's guide to over three thousand commonly available varieties. Each rose in the handbook is assigned a rating from 0 to 10, based on a survey of ARS members taken every three years. This small booklet contains a wealth of information, such as type of rose and color, to help you select new varieties for your garden.

The ARS maintains a lending library at its headquarters, and as a member you are entitled to borrow any of its more than five thousand books, films, videotapes, and slide shows on roses, by mail or in person. Write for a description of what's available. On the grounds of the Shreveport, Louisiana, headquarters is a magnificent rose garden; for the address, see page 336.

Twice each year the ARS holds national conventions. Each convention features a rose show, garden tours, educational programs, and good "rose talk." Many professional hybridizers and rose producers attend, giving you a "sneak preview" of what's to come in the world of roses.

In addition to the conventions, the ARS sponsors tours and cruises to faraway places, and seminars on special topics. Once every three years members join with rose growers from all over the world at the meeting of the International Federation of Rose Societies. The meetings are held at a different location each time and are organized by volunteers from the host country.

The ARS maintains a number of committees to help members know and grow roses better. Staffed by volunteers from all over the country, these committees specialize in a variety of subjects. For instance, the Trial Grounds committee tests new varieties of large roses at the ARS gardens in Shreveport. The Miniature Rose Testing committee evaluates new miniatures in Shreveport and at several other locations. The New Products Evaluation committee reports on new insecticides, fungicides, sprayers, and other garden products. The Rose Registration committee approves all new variety names submitted by commercial hybridizers to make sure the name has not been used before, and if it has, that the older rose is out of commerce. There

are many other committees as well; you can receive a detailed listing by contacting ARS headquarters.

One of the ARS's most valuable activities is the Consulting Rosarian program, in which outstanding rose growers who are active ARS members serve as advisers-at-large to the rose-growing community. Consulting Rosarians share their knowledge and enthusiasm by giving talks, opening their gardens to visitors, and traveling to neighboring gardens to give advice.

If you are like many people who have become dedicated to the hobby of rose growing, eventually you may wish to exhibit your roses at ARS-sponsored rose shows. (See the next section for details.)

Judges evaluate entries at an American Rose Society show. Training and accrediting judges is among the many activities of the ARS.

And some ardent exhibiters go on to the next step—becoming a judge. The ARS trains and accredits rose judges from among its members in all areas of the country so that there be will no shortage of qualified judges for local rose shows.

In addition to the ARS's national activities, the 18 regional districts and their scores of local chapters sponsor events of their own. Every district has a yearly convention that includes a rose show, programs, tours, awards, and social events. Most districts publish newsletters and many hold winter meetings to keep enthusiasm high while roses hibernate under the snow. Many local chapters within each district are also active, sponsoring their own monthly meetings, newsletters, shows, and demonstrations. Their members often help out at public gardens, answer questions at flower shows, garden centers, and libraries, and do whatever else they can to foster interest in roses.

Single blooms at a rose show receive points for form, color, substance, stem and foliage, and other attributes. Judges tally the points to determine the winners.

If you want to join a local rose group, which is separate from membership in the ARS, there is probably one less than an hour's drive from your home. If you can't locate one through community notices in your newspaper or on the radio, contact the ARS; they will put you in touch with the right people.

For membership or other information, contact the ARS. See page 339 for the address and telephone number.

EXHIBITING AND JUDGING ROSES

*M*ost people who become active in rose societies eventually become interested in exhibiting their roses. The lure of ribbons and trophies, and the chance to compare

their achievements with those of others, are hard to resist.

If you are interested in exhibiting your roses, you will find that there are many opportunities. In addition to local, regional, and national shows sponsored by the ARS, many garden clubs and state fairs have rose sections in their flower shows. These can take place anytime during rose-blooming season and are often advertised in local newspapers and on the radio. The ARS publishes the dates and locations of its rose shows in its monthly magazine.

Rose shows are usually held indoors at shopping malls, schools, libraries, and other public buildings. Exhibitors arrive early in the morning, usually about 6 A.M., and spend three or four hours arranging tables and setting out cut roses in clear glass bottles or vases. Roses are often positioned alphabetically by class (such as floribunda, hybrid tea, and so on). Judging the roses begins when the exhibits are ready, and is closed to the public, if feasible. Judges trained and accredited by the ARS work their way among the entries, usually in teams of three. The number of teams depends on the size of the show; a large national show may have as many as two dozen teams. Judges award blue (first prize), red (second prize), yellow (third prize), and sometimes white (honorable mention) ribbons by variety within each class. Only one blue ribbon is awarded per class and variety, but there can be numerous second and third prizes if the entries warrant it. After the judging is completed, the exhibitors and the public are allowed to view and enjoy the show.

After all the ribbons have been awarded, the blue-ribbon winners undergo a second round of judging. From among the one-bloom-per-stem, disbudded hybrid teas, grandifloras, and climbing hybrid teas exclusively, the judges select a grand-prize winner known as the Queen of the Show. Second- and third-place winners from these classes are often chosen as well, and are usually called the King and the Princess of the Show. Together with the best floribunda spray, grandiflora spray, one-bloom-per-stem miniature, miniature spray, old garden rose, polyantha, climber, and shrub (which are ineligible for the grand prize), these winners are placed on a separate table known as the Court of Honor. The winners of the Challenge Classes (see below) are also exhibited on this table.

JUDGING CRITERIA

To be a good exhibitor, you need to know what the judges are looking for when they decide the winners. For hybrid teas, grandifloras, floribundas, and miniatures there are two main sets of judging criteria: one for single blooms and another for multiple blooms. Polyanthas, climbers, shrub roses, and old garden roses are judged separately by class, without regard to the number of blooms. Additional categories called Challenge Classes evaluate groups of cuttings as a whole.

SINGLE BLOOMS   When judges turn a critical eye to roses that are eligible for Queen of the Show, they use the set of guidelines below, awarding up to the maximum number of points for each attribute. The flower with the most points is the winner. Miniatures, floribundas, and climbers (other than climbing hybrid teas) that are exhibited with single blooms are judged in the same way, although they are not eligible for Queen of the Show.

Form—25 points. An exhibition rose is in its ideal form when it is one-half to three-quarters open. When viewed from the top, the outline of the bloom is circular, with the petals arrayed symmetrically within the circle. The stamens at the center of the rose must not be visible. When the flower is viewed from the side, it should be triangular in form—pointed at the top and flat at the base.

The grand-prize winner, known as the Queen of the Show, is exhibited alongside runners-up (called the King and Princess) on a table known as the Court of Honor. Only one-bloom-per-stem entries are eligible for these top awards.

Color—20 points. The rose must be as close to its ideal color as possible, free of the bleaching or darkening caused by adverse weather conditions or refrigeration. There should be no green or white streaks on the petals, and no marks or spots from rain or spray residue.

Substance—15 points. Substance refers to the crispness, texture, firmness, thickness, and toughness of the petals. A newly cut rose that has been properly conditioned will have excellent substance. As a cut rose ages, it naturally loses some of its substance, and will not be as eligible for a high award as a newly cut rose.

Stem and Foliage—20 points. The stem should be straight and strong, and the foliage free of dirt, disease, insect infestation, spray residue, and cuts and holes. The foliage should also be large and healthy-looking without being overgrown. There should be at least two five-leaflet leaves on the stem, although there can be many more. The foliage should be evenly placed around the stem, so that if you look down on the exhibit, the foliage makes an evenly balanced background for the bloom.

Balance and Proportion—10 points. The size of the flower should be in proportion to the length of the stem. In other words, a small flower should not be shown on a very long stem, nor should a large flower be shown on a short stem. There are no exact rules here; evaluation is subjective.

Size—10 points. This refers to the size of the flower. The bigger the better.

MULTIPLE BLOOMS   More than one flower blooming on a stem is called a spray. Sprays are found on hybrid teas, grandifloras, floribundas, miniatures, polyanthas, and climbers. The individual flowers in sprays are judged by the same criteria as single flowers, and additionally by how they appear in relation to one another.

Each flower on a winning hybrid tea or grandiflora spray must have the ideal form, color, substance, size, and so forth required of a one-bloom-per-stem specimen. What's more, all the flowers in the spray must be arranged in a pleasing, balanced way. Judges look for how the flowers open according to the variety; the flowers of some varieties open all at once whereas others open in stages.

The flowers in a floribunda spray should have an overall form, or outline, that is pleasing from the side. It may be rounded, flat, or dome shaped, but it should be symmetrical. No flowers in the spray should protrude above or beyond this outline. Sprays of polyanthas, climbers, and miniature roses are judged in the same way as floribunda sprays.

Old garden and shrub roses may be exhibited either with a single bloom or with multiple blooms, depending on the way the plant naturally flowers. They are awarded blue ribbons if they have a fully open, circular form and if they are fresh and have good substance. Because most of these plants naturally have short stems, the "balance and proportion" category is not weighed as heavily as it is with modern roses. It is possible for a rose to have a large spray on a short stem and still win an award.

CHALLENGE CLASSES   Rose shows sponsored by rose societies also award trophies in categories called Challenge Classes. Challenge Classes usually call for a collection of roses, with each bloom standing in a separate container. In evaluating them, the judges first apply the criteria for judging individual flowers, sprays, or clusters, and then assesses 10 additional points per bloom for how the collection looks as a whole. Winning entries are those collections whose roses have complementary colors, and are ideally the same size and at the same stage of development. The more closely matched the individual flowers in the collection are, the better the chance that the collection will win the trophy.

READING ROSES FOR AN EXHIBIT

Once you understand what the judges will be looking for, you can proceed with the task of growing and grooming roses that are as close as possible to the ideal. Producing show-quality roses can take a lot of effort, but once you have experienced the exhilaration of winning your first ribbon or trophy, you'll probably want to work even harder for the next one.

Exhibiting starts in the garden. If you do not grow healthy plants and give them the care they need, they will not produce award-winning roses. In addition to conscientious plant care, serious exhibitors apply several techniques to improve their roses in the months and days before a show. You can easily do the same in your garden. If the spring has been cold, delay applying summer mulch until the ground has completely warmed up so that growth will not be retarded. If you will be entering the roses in competition for Queen of the Show, disbud hybrid teas, grandifloras, and climbing hybrid teas as soon as side growth appears (see the instructions on page 133).

This grouping of floribunda sprays and hybrid teas is the winner of the New Zealand Kiwi Award, one of several Challenge Classes at a national show.

*Left: The Nicholson
Perpetual Challenge
Bowl, the highest
award of the ARS,
goes to the best
collection of nine
different hybrid teas
in exhibition form.*

*Right: Blooms on
bushes can be covered
with plastic bags
to shield them from
light rain just before
a show.*

About ten days before the show, fertilize the plants with a soluble plant food such as 20-20-20 or 15-30-15 fertilizer. This will make the foliage healthier looking, give more color and substance to the flowers, and sometimes speed up their development.

If bad weather threatens just before a show, blooms can be protected by covering them loosely with a plastic bag and sealing the bag with a twist-tie so it does not blow away.

The next step is to cut the flowers to take to the rose show. For advice on cutting, see page 190. Stems must have at least two five-leaflet leaves but may have many more, as long as the stem length is in proportion to the size of the flower. However, stems must be no longer than 18 inches from the base of the stem to the base of the flower. They can be cut from the garden a little longer than 18 inches, and adjustments made at the show. As you cut your stems, write the variety name on a tag of paper and attach it loosely to the stem. The tags can be attached with string, but the easiest way is to cut the tags into long, rectangular strips. Make a slit at one end of the strip, and pull the other end of the paper through the slit as you wrap the strip around the stem.

Cutting for a rose show usually takes place the day before the show, unless you have a refrigerator in which you can store your roses. Most refrigerated roses retain their show quality for up to about five days as long as there is no food in the refrigerator. If food is present, especially fruit, roses will open more quickly and will not retain their show quality. Moreover, refrigeration can discolor some flowers, primarily reds and oranges. If this happens, they will be penalized by the judges. Roses keep best if they are stored standing up in a bucket of water in a refrigerator. Take care not to submerge any leaves, which will foul the water. Some exhibitors wrap entire stems and flowers in plastic, refrigerate them out of water, and then place them in water the night before the show. This method has limited success because the roses often dehydrate too much and will not rehydrate enough to be exhibited. Research is still being done on this method.

If you have a large number of entries, you'll find it easier and more efficient to do most of the preparation at home during the days before the show. In addition to cutting and labeling your roses, you can clean the foliage and fill out the show entry tags at home. These tags are provided by the rose society or sponsor and can usually be obtained in advance of the show. Using waterproof ink, you write in the name of the rose, the class in which it is being exhibited (hybrid tea, floribunda, etc.), and your name. Each tag is tied to the neck of the bottle holding the rose and is folded over so that your name is not visible during judging.

At most rose shows, roses are exhibited in clear glass bottles. Find out whether the sponsor will supply the bottles or whether you must furnish your own. Bottles that are provided by the sponsor are often available before the show. You will save time by putting your rose specimens in the bottles at home. Be sure to fill the bottle to the neck to keep the specimen from drying out. A floral preservative can be added to the water (see page 192).

Rose shows always follow a schedule, which is usually available from the sponsor at least a month before the show. You must follow the instructions in the schedule to the letter, or your entry may be disqualified. For example, if the instructions say that a Challenge Class calls for three dark red hybrid teas, you cannot enter two dark reds and one medium red.

Other things that can disqualify a rose from competition include misnaming the rose on the entry tag; entering the rose in the wrong class, or section, in the show; employing cosmetic substances such as pigments, oil, glue, or wires; and showing roses not registered with the American Rose Society (this rule is often ignored

at garden club and state fair shows). These and other rules are outlined in the instructions.

Rose shows always specify a time for making entries (for example, from 6 A.M. to 10 A.M.). Plan to arrive at the rose show early, so that you will have enough time to place all of your entries on the show tables. It is also cooler in the early morning, so the roses will suffer less from heat in transit. If your car is air conditioned, cool it off first and then keep the air conditioner running as you drive to the show. Placing small plastic bags over the flowers (the bags do not need to be sealed) will help them retain moisture during the trip. If you must travel a long distance to the show, your roses will keep much better if they are transported in an ice chest or other insulated box containing frozen

Last-minute grooming can transform a less-than-perfect bloom into a winner. Here, an exhibitor inserts cotton swabs between rows of petals to train them open in a desired shape.

Top: Groomed to perfection, roses await judging at a national show.

Bottom: Like beauty contestants, roses undergo painstaking last-minute prepping. These hybrid teas sit on an exhibitor's grooming table before entry in the show.

ice packs (be sure the blooms do not touch the ice). If the insulated box is not large enough to let roses stand up in their bottles, place each rose in an orchid tube. Orchid tubes, which are available from florist supply stores, are made of plastic or glass tubes resembling test tubes. The stems are placed in water in the tubes and held in place by a rubber stopper, which has a hole for the stem. If you don't have an insulated box, place the stems in ice water before you transport them if the trip is long.

As you make entries, keep the judging criteria in mind. If the form of a rose is not perfect, you may be able to groom it into shape by removing one or two petals. It is sometimes possible to shift a petal around in front of another petal so that the form is more symmetrical. If a rose has not opened enough, you can usually open it more by warming the outside of the rose for a few minutes between your fingertips and then gently pulling the petals down. The rose will also open more quickly if you place it in the sun or in warm water, either at home or after you get to the show. Dust and insects can be cleaned away with an artist's brush. Torn or damaged foliage can sometimes be manicured with small scissors. It is important not to smoke while getting your roses ready; cigarette smoke contains chemicals that cause flowers to open more quickly.

Sometimes a stem refuses to stand up straight in the bottle, which will detract from its beauty and probably cause the judges to bypass it. In such an instance, it is acceptable to wedge the stem with a piece of folded paper towel (as long as the paper does not touch and absorb water), a ball of aluminum foil, or wadded plastic wrap. If you must use a wedge, try to place it so that it does not protrude awkwardly above the lip of the bottle.

After you have groomed the rose for exhibit, make sure the paper identification tag that you placed on the rose at home is removed, that the entry tag is attached to the bottle with a twist-tie or rubber band, and that the rose is entered in the correct class in the show. In a few hours, after judging is over, you'll know whether your efforts have paid off.

Top-Rated Exhibition Roses

Some roses are better for showing than others, either because they last longer as cut flowers or because they naturally have strong canes, large foliage, and ideally formed flowers. Each year, the Golden Triangle Rose Society of Southeast Texas compiles a list of the top exhibition roses, based on judging results submitted by rose societies all over the country. If you wish to grow roses for exhibiting, the varieties on this list will give you the best results. For 1991, the top exhibition roses, in descending order, were as follows.

Hybrid Teas	Grandifloras	Floribundas	Miniatures
Touch of Class	Gold Medal	Showbiz	Jean Kenneally
Keepsake		Europeana	Snow Bride
Olympiad		Playgirl	Minnie Pearl
Uncle Joe		First Edition	Pierrine
Folklore		Sexy Rexy	Kingig
Color Magic		Playboy	Party Girl
Pristine		Sun Flare	Black Jade
Double Delight		Iceberg	Rainbow's End
Dublin		French Lace	Olympic Gold
Crystalline		Escapade	Luis Desamero
Lynette		Little Darling	June Laver
Elizabeth Taylor		Permanent Wave	Little Jackie
Royal Highness		Korikole	Old Glory
Suffolk		Ivory Fashion	Irresistible
Cary Grant		Gene Boerner	Red Beauty
Bride's Dream		Nana Mouskouri	Loving Touch
Lanvin		Simplicity	Pucker Up
White Masterpiece			Dreamglo
Captain Harry Stebbings			Ruby Pendant
Honor			Rise 'n' Shine
Elina			Sweet Pickens
Peter Frankenfeld			Cheer Up

PRESERVING ROSES

*A*las for rose lovers, the life of a cut rose is short and the time between blooming periods is often long. Fortunately, roses can be preserved in several ways to extend their beauty: They can be dried for arrangements, pressed for display in picture frames, or blended to make fragrant potpourris. All you need are a few simple ingredients and minimal tools and supplies. The results of your efforts can look and smell marvelous, and can last for years.

Roses for preserving can be picked anytime during the season, and are best picked in the morning after the sun has dried the dew. You can cut and preserve roses all summer, and then make home decorations and gifts with them during the winter months. Flowers for drying should be at the peak of perfection when cut; freshness is also critical with roses for pressing and for potpourri.

Roses should be at their peak when cut for drying or pressing. Pink and yellow roses retain their color best.

DRIED FLOWERS

Both the flowers and the foliage of roses can be dried to make charming arrangements for display around the house. Although many different types of roses can be dried, miniature roses are the most popular because their small flowers dry more easily than larger roses and retain their shape and color better. Along with size, color is an important consideration when choosing roses for drying. Many white roses turn brown when dried, many red roses turn quite black, and some orange roses turn dark at the tips of their petals. Pinks and yellows are a better choice because most of them retain their original color. Even if you are fairly sure you can anticipate the results, you may want to experiment with a few flowers before drying a large batch.

Silica gel is the material that dries roses best. It is a white, crystalline substance resembling table sugar and has the capacity to absorb large quantities of moisture. Sealed into small packets, it is the material sold by photo supply companies for protecting camera equipment. Larger quantities for flower drying are sold at craft and flower shops. A 1½-pound canister contains enough silica gel to dry several small flowers at once, and it may be reactivated and reused many times. Many brands of silica gel contain small blue indicator crystals that turn pink when it is time to reactivate the substance. To do this, simply spread the silica gel in a shallow, ovenproof container and bake it for 30 minutes to an hour at 250° F, until the crystals turn blue again; or dry it in the microwave for a minute or two.

To dry roses, pick flowers that are as perfect as possible, and that are dry, free of insects and debris, and at the desired stage of development. If possible, try to cut flowers with 2 inches of stem to make arranging easier. You can dry anything from tiny buds to fully opened flowers with leaves.

Then select a wide, flat-bottomed container with a tight-fitting cover, such as an imported-cookie tin, and spread a 1-inch layer of silica gel in the bottom. Lay the roses on top of it with the flowers facing up, cutting the stems if necessary so as not to bend the flowers over. Take care that none of the flowers touch. Foliage can be dried on the stem, but there is a chance it will break off later on. A better idea is to dry foliage separately from the flowers, laying it flat on silica gel beside them. Cover everything completely with more silica gel, making sure to fill in the flowers with silica gel, and then seal the container tightly for about a week. Flowers dry more uniformly if flowers of the same size are dried together. If you want to dry other types of flowers to use with roses, such as zinnias, marigolds, or asters, it is best to dry them separately, as drying times may vary.

When the roses and the leaves are fully dried, they will feel crisp or papery to the touch. Remove them carefully from the container and gently blow away any silica gel that has stuck to them. If any crystals remain, dust them away lightly with an artist's brush.

A few tricks will help you achieve better and longer-lasting results. Sepals curl as they dry, so if you cut them off before immersing the flowers in silica gel, the result will be more attractive. After a flower has dried, you can insert floral wire into its base and wrap it around the stem. This strengthens the stem and makes it easier to arrange the blooms. If you are leaving a stem on the flower, it's better to insert the wire through the stem before drying, as the stem would be more likely to break after drying. To strengthen a dried rose, apply a few drops of white glue to the undersides of the outer petals to make them less likely to fall off. To make a dried rose less brittle and also less likely to reabsorb moisture, spray it with clear plastic available from art supply stores, or dip it in warm, melted paraffin, which will give the rose a waxy coating.

You can also dry roses in a microwave oven; in fact, the resulting color and shape of the flowers will actually be better than if the roses are dried in a tin. It's best to dry only one flower at a time to avoid crowding and overdrying. First, dry and heat the silica gel at the high setting for about a minute. Then prepare the roses as described above, using an uncovered microwavable container. (Omit metal floral wire, which may cause arcing.) Since microwave ovens vary, it is impossible to give exact times. Start with one minute at the high setting. If that is not enough, dry for another minute. If the microwave lacks a rotating platter inside, stop the oven after 30 seconds and rotate the container so that the flowers dry evenly. Cool the flowers for 20 to 30 minutes and remove them from the silica gel.

Roses can also be dried in white cornmeal mixed with borax, or fine sand mixed with borax. However, drying takes twice as long as silica gel and is not as satisfactory, since the materials tend to cake on the flowers and the flowers are more likely to develop burn spots. Follow the same steps as for silica gel, but place flowers face down rather than face up and leave the container open. All in all, silica gel is far superior. Roses do not air-dry satisfactorily.

Dried roses are arranged in the same way as fresh roses, with several additional considerations. First, you do not need to worry about water; in fact, placing them in water will ruin them. Containers, floral foam, or pinholders can be used to support the stems. If the stems are weak and no supporting wire is in place, you can use wire to tie them to florist picks (pieces of wood that resemble large toothpicks, available at florist supply stores), or insert wire through the base of the flower and twist it around the stem. Wire and picks can be hidden if necessary with self-adhesive green tape.

Roses can be combined with many other dried flowers—asters, baby's breath, marigolds, yarrow, and zinnias, as well as combined with other types of foliage. Dried roses can also be wired onto wreaths and garlands. A dried arrangement can last for many years, depending on the humidity in the room. If it gets dusty, brush the dust off gently with a feather duster or an artist's brush. In humid climates protect the arrangement in a glass bell jar.

PRESSED ROSES

Pressed roses make lovely material for small framed "pictures," collages, or gift cards. Although many kinds of roses can be pressed, the best results are obtained with single flowers or those with fewer than 12 to 15 petals. Buds may also be pressed. Pick the flowers or buds when they are fresh and dry, and press them immediately.

Roses can be pressed in a heavy book or in a flower press. Pressing by either method takes about two weeks.

If you are using a book, place the rose on a piece of blotting paper, arranging its leaves and petals as you want them to look when they are finished. Petals can overlap or be arranged so that they do not touch; just make sure that they are lying flat and are not curled under. Place a second piece of blotting paper over the material to be pressed, close the book, and weight it with more books or some other heavy item. Check the blotting paper every two or three days to see if it is wet. If it is, replace it and return the material to the book. Several layers can be pressed in the same book, and flowers can be pressed all summer, stored in an airtight container after pressing, and the pictures or other items made later.

A flower press usually consists of two sheets of wood that clamp tightly together. If you cannot find one for sale at a gift shop or craft store, you can make your own inexpensively out of plywood; simply cut two identical boards, drill matching holes at the corners, and attach the boards with bolts and wing nuts. The main advantage of a flower press over a book is that it can press more layers of thicker flowers at a time.

To prepare roses for a flower press, place them between pieces of blotting paper and separate each layer with a sheet of corrugated cardboard. Carefully insert this stack into the press and tighten the wing nuts evenly. As with the book method, check the pressed materials every few days and change the paper if it is wet. Most material will be completely dry in about two weeks.

To make a pressed-flower picture, buy a picture frame with a glass covering and a stiff backing. Using white household glue, cover the backing with a fabric of the color you desire; velveteen is excellent, although any type of heavy material can be used. Sketch out your design first and then, using tweezers to handle the flowers and the foliage, set them in place on the fabric with white household glue. A toothpick or a small brush can be used to apply the glue evenly and lightly. Once the arrangement is finished and the glue has dried, place the glass and the rest of the frame in place, and hang it up to enjoy it, or give it as a gift.

Cards and other items are made in the same way. After the design is finished, spray it with clear plastic available from art supply stores to protect it.

POTPOURRI

Potpourri is a mixture of dried rose petals, aromatic oils, other scents derived from herbs or spices, sometimes other dried flowers, and a fixative to retain the aroma. Although potpourris can be made with flowers other than roses, roses are traditionally the main ingredient. The word *potpourri* is a French term meaning "rotten pot," which derives from the

original practice of placing rose petals in a container to ripen and age.

Although it is tempting to enjoy roses in the garden and then collect the petals for potpourri as they start to drop, this method is not satisfactory because the petals are past their peak and will not dry and retain their fragrance properly. Any type of rose of any color can be used to make potpourri; just be sure to use fragrant roses.

Today, potpourri is made by two methods—the dry method and the moist method. The dry method, which uses only thoroughly dried rose petals, makes potpourri displayed in glass bowls and in sachets to perfume lingerie drawers. Potpourri in glass bowls can last for 10 years or more, whereas that in sachets usually loses its fragrance after 2 years or so. The moist method, using partially dried petals, creates potpourri that is less attractive to view but whose scent lasts much longer—up to 50 years. Moist potpourri is used in glass bowls as well.

Aromatic oils, fixatives, dried flowers, and other ingredients necessary to make potpourri are available from craft stores and specialty shops or by mail order.

DRY POTPOURRI   Gather petals from fragrant roses after the morning dew has dried, and spread them on an elevated screen out of the sunlight and in a warm, dry, airy place. Drying will take several days to a week, depending on heat and humidity. The petals should be dry enough that they break easily when bent. If you cannot dry enough petals at once, store the dried petals in an airtight glass jar until you have enough.

In a large glass or wooden bowl, mix 1 quart of dried petals with about 1 ounce by weight of dried herbs or spices of the scent you desire—for example, allspice, cinnamon, cloves, lemon verbena, or mint. You may also add other dried flowers; carnations, lavender, and orange blossoms are most common, as they retain their scent long after drying. Place

Roses are the traditional main ingredient of potpourri. Any type of rose may be used, as long as it is fragrant.

Cut roses last only a few days, but their scent can linger for up to 50 years when preserved in a moist potpourri.

several drops of aromatic oil on 2 ounces of fixative such as orris root or benzoin (congealed resin from the styrax tree) and gently blend this into the rose petals and spice/herb mix with a wooden spoon. Use chunks of fixative rather than powder, as the latter can cling to the container and cloud the glass. Aromatic oils of cinnamon, cloves, lavender, lemon, rose, and sandalwood are the ones most often used.

Store the mixture in a dark, cool place in an airtight container, stirring or shaking often. Test the scents periodically. They will smell harsh at first; this is natural—do not try to compensate by adding other fragrances to the mix. After 3 to 12 weeks aging will be complete and the mixture will have a pleasant aroma. Place the potpourri in a covered glass container, adding other dried flowers for color. Remove the cover when you wish to scent the room.

There are thousands of potpourri recipes. From Caswell-Massey Co., Ltd., of New York, the country's oldest perfumer and purveyor of spices and essential oils, comes this recipe for dry potpourri. All plant material should be dried before use.

4 ounces dried rose petals (about 1 quart volume)
2 ounces lavender flowers or buds
4 ounces coriander leaves
4 ounces chopped orris root
½ ounce ground cinnamon
½ ounce ground mace
¼ ounce ground cloves
¼ ounce table salt
¼ ounce oil of lavender
¼ ounce oil of cinnamon
¼ ounce oil of cloves
¼ ounce oil of rose
½ ounce tincture of musk

MOIST POTPOURRI   To make moist potpourri, dry rose petals until they are limp but not completely dry. Mix them with the dried herbs and spices whose scents you desire, and then place a 2-inch layer of the mixture into a ceramic or glass bowl. Add a thin layer of non-iodized salt, then two more inches of petals, and repeat until the bowl is full. Press the mixture down with a weight, and mix daily. The mixture will be completely aged in about two weeks.

Fixative is not needed—the salt absorbs and retains the scents. If the mixture loses some of its scent, it can be revived with a few drops of brandy.

There are many variations on the theme. The following is a nineteenth-century list of ingredients.

3 handfuls fragrant rose petals
3 handfuls orange blossoms or other fragrant flower
3 handfuls carnation petals
1 handful chopped marjoram leaves
1 handful chopped lemon thyme leaves
6 sweet bay leaves
1 grated lemon rind
25 crushed cloves
1 handful myrtle leaves
½ handful spearmint leaves
½ handful lavender flowers

ROSES IN FOOD AND DRINK

*T*he gardener who likes to cook will find that roses can be incorporated in many foods and beverages. People have been cooking with roses since ancient times. Victorian hostesses often served rose petal sandwiches at teatime, and today edible flowers of all kinds have enjoyed a comeback in the kitchen. Rose hips and rose water, too, are ingredients in a variety of intriguing recipes. The following are a few tasty ideas.

ROSE PETAL RECIPES

The petals of any fragrant roses can make a truly delicious addition to recipes. Fresh or candied rose petals can also serve as decorations and garnishes. Fresh petals contribute a limp, velvety texture and a delicate flavor that varies in strength with their scent; however, they may not taste exactly the way they smell.

For the most flavorful recipes, cook with fresh, fragrant rose petals that have not been sprayed with insecticide or fungicide. Dark petals have the strongest flavor; light pink ones, the most delicate. Old garden roses generally have a stronger flavor than modern roses. If the scent is unusually weak, you can add more petals to compensate.

You prepare rose petals the same way for every recipe. Cut the flowers in the morning after the dew has dried and remove the petals from the flowers. (Fallen petals are not recommended, given that rose petals are perishable and the subtlety of their flavor is quickly lost.) With scissors, cut away the white bases of the petals, because they have a bitter taste. If the recipe calls for chopped petals, cut them into pieces about ¼ to ½ inch square. One medium-sized rose yields about a cup of whole petals.

ROSE PETAL CAKE

Makes one 2-layer cake.

This unusual cake has a delightful flavor just suggestive of rose petals. Light pink petals give the white cake and the whipped cream a delicate hint of color.

> ½ cup plus 2 tablespoons butter or
>   margarine
> 2½ cups cake flour
> ½ teaspoon salt
> 1 tablespoon baking powder
> 1½ cups sugar
> ¾ cup milk
> 3 egg whites
> 1 tablespoon rum or brandy (or 1
>   teaspoon rum or brandy flavoring)
> ½ cup coarsely chopped rose petals
>   (light pink suggested for delicate color
>   and flavor)
> ½ cup sliced almonds, toasted in oven
>   until golden

Frosting:

> 2 cups whipping cream
> 1 tablespoon rum or brandy (or 1
>   teaspoon rum or brandy flavoring)
> 1 teaspoon vanilla
> ⅓ cup sugar
> ¼ cup sliced almonds, toasted in oven
>   until golden
>   Candied rose petals (optional, see
>   recipe)

Preheat oven to 350° F. Cream butter or margarine in a mixing bowl until soft. Sift cake flour with salt, baking powder, and sugar. Combine dry mixture and milk in thirds, mixing after each addition with an electric beater. Beat on low speed, or by hand, until the mixture is well blended. Add egg whites and mix at low speed until smooth. Finally, add rum or brandy, rose petals, and almonds, and blend.

Pour batter into two 8-inch round cake pans that have been greased and lightly floured. Bake for 25 minutes, or until the cake springs back when touched lightly.

To make the frosting, whip cream with rum or brandy and vanilla until mixture is almost stiff. Add sugar and continue whipping until stiff peaks are formed. Apply one third of the frosting between layers, one third to sides, and one third to top. Form rosettes with a pastry bag. Decorate with almonds and candied rose petals (if desired).

ROSE PETAL JELLY
Makes 4 pints.
The flavor of roses is pronounced yet delicate in this wonderful jelly. Use dark red petals for a clear, bright red color.

> 4 quarts rose petals (16 cups)
> 2 quarts water (8 cups)
> 7 cups sugar
> 4 tablespoons fresh lemon juice
> 6 ounces liquid pectin
>   Food coloring (optional)

Boil rose petals and water together for 10 to 20 minutes, or until about half the liquid has boiled off. Strain through a fine sieve into a bowl, pressing on the rose petals to extract as much liquid as possible. Measure 3 cups of liquid, add sugar, stir to combine, and bring to a boil. (You may discard the remaining liquid.) Add lemon juice and pectin, and boil for 1 minute, stirring constantly.

Remove from heat, add food coloring if desired (use a color that enhances the color already present), and pour into sterilized jars, filling to ⅛ inch of the top. Seal with paraffin, or use vacuum lids. If using vacuum lids, cover immediately with flat lids, and screw tops on tightly. Turn upside down for 5 minutes, then turn right side up. After 1 hour, check that seals appear intact.

ROSE PETAL TEA
Makes 1 quart.
With more character than most "herb" teas, this light beverage has the flavor of roses with hints of nutmeg and orange. Brew fragrant, deep pink petals for a fine flavor and a lovely dark pink color.

> ½ cup tightly packed rose petals
> ⅛ teaspoon ground nutmeg
> 1 teaspoon sugar
> ¼ orange, peeled and coarsely chopped
> 1 quart water

Place rose petals, nutmeg, sugar, and chopped orange into a pitcher. Pour boiling water over petals and steep for 5 minutes. Strain. Serve hot or cold.

CANDIED ROSE PETALS
Makes 2 dozen petals.
Candied flower petals were a favorite treat in Victorian times. This easy-to-make confection can decorate cakes, petits fours, and candied fruits.

> 24 small, colorful, well-formed rose petals
> 2 egg whites, slightly beaten
> 1 cup superfine sugar

Brush both sides of the petals with a thin coating of egg white. Sprinkle both sides lightly with superfine sugar and place on a tray sprinkled with additional sugar. Sift a bit more sugar over the top to lightly cover any bare spots. Allow to set overnight at room temperature, and use within a few days.

ROSE HIP RECIPES

Rose hips, the fruits of roses, are not only tangy and sweet in flavor but are also high in vitamin C—ounce for ounce, as much as 100 times that of citrus fruits. Rose hips are gathered in the fall, usually after the first frost, when they are fully ripe and bright red or orange. Do not use hips from plants that have been treated with systemic pesticides.

For recipes requiring prepared hips, cut the stems and the leaves from the bases of the hips, and remove the shriveled blossom ends from the tops. Wash the hips well and cut them in half down the center with a knife. Remove the seeds and keep them if you want to experiment with germination (see the section beginning on page 232). About 40 medium-sized whole hips will fill 2 cups.

To preserve the vitamin C, chill the hips until you are ready to use them. When cooking, avoid copper or aluminum utensils and containers, which can react chemically with the ascorbic acid in the hips and thus reduce vitamin C content considerably. Instead, use implements made of wood, stainless steel, glass, plastic, or porcelain.

ROSE HIP JELLY
Makes about 2 pints.
The pungent rose hip flavor comes through clearly in this jelly without being overpowering, as it is in some other rose hip recipes.

> 1 quart prepared rose hips (4 cups)
> 6 cups water
> 5 tart apples, unpeeled and coarsely
>   chopped
> ¼ cup fresh lemon juice

> 1 teaspoon cloves
> 7 cups sugar
> 6 ounces liquid pectin

Bring rose hips, water, apples, lemon juice, and cloves to a boil, and boil for 30 minutes. Strain through several layers of cheesecloth. Measure 3 cups of the juice with sugar, and bring to a full, rolling boil. Add the liquid pectin, stirring constantly, and bring to a second boil. Boil for 1 minute. Fill jars to ⅛ inch of the top. Wipe jar threads clean and cover with paraffin or flat vacuum lids, screwing tops on tightly. Invert for 5 minutes, then turn upright. After 1 hour, check that seals appear intact.

ROSE HIP SOUP
Makes six ½-cup servings.
This variation on a Scandinavian recipe is rich and distinctive, with a deep amber color. Serve it for dessert or as a first course with a light main dish such as poultry.

Rose hips are the prime ingredient of this unusual soup, which combines their tangy flavor with the taste of lemon, cinnamon, almonds, and ginger.

5 cups prepared rose hips
7 cups water
⅛ teaspoon salt
½ cup sugar
½ teaspoon vanilla
2 2½-inch cinnamon sticks
2 tablespoons cornstarch, mixed with
    ¼ cup water
½ cup slivered almonds (toasted in oven
    until golden)
2 teaspoons fresh lemon juice
½ teaspoon ground ginger
3 tablespoons sour cream
1½ teaspoons grated lemon rind

Combine rose hips, water, salt, sugar, vanilla, and cinnamon sticks in a saucepan and bring to a boil. Boil for 20 minutes, then strain through a fine sieve lined with several layers of cheesecloth. Return to heat and bring to a boil. Stir in cornstarch and water mixture, almonds, lemon juice, and ginger, and bring to a boil. Reduce heat and cook for 2 minutes, stirring constantly. Top each serving with ½ tablespoon sour cream and ¼ teaspoon grated lemon rind. Serve warm or chilled.

ROSE WATER RECIPES

Rose water (often called rose flower water on labels) is water with a slight fragrance and flavor of roses. It is made by distilling rose petals in water. As the water is distilled, the fragrant oils from the rose petals are carried over with the water. It is difficult to make without distilling apparatus and is best purchased ready-made at specialty stores, natural food stores, or some old-fashioned drugstores. If you cannot find it, use rose extract, which is sometimes sold in the baking section at supermarkets. To approximate rose water for cooking, dilute the rose extract with 18 parts of water.

Rose water is used primarily in cakes, cookies, pies, and other desserts. When used in cooking, it can lose its flavor, so add it at the last possible moment.

ROSE WATER SYRUP
Makes 2 pints.
The rose flavor in this very sweet syrup is quite decided, making it stand out when served with pancakes, pound cake, fresh fruit, or ice cream.

4 cups sugar
2 cups water
2 cups light corn syrup
3 tablespoons rose flower water
1 teaspoon fresh lemon juice
    Red food coloring

Simmer the sugar, water, and corn syrup for 20 minutes. When cool, add the rose flower water, lemon juice, and enough food coloring to tint the syrup pink or red, as desired. Stir to combine and place in a sterilized bottle. Screw cap on tightly. Store in refrigerator.

OTHER COOKING IDEAS FOR ROSES

The uses of roses in the kitchen are limited only by your imagination. You can line the bottom of a cake pan with rose petals before pouring in prepared batter to make an upside-down rose cake. (This works best with white or yellow cakes.) You can also substitute rose extract in many recipes that call for vanilla, lemon, or almond extract. Use chopped rose petals as a garnish for omelets, or line salad bowls with whole petals. Rose petals can also be included in fruit salads.

Honey can be flavored with rose petals, and rose water can be combined with honey, butter, anise, saffron, or sage and used to baste poultry. Rose-flavored vinegar can be made by soaking 1 cup of rose petals in 1 pint of white vinegar and straining it after 10 days.

Rose petals can be steeped in brandy for three to four weeks, and then the brandy can be used in flaming dishes, custards, sauces, and puddings, or as a dessert topping.

ROSES IN COSMETICS

Roses have been used since ancient times to scent perfumes; attar of roses is the traditional source of the rose scent. This yellow-green semisolid is distilled from rose petals and is literally worth its weight in gold, as it takes 4,000 to 5,000 pounds of petals to make a pound of attar. Only one drop is needed to scent several ounces of perfume.

Attar was made by the Persians as long ago as the first century B.C., but the industry is now centered in Bulgaria. Flowers from fragrant damask roses are harvested following a May festival and are steam distilled.

Because making attar of roses requires special apparatus, the semisolid is difficult to produce outside a laboratory. However, you can make small quantities at home by filling a wide-mouthed ceramic jar with fragrant rose petals and covering them with water. Place the jar in the sun during the day, preferably outdoors, and cover it at night. In several days you will see small yellow-green globules of oil floating on the surface of the water. In about a week there should be enough of the oil to harvest. Absorb it with a cotton ball or swab, being careful not to absorb any water, and squeeze the oil into a vial. You won't get much, but you will get a few drops of strongly and deliciously scented oil.

Rose water and glycerin is a time-honored skin moisturizer. You can buy it ready made at cosmetics stores, or you can make your own by mixing together three parts rose water and two parts glycerin.

Sachets filled with dry potpourri impart a light scent to nearby objects. You can make a more concentrated fragrance by steeping fresh rose petals in water to extract their oil.

A professional garden photographer trips a cable release while holding a diffuser to soften the light. A gold reflector fills in shadows; the gray card is a reference for light readings.

PHOTOGRAPHING ROSES

O f all the sidelines you can pursue in the hobby of rose growing, photography may well be the most rewarding. In summer, when roses are at their peak, few activities are more pleasant than visiting a magnificent rose garden to capture its magic on film. The craft of photography has many subtleties that can take a lifetime to explore, and some photographers who master these eventually turn their hobby into a lucrative profession. Whatever your ambition, a well-taken photograph is a lasting token of the beauty of your roses, one that can brighten your home, make a welcome gift, or win acclaim in contests and publications.

Technical know-how is critical, but so is an artistic sense. Study photographs and books on photography to glean the essence of composition and for inspiration in presenting a subject in new ways.

CAMERA BASICS

In order to reproduce your vision successfully, you need to understand a few basic things about the way cameras work. Three of the most important concepts are shutter speed, aperture, and depth of field. All are interrelated: Each depends on or affects the others.

Shutter speed is the length of time the shutter (a movable barrier inside the camera) stays open to expose the film. On most cameras, shutter speed can vary from one-thousandth of a second to several seconds or more. Other things being equal, the more light there is, the less time the shutter needs to stay open to expose the film. With the faster shutter speeds (those faster than $1/250$ of a second), exposure takes place so quickly that accidental movement of the camera or subject does not register on the film. A fast shutter speed is therefore desirable, but it is not always possible if the lighting is low.

Aperture refers to the opening in the lens through which light reaches the film. On most lenses the aperture can be made wider or narrower to admit more or less light. Other things being equal, the less light there is, the wider the aperture you need. Aperture is adjusted in numbered increments called f-stops, the range of which varies with the lens. A typical range is from $f/1.4$, the widest aperture, to $f/32$, the narrowest.

Aperture and shutter speed are reciprocal. Given the same lighting and film, a fast shutter speed requires a wide aperture whereas a slow shutter speed requires

Left: Photographed at f/16, the floribunda 'Matangi' is almost completely in focus.

Right: The same flower at f/4 has fewer petals in focus.

a narrow one. Both settings expose the film to the same amount of light.

Along with the amount of light entering through the lens, aperture also controls the range within which objects are in focus. This is known as depth of field. Owing to the laws of optics, narrower apertures make for greater depths of field and wider apertures make for shallower depths of field. Thus, a nearby rose photographed at a narrow aperture of $f/16$ would have more of its petals in focus than one photographed at a wide aperture of $f/4$. Depth of field is a critical consideration when taking close-ups of roses, since it is desirable that the entire flower be in sharp focus.

CHOOSING A CAMERA AND FILM

Although you can take a successful photograph with almost any camera, it is easier if you have a good one. Choose one of the many excellent 35 mm single-lens reflex (SLR) cameras, which let you look directly through the lens when composing photographs. Less expensive rangefinder cameras make you look through a separate viewer. This means that when you take close-ups, the slight offset between lens and viewer may result in photographs that are off-center.

Automatic "snapshot" cameras are fine for photographing rose gardens, but

their lenses will not allow you to get near enough to a flower to take a close-up. There are cameras that take photographs in formats larger than 35 mm, such as 2¼ inch by 2¼ inch; these give excellent results, but are usually much more expensive. The 35 mm SLR cameras sold today are so good that buying a more expensive camera is not necessary to take good photographs.

Many cameras today are fully automatic, setting the shutter speed and aperture and even focusing for you. However, it is important that the camera have manual overrides, since the automatic setting may sometimes be inappropriate. For example, a white rose photographed in shade with an automatic setting might have a grayish or yellowish cast because the light meter inside the camera is fooled. To make the rose appear pure white, you must override the automatic feature and overexpose by ½ to 1 f-stop if you are using slide film; for print film, you would overexpose by the same amount. Similarly, in bright sun using slide film, the automatic features of the camera would likely overexpose a white or pale yellow rose and wash out its detail; with print film, the flower would also be overexposed. To compensate manually, you would underexpose by ½ to 1 f-stop for slide film and do the same for print film. Slides of close-ups of dark red roses are often better if slightly overexposed.

Basic equipment for rose photography includes a tripod, a cable release, a macro lens, a haze filter, lens tissue, assorted films, a gray card, and scissors to snip off dead blooms.

Many newer cameras have automatic focusing features. Although easy to use, cameras with these features sometimes do not focus on what you have chosen as the focal point of the photograph. It is thus important that these cameras, too, have a manual override.

Most SLR cameras come with a 50 mm lens (the measurement refers to the focal length), which is suitable for general landscape photography. To take close-ups, you will need a macro lens, which usually has a focal length of about 100 mm. (Telephoto lenses also have long focal lengths, but are not designed for close-up photography.) It is best to buy a lens of the same brand as your camera so that you will have no problem fitting it to the camera body. Also, there are other, less expensive accessories you can buy to take close-ups, including extension tubes, rings, and close-up lenses that fit over your regular lens. However, a macro lens is the easiest to use and produces the best photographs.

Many photographers use zoom lenses. With a zoom lens, you can change the focal length of the lens, thereby changing the subject's size and apparent distance in the viewfinder. Zoom lenses are useful when you need to eliminate a distracting background but are not willing or able to move closer to the subject. Zoom lenses also enable you to carry fewer lenses; lenses are heavy, and lugging a lot of them around can be backbreaking.

The choice of film is personal, so it is worth your while to experiment with several varieties. Each has a character of its own. Some, such as Kodak's Ektachrome, produce photographs with cool to neutral tones, whereas others, such as Kodachrome, Fujichrome, and Agfachrome, are comparatively warmer. However, Kodachrome uses a different processing system than the others mentioned, one that is not always available in remote areas or in "instant print" stores. In some circumstances your choice of film may also be influenced by the subject matter. For example, some lavender flowers are difficult to photograph because they come out looking pink. A film such as Ektachrome would be a good choice because it would not exaggerate the pink color.

All film is sold according to its sensitivity to light, which is indicated on the package by a number called the ISO rating (formerly the ASA rating). The more light-sensitive the film, the higher its ISO rating. A slow film—one that is relatively insensitive to light—typically has an ISO rating of between 25 and 100;

a medium-speed film has a rating between 100 and 400; and a fast film has a rating of 400 or higher.

Each film speed has its trade-offs. Slow films usually have less grain and greater color saturation, producing richer and more finely detailed photographs. Because of their comparative insensitivity to light, however, they must be used with slower shutter speeds. Unless the air is still and you are using a tripod, you risk taking pictures that are blurred by wind or camera movement. Also, slow films are less suitable when lighting is low, because they limit you to wider apertures and thus to shallower depths of field. They may even prevent you from taking pictures at all. The best compromise, especially for close-up photography, is medium-speed film with an ISO rating of 200. The grain and color saturation will be quite acceptable, and you can shoot at speeds fast enough to avoid the danger of wind or camera movement. You will also be able to use the aperture that gives you the best depth of field.

Another choice you must make is between slide film and print film. Most professionals use only slide film because slides have better color fidelity and are thus preferred by publications and agencies. Many photography contests also limit entries to slides, and you will need slides if you want to project your photographs for friends. Slides can always be made into prints if you wish to hang your best photos on the wall. The main advantage of print film over slide film is that print film is more forgiving of over- and underexposure.

Film also comes in varying lengths, typically 12, 24, or 36 exposures. If you expect to take many photos at one time, 36 exposure is best because it is more economical and needs to be changed less frequently. If you will be taking only a few photos, use smaller rolls so that the film does not sit in the camera too long before it is developed.

TECHNIQUES FOR GARDEN PHOTOGRAPHY

Good garden photography is the product of many factors, ranging from the condition of the plants to the quality of light and the presence of disturbing breezes. Good composition, in conjunction with fine control over focusing and depth of field, is what separates the good photos from the bad. With the proper techniques and equipment (and a little luck and practice), you can produce photographs good enough to hang on the wall.

The exquisite texture, form, and shadowing of roses make them glorious subjects for close-up photography. Taking good close-ups has its challenges, however. The slightest movement by the wind or an unsteady hand can produce blurred results. An unsteady hand can be remedied with a tripod, but there is little you can do about the wind except wait until it stops. A limited solution is to carry a large board to use as a windbreak, but this will not protect completely against stray gusts.

When purchasing a tripod, choose one that is sturdy, since one that is too flimsy can move in the wind. Almost every camera has a threaded hole at the bottom that lets you attach it to a bolt at the top of the

Lavender roses such as the floribunda 'Lilac Dawn' tend to photograph too pink because the film registers light frequencies that the eye cannot see.

tripod. Once it is attached, you can make the camera level by lengthening or shortening the tripod's legs. With practice, you'll learn to do this quickly; some tripods have a built-in level to assist you.

It's a good idea to use a cable release with a tripod. This is a length of flexible cable with a plunger at one end and a threaded shaft at the other end that attaches to the camera's shutter-release button. A cable release enables you to trip the shutter without touching the camera, thus preventing any camera movement. This is especially important when you are using slow shutter speeds.

If you do not have a tripod, you can keep the camera relatively stable by holding the camera body with your right hand and the lens with your left. Keep your elbows tucked against your body for additional stability. When you are ready to take the picture, hold your breath and slowly press and release the shutter button with your right index finger.

It is important to focus your picture so that its center of interest is sharp and clear. If you focus at a point about one third of the way into the field of view (whether you are taking landscape shots or close-ups), your entire photograph should be in focus—unless, of course, you are using an aperture that gives you only a limited depth of field. Before taking the picture, you can test the depth of field by depressing the preview button, which exists in some form on most SLR cameras. This shows you precisely what will be in focus at the selected aperture.

Most of the time it is best to take pictures using as small an aperture as your exposure will allow, so that as much of the photograph will be in focus as possible. But there are times when a wider aperture, with a shallower depth of field, can prove useful. For example, you can place a rose in focus and the background out of focus so that the background will not be too distracting. Whenever possible, try to take close-up photos of roses at an *f*-stop of *f*/11 to *f*/16. This will normally keep an entire rose in focus while pleasantly blurring the background. Bear in mind, though, that these narrow apertures will require slower shutter speeds that may cause blurring if light is low or you are not using a tripod. (It is a rule of thumb that you need a tripod when shooting at speeds slower than $1/60$ of a second with 50 mm lenses, and $1/125$ of a second with 100 mm lenses.)

Many professional photographers carry paper, wood, or cloth backgrounds with them to block out distractions behind the rose, especially when taking close-ups. This is not necessary, but can be done if you choose. Velvet is the best background material because it does not reflect light. Choose a color that harmonizes with that of the rose and with the effect you wish to achieve.

When taking pictures, most professional photographers use a technique called bracketing. They take a photo at 1 *f*-stop below the setting recommended by their light meter, another at the recommended setting, and then another at $1/2$ to 1 *f*-stop above the meter reading. That way, they are assured of at least one correct exposure.

Many professional photographers also use various filters to obtain special effects. Available at camera stores, these either screw onto the camera lens or fit over it in a holder. Filters can soften light or change its color. For landscape shots, there are filters with blue tops and clear bottoms that darken the sky without altering the rest of the subject. There are also filters that simulate sunsets. Other filters put a background around the subject, such as a colored heart or circle, or add interesting visual effects, such as starbursts or multiple images.

Timing is important. Most professional photographers like to work before 10 A.M. and after 2 P.M., because bright midday sun gives off flat light and causes harsh shadows. If you must work at midday,

you can fill in shadow areas with a reflector (available at camera stores) placed above or at the side of the rose where it will reflect light onto the plant. Another alternative is to use a flash, which will also eliminate shadows. A piece of thin white cloth or translucent plastic, placed between the sun and the subject, will soften the light. Called a diffuser, this can be purchased at a camera store or made at home by stretching the material over a wooden frame. If you photograph on a bright, overcast day, you can take excellent pictures all day without harsh light or shadows to worry about.

To deepen color saturation and to prevent stray light from entering the lens, especially in the bright sun, always use a lens hood. This can be a flexible rubber ring that screws onto the end of the lens to shade it from the sun, or a rigid piece of metal or plastic that extends from and encircles the lens; you should purchase one when you buy your camera and lens.

If you take photos very early in the morning or very late in the afternoon, you will find that the color in the photographs is not the same as your eye perceived it. This is especially dramatic in the afternoon, when orange and red tones increase. Of course, this can work to your advantage if you want to increase the amount of red and orange in your pictures.

Most instruction books tell you to take photographs with the sun at your back. However, you can take some very interesting pictures with the sun hitting the flower from the side or even from behind, making the petals appear almost translucent. This technique works best with light-colored flowers.

When composing a close-up photograph, look carefully through the viewfinder. Try to fill the frame with the flower without cutting off any of the petal edges. Sometimes a horizontal photo will accomplish this better, whereas at other times the photo should be vertical. After you have composed the picture, look all around in the viewfinder to make sure there are no distractions in the background. This is important when taking garden shots too. Look carefully for trash cans, garden hoses, and other unsightly objects that you may not have noticed when you were studying the roses.

When taking a landscape shot, mentally divide the photo into thirds, both horizontally and vertically. Your focal point should be at any of the places where the lines intersect. This will make your photograph more pleasing, and will give it greater impact, than if its focal point is centered.

Photographs of gardens are also more attractive if the scene is framed by a tree, bench, or other garden feature. Photographing a row of rosebushes at an angle rather than straight on leads the viewer into the photo and gives a more three-dimensional effect. If a garden contains many red flowers, underexpose it by ½ to 1 *f*-stop or the red flowers will stand out like beacons rather than blend with the landscape. This is the reverse of the advice about taking close-up slides of red roses, which should be overexposed so that they are not too dark.

The best time to photograph a rose close up is when it has reached the stage of development that would win it a ribbon at a rose show. For example, a hybrid tea

The red and orange tones of late afternoon distort rose colors but can lend drama to a photograph.

223

looks best when it is one-half to three-quarters open, with petals arranged symmetrically around the center and the central stamens not visible. The flower should otherwise be as perfect as possible, with ideal color, substance, stem and foliage, balance, and size. For details, see the discussion of judging criteria on page 201. You can groom the roses you photograph just as you would roses to be entered in a show. Before you snap the picture, clean any dirty foliage, remove ripped petals, and shape the rose gently with your fingers if it is not as good as it could be.

As you take photographs and experiment with films, shutter speeds, and apertures, make note of the combinations you try. That way you can learn what works best for you.

If you wish to frame your prints, you can take them to a professional framer or frame them yourself. Art supply stores sell mats in a variety of colors, which can be used as a border for the photo before it is framed; choose one in a color that complements that of the flower, if you wish. Art supply stores also sell spray adhesive, which is the easiest way to attach the photo to the mat or background. You can also buy cardboard with adhesive already applied to it for mounting photographs. It is not necessary to have glass in front of a photo, but if you do want a frame with glass, choose a nonglare glass to prevent distracting reflection.

FESTIVALS OF ROSES

*T*he love of roses has led many groups and communities to organize festivals around this most beautiful of flowers. Everyone from avid rose growers to apartment dwellers who have never gardened can enjoy these exuberant festivities. If you cannot attend in person, you can likely view one or more of them on television.

Perhaps the best-known North American rose revelry is the Rose Bowl parade, more properly called the Tournament of Roses parade. Each year, in the early morning hours of New Year's Day, tens of thousands of people line the streets of Pasadena, California, to view the parade that precedes the football game. The Tournament of Roses is said to be the largest floral extravaganza in the world. Along with marching bands, equestrians, and a beauty queen, the festival features some sixty floats, each of which must be covered with fresh flowers, including roses and other blooms—for a total of about twenty million blooms. Float builders have a special challenge, as they have only a short time to place the perishable flowers on the prebuilt floats.

In 1989 the pink-flowering grandiflora 'Tournament of Roses' was named in honor of the hundredth anniversary of the festival. An earlier tribute to the annual event was 'Rose Parade', a pink floribunda introduced in 1975 (but not readily available for sale).

The Portland Rose Festival Parade in Oregon is one of many grand events of the Portland Rose Festival, a civic celebration of the rose that takes place each June. Begun in 1907 as a three-day adjunct of the Portland Rose Society's annual rose show, it has grown into a seventeen-day extravaganza celebrating the place that calls itself The City of Roses. The parade of thirty flower-covered floats highlights a festival that includes street fairs, concerts, Indianapolis-style car racing, ski racing on nearby Mount Hood, an air show, hot-air ballooning, and visits from the U.S. and Canadian naval fleets, in addition to the rose show. One of Portland's biggest department stores devotes a large section to dresses made of rose-print fabrics, which are de rigueur for the festivities.

During the last week in April, another City of Roses—Thomasville, Georgia—sponsors its own annual Rose Festival. Begun in 1921 as a humble display of roses at a local department store, the festival now attracts more than sixty thousand visitors. Events include a rose show, floral parades, a circus, a clown contest, footraces, and tours of local antebellum mansions.

Most of the roses produced outdoors in the United States are grown in Texas, California, Arizona, and Oregon. Each fall, the capitals of the nation's two leading rose-producing areas—Wasco, California, and Tyler, Texas—celebrate roses with local festivals. Wasco's celebration, the Wasco Rose Festival, which takes place the weekend after Labor Day, features a parade, a beauty contest, a rose show, an art exhibit, a barbecue, and tours of the local rose fields by bus or plane. The Tyler Rose Festival, held during the second or third week in October, brings out the whole town to celebrate. Events include the Queen's Tea (an afternoon party feting the Rose Queen and her Court), an art show, tours of the Tyler rose garden, a rose show, and a parade. The selection of the Rose Queen and her Court and the parade that follows are the equivalent of a debutante ball, with the beautiful young women of Tyler bedecked in elaborate gowns. The city of Tyler is also completing plans for a rose museum to house artifacts relating to the history of the rose.

Perhaps the oldest American rose tradition dates back to the time of William Penn, whose family rented out parcels of land in what is now Pennsylvania for the annual fee of one red rose. For many years the Conard Pyle Company (which markets Star Roses) of West Grove, Pennsylvania, held an annual celebration known as Red Rose Rent Day, a gathering of amateur and professional rose growers who witnessed payment of the "rent" and the introduction of new rose varieties. The celebration was discontinued in 1985, but its many attendees remember it fondly.

The Tournament of Roses parade has taken place every January for more than a century. Today's extravagant motorized floats are a far cry from the simple rose-festooned carriages of 1891.

Tree roses for the commercial market grow in a California field.

CHAPTER EIGHT

CREATING AND MULTIPLYING ROSES

ave you ever wondered how the roses in your garden were created and marketed? Have you ever wanted to try your hand at hybridizing? As rose breeders are well aware, it is easy to produce a new variety but far more difficult to achieve real novelty. In these pages you will learn how professional hybridizers create new roses, and how you can experiment with this fascinating process.

*M*ost people who grow roses seldom stop to wonder where they came from; they are simply content to plant and enjoy them. But if you have been growing roses for a while, you may find that you are curious about how new roses are created, how they are named, and how they are grown for the market. You may even wish to try your hand at creating and multiplying roses of your own.

This chapter describes several methods of hybridizing and propagating roses for the home garden. It also takes you behind the scenes to learn how commercial growers create and produce roses in quantity. Lists of the best commercial roses follow, along with brief profiles of some of the outstanding hybridizers who created them.

HYBRIDIZING A NEW VARIETY

*P*eople who grow roses often try to produce their own varieties, even if just for the fun of it. Although professionals estimate that the chance of creating a rose with commercial value is about 1 in 10,000, amateurs often derive sufficient pleasure from trying; some have actually gone on to see their varieties marketed.

The creation of a new rose variety begins with hybridizing—fertilization of the female parts of one variety with the male pollen of another. Each seed produced by this union can grow into a plant resembling one or both of its parents, or possessing any combination of traits from its earlier ancestors. Because parent roses

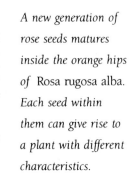

A new generation of rose seeds matures inside the orange hips of Rosa rugosa alba. *Each seed within them can give rise to a plant with different characteristics.*

may themselves be the products of complex hybridization, there are millions of potential variations.

Both amateur and professional breeders apply the same techniques to create a new rose; the professional, however, will take this work several steps further, undertaking field trials to establish a performance record before the new variety goes on the market. If you would like to experiment with hybridizing, you can do so with minimal effort and little in the way of equipment or materials. If you make your crosses outdoors in early summer, you will have seeds by fall for planting the following winter or spring. If you are lucky enough to have a greenhouse, you will be able to make crosses and start seeds throughout the year.

MAKING A SUCCESSFUL CROSS

Hybridizing roses is an unpredictable process. Because roses carry the genes for millions of traits—not all of which are expressed by the plant—it is impossible to tell in advance which set of traits a given offspring will manifest. A plant can exhibit the traits of one of its parents, both of them, neither of them, or a blending of the two. A dominant trait is one that will appear in offspring even if only one parent passes it on. A recessive trait is one that must come from both parents.

For example, fragrance seems to be a recessive trait (or possibly, some genes affecting fragrance are recessive). Thus a rose will be scented only if both of its parents have passed on the genes for fragrance. (The parents themselves need not be scented; they need only possess and transmit the fragrance genes.) The inheritance of color is more ambiguous. Two red roses crossed together usually produce red offspring; however, the color produced by crossing a red rose with a pink or yellow rose is anyone's guess. It

can be a blending of the parents' colors, or it may be a completely different color.

Botanists still do not know the exact mechanisms by which rose genes are inherited and expressed, nor the roles that many rose genes play. Until rose genetics is better understood, creating new roses with the desired characteristics will remain a matter of trial and error. Hybridizing today is as much a matter of throwing out combinations that don't work as it is fostering combinations that do.

Before making a cross, a hybridizer selects the parent plants, taking into account their color, form, hardiness, disease resistance, fragrance, and other characteristics. However, the presence of good traits in the parent plants is no guarantee that the offspring will exhibit

To prevent self-pollination, hybridizers have removed this rose's pollen-bearing male anthers before brushing its female stigmas with pollen from another plant.

them. Modern roses are of such complex and mixed ancestry that almost anything can happen—and usually does.

With experience, hybridizers learn that some varieties make good female parents, others make better male parents, and still others can be used as either mother or father. The same variety is rarely if ever used for both roles. After the parents are selected, the hybridizer removes the outer petals of the parent flowers in order to expose their reproductive organs.

To prevent self-pollination, which will interfere with the selected cross, the pollen-producing anthers are removed from the rose designated as the mother flower. This flower is then covered with a plastic bag to prevent cross-pollination by insects or the wind.

On the rose designated as the father, the stamens are picked off, labeled, and stored in an airtight container in a refrigerator. After about a day they release their pollen and can be discarded; the powdery yellow pollen remains in storage in the airtight container until it is used.

Top: Pollen is removed from flowers of the plant designated as the father.

Bottom: Selected pollen is brushed onto a flower of the mother plant, which is tagged to identify the cross.

About a day after the stamens have been removed from the female flower, a sticky substance appears on the stigma. This is the signal that the female is ready to receive pollen. The pollen of the selected male parent is then brushed onto the stigma with a fingertip or a small brush. A label detailing the parentage of the rose and the date of pollination is attached to the stem, and the pollinated flower is enclosed in a bag to protect it from further pollination. If fertilization occurs (it does not always happen), the ovary swells and the hip forms as the seeds develop. After the hip ripens in several months, it is harvested from the plant and its seeds are removed for germination. They can be planted right away, but more will germinate if you first subject them to the cold treatment known as stratification; see page 232 for instructions.

Owing to the permutations of heredity, the new plants that grow from these seeds are usually as different from their parents as they are from each other. The first flowers of these new plants appear within seven months to a year after the initial cross has been made. But since these early blooms are often slightly different in form from those of a mature plant, it is sometimes necessary to wait for several bloom cycles to determine whether a new rose has any potential.

If it does, an amateur hybridizer will either bud the variety or let it grow on its own roots. Professionals will bud every variety that looks promising for two reasons: to test whether the new rose can be budded successfully (a requirement for mass production) and to see how the rose grows and flowers after being budded, since budded roses may perform differently than those grown on their own roots. Successful crosses are selected for further testing.

Top: Applied to the stigma with a brush, dustlike pollen grains grow pollen tubes to fertilize ovules in the ovary.

Bottom: Seeds from a cross develop inside the ovary, which has swollen to form a hip. If spectacular, plants from one of these seeds could reach the market in 7 to 10 years.

Seeds within a rose hip can range in size and number, depending on the variety. This hip contains just a few large seeds.

STARTING ROSES FROM SEED

*I*f they are to enjoy the fruit of their hybridizing efforts, both amateur and professional breeders must be adept at growing seeds. Growing roses from seeds is not difficult and requires a minimum of equipment. This includes pots, sowing flats, and ideally a greenhouse or fluorescent lights, or both. If you do not own a greenhouse, you can grow seeds on a windowsill, under lights in the basement, or outdoors in containers or the ground.

About one year will have passed from the time a cross is made until the seedling of a new variety first blooms. This may seem like a long time, but for most growers the prospect of beholding a new and unusual variety makes the wait worthwhile.

To harvest the seeds from a rose plant, cut the hips from the plants when they are ready, wash them well, and cut them in half with a knife. The round to oval, slightly pointed white seeds, which are about ⅛ inch long, can then be easily removed. There may be 1 to 50 seeds in a hip. Next, wash the seeds in a kitchen strainer so that they will not go down the drain accidentally.

Although rose seeds can be sown as soon as they are harvested, germination is usually more successful if they are placed in the refrigerator in an airtight jar or plastic bag, between layers of moist sphagnum peat moss, moist paper toweling, or moist tissue, for six to eight weeks before sowing. This process, known as stratification, simulates the cold of a natural winter, priming the seeds to sprout. After the cold treatment, use tweezers to remove the seeds from the sphagnum peat moss or paper. Before sowing the seeds, you may wish to test them for viability, or the ability to germinate. To do this, place them in a container of water. Those that are not viable will float to the top and can be discarded.

Seedlings often succumb to a disease known as damping off, caused by one or more fungi that are present in most garden soils. Seedlings that have succumbed to damping off suddenly wilt and fall over soon after they have germinated. There is no cure for damping off, so prevention is the only remedy. Use a sterilized, soilless sowing mixture such as the ones recommended for indoor plants (see page 172).

Sow the seeds in a wide, shallow container filled with about 4 inches of medium, burying them ¼ inch deep. Rose seeds germinate best under greenhouse conditions; if you do not have a greenhouse, cover the seed flats with clear plastic or glass, or place the flat in a clear plastic bag, to keep the medium moist and the humidity high until the seeds germinate. If condensation forms on the glass or plastic, remove the glass or plastic for a few minutes to dry out the medium slightly and to prevent diseases. Rose seeds germinate best at temperatures between 50° and 55° F, but will germinate at temperatures as high as 60° F. Place the flats in bright light but not full sun for as many hours as possible, or keep them 6 to 10 inches below fluorescent lights that are kept on continuously until the seeds germinate.

Germination time can vary from three weeks to four months or longer. When you see short stems with two seed leaves called cotyledons, remove the plastic bag and move the containers into as many hours of full sun as you can provide, or under fluorescent lights. Follow the instructions for growing miniature roses under lights (see page 176).

After the seeds have germinated, check them every day to see if the medium is dry and if they need water. Avoid watering in any way that will dislodge or uproot young seedlings. A good method

is to use a very fine mist or spray, or to set the container in a tray of water and let it soak up moisture from the bottom. Once all the seedlings are growing, ensure steady growth by adding soluble fertilizer such as 20-20-20 or 15-30-15 to the irrigation water once a week at one quarter the recommended strength.

When seedlings have produced three sets of compound leaves, they're ready to transplant into individual pots. First, moisten the medium in the original container. Then fill 2-inch plastic or peat pots with moistened growing medium and make a hole the depth of the roots at the center of pot. The ideal tool for this is a probe known as a dibble (available at garden centers and greenhouse supply stores), but a pencil will also work. With a wooden plant label or a spoon handle, gently lift out the tiny plants, disturbing the roots as little as possible.

Holding the seedling by the leaves—never by the stem—lower it into the pot and firm gently around the roots. Continue to provide light, water, and fertilizer as before.

A more convenient alternative to sowing seeds in a large container is to plant them directly into individual 2-inch pots filled with growing medium. This saves a transplanting step and reduces the need to handle the delicate seedlings. It also usually produces larger plants by the end of the first year. When a plant is about 4 inches tall, transfer the entire soil ball to a 4-inch pot and fill the extra space with potting medium.

It is also possible to sow rose seeds directly into the garden. Prepare the soil as described in Chapter 4, and sow the seeds either in late fall or in early spring for germination in mid to late spring. The cold weather will not harm the seeds; in fact, it helps them germinate. Sow seeds ½ inch deep and 1 inch apart, in rows 2½ inches apart.

Make sure that the seed beds never dry out. Once the seeds have germinated, continue to water and start to administer light applications of soluble fertilizer such as 20-20-20 or 15-30-15, applied at one quarter the recommendations on the label once a week, until the plants produce their first blooms. The first flowers will appear by the time the seedling is 4 to 5 inches high, about six to eight weeks after germination. Don't be disappointed if the first flowers are not exciting; they are often not representative of mature blooms. After the plant has bloomed several times, you can decide whether you want to keep or discard it.

If a seedling shows promise—for example, if it is a color you like or has good flower form—it can be moved to a permanent place in the garden and either left to grow on its own roots or grafted to a more robust understock (see the next section). If practical, it's a good idea to let your rose grow from its own roots, for two reasons. First, own-root roses are never plagued by suckers that grow from the understock and steal the plant's energy. Second, vigorous and hardy varieties will often grow faster, bloom better, and survive winter more easily on their own roots than on the roots of an equally vigorous understock. On the other hand, roses that are tender or do not grow well on their own roots will thrive far better if budded. There's no reliable way to predict whether a newly hybridized variety will be hardy or vigorous. If you grow it on its own roots and it does not grow well, try budding it and see what happens.

PROPAGATING ROSE PLANTS BY BUDDING

*B*udding is the method of propagation most often used to reproduce large modern bush roses. Unlike propagation by seeds, this asexual method produces a plant identical to the parent. Many roses are difficult to grow from stem cuttings (another asexual method, described in the next section), and many that do take root from cuttings will not be as vigorous or as hardy as those that are budded.

Budding is a type of grafting in which a growth bud (sometimes called a bud eye) from the variety to be reproduced is joined together with roots of a different variety, known as an understock. In the process of budding, one bud is grafted to the main cane of the understock at a point just above the ground. Budding increases the vigor and hardiness of a variety, and is often the only reliable method of propagation. The only disadvantage of budding is that the process takes longer than rooting cuttings, requiring two years to produce a new plant.

Two major understocks—'Dr. Huey' and *Rosa multiflora*— are used in the United States because they thrive in the wide range of climates and soil conditions. Two other understocks occasionally used are *R. manettii* and *R.* × *odorata*.

'Dr. Huey' and *R. multiflora* are rarely grown in their own right. The flowers of 'Dr. Huey' are undistinguished, and *R. multiflora,* although it produces pretty flowers, grows so rank that most people consider it a weed. *R. manettii* is sometimes grown in gardens, although it is quite large and unruly, and *R.* × *odorata* is often seen in old-rose collections, as it is the original tea rose.

'Dr. Huey' grows best in the irrigated desert soils where most commercial roses are grown, and therefore is by far the most popular understock. Its pliable bark makes budding easier, and it forms a good union with nearly all varieties. It produces a strong, hardy root system that tends to refrain from producing suckers (unwanted shoots from underground portions of the plant). It also has fewer thorns than *R. multiflora,* making it easier to work with.

R. multiflora is vigorous and is the hardier understock. It grows as well in Minnesota as it does in Arizona, and almost all roses bud well to it. It is the second most popular understock, mainly because 'Dr. Huey' grows better in commercial fields in irrigated dry areas, where most of the country's roses are produced. *R. multiflora* is used extensively in areas with acid soil, such as Texas and Oregon. Its major disadvantages are that it is harder to work with and more prone to mite infestation.

R. manettii and *R. × odorata* are extremely tender plants and can be used as understock only where there is no frost during the winter. However, they are excellent understocks for greenhouse roses.

In Europe and Canada some rose producers use *R. canina* as an understock because of its extreme cold-hardiness. However, it forms a brittle bud union and tends to dwarf the variety budded to it.

Amateurs who want to bud their own plants can purchase understock from a few retail mail-order nurseries (see pages 340 and 341), or through a local rose society that can buy in quantity from a wholesale source. Once you have acquired understock, you can root it as you would any other rose (see the next section), and then either bud directly onto the rooted plants or save a plant or two to use as stock for future cuttings. If you don't wish to purchase understock, you can propagate it from any hardy, vigorous variety—preferably a species rose or other old garden rose—that you may have in the garden. It is also possible to collect and grow rose seeds from the wild.

A crop of 'Dr. Huey' understock will become the foundation for commercially budded roses. Understocks are chosen for their vigorous growth and the ease with which other varieties can be grafted to them.

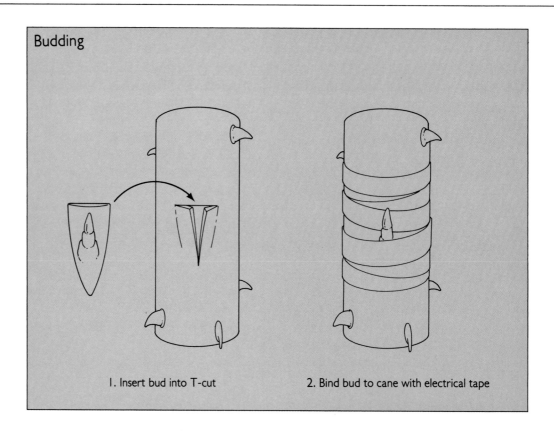

Budding

1. Insert bud into T-cut   2. Bind bud to cane with electrical tape

If understock is planted in the ground, leave about 12 inches between plants in rows 2 feet apart. Many backyard gardeners who like to bud roses find it is easier to grow the understock, do the budding, and grow the new plant to maturity in a container.

The best period for budding is from early to late summer, because the bud has time to "take" before cold weather. Before budding, be sure to water the understock thoroughly so that it will contain enough internal moisture to allow bark to pull away easily. To prepare the understock, make an inch-long vertical cut into the bark of the main cane at the base of the plant, cutting through to but not into the wood. You can use any small, sharp knife, or you can purchase a budding knife at a garden center. Then make a horizontal cut at the top of the vertical cut to create a T-shaped incision. The horizontal cut should reach about a third of the way around the cane. The bark should pull away from

the wood easily. If it does not, it may be too early in the season; wait a few weeks and try again on the same cane. (The first cut will gradually heal itself; no sealant is needed.)

To prepare the bud, select a stem on the plant to be budded (called the budwood) and, with a sharp knife, cut out a shield-shaped layer of stem containing a large bud. Cut through the bark and slightly into the wood, cutting from top to bottom and taking as thin a slice of wood as you can. The cut should extend from 1 inch above the bud to ½ inch below it, skirting the bud eye by about ⅛ to 3/16 inch on each side. Then take the bud (often called the shield) and insert it into the T-cut you made in the understock. If the shield is too long for this opening, trim the shield above the bud eye with scissors or a budding knife. Finally, bind the shield and understock together by wrapping electrical tape or a cut rubber band around the cane several times, leaving the bud eye exposed. Be sure to overlap the tape or rubber band to keep water from getting behind the shield. Keeping the soil moist after making the graft helps the bud unite with the understock.

The bud will lie dormant during the first season and will start to grow the following spring. When the bud starts to grow and a stem starts to develop, remove the tape or rubber band.

All the top growth of the understock should be cut away at this time, to a point just above where the bud has started to grow. Now, only the grafted variety will be making top growth on its new roots.

If budding has not been successful—that is, if the bud did not grow—the plant can be rebudded on the opposite side of the cane.

It often happens that unwanted shoots called suckers will develop from the understock below the bud union, the point at which the budded variety starts to grow. These shoots must be removed as soon as they appear, or the understock will eventually outgrow the plant that has been budded to it.

PROPAGATING ROSES FROM STEM CUTTINGS

One of the simplest techniques of propagating new roses is to cut off pieces of stem and plant them directly into a growing medium, where they will eventually take root. Commercial growers use stem cuttings primarily to multiply miniature and old garden roses, which take root readily by this method. However, some large modern bush roses, especially the larger and more vigorous varieties, can also be rooted from stem cuttings. Like budding, rooting stem cuttings is an asexual method of propagation that produces plants identical to the parent.

Rooting Stem Cuttings Indoors

1. Let top two 5-leaflet leaves remain; pull off lower leaves, being careful not to damage buds. Dip in root hormone stimulant.

2. Set cuttings into damp soil mix.

3. Seal in plastic bag until cutting is firmly rooted, about 5–8 weeks.

To take a stem cutting, use pruning shears to cut a 4- to 6-inch length of stem, making sure that the cutting has at least four five-leaflet leaves. Make the cut at a 45-degree angle, just above the highest leaf that will be left on the plant. It is sometimes possible to cut a longer stem and make two cuttings out of it, but the upper portion will usually root better.

The best time to take the cuttings is right after the flowers have faded, when the wood of the stem is neither too soft nor too hard and will thus take root readily. Remove the two lowest leaves from the cutting, and all its flowers and flower buds, and poke the cutting into a container of soilless medium. Make sure that the medium covers the two nodes from which leaves were removed. Use your fingers to firm the medium around the cutting.

Cuttings will root more quickly if you dust their bases with powdered rooting hormone before placing them in the medium. Rooting hormone is a powder available in packets or jars at garden centers. Cuttings that are started indoors will root faster if heated gently from the bottom. You can supply this warmth with a heating coil, a special electrical device sold at garden centers and through seed catalogs, or by placing the cuttings on top of a warm appliance.

If you are rooting cuttings in the house, place the container in a plastic bag and set it in bright light but not direct sun. Remove the plastic bag for a few minutes each day to circulate the air and prevent disease. After several weeks test the cutting for signs of root growth by tugging lightly at the stem. If it offers resistance, the cutting has rooted. Remove both the plastic bag and the source of heat. But if the cutting pulls out freely, replace the bag and wait several weeks more before testing the cutting again.

If you have access to a greenhouse, so much the better; its moist environment

Stem cuttings grow into new plants that are identical to the parent. Commercial growers use this method to propagate miniature and old garden roses, which can grow vigorously on their own roots.

is exactly what young cuttings need. You do not need to place them in plastic bags, but frequent misting helps them root more quickly.

Rose cuttings can also be rooted outdoors in beds of well-prepared soil, as long as the beds are not in full sun. Prepare the cuttings as you would for rooting in containers, and keep the air around them moist until they take root. You can do this by daily misting or by covering plants with plastic film stretched over a frame or glass jars. The plastic or glass will retain much of the soil moisture, but check for dryness and add water as soon as the ground starts to dry out. Test the cuttings for rooting as described above; when rooting is complete, remove the plastic or glass. Apply extra winter protection to get the plants through the first winter (see page 154), because young rooted cuttings are more vulnerable to the cold than mature plants. Cuttings can be moved to their permanent positions the following spring.

GROWING NEW PLANTS BY LAYERING

*L*ayering is a method of asexual propagation in which the stems of roses with supple canes are buried underground until new roots grow from them; these canes are then severed from the parent plant. To propagate a plant by layering, choose one whose canes can be bent over to the ground—these will be primarily climbers or some of the old garden roses. Select a cane and mark a point about a foot in from the end, and notice where this point falls when you bend the cane to the ground. Here is where you will encourage the new roots to grow. Improve the soil in this area as if you were planting a new rose.

Next, just above a growth bud near the marked point on the cane, make a slanting cut halfway into the underside of the cane. Place a small piece of wood such as a toothpick or a matchstick into the cut to wedge it open. Apply rooting hormone to the cut, and remove any adjacent leaves. With a wire or a stick, firmly anchor the cut section of cane under about 3 inches of prepared soil, then cover the area with a mound of soil 4 inches high. Both ends of the cane should protrude from the mound. Keep the area moist until new roots grow. The time this takes depends on the variety of rose, but you can expect that a cane layered this summer will be ready to sever from the parent plant by the following summer.

When new growth appears at the end of the cane, dig gently under the soil to see whether roots are growing. If they are, cut the new plant free with pruning shears and transplant it.

REPRODUCING ROSES BY DIVISION

*D*ivision is the least popular method of reproducing roses, because it cannot be accomplished with budded varieties. However, it can be done with any rose that is growing on its own roots. A rose is divided by cutting it in half lengthwise, thus making two plants from one. Division can also be used to thin old, overgrown plants. Roses should be divided in early spring or late fall when the plants are dormant; in warm climates plants should be divided in winter.

To divide a rosebush, carefully dig it from the ground after a thorough watering and examine it closely for a logical place to make the division. The goal is to split the plant lengthwise so that each half will have an equal number of canes

Tree roses take longer to mass-produce than bush roses because they involve two grafts: one to join the understock to a long stem, and another to graft the desired variety to the top.

and roots. With a sharp knife or a pruning saw, carefully sever the plant in half by cutting through its crown. Then brush on tree wound paint or orange shellac over the exposed areas. Tree wound paints are available at garden centers, orange shellac at hardware stores. You can replant the two divisions as soon as the sealant has dried.

COMMERCIAL PRODUCTION OF ROSES

As they browse through a rose catalog or visit a garden center, most people are unaware of the route these plants have taken to reach the market. Seeing apparently lifeless bundles of roots and canes, they may wonder why the roses have such exorbitant price tags. However, once they realize how much

time and expense are involved in producing roses commercially, they have a better appreciation of their new treasures. Knowing how the professionals produce plants is also instructive to amateurs who wish to propagate roses of their own.

A new rose hybrid passes through four phases of development before it reaches the market: field testing and stock buildup; naming; registration and patenting; and mass production. In addition, some nurseries test the market further by distributing new roses to amateur gardeners for evaluation. Once the new variety is ready for the market, advertising and distribution follow.

TESTING AND STOCK BUILDUP

For the professional rose grower, the first step after hybridizing is field testing and evaluation. Of the 100,000 different seedlings a professional may have hybridized in a year, only a thousand of the best varieties may be budded for field testing. After these have been evaluated, the best 50 to 100 varieties are chosen for further trials. This culling continues for at least two to four more years, after which one or two varieties might be commercially introduced.

Once a new variety has been selected for introduction, the next step is to build up enough plants for the market. This process may take as long as four years. In the first year, budwood from each plant remaining from the evaluation process will provide enough bud eyes to propagate 10 more plants. By the second year, the original plants will have grown larger, producing enough bud eyes for 20 plants. Their first offspring will each propagate 10 more plants. As the original plants grow in size, they can be counted on to produce enough bud eyes for 40 to 50 more plants, and each successive year their offspring will be able to produce more and more bud eyes. A large rose producer strives to have enough bud eyes to propagate 250,000 plants before introducing a new variety.

All told, the progress of a new rose from hybridization to market may take 7 to 10 years. Miniature roses take less time because they bloom and grow faster, and because they don't need to be budded; but the procedure is similarly demanding.

Any amateur rose grower who thinks he or she has a rose worthy of introduction should contact one or more of the large rose nurseries for evaluation. It has happened more than once that an amateur has been very successful in bringing a new rose to market.

HOW ROSES ARE NAMED

Once a new variety has been selected for marketing, and while the stock is being built up, an important next step is to give it a name. Because roses are sold in the dormant state when little about them looks appealing, a colorful name can make the difference between brisk sales and oblivion. For example, after the Jackson and Perkins Company first introduced the hybrid tea 'Jadis', it sold poorly and was dropped from sale. About 15 years later it was renamed 'Fragrant Memory' and returned to the marketplace, where it is now selling better. The hybrid perpetual 'American Beauty', a famous greenhouse variety, languished in obscurity until its original name, 'Madame Ferdinand Jamin', was given a patriotic replacement.

Most rose names fall into one of four categories, referred to by the trade as descriptive, complimentary, commemorative, and commercial. A descriptive name is apt, witty, or evocative, relating to some quality of the rose. Many descriptive names arise straightforwardly from the rose's color, scent, or form; for example, 'Crimson Glory' (a velvety red rose) and 'Dainty Bess' (a delicate five-petaled rose). Other names refer to these

Miniature roses grow outdoors under shade cloth at a California rose nursery. Because they do not need to be budded, they take less time to mass-produce than bush roses.

Deane', for the doctor who removed his tonsils.

Commemorative roses celebrate famous events. Examples are 'Sutter's Gold', commemorating the hundredth anniversary of the discovery of gold at Sutter's Mill in California; 'Diamond Jubilee', toasting Jackson and Perkins's seventy-fifth anniversary; and 'Tournament of Roses', celebrating the annual parade. Others, such as 'New Yorker' and 'Shreveport', honor cities. A number of commemorative roses are named for holidays, such as 'White Christmas' and 'Easter Morning'.

Commercial rose names are paid for by various companies as a form of self-promotion—a practice that is now more common in Europe than in the United States. Past examples are 'Daily Sketch' (a former London newspaper), 'Silent Night' (a British mattress company), and 'Chrysler Imperial' (an American car model). Some European commercial names that are unfamiliar to Americans have been changed when the roses were introduced in the United States.

Sometimes breeders nickname their roses as they evaluate them, and the names stick. A few of these are 'Eiffel Tower', 'Matterhorn', and 'Duet'.

REGISTRATION AND PATENTING

While stock is building up and marketing plans are being drawn, the nursery does the paperwork to establish the rose as a commercial property. Although it is not a requirement, most hybridizers register their variety names with the International Registration Authority for Roses (IRAR), which is administered internationally by the American Rose Society. Registration was introduced to eliminate the giving of many names to the same rose—a practice that once confounded rose buyers. To be accepted for registration, a name must not be in use by another registered

The hybridizer of 'Chrysler Imperial', a 1952 hybrid tea, received a free automobile in return for helping to promote the car line.

attributes indirectly—for example, 'Olé' (a ruffled orange-red) and 'Arizona' (a blend of desert-sunset colors).

Complimentary names honor prominent people in show business, the arts, politics, society, or the rose world itself. Others are named for people who are significant only to the namer of the rose. For example, well-known hybridizer Sam McGredy IV named a rose, 'Hector

rose unless it can be proved that the older variety has become extinct. This is difficult to do, since no one knows with certainty which older varieties are still growing in private gardens. Hybridizers make a point of registering their most promising new varieties, because a rose must be registered in order to be exhibited at rose shows.

In addition to registration with the IRAR, some variety names are trademarked. This practice is required in some foreign countries but not in the United States, although some U.S. growers do so anyway. Registering a name as a trademark legally precludes others from using it.

When hybridizers wish to protect the plant itself from unauthorized reproduction and sale, they go to the effort of obtaining a patent. A patent gives patent holders sole rights over the variety for 17 years, during which they are entitled to royalties on every rose of this variety that is sold.

The first step in patenting a rose is to obtain an application from the U.S. Patent and Trademark Office in Washington, D.C. On the application the patent seeker must state the name of the new variety and describe it completely enough to distinguish it from its ancestors and from all other known varieties. The patent seeker must also submit color photographs of the plant and declare that he or she did in fact hybridize it. There is also a substantial filing fee. It is also possible to patent a sport, or mutation, that has been discovered; in addition to supplying the information mentioned above, the patent seeker must describe the location and environment where the sport was found.

It is possible to patent a rose yourself, but far easier to do so with the help of a patent attorney. However, you would undoubtedly not want to invest the time and expense to obtain a patent unless the variety showed strong commercial promise.

MASS-PRODUCING BUDDED ROSES

Commercial rose growers harvest some fifty million modern bush roses and climbers each year from tens of thousands of acres of fields, primarily in Texas, California, Arizona, and Oregon. Production of these plants is a labor-intensive, multistep process that takes two years.

A budded rose crop starts with the propagation and growth of the understock. In the fall cuttings of understock are taken from stock plants or from the top growth of previously budded plants, and prepared for rooting. During the preparation process, 9-inch lengths of stem are cut from the understock plants and all but the top two or three buds are removed. Doing this helps discourage the understock from developing suckers after it has been budded.

In early winter cuttings are planted into the fields where the budded varieties will be produced. Typically, the plants are set 3 inches into the soil with about 9 inches between plants, in rows that are 4 feet apart. Often, a piece of black plastic is first laid along each row and the cuttings are planted into holes in the plastic; this helps keep weeds from sprouting and holds moisture in the soil. Over the late winter and early spring, the cuttings take root and start to grow vigorously.

Depending on the location and climate, the grower chooses either R. multiflora or 'Dr. Huey' as the understock. Occasionally a producer will bud to understock of R. multiflora that has been grown from seeds instead of from cuttings. ('Dr. Huey' cannot be propagated from seeds.) The reason is that viruses are freely transmitted to the budded varieties through cuttings; viruses, however, are not present in seeds. It is not a common commercial practice, since it takes much longer to grow understock from seeds

Left: Budwood is harvested for grafting.

Right: Lengths of budwood are deleafed (top) and dethorned (bottom).

than from cuttings, and because it does not produce as good a root system. Nevertheless, many amateurs opt for this method to deter viruses.

While the understock is being readied, the budwood (cuttings from which buds will be taken) is harvested and prepared, and buds cut from it for future insertion into the understock. First, budwood is cut from stock plants during the fall in 10- to 12-inch lengths, wrapped in wet burlap, and placed in a cool room where workers remove the thorns and the foliage. The budwood is then dipped in fungicide,

wrapped in wet newspaper, and wrapped again in dry newspaper and plastic. After being labeled with the variety names, the budwood is stored in a refrigerated room at 28° to 30° F until early the following summer. The budwood is then removed from storage and the buds are cut from it. Amateurs who cut budwood in the fall can also use this method of storage.

Diseases of understocks and budwood in the rose fields are kept to a minimum by practicing good sanitation in the cutting room. Knives, saws, benches, and even the floor are washed several times

A shield-shaped cutting from a length of budwood has been inserted into a T-shaped cut in the understock.

A newly inserted bud is wrapped and tied.

daily with a formaldehyde solution that reduces transmission of crown gall, a bacterial disease. (Amateur rose growers who do not wish to use formaldehyde can disinfect with a 10 percent bleach solution.) Since most root stocks have been grown in a fungus-free setting, the only remaining worry is viruses. Professional growers use a heat treatment known as virus-indexing to produce virus-free understocks.

The actual budding begins during the first summer. It is accomplished by a two-member team—one member who makes a T-shaped cut on each plant and inserts the bud to be grafted, and another who ties the bud firmly in place. A good team can bud 3,000 to 5,000 plants per day. After budding, the top of the understock plant continues to grow, storing food in the root system. In warm areas buds are left exposed over the winter, but in colder climates the grafts are covered with soil to prevent winter damage.

Buds usually start to grow vigorously at the beginning of the second season, at which time all of the top growth of the understock is removed. To accomplish

The tops of year-old grafted roses are cut off to obtain stems for further budding.

this quickly some commercial growers use a type of mower that grinds or chops the tops and throws them to the ground to function as a mulch. The mower cuts 6 inches above the bud, and the rest of the top growth is then pruned away by hand. Other commercial growers remove the tops of the understock plants completely by hand.

The budded portion of the plant continues to grow energetically. During the summer months, the newly grown canes are pruned to prevent their tops from breaking off and to encourage them to branch. Plants also receive water, fertilizer, and protection against insects and diseases.

All roses are harvested in the fall. In some areas of the country, the leaves fall off naturally; in others, they are removed after harvesting. Digging is done by a machine with a large U-shaped blade that cuts at the required depth, loosens the soil, and lifts the plants out of the ground.

Teams of workers follow the digging machine to pick up and bundle roses for delivery to cold storage.

At the cold storage facility, the roses are placed onto a conveyor belt where they pass before workers who grade them, label them, and tie them into bundles, usually of 10 plants. After bundling, the tops of the canes are cut to a uniform length with a band saw. Roses are then placed into bins and stored in warehouses that are held at 32° to 40° F and kept very humid. At a major facility, approximately 140,000 rosebushes may be processed, graded, pruned, labeled, tied, and stored in one day. The plants remain in cold storage through the fall and winter until shipping begins in the winter or spring.

The finished product is processed and delivered in one of several ways. Roses destined for sale as bare-root stock have their roots wrapped in moist sphagnum peat moss and plastic and are shipped directly to mail-order customers; a lesser number are sent to garden centers for sale. Roses that will be sold in containers are planted into boxes and shipped, mainly to garden centers. Although some other shrubs are produced as balled-and-burlapped plants, this method is rarely if ever used for roses.

Tree roses are complicated and time consuming to produce, requiring two budding operations and a three-year growth period, which makes them more costly than bush roses. Onto a root of the same type of understock used for bush roses, growers bud a stem of *R. multiflora, R. rugosa,* or 'De la Grifferaie' (a robust variety of uncertain parentage that is believed to be a *R. mutiflora* hybrid). These roses are used because they make strong, straight stems. Then stock from the variety that will produce the flowers is budded onto the top of the stem; this stock can be from any variety of bush rose. To harvest tree roses, growers use a special high tractor that can pass over the plants as it digs the roots. These plants are stored, shipped, and sold in the same manner as bush roses.

Although most large modern rosebushes are currently propagated by budding, commercial growers hope to turn increasingly to cuttings and tissue culture (cloning of new plants from small pieces of plant tissue) for mass production. Propagation from cuttings is less laborious than budding, and tissue culture can yield more disease-free plants. For the moment, though, more research must be done before these methods can become economical.

MASS-PRODUCING OWN-ROOT ROSES

Each year millions of miniature and old garden roses are propagated in fields and greenhouses throughout the country. These operations range from small "mom-and-pop" operations to large greenhouse production facilities.

Miniature roses are almost always grown from cuttings because they root easily, and because they are cold hardy and vigorous enough that they do not need to be budded. Most are commercially produced in greenhouses, because of the small size of the plants and because production can be a year-round effort. A smaller number are grown in fields and are harvested, stored, shipped, and sold by the same methods as larger roses.

Old garden roses and species roses are grown mostly by small specialty growers because the demand for these roses is limited. They are usually grown in fields, from plants that have been propagated from stem cuttings rather than by budding. These plants root readily and most are hardy and vigorous enough that they do not benefit from being budded. They are harvested after a one- or two-year growing period and processed and stored like any other rose. Most of these roses are sold through mail-order nurseries.

Rose of the Year

Each year since 1959, the Jackson and Perkins Company, the largest rose nursery in the United States, selects the most outstanding of its new varieties as Rose of the Year. Some of these have been products of Jackson and Perkins's American hybridizers, whereas others are outstanding new roses from Europe. To date, all have been hybrid teas. (The winners for 1964, 1966, 1971, 1972, and 1975 are not listed because they are no longer commercially available. There were two winners for 1984.)

Variety	Color	Year of Award
Kordes' Perfecta	Ivory and red	1959
Hawaii	Orange-coral	1960
Americana	Medium red	1961
South Seas	Coral-pink	1962
Tropicana	Orange-red	1963
Polynesian Sunset	Coral-orange	1965
Valencia	Apricot-orange	1967
Fragrant Cloud	Coral-red	1968
Proud Land	Dark red	1969
Irish Gold	Pale yellow	1970
Medallion	Apricot and buff	1973
Red Masterpiece	Dark red	1974
Promise	Light pink	1976
New Day	Rich yellow	1977
Pristine	White and pink	1978
American Pride	Dark red	1979
Honor	White	1980
Madras	Rose and cerise	1981
Fascination	Pink blend	1982
Tribute	Cerise	1983
Sunbright	Yellow	1984
Grand Masterpiece	Medium red	1984
Milestone	Orange and red blend	1985
Headliner	Red and white	1986
Summer Dream	Shell pink	1987
American Spirit	Bright red	1988
Graceland	Yellow	1989
White Delight	Ivory and pink	1990
Dynasty	Orange and yellow	1991
Unforgettable	Pink	1992

AWARDS FOR OUTSTANDING ROSES

*A*ll rose hybrids are not created equal. Some have lovely flowers but succumb easily to cold or diseases. Others are vigorous but have lackluster growth habits or uninspiring blooms. To assist consumers in selecting the best varieties, rose growers present a number of annual awards. You'll often see these awards referred to in catalog descriptions of roses.

The following are lists of recipients of the major awards given to roses in the United States. Listings are current as of mid-1991. Some of these roses were hybridized by U.S. plant breeders, others by foreign breeders. Note that these lists include only roses that are commercially available; excellent varieties of older roses still exist, but may no longer be sold. Among the roses that are listed, some are not widely available; they are thus not included in the plant descriptions in Chapter 10.

When looking through rose catalogs, you will often see references to awards from other countries. These include the Bagatelle Gold Medal (France), the Geneva Gold Medal (Switzerland), the Royal National Rose Society Gold Medal (Great Britain), the Rome Gold Medal (Italy), the Madrid Gold Medal (Spain), and The Hague Gold Medal and Golden Rose (the Netherlands). Many of these European winners are available in the United States. Foreign awards reflect some specialized adaptations that American rose growers might find useful. For example, winners of the Royal National Rose Society Gold Medal would probably grow well in the Pacific Northwest, whose climate is close to that of England; but these same roses might not grow very well in the Deep South.

The prestigious All-America Rose Selections award honors the year's best introductions. The grandiflora 'New Year' was one of three winners for 1987.

James Alexander Gamble Fragrance Medal

The American Rose Society awards this medal to outstanding varieties of fragrant roses. Here is a list of winners since the award began in 1961; awards are not given every year.

Variety	Class	Color	Year of Award
Crimson Glory	Hybrid tea	Crimson-red	1961
Tiffany	Hybrid tea	Light pink	1962
Chrysler Imperial	Hybrid tea	Crimson-red	1965
Sutter's Gold	Hybrid tea	Golden yellow	1966
Granada	Hybrid tea	Red and yellow	1968
Fragrant Cloud	Hybrid tea	Orange-red	1970
Papa Meilland	Hybrid tea	Deep red	1974
Sunsprite	Floribunda	Bright yellow	1979
Double Delight	Hybrid tea	Red and white	1986

All-America Rose Selections

All-America Rose Selections, Inc. (AARS) is an association of U.S. rose producers who evaluate new varieties and lend their stamp of approval to the most worthy ones. The organization was founded in 1938 to guide amateur gardeners to the best of the many new varieties introduced each year. The first awards were made in 1940, but these older varieties are no longer commercially available. AARS does not market roses directly; rather, its member firms sell the winning varieties to the public

and pay an assessment fee back to AARS for every plant sold. Although AARS cooperates with the American Rose Society, there is no official link between them. Most rose growers regard the AARS designation as the highest honor a rose can win.

To evaluate a new variety, the AARS tests sample plants for a two-year period at 26 locations throughout the country. The locations are chosen to represent a wide range of soils and climates. Four times during the evaluation period, roses are

scored in a number of categories including vigor, growth habit, hardiness, disease resistance, foliage, flower production, bud and flower form, opening and finishing color, fragrance, stem strength, overall value, and novelty. After the test period, the scores are compiled and the selections made.

The following roses have been designated as worthy of the AARS award. You will find that most are rated highly by the American Rose Society as well.

Variety	Class, Color	Year of Award	Variety	Class, Color	Year of Award
Charlotte Armstrong	HT, Cerise	1941	Fire King	F, Vermillion	1960
Fred Edmunds	HT, Apricot	1944	Garden Party	HT, White	1960
Lowell Thomas	HT, Butter yellow	1944	Sarabande	F, Scarlet-orange	1960
Floradora	F, Salmon-rose	1945	Duet	HT, Salmon-pink	1961
Mirandy	HT, Crimson-red	1945	Pink Parfait	Gr, Light pink	1961
Peace	HT, Pale gold	1946	Christian Dior	HT, Crimson-scarlet	1962
Rubaiyat	HT, Cerise	1947	Golden Slippers	F, Orange-gold	1962
Diamond Jubilee	HT, Buff	1948	John S. Armstrong	Gr, Deep red	1962
High Noon	Cl HT, Yellow	1948	King's Ransom	HT, Chrome yellow	1962
Nocturne	HT, Dark red	1948	Royal Highness	HT, Clear pink	1963
Pinkie	F, Light rose pink	1948	Tropicana	HT, Orange-red	1963
Forty-niner	HT, Red and yellow	1949	Granada	HT, Red and yellow	1964
Fashion	F, Coral-pink	1950	Saratoga	F, White	1964
Sutter's Gold	HT, Golden yellow	1950	Camelot	Gr, Shrimp pink	1965
Helen Traubel	HT, Apricot-pink	1952	Mister Lincoln	HT, Deep red	1965
Vogue	F, Cherry coral	1952	American Heritage	HT, Ivory and carmine	1966
Chrysler Imperial	HT, Crimson-red	1953	Apricot Nectar	F, Apricot	1966
Ma Perkins	F, Coral-pink	1953	Matterhorn	HT, White	1966
Mojave	HT, Apricot-orange	1954	Bewitched	HT, Clear Pink	1967
Jiminy Cricket	F, Coral-orange	1955	Gay Princess	F, Shell pink	1967
Queen Elizabeth	Gr, Clear pink	1955	Lucky Lady	Gr, Shrimp pink	1967
Tiffany	HT, Light pink	1955	Roman Holiday	F, Orange-red	1967
Circus	F, Yellow and red	1956	Europeana	F, Red	1968
Golden Showers	Cl, Daffodil yellow	1957	Miss All-American Beauty	HT, Pink	1968
Gold Cup	F, Golden yellow	1958			
White Knight	HT, White	1958	Scarlet Knight	Gr, Scarlet-red	1968
Ivory Fashion	F, Ivory	1959	Angel Face	F, Lavender	1969

All-America Rose Selections (*continued*)

Variety	Class, Color	Year of Award	Variety	Class, Color	Year of Award
Comanche	Gr, Scarlet-orange	1969	Brandy	HT, Golden apricot	1982
Gene Boerner	F, Pink	1969	French Lace	F, Ivory	1982
Pascali	HT, White	1969	Mon Cheri	HT, Pink and red	1982
First Prize	HT, Pink blend	1970	Shreveport	Gr, Orange blend	1982
Aquarius	Gr, Pink blend	1971	Sun Flare	F, Bright yellow	1983
Command Performance	HT, Orange-red	1971	Sweet Surrender	HT, Silvery pink	1983
			Impatient	F, Orange-red	1984
Redgold	F, Red and yellow	1971	Intrigue	F, Deep plum	1984
Apollo	HT, Sunrise yellow	1972	Olympiad	HT, Clear crimson	1984
Portrait	HT, Pink	1972	Showbiz	F, Scarlet	1985
Electron	HT, Rose-pink	1973	Broadway	HT, Red, pink, and yellow	1986
Gypsy	HT, Orange-red	1973			
Medallion	HT, Apricot-pink	1973	Touch of Class	HT, Coral-pink and cream	1986
Bahia	F, Orange-pink	1974			
Bon-Bon	F, Pink and white	1974	Voodoo	HT, Yellow, orange, and red	1986
Perfume Delight	HT, Clear pink	1974			
Arizona	Gr, Bronze and copper	1975	Bonica '82	S, Pink	1987
			New Year	Gr, Tangerine	1987
Oregold	HT, Yellow	1975	Sheer Bliss	HT, White and pink	1987
Rose Parade	F, Pink	1975	Amber Queen	F, Apricot	1988
America	Cl, Salmon	1976	Mikado	HT, Red, pink, and yellow	1988
Cathedral	F, Golden apricot	1976			
Seashell	HT, Peach and salmon	1976	Prima Donna	Gr, Deep pink	1988
Yankee Doodle	HT, Sherbet orange	1976	Class Act	F, White	1989
Double Delight	HT, Red and white	1977	Debut	Min, Red and white	1989
First Edition	F, Coral	1977	New Beginning	Min, Orange and yellow	1989
Prominent	Gr, Hot orange	1977			
Charisma	F, Red and yellow	1978	Tournament of Roses	Gr, Coral-pink	1989
Color Magic	HT, Coral blend	1978	Pleasure	F, Coral-pink	1990
Friendship	HT, Pink	1979	Carefree Wonder	S, Pink and cream	1991
Paradise	HT, Lavender	1979	Perfect Moment	HT, Yellow and red	1991
Sundowner	Gr, Orange	1979	Sheer Elegance	HT, Pink and salmon	1991
Love	Gr, Red and white	1980	Shining Hour	Gr, Yellow	1991
Honor	HT, White	1980	All That Jazz	S, Coral-salmon	1992
Cherish	F, Shell pink	1980	Brigadoon	HT, Coral-pink and cream	1992
Bing Crosby	HT, Orange	1981			
Marina	F, Coral-orange	1981	Pride 'n' Joy	Min, Orange and yellow	1992
White Lightnin'	Gr, White	1981			

HT = Hybrid tea, F = Floribunda, Gr = Grandiflora, Cl = Climber, Cl HT = Climbing hybrid tea, S = Shrub, Min = Miniature

American Rose Society Award of Excellence

Since 1975 the American Rose Society has administered a testing program for miniature roses at six locations across the country. The most outstanding entries receive the ARS Award of Excellence. Here is a list of the winners to date.

Variety	Color	Year of Award	Variety	Color	Year of Award
Beauty Secret	Medium red	1975	Cupcake	Clear pink	1983
Judy Fischer	Rosy pink	1975	Hombre	Pink blend	1983
Lavender Lace	Lavender	1975	Snow Bride	White and yellow	1983
Magic Carrousel	White and red	1975	Valerie Jeanne	Magenta-pink	1983
Mary Marshall	Orange blend	1975	Baby Eclipse	Medium yellow	1984
Over the Rainbow	Red and yellow	1975	Hot Shot	Orange-red	1984
Sheri Anne	Orange-red	1975	Julie Ann	Vermillion	1984
Starglo	White	1975	Little Jackie	Pink, orange, and yellow	1984
Toy Clown	White and red	1975			
White Angel	White	1975	Black Jade	Dark red	1985
Hula Girl	Orange blend	1976	Centerpiece	Medium to dark red	1985
Peachy White	White	1976			
Red Cascade	Rich red	1976	Jennifer	Porcelain pink	1985
Jeanne Lajoie	Medium pink	1977	Loving Touch	Light apricot	1985
Peaches 'n' Cream	Peach and cream	1977	Winsome	Bright lilac	1985
Avandel	Yellow, peach, and pink	1978	Jean Kenneally	Apricot	1986
Gloriglo	Orange blend	1978	Rainbow's End	Yellow and red	1986
Humdinger	Orange-red	1978	Ring of Fire	Yellow and red	1987
Rise 'n' Shine	Clear yellow	1978	Sequoia Gold	Medium yellow	1987
Cuddles	Deep coral-pink	1979	Old Glory	Flag red	1988
Puppy Love	Orange, pink, and yellow	1979	Heavenly Days	Apricot and yellow	1988
			Dee Bennett	Orange blend	1989
Red Flush	Medium red	1979	Jim Dandy	Red blend	1989
Zinger	Medium red	1979	Night Hawk	Medium red	1989
Holy Toledo	Orange and yellow	1980	Tipper	Medium pink	1989
Pink Petticoat	Pink blend	1980	Regine	Pink blend	1990
Pacesetter	White	1981	Golden Halo	Medium yellow	1991
Party Girl	Apricot, yellow, and salmon	1981	Good Morning America	Medium yellow	1991
Center Gold	Deep yellow	1982	Just For You	Deep pink	1991
Cornsilk	Cornsilk yellow	1983	Suzy	Medium pink	1991

American Rose Society Trial Ground Winners

The nation's largest organization of amateur rose growers maintains a test garden at its Shreveport, Louisiana, headquarters where new roses are evaluated. As with the AARS evaluation, the American Rose Society's trial period lasts two years, and follows the same general guidelines for selecting winners. Although the trial grounds are open to any ARS member, including its few professional hybridizers, they are used primarily by amateurs. Many of the award winners have gone on to see their roses commercially introduced, which is perhaps the most thrilling experience an amateur hybridizer can have.

The following is a list of award-winning ARS roses that are available for purchase. (Roses from years not listed have never been introduced; many of these have not even been named.)

Variety	Class	Color	Year of Award
Flaming Beauty	Hybrid tea	Red blend	1979
Pelé	Climbing hybrid tea	White	1980
Megan Dolan*	Hybrid tea	Pink blend	1981
Dolly Parton	Hybrid tea	Orange-red	1982
Dallas Gold	Hybrid tea	Yellow blend	1984
Rejoice	Grandiflora	Pink blend	1985

* Best grown in a greenhouse

Left: The hybrid tea 'Honor' was the 1980 Rose of the Year and an All-America Rose Selection.

Right: 'Sarabande', a floribunda, was a 1960 AARS winner.

THE WORLD'S LEADING HYBRIDIZERS

*T*he rose that catches your eye in a catalog or at a nursery may well be the product of a lifelong quest by a particular hybridizer. Indeed, several family dynasties have continued this work over a span of generations. Each breeder tends to have an area of special interest. Some concentrate on landscape appeal, whereas others make great effort to develop hardy roses. Some specialize in hybrid teas; others focus on floribundas or grandifloras. Simply knowing who hybridized a particular rose can tell you a great deal about the characteristics it is likely to exhibit. For example, roses from the Danish breeder Svend Poulsen, who hybridized the floribunda 'Else Poulsen', are very winter hardy. Planting several roses from a single breeder can shed light on the evolution of a hybridizer's tastes and priorities over the years.

Many hybridizers have their own nurseries; others are employees of nurseries that market roses. Many rose catalogs include the name of the hybridizer in their descriptive copy. If they do not, you can look it up in *Modern Roses* or the *Combined Rose List* (see page 281). Descriptions of rose varieties in Chapter 10 also include the names of hybridizers.

Some outstanding hybridizers are profiled in the sections that follow. These men and women and their companies have made the most significant contributions to today's rose industry.

EUROPEANS

Patrick Dickson and his son Colin are the fifth and sixth generation of a Northern Ireland family that has been breeding roses since 1836 at their firm Dickson Nursery Ltd. A story goes that during the nineteenth century, Alexander Dickson, Jr., developed a blue rose; but when Alexander, Sr., learned of it he destroyed his son's stock, saying that a blue rose would profane public taste. Although the Dicksons have produced a large number of hybrid teas, grandifloras, and floribundas, they believe that there will be only marginal improvements in rose breeding unless new blood is introduced from outside the current range of modern roses, such as from species roses and shrubs. Like other breeders, the Dicksons are experimenting with shrub roses and are looking for new varieties among the different classes of roses to use as ground covers, and for hedging and patios. Among Dickson Nursery's best roses are 'Irish Gold', 'Precious Platinum', 'Red Devil', and 'Sea Pearl'. These roses are available in the United States from a number of mail-order companies and wholesalers. For mail-order addresses, see page 340.

Jack Harkness of England began breeding roses in 1939, but owing to war and other interruptions he did not open his first breeding station until 1962. In this short time his list of introductions has been long, notably including the floribunda 'Amber Queen', a 1988 AARS winner that is widely available in the United States. The goals of his nursery, R. Harkness and Company Ltd., are to create better roses for ground cover, and to breed roses in the amber, orange, and bronze color ranges. Harkness is also interested in improving species and shrub roses, and would like to see the introduction of some new varieties that fit into the old garden rose class.

The Kordes family of Germany has been breeding roses since 1887. Their breeding goals, in order of priority, are hardiness, disease resistance, color, form, and fragrance. In 1952 a significant introduction of the family was *Rosa kordesii*, a frost-resistant shrub that flowers several times a year and has been used to produce

many free-flowering landscape plants. The largest rose grower in Europe, W. Kordes' Söhne also has many excellent floribundas and hybrid teas to its credit. Plant breeding is now carried on by Wilhelm Kordes, the great-grandson and namesake of the founder. The list of good varieties from Kordes is a staggering one, and includes 'Folklore', 'Iceberg', 'Seashell', 'Shreveport', and 'Sunsprite'. In the United States Kordes roses are sold at numerous garden centers and through mail-order catalogs.

The McGredy family has been hybridizing roses since 1880. Sam McGredy IV, a member of the fourth generation, is a former Northern Irelander who has relocated McGredy Roses International to New Zealand.

He breeds for unusual colors and for roses that can be used as landscape plants, especially as ground covers, which he calls "creepy crawlies." He's had the most fun with his "hand-painted" series, a group of roses in which each flower on a single plant has a slightly different coloring, as though it has been tinted by hand. Some of the roses in this group are 'Eyepaint', 'Matangi', 'Old Master', and 'Picasso', all floribundas.

Other well-known McGredy introductions are 'Electron', 'New Year', 'Olympiad', and 'Red Lion', all of which are available from a large number of sources in the United States.

The Meilland family is perhaps best known for the hybrid tea 'Peace', introduced in 1945, although five generations of Meillands have produced many other

Hybridizers have particular goals in mind when they cross different varieties. Some strive for healthier, hardier plants while others pursue certain colors or plant forms.

The Danish breeder Svend Poulsen introduced the first floribundas in 1924. Shown here is the vigorous 'Poulsen's Bedder'.

excellent roses since 1850. Located in Cap d'Antibes on the French Riviera, the Meilland business, which is known as Universal Rose Selections, strives for roses with wide appeal that can be used in massed plantings. Toward that goal the Meillands have introduced a group of shrub roses and ground covers known as the Meidilands, which include the popular shrub 'Bonica '82'. Meilland roses are available from a large number of mail-order nurseries, and many are sold through garden centers under the trade name Star Roses.

The Poulsen family of Denmark began breeding plants in 1878, making its first great impact when Svend Poulsen introduced the first floribundas, 'Else Poulsen' and 'Kirsten Poulsen', in 1924. Under

the management of son Niels and his granddaughter Pernille, Poulsen Roser APS has had one major goal—roses that are exceptionally hardy. The Poulsens are now breeding toward more everblooming shrub roses and climbers, new colors, and roses for the landscape. Roses by Fred Edmunds, Inc., carries several good Poulsen varieties.

The German firm Rosen Tantau, one of Europe's largest rose hybridizers and growers, is responsible for color breakthroughs such as 'Tropicana' (the first orange-red hybrid tea), 'Fragrant Cloud' (orange-red with striking dusky shading), and 'Blue Moon' (the lavender rose that most nearly approaches blue). Founded in 1906 by Mathias Tantau, Sr., the firm is now run by his son Mathias, Jr., whose

goals are compact, bushy plants with excellent fragrance and cold hardiness. Tantau roses are widely available in the United States.

AMERICANS

Rose hybridizing in the United States has not been the family affair it has been in Europe. At Jackson and Perkins Company, in Medford, Oregon, the largest rose nursery in the United States, the late Gene Boerner made notable strides in improving the floribunda. He was followed by the recently retired William A. Warriner, who created magnificent hybrid teas, many bicolored or changing in color as they age.

Herb Swim, who died in 1989, created at least 129 varieties and won numerous awards in the United States and abroad. Associated over the years with Armstrong Nurseries of Somis, California, and Weeks Roses of Ontario, California, he devoted his best efforts to hybrid teas with magnificent form and fragrance, including 'Brandy', 'Double Delight', 'Duet', 'Garden Party', 'Summer Sunshine', and 'White Lightnin''. At Weeks Roses he worked with proprietor Ollie Weeks, who on his own produced a large number of exhibition-type hybrid teas, including 'Paradise' and 'Sweet Surrender'.

Ralph Moore, affectionately known as Mister Miniature, has been responsible for transforming the miniature rose from a limited novelty into a serious and wide-ranging genre. Since 1937 Moore has introduced over two hundred miniatures through his Sequoia Nurseries in Visalia, California. His breakthroughs have included striped miniatures and crosses between miniatures and moss roses. A recent goal is miniatures for ground covers. His introductions include 'Gold Coin', 'Judy Fishcher', 'Lavender Jewel', 'Mary Marshall', 'Over the Rainbow', and 'Rise 'n' Shine'.

Moore has given inspiration to many other miniature-rose breeders, the most notable being F. Harmon Saville of Nor'East Miniature Roses (Rowley, Massachusetts), Nels Jolly of Rosehill Farm (Galena, Maryland), Ernest Williams of Mini Roses of Texas (Denton, Texas), and the amateur breeder Frank Benardella (Old Tappan, New Jersey).

The hybrid tea 'Brandy' was one of the many creations of American Herb Swim.

*R*aindrops on
roses look
appealing, but alas,
they promote fungal
diseases.

CHAPTER NINE

LIVING WITH ROSES AND NATURE

*E*ven the most fastidious gardeners accept
the reality that diseases, insects, and other
inhabitants of the natural world will
eventually inflict harm upon their roses.
But they take solace from the fact that
few of these are devastating if prevented or
treated in time. This chapter describes
the major ills that can beset roses, and how
to keep them in check.

Drip irrigation with a micropore hose helps prevent fungal diseases by keeping the foliage dry. A mulch of wood chips holds down weeds that can harbor diseases and pests.

Whether we like it or not, nature has a way of interfering with our desire to grow perfect roses. Choosing disease-resistant varieties, keeping plants well watered and nourished, and practicing good garden hygiene are important steps in maintaining a healthy rose garden. But even the best-kept gardens are not invincible. Inevitably, some insects and diseases will attack.

Roses are especially susceptible to diseases—particularly powdery mildew and black spot. These are most severe where humidity or rainfall is high, or where air circulation is poor. Semitransparent aphids, iridescent Japanese beetles, and tiny spider mites are other common

banes. Diseases and pests such as these can spoil or even kill your roses if not dealt with appropriately.

Fortunately, it is possible to prevent or cure many of the ills that can beset a rose garden. This chapter suggests ways to keep problems from starting, and to solve them if they do.

CONTROLLING DISEASES

Roses are susceptible to a variety of fungal, viral, and bacterial diseases whose effects can range from disfigurement of the leaves to outright killing of the plant. Since most diseases are hard

to cure, it is usually easier to prevent them from taking hold in the first place. Because well-maintained plants are less likely to succumb to diseases than weak ones, you can help ensure the health of your roses by caring for them properly. Follow the recommendations for watering, fertilizing, and pruning your roses, as outlined in Chapter 5. If you live where one or more rose diseases are common, you may wish to plant only disease-resistant varieties; a list of these appears on page 68.

Apart from practicing good garden hygiene and choosing disease-resistant plants, the best way to keep your roses from contracting diseases is to limit their exposure to the agents that spread them. Diseases are spread by air, water, and soil; by insects; and by direct contact with diseased plant material. Although you cannot shut your roses away from these influences completely, you can at least exert some control over them. For instance, watering your roses by drip irrigation rather than by an overhead method can help control black spot and other fungal diseases, which grow quickly under moist conditions. If you must water from above, do so in the morning to give leaves and flowers a chance to dry by nightfall. Applying a mulch prevents water from splashing onto plants from the ground during rain or irrigation and contaminating them with disease spores from the ground.

Good air circulation can also hold back mildew and other diseases by keeping plants dry and by not allowing disease spores to take hold. To enhance air circulation, do not plant your rosebushes too close together (see page 111 for spacing guidelines), and do not let them grow into one another if they become large. It also helps to keep the centers of the plants open through pruning (see the instructions in Chapter 5).

Weeds can harbor many diseases, such as black spot and mildew, and disease-carrying insects, such as Japanese beetles and leafhoppers. You can eliminate this potential breeding ground by keeping weeds in check. If your garden has a large number of weeds, use a mulch or pre-emergent herbicide to control them; see Chapter 5 for information. Insects known to be disease carriers can be eradicated with sprays or, if practical, picked from plants by hand or knocked off with a jet of water.

To keep diseases from spreading among your roses by direct contact, prune away and destroy diseased parts of plants, and pick up diseased leaves as soon as they fall.

Some disease organisms, such as crown gall, are soil borne. Many have no means of prevention or cure, so when a rosebush becomes infected, the only remedy is to replace both it and the surrounding soil. Diagnosis and treatment of specific diseases is described later in this chapter, beginning on page 266.

CONTROLLING INSECTS AND OTHER PESTS

*H*undreds of kinds of insects live in a typical garden, but only about a dozen regularly cause damage to roses. Indeed, some, such as lady beetles, are beneficial because they consume harmful insects. Although the variety of attackers is small, the damage they do can be extensive. Left unchecked in a rose garden, these insects can chew holes in leaves and flowers, suck vital juices from the plants, spread diseases, and even kill the plants altogether. Insect control is therefore essential to a healthy, productive rose garden.

As with diseases, the best way to reduce the chance of an insect attack is to practice good garden hygiene. Insects often live and lay eggs in weeds, so it is vital to keep the garden free of these breeding sites. Cleaning up garden debris as it accumulates, and destroying it each fall so that insects and their eggs cannot overwinter, also reduces the insect threat. Even the tidiest garden can harbor destructive insects, so it is wise to keep an eye out for early signs of infestation. Catching a problem early can save your garden from serious damage.

Once you have identified an insect problem, you may choose to fight back with insecticides. Some insects, such as aphids, can be dislodged from the plants by a jet of water, but application of insecticides is almost always a necessity at some time. Some of these insecticides, such as insecticidal soaps and pyrethrin sprays, are biological in origin. Others are synthetic formulations. These are usually stronger and longer lasting than organic agents, and should be used with care around birds and pets.

Insecticides of both types are classed as either contact or systemic. Contact insecticides are absorbed through the insects' bodies and must be sprayed onto them directly. Horticultural oil and insecticidal soap are a type of contact insecticide that kills insects by smothering them or their eggs with a film. Systemic insecticides are applied to plants and taken up through their roots or leaves; insects are poisoned as they feast on plant parts. The type of insecticide you choose depends to a great extent on what works best in killing the insect that is causing the problem; see the recommendations on pages 269 to 274. Some insecticides, such as Orthene®, work both systemically and by contact.

In addition to insecticides, you may need to use miticides in your garden. These are formulated especially to control spider mites, tiny eight-legged relatives of spiders that disfigure leaves and flower buds with grayish webs. Like spiders, mites are technically not insects. Although some insecticides are effective against them, miticides are usually applied to kill them.

The other major pests of roses are nematodes, small worms that are treated with chemicals known as nematicides. A few are available to the homeowner, but the majority can be purchased and applied only by licensed pesticide applicators.

Insecticides, miticides, and nematicides are best used at the first sign of infestation; spraying to prevent attack rarely works, and is costly as well. It also can destroy natural predators and other beneficial insects. In addition, these products can unnecessarily cause pests to build up an immunity, so that these controls will not work when you need them.

Some rose growers prefer not to use any chemicals in their gardens, and instead rely on natural predators to control destructive insects. These helpful species include lady beetles (sometimes called ladybird beetles or ladybugs), assassin bugs, green lacewings, praying mantids, parasitic wasps, and predatory mites. The drawback to these insects is that once they have eaten the pests in your garden, they will move on to other gardens in search of food. As a result, their effectiveness may not last long. You can purchase these insects by mail order (see page 341). In addition to insects, you can also buy a number of other natural controls for insects and diseases, such as biological insecticides and fungicides.

SPRAYERS

Although a few insecticides and fungicides are poured into the ground or applied in dry form to it, most are applied directly to the foliage as a spray. Ready-to-use products often come with built-in sprayers, but for larger gardens it is more economical to purchase a sprayer and chemical concentrates to dilute yourself.

There are several different types of sprayers, all widely available at garden

centers and hardware stores. A compression sprayer has a tank for the spray solution (usually holding 1½ to 2 gallons), a plunger to compress air into the container, and a piece of tubing with a nozzle at the end. Pressure in the tank delivers a spray. Both metal and plastic types are available; plastic ones are lighter in weight and resist corrosion, which makes them easier to clean. All in all, compression sprayers are the most convenient and popular type.

Some small sprayers are driven by rechargeable batteries that eliminate the need for hand pumping. Overnight charging will power most of these for 45 minutes—enough time to spray the average garden. Some older types of aerosol sprayers have plungers that are operated by hand; these do not deliver as even a spray as the compression or battery-driven sprayers.

Other kinds of sprayers, called hose-end sprayers, are designed to be attached to the end of a garden hose. Most consist of a nozzle and a detachable plastic bottle that holds a concentrated solution of insecticide or fungicide. Water from the

hose siphons and dilutes the concentrate and propels the mixture through the nozzle. This is the least convenient sprayer to use, since you must drag a hose around—an inconvenience in a large or crowded garden. This type of sprayer may also distribute the concentrate unevenly. Siphon injectors of the type used to apply large amounts of liquid fertilizer (see Chapter 5) can also be used to apply spray materials.

Some sprayers have long tubular or sliding attachments called trombones that make it easy to spray tall rose plants that are trained on trellises and arbors. These trombone-action sprayers are pumps, not compression sprayers, and pump solution out of a bucket. Tank sprayers that roll on wheels are also available, and are convenient in very large gardens; some have motorized compressors.

Garden centers also sell dusters for applying powdered insecticides and fungicides; they are tubular devices with a plunger at one end. However, in recent years they have given way to sprayers, since spraying liquid is a more even and effective way to apply materials.

Fungicides and insecticides are applied to roses with a sprayer. Fungicides are often sprayed preventively, but insecticides are not used until pests appear.

Spraying Tips

Before you use a sprayer for the first time, be sure to read the instructions accompanying it. Sprayers differ in design and operation, so it is important to follow the instructions carefully. Here are some general pointers.

—Make sure plants are well watered before you spray, since damage is more likely to occur to dry leaves than to moist, turgid ones. Never spray on a windy day, as too much of your spray will be blown away, perhaps onto plants that may be damaged by the product.

—Spray both the upper and lower leaf surfaces until the spray starts to run off the leaf. Nozzles on some sprayers can be adjusted to produce different droplet sizes; the finer the spray, the more even the coverage.

—When applying dormant sprays, make sure the canes are completely covered with spray. Also cover the ground around the bases of the plants.

—When using a compression sprayer, you will need to repump it once or twice during spraying to keep the pressure high enough to deliver a fine spray.

—If the sprayer contains powdered material in suspension, you may need to shake it several times during spraying to keep the material evenly dispersed in the water. Adding a squirt of liquid dish detergent to the water in the sprayer if powdered material is being used, either in suspension or in solution, helps it to better adhere to the leaves of the plants. Liquid concentrates often contain a material that helps the active ingredient to adhere to the leaves, so liquid dish detergent is usually not necessary when using them.

—When spraying a chemical that is toxic (the label will give this warning), wear a mask, gloves, and protective clothing, and change your clothes and take a shower as soon as you have finished the job.

—Never apply insecticides or fungicides with a sprayer that has been used to apply weed killers, unless you have thoroughly washed the sprayer with soap and rinsed it well with water. Residues of weed killer remaining in the sprayer can harm or kill your plants. To avoid this possibility, it's a good idea to have a separate sprayer for weed killers.

—Keep your sprayer in good working order by cleaning and maintaining it properly. Nozzle apertures are small and clog easily; after each use, fill the sprayer with plain water and spray it through the nozzle to flush out any residue. If the nozzle becomes clogged, clean it by poking a thin wire through it. If you have a compression sprayer, you may need to apply light oil to its pump cylinder from time to time to keep it working smoothly.

APPLYING PESTICIDES

Once you have diagnosed your insect and disease problems, you can determine what spray material to use by studying the listings in this chapter, asking at your local garden center, or consulting your county agricultural extension. Some of these products are sprayed directly onto the plants; others are applied to the ground. Dormant sprays are applied in early spring before the plants show signs of life; other formulations are applied throughout the growing season at intervals specified on their labels.

Insecticides, fungicides, and other chemicals are usually available wherever gardening supplies are sold. Many are concentrates that must be diluted with water before you use them. Some of these are liquids; others are powders or granules that either dissolve in water or go into suspension. Several products come fully diluted and ready to use, and are convenient if you have only a few plants. For large gardens, however, concentrates are much less expensive.

When working with concentrates, read the label carefully and dilute the substance exactly as directed. Determine how much water you will need and add one quarter of it to the empty sprayer (hot water works best to dissolve dry materials). Then add the concentrate and mix well by agitating the sprayer. Pour in the remaining water and mix again, making sure the ingredients are fully dissolved or suspended before spraying. The label also tells you how often repeat treatment may be needed. Fungicides are usually needed every 7 to 10 days throughout the growing season. Insect sprays should be applied as directed on the label; spray should usually stop when there are no more signs of infestation.

It is possible to mix different products together—for example, an insecticide and a fungicide—so that more than one treatment is applied at a time. Before mixing two products, however, make sure that the directions on both labels recommend this; if the mixing directions seem too complicated, you may choose to apply the products separately. If you are combining a powder and a liquid, add the powder first to one quarter of the total water needed. After mixing, add the liquid before adding the rest of the water. Label instructions give dilution rates in units (such as tablespoons) per gallon of water. When combining products, dilute each one as if it were the only ingredient; do not increase the total amount of the water.

Always mix chemicals outdoors in a well-ventilated area and do not eat, drink, or smoke while handling them. When using hazardous chemicals (a hazard warning appears on the label), wear gloves, goggles, and protective clothing. Remove the safety gear and take a shower as soon as you have finished spraying. Never reuse a spray solution; mix only what you need for one application. Do not dispose of leftover pesticide in the trash. If you have finished spraying your roses, you can spray the remainder on other plants that are listed on the product label. Always wrap empty containers in newspaper and discard them in the trash; never burn or incinerate them.

Most fungicides work better in water that is slightly acidic. You can determine the pH of your water with a pH test kit available from swimming pool suppliers, or by calling the local water authority. If your water is neutral or alkaline, you may wish to adjust it. Adding 1 to 2 tablespoons of white vinegar per gallon will lower its pH toward the slightly acid range (6.0 to 6.5).

Do not buy more pesticides than you will use in a year or two, as chemicals can lose their effectiveness over time. Always store products in the original container where children cannot reach them; if possible, lock them away. Also keep them out of the sun and heat.

IDENTIFYING AND TREATING PROBLEMS

*B*efore you can take action against insects and diseases, you need to know which ones you are facing. This section describes the most common attackers of roses, and describes symptoms and recommended treatments. Most insect and disease problems are easy to identify and are easily distinguished from cultural problems such as nutrient deficiencies. (Symptoms of nutrient deficiencies are outlined on page 152.)

The problems discussed here pertain to roses grown outdoors, although some of these problems also occur indoors. For a discussion of indoor pests and diseases, refer to Chapter 6.

A ladybird beetle is a welcome guest on the grandiflora 'Queen Elizabeth', where it busies itself eating aphids. Only a few insects harm roses; others are quite helpful.

DISEASES

A regular program of preventive spraying can keep many diseases from gaining a foothold. Indeed, preventive spraying is almost always better than waiting until a disease takes hold and trying to cure it then. Spraying should begin as soon as the plants have leafed out fully in mid-spring. (The exception is dormant spraying, which is performed before the leaves unfold.) In most instances, spraying should be repeated every 7 to 10 days throughout the growing season. Most rose diseases can spread from plant to plant, so their swift eradication from one plant keeps the entire garden from becoming infected.

The exact measures to take depend on the diseases you expect to encounter. Most rose diseases are caused by fungi, thus a fungicidal spray is the most common method of prevention and treatment. To ensure proper treatment, however, accurate diagnosis is essential. The photographs and descriptions that follow will help you identify common rose diseases. If you have a problem you cannot identify, a garden center or county agricultural extension will be able to help. Once you know what you are dealing with, follow the recommendations here or ask a garden center to recommend products and techniques to help you solve the problem. Note that the chemicals recommended here are active ingredients. They may be contained in several different products.

BLACK SPOT
Category: Fungal disease
Symptoms: Round black spots appear on the upper sides of the leaves; the spots are often surrounded by yellow halos. As the spots become larger and start growing together, the leaves turn yellow and fall from the plant. Black spot is a very serious disease prevalent in all areas of the country, but is less serious in the semiarid Southwest.
Treatment: Once established, black spot cannot be cured; therefore its spread must be prevented. As a preventive measure, spray every 7 to 10 days with a fungicide such as captan, maneb, chlorothalonil, or Funginex®, starting in midspring. A dust or a spray of sulfur every 7 to 14 days will also control black spot. If the disease does occur, remove any damaged leaves, pick up and discard all leaves that have fallen to the ground, and continue spraying the entire garden to control its spread. Water early in the day and, if possible, avoid overhead watering until the disease is under control. To eradicate disease spores that have overwintered on the canes, prune back infected plants heavily in the spring before the leaves appear, and apply a dormant spray of lime-sulfur before the canes start to leaf out.

Black spot, a fungal disease, is a widespread bane of roses.

The soil-borne bacterium that causes crown gall produces rounded, corky growths. There is no easy cure for this disease.

BOTRYTIS BLIGHT
(Also called gray mold)
Category: Fungal disease
Symptoms: Leaves, stems, and growing tips turn black. Flower buds turn black and may not open; if they do open, the flowers may be streaked or flecked with yellow or brown and are covered with a gray fuzzy growth. Botrytis blight is a moderately serious disease most prevalent when the weather is cool and damp.
Treatment: Avoid watering at night and improve air circulation by pruning the centers of the plants open, and by not overcrowding. Cut away and discard any infected plant parts. Spray the entire plant with a fungicide such as benomyl, thiram, or chlorothalonil to control the disease and keep it from spreading to other plants.

CANKER
Category: Fungal disease
Symptoms: Red, brown, or black spots that are sunken and elongated appear along canes and stems, especially in early to midspring. Cracks may appear within the spots. The spots enlarge and eventually encircle the canes, killing them. Canker is a widespread disease often caused by mechanical injury to the canes.
Treatment: There are no chemical preventives or controls for canker. Prune away canes below the infection.

CROWN GALL
Category: Bacterial disease
Symptoms: Rounded, sometimes corky growths, light green to light tan, appear on roots or on the bud union; the growths turn brown and woody as they age. Roses may fail to grow, have very small leaves, produce few flower buds, and possibly die. Crown gall is no longer as serious a disease as it once was, because commercial growers have instituted sanitary measures that prevent the disease from infecting plants in the nursery.
Treatment: There are no commercial chemical controls for crown gall, which is caused by a soil-borne bacterium. Small galls can be pruned out with a sharp knife or pruning shears; sterilize the blades with alcohol after each cut. In serious cases dig up the plant and discard it, and replace the soil around the roots.

Mosaic is a set of symptoms caused by any of several viruses.

MOSAIC

Category: Viral disease

Symptoms: Leaves become mottled, streaked, or spotted with circles of yellow or light green, or develop a pattern of yellow netting. Leaves may curl and plants are sometimes stunted in their growth. Mosaic is most common in areas along the Pacific coast.

Treatment: Unfortunately, there are no chemical controls for mosaic disease. To halt the disease you must remove and discard severely infected plants; if this is not done, the disease can eventually kill the infected plant and may be spread to others by feeding insects. In mild cases the symptoms sometimes disappear by themselves.

POWDERY MILDEW

Category: Fungal disease

Symptoms: Dusty white or gray powder coats leaves, stems, and flower buds. Leaves become curled, twisted, or distorted, turn yellow, and fall. Flower buds may fail to open or, if they do, they may produce distorted flowers. Powdery mildew is a serious disease that can occur at any time of year, but it takes hold most often when days are warm and nights are cool.

Treatment: To prevent powdery mildew, spray the entire plant every 7 to 10 days, beginning in midspring, with a fungicide such as benomyl, fenarimol, or Funginex®. A dormant spray of lime-sulfur in early spring before the leaves appear further helps to control powdery mildew. Improving air circulation and watering early in the day also helps to control the disease.

If the disease does occur, remove and destroy all infected leaves, and continue spraying the entire plant to prevent the spread of the disease. Fungicides containing sulfur applied every 7 to 14 days will eradicate mildew, but should not be applied if the temperature is over 85° F, or the leaves will burn.

DOWNY MILDEW

Category: Fungal disease

Symptoms: Irregular purple blotches appear on stems and leaves; foliage suddenly turns yellow and drops from the plant. Flower buds and flowers are deformed. Downy mildew is not a common disease but can become troublesome when the weather is cool and damp.

Treatment: Prune back defoliated canes. Spray the entire plant with maneb or zineb every seven days until the symptoms disappear.

RUST

Category: Fungal disease

Symptoms: Tops of leaves turn pale green or yellow; undersides are covered with small spots of orange powder. Infected leaves may wilt or curl. Rust is a serious disease that is most prevalent in the Pacific Northwest, where the climate is cool and humid.

Treatment: Prevent rust by spraying the entire plant with lime-sulfur in early spring when plants are still dormant; beginning in midspring, apply a fungicide such as Funginex® every 10 days. Water early in the day. If symptoms occur, remove infected leaves and clean up any fallen leaves and stems, and continue spraying while cool and humid conditions persist.

SPOT ANTHRACNOSE

Category: Fungal disease

Symptoms: Small red, brown, or purple spots form on the upper surfaces of leaves. Eventually the center of the spot dries out, turns white, and may fall from the leaf, leaving a hole. Leaves eventually turn yellow and fall from the plant. Spot anthracnose is a moderately serious disease that can occur anywhere; it usually affects climbers more than other classes of roses.

Treatment: Spray the entire plant with a fungicide such as maneb or chlorothalonil every seven days, starting as soon as symptoms appear. Avoid overhead watering and continue to spray until symptoms are gone.

INSECTS AND OTHER SMALL PESTS

To treat an insect or pest problem effectively, you need to know exactly what you are dealing with. Many insects are large and highly visible, making them easy to identify. Others are so small or elusive that they can be identified only by the symptoms they leave. The following information describes telltale signs of the small pests that most often trouble roses. If you have a problem you cannot identify, ask your local garden center or county agricultural extension for help.

Left: Powdery mildew occurs most often when warm days are followed by cool nights.

Right: Rust, another fungal disease, is a serious problem in the Northwest.

Unlike the control of diseases, which is largely preventive, spraying to eradicate insects is carried on when symptoms occur. It is therefore important to walk through the rose garden on a regular basis to spot small infestations before they spread to all of your plants. Once the problem has been eradicated, spraying can cease.

APHIDS
Category: Insect
Symptoms: Small, semitransparent, ⅛-inch insects; green or sometimes yellow, black, red, or brown; cluster on buds, leaves, and stems and suck the juices of the plants. Leaves curl, wither and may turn yellow, and a clear, shiny substance appears on them. A sooty black mold is sometimes present on the leaves as well. Flower buds wither or become distorted. Aphids are common and widespread.
Treatment: As soon as signs of infestation appear, spray infested plants with diazinon, malathion, methoxychlor, Orthene®, Sevin®, pyrethrins, or insecticidal soap; or apply granules of disulfoton to the ground. Spraying leafless canes with horticultural oil in the spring smothers aphid eggs. A strong stream of water knocks some of the aphids off the plants, but does not kill them. Lady beetles in the garden can also help control, but not eradicate, aphids. Controlling aphids controls the sooty black mold.

CANE BORERS
Category: Insect
Symptoms: Foliage is small or sparse, and leaves turn yellow, wilt, and die. Growth slows or stops as growing tips and canes wilt. Looking like a caterpillar, this insect can measure up to 1 inch long and is located within the canes, usually where a swelling of the cane is visible. Cane borers enter roses through wounds or through pruned stem tips; the entry holes are usually apparent. Cane borers are a moderately serious insect pest.
Treatment: Prune away the cane to below the infested area, and discard it. Locate entry holes on canes and paint the holes with lindane or another insecticide for borer control. In areas where borers are common, seal all newly pruned cane tips with tree wound paint, orange shellac, or water-insoluble glue to keep the borers out.

CATERPILLARS
Category: Insect
Symptoms: Large holes appear in leaves and entire leaves may be consumed. Holes appear in the bottoms of flower buds. Greenish or yellowish wormlike larvae of various insects in varying sizes are usually visible on plants. Caterpillars are

Aphids cling to buds, stems, and leaves to suck juices from the plant.

widespread and can do serious damage. *Treatment:* Large caterpillars can be hand-picked and destroyed. An alternative is to use a contact insecticide such as Sevin® or a systemic insecticide such as Orthene®, spraying it over the entire plant; or spray the entire plant with *Bacillus thuringiensis* (abbreviated Bt), a bacterium that kills caterpillars but is harmless to plants and animals. Bt is contained in several commercial sprays.

JAPANESE BEETLES
Category: Insect
Symptoms: Small, round holes appear in flowers and sometimes leaves. Insects ½ inch long with hard shells of copper and green are visible. Roses with light-colored flowers tend to be the most susceptible to attack. Japanese beetles are very serious pests, primarily in the eastern half of the United States.
Treatment: Keep the garden weed free, as adult beetles often hide in weeds. Small infestations can be controlled by picking off beetles by hand. Insecticides such as Orthene®, Sevin®, or methoxychlor can be used; spray them on the infested parts of the plant. Milky spore disease, a biological product that is applied to the soil, destroys the beetles in their larval stage before they emerge from the soil as adults. The chemical insecticides diazinon, isofenphos, and chlorpyrifos also kill larvae. Traps for adult beetles have limited effectiveness; their attractants may actually lure more beetles from your neighbors' gardens and not all of them may be trapped.

LEAFCUTTER BEES
Category: Insect
Symptoms: Small, almost perfect semicircles and circles are cut into leaf margins. The ½-inch bees may sometimes be seen; they are black, blue, or purple, and shiny. The bees do not eat the foliage, but instead use the pieces they have cut to build their nests. They can be found all

Top: The Io caterpillar likes to dine on rose leaves. This and other caterpillars can do great damage.

Center: Japanese beetles are a serious pest in eastern states. They eat holes in flowers and leaves.

Bottom: Leafcutter bees slice off pieces of leaf to incorporate in their nests.

Left: Small and difficult to spot, midge insects wreak sudden destruction on buds and stems.

Right: Rose scales are small shell-covered insects that cluster on canes to suck their sap.

over the country, although they are not a serious pest.

Treatment: Prune away any canes that have damaged foliage. Chemical sprays are not recommended, as leafcutter bees are otherwise beneficial for pollination.

LEAFHOPPERS

Category: Insect

Symptoms: Leaves turn yellow, starting at the edges, or are speckled with tiny dots; they eventually curl up and die. Wedge-shaped, ⅛-inch insects colored light green, yellow, white, or gray are visible, and jump very quickly when disturbed. They are widespread and do the most serious damage in the fall.

Treatment: Remove damaged leaves and spray plants with insecticidal soap or with pyrethrins; or spray with diazinon, methoxychlor, or Orthene®. Disulfoton, a granular insecticide, is also effective when applied to the ground; diazinon may also be applied to the ground in granular form. In autumn rake up all fallen leaves and remove all weeds, as leafhopper eggs can overwinter in debris left on the ground.

MIDGE

Category: Insect

Symptoms: Flower buds suddenly turn black and die. The stems below the affected flower buds and the leaves around the affected flower buds may also take on a burned appearance. These insects are very small (¹/₂₀ inch long) and are quite difficult to spot. They are widespread and work with sudden devastation, usually in mid or late summer.

Treatment: Prune away and discard any infested flower buds and stems. Apply a granular insecticide such as diazinon to the ground around the bases of the plants and spray the tops of plants with diazinon or Orthene® as well.

NEMATODES

Category: Worm

Symptoms: Plant growth slows, and leaves and flowers are smaller than normal. Leaves may suddenly lose their color, wilt, and die. Digging up the plants reveals discolored, swollen, and knotted roots. Nematodes are too small to be seen without a microscope, and only a soil test can definitively confirm their presence. Nematodes are moderately serious pests found in all parts of the United States, especially around farmlands.

Treatment: There are few effective chemical controls available to the home gardener, metam-sodium being the major exception, but a licensed pesticide applicator can treat the soil for you with other materials; look in the yellow pages under Landscape Gardeners. If the soil is not treated, remove and destroy infested plants, replace the surrounding soil, and do not replant roses in the same spot for three years. Large plantings of marigolds around rosebushes help keep nematodes out of the area.

ROSE SCALE

Category: Insect

Symptoms: Plants stop growing, and growing tips die back. Leaves turn yellow and fall from the plant, and the plants do not flower. Clusters of round or oval $1/10$-inch insects with crusty white, gray, or brown shells are visible on the canes. Rose scale is a moderately serious pest that is widespread.

Treatment: Prune out any dead or severely infested canes. Prevent by spraying leafless canes with horticultural oil in early spring. If infestations appear, spray the canes with insecticidal soap, malathion, or Orthene® until symptoms are gone.

ROSE SLUGS

Category: Insect

Symptoms: Small, rounded holes appear in the foliage and eventually the entire leaf blade between the veins is consumed. Rose slugs, the larvae of sawfly wasps, are ½ inch long, light green, short legged, and shaped like caterpillars. (They are unrelated to common garden slugs, which are mollusks.) It may be necessary to examine the undersides of the leaves to find them. They are serious pests found throughout most of the United States.

Treatment: Spray leaves with a contact insecticide such as Sevin®, making sure the insecticide covers the undersides of the leaves. Small infestations can be removed by hand.

SPIDER MITES

Category: Arachnid

Symptoms: Leaves become dry and speckled with yellow and take on a dull bronze sheen. Small black spots are evident on the undersides of leaves; mites themselves are only about $1/150$ of an inch long. Webbing appears on leaves and flower buds as the infestation advances. Mites are a widespread, serious problem, especially when the weather is hot and dry.

Top: Rose slugs, the larvae of saw wasps, consume the portions of leaf between the veins.

Bottom: Tiny eight-legged spider mites discolor rose leaves as they suck juices from the undersides. Fine webs may appear.

Treatment: Keep the garden weed free, as adult mites hibernate in weeds. At first sign of infestation, spray with a miticide such as dicofol, abamectin, or hexakis three times, waiting three days between each application. Or spray with an insecticide such as malathion, diazinon, or Orthene®, following the same schedule. Disulfoton insecticide also controls spider mites. Apply it to the soil in granular form and water it in. Mites often build up a resistance to a miticide or insecticide, so it is wise to rotate among them. Misting the undersides of the leaves with water helps to deter spider mites.

THRIPS

Category: Insect

Symptoms: Leaves curl, and leaf margins turn white, yellow, or brown. Flower buds are discolored and bent over, and may not open; flowers that do not open may have bumpy petals streaked in brown. The insects themselves are small and difficult to see. White and pastel roses are the most susceptible to attack.

Treatment: Remove and destroy any affected flowers or buds. Spray the tops of rosebushes with insecticidal soap, diazinon, Sevin®, malathion, methoxychlor, or Orthene®, following directions on the product label. Also spray the soil litter around the bush, where young adults mature.

RODENTS AND OTHER ANIMALS

A number of animals can be a menace to rose gardens, especially in rural areas. Though no method is completely effective, there are measures you can take to reduce the damage these animals do.

A great deal of trouble is caused by rabbits and deer, which gnaw on rose canes, especially in winter, and eat foliage and flowers during the growing season. One way to deter rabbits is to build a fence of fine chicken wire around the entire rose garden, or wrap individual plants in chicken wire. The barrier should be 2 feet high and should extend at least 6 inches below the ground. Check the fence often for any signs of burrowing below the fence line, and add additional protection if it occurs. Outdoor cats can also help keep rabbits away from the planting area. Deer can be deterred by 7- to 8-foot electric fences, by 7- to 8-foot fences made of chicken wire or netting, or by fences of any height that have an angled extension jutting 8 feet out from them to prevent the deer from jumping the fence. Dogs may keep deer away from the area as well.

Setting out winter feed for animals will sometimes lure them away from your roses. Put out apples, corn, seeds, or nuts. Deer can be deterred by some plants used as barriers, including cedar,

Usually too small to see, thrips are evident from bent and discolored flower buds that fail to open.

daffodils, eucalyptus, fir, foxglove, iris, juniper, Oregon grape holly, poppy, tulips, and zinnia. Deer avoid these plants because they do not like their taste.

Burrowing animals such as moles, voles, and gophers eat roots and push plants out of the ground as they tunnel under them. To control gophers, locate their main tunnels by locating the entrance holes, and set traps inside them. They can also be killed by bombs or chemicals you can buy at the garden center. Underground barriers such as vinyl siding set around planting holes or beds are somewhat effective. A professional exterminator may be necessary in the most severe cases.

Moles dig tunnels but do not live in them permanently. Step on a mole hill as soon as you see it (you'll recognize a mound of soil pushed up from ground level) to collapse the underlying tunnel and bring disturbed plant roots back into

contact with the soil. Traps and baits have very limited effectiveness. Moles eat insects, especially ants and grubs, so controlling the insects will control the moles to a degree.

Voles and field mice live in abandoned gopher and mole tunnels and emerge to feed on the aboveground parts of plants. Cats can be a great help here, as can mouse and rat traps.

Garden centers sell a variety of commercial repellents and poisons to deter animal marauders. You can also make your own repellents by soaking strips of heavy cloth in creosote or Tabasco sauce and hanging them near the rose garden. These are most effective against deer, although probably none is as effective as commercial repellents. If you use creosote, keep it away from rose plants, as it kills the stems and foliage. Dried blood and mothballs placed in their tunnels will sometimes deter burrowing animals.

A protective circle of chicken wire keeps roses safe from small rabbits, but is too short to deter larger rabbits and deer. Surprisingly, thorns give roses little protection against these hungry animals.

The climber 'Joseph's Coat' has blooms that change color as they age.

CHAPTER TEN

THE WORLD'S FINEST ROSES

o rose lovers, the arrival of a colorful mail-order catalog is one of life's great pleasures— yet it is also something of a torment. A rose that looks good on paper may prove unworthy in the garden; conversely, a photograph may not do justice to the original. What's more, roses are highly variable; their performance can change with the climate, the soil, and other factors. How, then, to single out the best? In these pages you will find a selection of good-looking roses that thrive in a wide range of environments.

*W*ith thousands of varieties available for sale, choosing the right rose might seem like a mind-boggling process. The pages that follow describe the most outstanding roses that are commercially available in the United States and Canada. Roses are listed alphabetically within each class (such as hybrid tea or floribunda). The name of each variety is followed by the hybridizer's surname, the year the plant was introduced, its flower color code, and a description of its characteristics. Also indicated are the rating the American Rose Society (ARS) has given the plant and any outstanding awards it has won.

The names of hybridizers have historical interest for rose buffs, and can also provide clues about qualities of the rose. For example, William Warriner's roses are often tender, while roses hybridized by the Poulsen family are usually winter hardy. Sam McGredy IV hybridizes many roses for landscape effect. See page 254 for descriptions of leading hybridizers.

The year of introduction, listed next, can provide further information about a rose's place in history. But do not be misled into thinking that a newer rose is better than an older one. Many of the older hybrid teas are still among the best, although some of the newer ones exhibit interesting color combinations not found in older roses, as well as improved hardiness or disease resistance.

Hybrid teas crowd a rose lover's garden, as if straining to escape its boxwood edging.

Following the introduction date is a letter code for the color class assigned to the rose by the American Rose Society. This information is essential if you want to exhibit roses.

Next, you'll find a complete description of the variety, including the form of its flowers and the number of petals. The term *high centered* means that the center of the open flower is higher than the edges, forming a triangular shape when viewed from the side. This shape is sometimes referred to as classic. The term *cup shaped* means that the center of the flower is on an even plane with its edges, and that the outline is semicircular when viewed from the side. The word *flat* means that the flower has so few petals that when fully open it looks flat from

Top: Members of William Warriner's award-winning wedding trio include the red-and- white grandiflora 'Love', the white hybrid tea 'Honor', and the pink floribunda 'Cherish'.

Bottom: Climbers and bush roses bloom against a latticework enclosure at New York's Brooklyn Botanic Garden.

the side. Cup-shaped and flat flowers are often referred to as decorative or informal. Roses are often described as having a reverse of a different color. The reverse is the outside of a petal. A few roses are described as quartered because they appear to be divided into distinct quadrants. Most roses have double flowers (with 25 to 45 petals); a lesser number are single (with 5 to 12 petals), semidouble (with 13 to 25 petals), or very double (with over 45 petals).

Also listed are plant form and size, and any special characteristics such as disease resistance, winter hardiness, and thorniness. If not mentioned, these traits are assumed to be average for that rose class. Similarly, if no fragrance is described, the rose has none.

At the end of each listing, you'll find the 1991 rating by the American Rose Society. ARS ratings, which rate all-around performance, range from 0 to 9.9; the higher the rating, the better the rose, in the opinion of this influential group and its members. If you stick with roses whose ARS rating is at least 7.0, you will rarely be disappointed. However, roses with lower ratings may still be worth growing for their historical or aesthetic interest.

Some roses are too new to have ratings; others have been assigned a provisional rating until their evaluation is complete. (But even established ratings are subject to change.) For yet other roses, ARS survey takers received too few responses to determine a rating. Any award received by a rose is also noted; for a description of each award and a list of its recipients, see pages 248 to 253.

The accompanying box explains the symbols and abbreviations that are used in the plant descriptions.

Abbreviations and Symbols

The following codes are used in these listings.

Color Classes

AB	apricot blend
DP	deep pink
DR	deep red
DY	deep yellow
LP	light pink
LY	light yellow
MB	mauve blend
MP	medium pink
MR	medium red
MY	medium yellow
OB	orange blend
OP	orange pink
OR	orange red
PB	pink blend
R	russet
RB	red blend
W	white, near white, and white blend
YB	yellow blend

American Rose Society Ratings

9.0–9.9	outstanding
8.0–8.9	excellent
7.0–7.9	good
6.0–6.9	fair
5.9 and lower	questionable (but may have historical interest)

Ratings Notes

(7.5)	still being evaluated; rating may change
+	too new to have a rating
%	too few responses to determine a rating

Awards

AARS	All-America Rose Selections
ARSTG	American Rose Society Trial Ground Winner
AOE	American Rose Society Award of Excellence
JAGFM	James Alexander Gable Fragrance Medal
ROY	Rose of the Year

FINDING OUT MORE

*S*ome of the roses described in these pages are very common; others may be harder to find. If the rose you want is not available locally, the mail-order nurseries on pages 340 and 341 provide a wide selection. If you have trouble locating a particular variety, a useful booklet called the *Combined Rose List* can help you track it down. Your local rose society may have a copy, or you can purchase one by mail from Beverly Dobson, 215 Harriman Road, Irvington, NY 10533. The booklet is updated annually.

If you're searching for old garden roses and older varieties not protected by patent, a good way to get these is from an acquaintance or a public garden that is willing to part with a cutting. Associations such as the Heritage Rose Foundation or the Heritage Roses Group may be able to direct you to a source; see page 339 for their addresses. A growing number of mail-order catalogs offer old roses for sale.

For more guidance in choosing roses to fit your gardening needs, see Chapter 2 of this book. You can also consult the American Rose Society's *Handbook for Selecting Roses*, sent free to all ARS members. Nonmembers can order the handbook for $1. Send your payment and a stamped #10 return envelope to: American Rose Society, Box 30,000, Shreveport, LA 71130. This is also the address to write for information about becoming a member.

Should you need to correspond with rose hybridizers regarding characteristics of their varieties, you'll find their names and addresses in the American Rose Society's *Modern Roses*. Your local chapter of the ARS can steer you to a copy, or you can purchase it by mail from the ARS. This valuable book is updated every few years; as of 1991, the latest edition was *Modern Roses 9*, published in 1986.

The Very Finest Roses

If your rose-growing experience is limited, you may feel somewhat daunted by the vast selection available. The varieties on this short, discriminating list have been chosen for both their beauty and their reliable performance. If you are uncertain about which roses to start with, you can't go wrong with one of these. For details about each variety, consult the listings in this chapter.

Hybrid Teas

Chicago Peace
Chrysler Imperial
Dainty Bess
Double Delight
Electron
Folklore
Fragrant Cloud
Garden Party
Mister Lincoln
Olympiad
Paradise
Tiffany
Touch of Class
Tropicana

Floribundas

Angel Face
Apricot Nectar
Europeana
First Edition
Gene Boerner
Iceberg
Simplicity
Sunsprite

Polyanthas

The Fairy

Grandifloras

Gold Medal
Pink Parfait
Queen Elizabeth

Miniatures

Beauty Secret
Cinderella
Cupcake
Dreamglo
Holy Toledo
Jean Kenneally
Lavender Jewel
Magic Carrousel
Mary Marshall
Over the Rainbow
Party Girl
Peaches 'n' Cream
Puppy Love
Rainbow's End
Rise 'n' Shine
Simplex
Starina
Toy Clown

Climbers

America
Blaze
Don Juan
Handel

Shrubs

Belinda
Bonica '82
Carefree Beauty
Dortmund
Golden Wings
Sparrieshoop

'Admiral Rodney'

'Blue Moon'

'Bobby Charlton'

HYBRID TEAS

To most rose lovers the hybrid tea represents the culmination of the quest for ideal form and coloring in a rose, with a classic high-centered form and colors that range from rich reds, yellows, and oranges to delicate whites, pinks, and lavenders, with exotic blends of all shades in between. To show off their large and exemplary flowers, most hybrid teas have long, strong stems that make them the most popular roses for cutting.

A cross between the exquisite but tender tea rose and the hardy hybrid perpetual, the hybrid tea embodies the best of both lineages, with often fragrant flowers that bloom repeatedly all summer on tolerably winter-hardy plants. Most hybrid teas produce one flower per stem, but a few bloom in sprays. Plant size and hardiness range according to variety. If hybrid teas have a weak point it is that the plant form is less useful for landscaping than that of floribundas, shrub roses, and miniatures.

'ADMIRAL RODNEY'.   Trew, 1973, PB. The flowers of 'Admiral Rodney' are soft, pale rose-pink, with a deeper coloration on the reverse sides of the petals. The highly fragrant blooms of this variety are 4 to 6 inches across, with 45 petals and an exquisite high-centered form. Large, glossy, dark green foliage resists most rose diseases except rust. Plants grow about 4 feet tall and exhibit good winter hardiness. This variety is at its best during its first flush of bloom. 6.3

'BIG PURPLE'.   Stephens, 1986, MB. As the name implies, these 35-petaled flowers are enormous—up to 6 inches across—and their color is true purple, like grape juice. In addition to their large size, the flowers also have a wonderful fragrance. The 4- to 5-foot plant has medium to dark green foliage with a grayish coating that helps keep the plant disease resistant. It is also quite hardy. If you want to exhibit this rose in an ARS show, you must label it 'Stephens' Big Purple', its proper registered name, although it is usually listed in catalogs as 'Big Purple.' (7.5)

'BLUE MOON'.   Tantau, 1964, MB. Although there has never been a blue rose, 'Blue Moon' comes closer than many others. Its close-to-blue lavender flowers have 40 petals and measure 3 to 4½ inches across. Plants grow 4 to 5 feet high. Like most lavender roses, 'Blue Moon' has a strong fragrance. It is also fairly winter hardy and has good disease resistance. 6.9

'BOBBY CHARLTON'.   Fryer, 1974, PB. The superbly formed, 6-inch flowers of this variety are deep pink on the insides of the petals and silvery on the outsides. The blooms, with 35 to 40 petals, also have a pleasant, spicy fragrance. They contrast nicely with the dark green, leathery leaves that have fairly good disease resistance, although they are somewhat prone to mildew. Plants grow about 5 feet tall. However, plants tend to be a little too tender in areas colder than Zone 7 unless they receive a lot of protection. 7.0

'BROADWAY'. Perry, 1986, YB. Blooms of 'Broadway' have 35 petals and are high centered, 4 to 5 inches across, and a lovely yellow with the petal edges tipped in pink. They also have a delicious fragrance. Plants grow 5 to 6 feet tall and are clothed with large, dark green, leathery foliage that resists disease. 'Broadway' also has better-than-average winter hardiness. 7.1 AARS

'Broadway'

'CANADIAN WHITE STAR'. Mander, 1980, W. As the 40 to 45 sparkling white petals of this variety open, they quill back in such a way that they form the outline of a multipointed star 3 to 4 inches across. The plants grow 5 to 6 feet tall and have medium to dark green, leathery, semiglossy leaves. Another identifying characteristic of this variety is its large, hooked thorns. For best results, grow this rose in coastal climates as it does not take well to heat. 6.5

'CARY GRANT'. Meilland, 1987, OB. Blooms of 'Cary Grant' are an eye-catching bright orange with a lighter reverse and have an excellent high-centered form and spicy fragrance. Flowers are 5 inches across and have 35 to 40 petals. Stems commendably firm for cutting are covered with dark green, glossy foliage on plants that can grow 4 to 5 feet tall. (7.5)

'CENTURY TWO'. Armstrong, 1971, MP. Long, pointed buds open into medium pink, double, cupped, slightly fragrant flowers that are 5 inches across. The bushy, upright plants grow 4 to 5 feet tall, with leathery foliage and good winter hardiness. Plants are somewhat mildew prone. 8.3

'Charlotte Armstrong'

'CHARLOTTE ARMSTRONG'. Lammerts, 1940, DP. Named for a member of one of the original rose-growing families in the United States, 'Charlotte Armstrong' is pretty in its own right but most revered as the parent of many of today's modern hybrid teas. The flowers are deep pink to light red with 35 petals, and measure 3½ to 4½ inches across. Blooms have a light tea fragrance and are loose and informal in shape. Plants can grow 5 to 6 feet tall and have dark green, leathery leaves. 7.2 AARS

'CHICAGO PEACE'. Johnston, 1962, PB. This sport of 'Peace' was discovered by a gardener in her backyard in Chicago. There have been many sports of 'Peace', but this one is the best. Like its parent, it has large, 5- to 6-inch, high-centered flowers with about 60 petals. But instead of being primarily yellow, as 'Peace' is, the blooms are a blend of deep rose pink, light pink, and apricot, with yellow at the base of the petals. Bushes grow 4½ to 5½ feet tall and have leathery, dark green shiny leaves that are prone to black spot. On the plus side, 'Chicago Peace' is very winter hardy. 8.2

'Chicago Peace'

'Color Magic'

'Command Performance'

'Dainty Bess'

'CHRISTIAN DIOR'. Meilland, 1958, MR. The formal, high-centered bud opens into a cupped, full, 4- to 6-inch flower with 50 to 60 petals. The clear, glowing, medium cherry red flowers can burn and turn black on the petal edges in hot, dry gardens, so it is best to grow 'Christian Dior' where there is afternoon shade. Plants grow 3½ to 5 feet tall and have large, leathery, semiglossy leaves on almost thornless canes. Plants can be prone to mildew. 7.0 AARS

'CHRYSLER IMPERIAL'. Lammerts, 1952, DR. Early advertisements for this rose pictured Chrysler automobiles, in consideration of which the breeder received a free car. This commercial arrangement raised the eyebrows of many rose hybridizers at the time. 'Chrysler Imperial' has long been popular for its classic hybrid tea form and very heavy fragrance. Flowers of deep red are 4½ to 5 inches across and have 40 to 50 petals. Plants grow 4 to 5 feet tall, and have thorny canes and dark green, semiglossy leaves. 'Chrysler Imperial' tends to mildew in cool, wet climates but otherwise has excellent disease resistance; it is also somewhat winter hardy. 8.5 AARS, JAGFM

'COLOR MAGIC'. Warriner, 1978, PB. As the flowers of 'Color Magic' mature, they change from ivory, to ivory tinged with light pink, to coral, and finally to dark pink. This color change is intensified by sunlight and high heat. The 5-inch-wide blooms with 20 to 30 petals are cupped when fully open, and are slightly fragrant. Bushes grow 3½ to 4 feet tall and bear large, dark green, semiglossy leaves that are fairly disease resistant. 'Color Magic' is extremely tender where winters are cold. 8.2 AARS

'COMMAND PERFORMANCE'. Lindquist, 1970, OR. Flowers of 'Command Performance' are 4 inches across when fully open, and the 25 petals reflex (curl under) in such a way that the rose eventually takes on a star-shaped appearance. Flowers are orange-red sometimes suffused with blue, and are highly fragrant. Leathery foliage clothes the upright, bushy, 5- to 6-foot plants. 7.1 AARS

'CRIMSON GLORY'. Kordes, 1935, DR. Although 'Crimson Glory' is a relatively old variety, it is still grown for its outstanding heavy fragrance. It has also been used extensively in hybridizing. Long, pointed buds open into cupped, decorative, dark red, velvety, 3- to 4-inch flowers with 30 petals. Blooms of 'Crimson Glory' take on a purple tinge as they fade. The foliage is leathery on compact, 3-foot, spreading plants. It is very prone to mildew. 7.2 JAGFM

'DAINTY BESS'. Archer, 1925, LP. With only five petals per flower, 'Dainty Bess' is one of the few single hybrid teas. The fragrant 3- to 4-inch flowers are a soft rose-pink set off by bright maroon stamens. The vigorous plants grow 4 to 5 feet tall and have leathery foliage and heavily thorned canes. 'Dainty Bess' looks delicate but is quite winter hardy. 8.8

'DIAMOND JUBILEE'. Boerner, 1947, YB. Named for the seventy-fifth anniversary of Jackson and Perkins Company, the largest rose nursery in the United States, 'Diamond Jubilee' has flowers of buff yellow to apricot. The blooms are 5 to 6 inches across, with 30 to 45 petals, a delightful fruity fragrance, and a cupped, decorative shape. Compact plants grow 3 to 4 feet tall and have dark green, leathery leaves. This rose was once classified as a floribunda, and it has the blooming characteristics of one, as it usually produces its flowers in sprays. 6.5 AARS

'DOLLY PARTON'. Winchel, 1984, OR. Like its show-business namesake, this rose is larger than life, with huge 6- to 7-inch double blooms that are extremely long lasting as cut flowers. Fragrance is exceptionally strong and spicy, and the bright orange-red blooms are attractively set off by dark green, slightly glossy leaves. Plants grow about 4 feet tall. Unfortunately, bloom production can be sparse and the plant is tender and prone to mildew. 7.2 ARSTG

'DOUBLE DELIGHT'. Swim and Ellis, 1977, RB. A delight both to look at and to smell, 'Double Delight' has a highly spicy fragrance and lovely 5½-inch flowers of white, edged in raspberry red. As the flower ages, the red edge extends further into the petal until the rose almost appears to be red. The blooms have 35 to 45 petals. Spreading, bushy plants grow 3 to 4 feet high. 8.8 AARS, JAGFM

'DUET'. Swim, 1960, MP. Generally blooming in sprays, 'Duet' has a long vase life and is therefore an excellent cut flower. The 4-inch blooms with 25 to 35 petals are a dusty coral-pink with darker tones on the undersides of the petals; flowers have an informal, decorative form. Flowers are fragrant and bloom on 4½- to 5½-foot plants that have leathery, medium green, hollylike leaves. 7.9 AARS

'DYNASTY'. Warriner, 1989, OB. Flowers of bright orange with flashing yellow on the reverse sides of the petals are 4 to 5 inches across with 30 petals. The most outstanding feature of this 5-foot-high variety is its long cutting stems. + ROY

'ELECTRON'. McGredy, 1970, DP. Called 'Mullard Jubilee' in Europe, in honor of an electronics company, 'Electron' has flowers of rich, deep, glowing electric pink with a very heavy fragrance. The circular flowers have 30 to 35 petals and open to 5 inches across. Repeating quickly all summer, 'Electron' has medium green, leathery leaves and extremely thorny canes. Compact, slightly spreading plants grow 2½ to 3½ feet high, making them good choices for the front of a bed, and have good winter hardiness. 7.9 AARS

'FIRST PRIZE'. Boerner, 1970, PB. 'First Prize' was well named, for it is a frequent winner at rose shows. Its tall light pink buds open into high-centered flowers that graduate from ivory at

'Double Delight'

'Electron'

'First Prize'

'Flaming Beauty'

'Fragrant Cloud'

'Fragrant Memory'

the bases of the petals to medium pink at the edges. The fragrant blooms have 30 to 35 petals and are 5 to 6 inches across when fully open. 'First Prize' makes a good vase flower if cut when the buds are tight, which will extend its life as a cut flower. The foliage of this 4- to 5-foot plant is attractively dark green and leathery but slightly prone to mildew. Plants are extremely tender as well. 8.9 AARS

'FLAMING BEAUTY'. Winchel, 1978, YB. One of the best commercial products to come from an amateur hybridizer, 'Flaming Beauty' has perfect, high-centered blooms of yellow brushed with reddish orange. The brightly colored double blooms are 4 inches across. Plants are 3 to 4 feet high and slightly spreading, with fair winter hardiness. Watch out for mildew, though. 7.0 ARSTG

'FOLKLORE'. Kordes, 1977, OB. This perfectly formed hybrid tea, excellent for exhibiting at rose shows, has flowers of soft orange, with orange-yellow on the reverse sides of the petals. Blooms of 'Folklore' are 4 to 4½ inches across and have 45 petals. A heavy fragrance makes it as good to smell as it is to look at. Leaves on the 5- to 6-foot plant are glossy and elongated and quite resistant to diseases. Plants also have better-than-average winter hardiness. 8.5

'FRAGRANT CLOUD'. Tantau, 1963, OR. Intensely fragrant, as its name denotes, 'Fragrant Cloud' is vivid orange-red with a shading of dull blue or gray on the petals. The 3½- to 5-inch flowers have 25 to 30 petals and often bloom in sprays, making it look more like a floribunda. High centered when first open, flowers become flat and decorative as they mature. The compact plants grow 3 to 4 feet high and have dark green, shiny foliage. 'Fragrant Cloud' has better-than-average disease resistance and is very winter hardy. 8.0 ROY, JAGFM

'FRAGRANT MEMORY'. Warriner, 1974, MP. Introduced in 1974 as 'Jadis', this rose was removed from the marketplace in 1979 because Jackson and Perkins thought the name was too difficult for most people to pronounce. It was reintroduced in 1989 with its present and more evocative name. One of the most fragrant roses ever hybridized, 'Fragrant Memory' has long, slender flowers of lively pink with a slight lavender fluorescence. When fully open, the 25-petaled flower measures 4½ to 5 inches across. Plants grow 3 to 5 feet tall and have long cutting stems and better-than-average hardiness. 7.0

'GARDEN PARTY'. Swim, 1959, W. With white, classically shaped flowers delicately edged in pink, 'Garden Party' has been a favorite for many years. The fragrant blooms are 5 to 6 inches across with 25 to 30 petals; they flower above medium green, semiglossy leaves on plants that grow to 5 feet high. Long lasting in the garden or when cut, 'Garden Party' is very winter hardy. It has better-than-average resistance to black spot, but is mildew prone. 8.5 AARS

'GRACELAND'. Warriner, 1989, MY. Exceptionally bright golden yellow color characterizes 'Graceland'. The high-centered flowers are 4 to 5 inches wide, with 30 to 35 ruffled petals; they bloom in sprays on long cutting stems. Plants grow 4 to 5 feet tall and have better-than-average disease resistance. (7.6) ROY

'GRANADA'. Lindquist, 1963, RB. Although classified as a red blend, 'Granada' is more precisely a blend of yellow, gold, pink, and red. Spicily fragrant 'Granada' has 18 to 25 petals and slender flowers that open from urn-shaped buds. Fully open flowers are 3 to 4 inches across. Plants grow 4 to 5 feet tall and are covered with dark green, leathery, crinkled, and serrated leaves on thorny canes. 'Granada' has better than average resistance to black spot, but is susceptible to mildew. 8.4 AARS, JAGFM

'Graceland'

'HEADLINER'. Warriner, 1985, PB. The petals of 'Headliner' are creamy white, blending to deep pink and then red at the edges. The inner petals have only a narrow band of color, while the outer petals are almost completely brushed in cerise. The petal count is high, at 40 to 60, and open blooms measure 4 inches across. The medium green leaves have good disease resistance and heavily cover a 5-foot plant. 7.6 ROY

'HELEN TRAUBEL'. Swim, 1951, PB. Rose growers often call this variety "Helen Trouble" because it often produces flowers with weak necks that cannot hold the flower upright. Nevertheless, the 5- to 6-inch flowers with 20 to 25 petals are decorative, fragrant, and a pretty apricot-pink. The foliage of this 5- to 6-foot plant is leathery and dull green. 6.0 AARS

'HONOR'. Warriner, 1980, W. A member of William Warriner's wedding trio 'Love', 'Honor', and 'Cherish' (a grandiflora, hybrid tea, and floribunda, respectively), this rose has long-lasting white to yellowish white flowers on long cutting stems. The slightly fragrant flowers have 20 to 25 petals and open to 3 to 4 inches wide. Fully opened, the flowers are cupped and loose. The upright plants grow 4 to 5 feet tall and often have slender canes and large, dark green, leathery leaves. 'Honor' has better-than-average disease resistance and winter hardiness, especially for a white rose. 7.4 AARS, ROY

'Headliner'

'INGRID BERGMAN'. Poulsen, 1983, DR. This rose commemorating the late Swedish-born actress has slightly fragrant blooms of dark red set off by dark green foliage. Flowers have 35 to 40 petals and open 4 to 5½ inches across. The most outstanding feature of this rose is its exceptional winter hardiness. Upright plants grow 4½ feet tall. 7.4

'IRISH GOLD'. Dickson, 1966, MY. Known in Europe as 'Grandpa Dickson' (after a patriarch of the Northern Ireland rose-breeding clan), 'Irish Gold' has clear, pale yellow flowers whose petals quill when the flower is open, giving it a star-shaped outline. Occasionally the petals have a pale pink edge. Flowers are

'Helen Traubel'

'John F. Kennedy'

'King's Ransom'

'La France'

5 to 6 inches across with 30 to 35 petals, and have a light, sweet fragrance. The bushy plants reach a height of 3 to 4½ feet and have leathery, glossy, dark green foliage. 7.0 ROY

'JOHN F. KENNEDY'. Boerner, 1965, W. Gene Boerner of Jackson and Perkins had planned to name this variety after himself, but following the assassination the company named it for the late president instead. (Boerner finally did immortalize himself with a floribunda, described in the next section.) The green-tinged buds of 'John F. Kennedy' open into 5- to 5½-inch white flowers of 45 to 50 petals. This variety is the most fragrant among popular white hybrid teas. Its disease-resistant foliage is dark green and leathery. Plants grow 4 to 5 feet tall. 6.0

'KEEPSAKE'. Kordes, 1981, PB. Called 'Esmeralda' in Europe, 'Keepsake' is a very fragrant rose whose plants produce blooms either singly or in sprays. The outsides of the petals are light pink, blending to darker pink at the edges; the insides of the petals blend from medium to dark pink. Blooms have 30 to 35 petals and open to 5 inches across. Plants are 4 to 6 feet tall with stout thorns and shiny, light green leaves. 'Keepsake' is quite winter hardy. 7.5

'KING'S RANSOM'. Morey, 1961, DY. Blooms of 'King's Ransom' are medium to deep yellow, and the color does not fade in the heat, which happens with many other yellow roses. Flowers are 4 to 5 inches wide with 35 to 40 petals. They have a pleasing fragrance and grow on long stems for cutting. Plants are 4½ to 5 feet tall with moderately thorny canes. 'King's Ransom' is reasonably winter hardy, a surprising attribute for a yellow rose, but is often slow to rebloom during the summer. 6.5 AARS

'KORDES' PERFECTA'. Kordes, 1957, PB. Urn-shaped buds of this highly fragrant rose open into 4½- to 5-inch very double flowers with 65 to 70 petals. The high-centered, slender blooms are creamy white, edged with red. As the temperature climbs, more red appears on the flowers, spreading downward from the edges. Cutting stems are long and strong on this 4- to 5-foot plant that has dark green, leathery, glossy foliage. 'Kordes' Perfecta' is a sparse bloomer but quite winter hardy. 6.5 ROY

'LADY X'. Meilland, 1966, MB. Long, pointed buds open into high-centered, slender, 4-inch double flowers of pale lavender that often have a pinkish cast. As the petals open they curl back on themselves, quill-like, to form a star shape. Unlike most lavender roses, 'Lady X' is not richly fragrant. Fairly disease resistant and a prolific bloomer, this is one of the tallest roses in its color class, reaching heights of 5 to 6 feet. 8.3

'LA FRANCE'. Guillot Fils, 1867, LP. Although no longer grown widely, this living heirloom is considered to be the first hybrid tea and thus the first modern rose. Its petals are silvery pink on the insides and brighter pink on the outsides, and its flowers are more decorative in shape than those of modern hybrid teas. The fragrant blooms measure 3 to 4½ inches across, with 60 petals. Plants grow 3 to 4 feet tall and have semiglossy leaves. 5.9

'LAS VEGAS'.   Kordes, 1981, OB. Evoking the desert colors of a Las Vegas sunrise, or the busy neon of its famous Strip, 'Las Vegas' has gleaming orange-yellow buds that open to reveal petals that are rich orange-red on the insides and golden yellow on the outsides. Flowers are 4 inches across, with 25 petals, and are deliciously fragrant. The medium green, glossy foliage is highly resistant to mildew and the 4- to 5-foot bushy plant is very hardy. 7.5

'MADAME VIOLET'.   Teranishi, 1981, MB. This robust, 4- to 5-foot plant with gray-green, semiglossy foliage is somewhat more disease resistant than average. Its high-centered, 3- to 4-inch flowers, which usually bloom in sprays, have 45 petals and open into a perfect spiral in shades of lilac with a pink tint. Plants bloom sparsely but are fairly winter hardy. 7.0

'MARIJKE KOOPMAN'.   Fryer, 1979, MP. The long pointed buds of this flower open into satiny pink, 4-inch flowers with 25 petals. The fragrant blooms usually appear in sprays of three to five and rebloom prolifically throughout the summer. Foliage is dark green and leathery, growing along stems with conspicuous red thorns. The vigorous plants reach about 4 feet in height. 7.8

'MISS ALL-AMERICAN BEAUTY'.   Meilland, 1967, DP. Known as 'Maria Callas' in Europe, 'Miss All-American Beauty' has 4- to 5-inch cupped flowers with 50 to 60 petals each. The highly fragrant blooms are such a deep pink color that they are almost red. Leaves are leathery on a bushy, 3- to 4-foot plant that is very winter hardy. 8.3 AARS

'MISTER LINCOLN'.   Swim and Weeks, 1964, DR. Although introduced nearly three decades ago, 'Mister Lincoln' is still regarded as one of the best red roses. Its velvety, dark red petals do not burn in the sun as easily as other red roses do and are very fragrant. The 4- to 5½-inch blooms have 30 to 40 petals and long stems for cutting. Leaves are dark green, leathery, and semiglossy. The 5- to 6-foot plant has better-than-average winter hardiness. 8.9 AARS

'MON CHERI'.   Christensen, 1981, RB. Opening from a bright pink bud, this 1982 All-America Rose Selection has petals whose edges darken to red as the flower matures. The 4½-inch blooms with 30 to 35 petals are more decorative than high centered, and have a light, spicy fragrance. The compact, spreading plants grow 2½ to 3 feet tall. 'Mon Cheri' repeats its blooming cycle extremely quickly, has better-than-average disease resistance, and is very winter hardy. 7.6 AARS

'OLYMPIAD'.   McGredy, 1984, MR. The official rose of the 1984 summer Olympics, and one of the best reds in recent years,

'Miss All-American Beauty'

'Mon Cheri'

'Olympiad'

'Papa Meilland'

'Paradise'

'Pascali'

'Olympiad' has 3- to 5-inch nonfading, 35-petaled flowers of bright medium red that repeat very quickly. It is good for cutting, as flowers are long lasting and stems are long and strong. Plants grow 4 to 5 feet high and have better-than-average winter hardiness as well as good disease resistance. 8.3 AARS

'OSIRIA'. Kordes, 1978, RB. Large (4- to 6-inch), well-formed, high-centered flowers with 50 to 60 petals are dark red on the inside of the petals and silvery white on the outside. The highly fragrant blooms repeat very quickly, especially for a large rose. Plants can grow 5 to 6 feet high, have dark green, semi-glossy, black spot–resistant foliage that is prone to mildew, and are very winter hardy. 7.2

'PAPA MEILLAND'. Meilland, 1963, DR. Pointed buds open into high-centered, 4- to 6-inch flowers with 35 petals. The color is rich, velvety crimson and the rose is one of the most fragrant. The leathery leaves are dull medium green on a 4- to 5-foot plant. 7.2 JAGFM

'PARADISE'. Weeks, 1978, MB. Deep mauve with red edges, 'Paradise' was a color breakthrough when first hybridized. Long buds open into high-centered, delectably fragrant flowers that have 25 to 30 petals and measure 3½ to 4½ inches across when fully open. The thorny plants grow 3 to 4½ feet high and are covered with dark green, glossy leaves. 'Paradise' is fairly winter hardy and disease resistant. 8.6 AARS

'PASCALI'. Lens, 1968, W. The flowers are small, about 3 inches across, but they are perfectly formed and high centered. The slightly fragrant, creamy white blooms have 30 petals and stand on strong cutting stems against dark green foliage. This is one white rose that resists rain spotting. Plants can grow 4 to 5 feet tall. 8.5 AARS

'PEACE'. Meilland, 1945, YB. Famous for its role as peace harbinger at the end of World War II (by coincidence, it was christened on the day Berlin fell), 'Peace' has 6- to 7-inch flowers of yellow edged in pink. Flowers have more than 50 petals, a high-centered form, and a light fragrance. Blooming best in early summer, 'Peace' has very shiny, leathery leaves that are prone to black spot. Plants can grow 5 to 6 feet tall and have better-than-average winter hardiness. 8.7 AARS

'PERFECT MOMENT'. Kordes, 1989, RB. 'Perfect Moment' has unique, flamboyant yellow-based flowers with red edges that stand out in a rose bed. The long-lasting flowers are high centered, 4 to 4½ inches across, and slightly fragrant, and have 35 petals. Plants grow 4½ feet tall and have dark green foliage with excellent disease resistance. + AARS

'PINK PEACE'. Meilland, 1959, MP. Like its parent, 'Peace', this very double rose has flowers with 50 to 65 petals that open to

6 inches across. Unlike its parent, 'Pink Peace' is a solid-colored medium to deep pink with a heavy fragrance. The flowers are rounded to cupped and decorative in shape. Plants grow 4½ to 5½ feet high, have medium green, dull, leathery leaves. They have better-than-average disease resistance and are winter hardy. 7.3

'POLARSTERN'.   Tantau, 1982, W. Massive creamy white buds tinged with yellow at their bases open into perfectly formed, high-centered 3- to 4-inch roses with 35 petals. The leaves are medium green and covered with a grayish waxy coating that virtually guarantees their disease resistance. Bushy plants grow 5 to 6 feet high and have good winter hardiness. 7.7

'PORTRAIT'.   Meyer, 1971, PB. Fragrant double flowers, 3 to 4 inches wide, are a lovely blend of ivory shading to light and dark pink toward the edges. The leaves are dark green and glossy, clothing a 5- to 6-foot plant that is very winter hardy. This rose is yet another successful innovation by an amateur breeder. 7.0 AARS

'PRECIOUS PLATINUM'.   Dickson, 1974, MR. The clear medium red flowers of 'Precious Platinum' are long lasting as cut flowers and repeat their bloom very quickly. Flowers are 3 to 4 inches wide, with 35 to 40 petals and a slight fragrance. The somewhat spreading plant with moderately thorny canes grows 4 feet tall and is quite winter hardy. Leaves are dark green, leathery, and shiny, with better-than-average disease resistance. 7.9

'PRINCESSE DE MONACO'.   Meilland, 1981, PB. This rose was named in honor of Grace Kelly and is sometimes known by that name in Europe. The petals of this flower are cream colored and edged in shades of pink to cerise. The 35-petaled, 4- to 6-inch flowers have the high-centered form and symmetrical swirl of petals that characterize exhibition-quality blooms. Flowers are deliciously fragrant as well. Foliage is large, dark green, and glossy on a bushy, 3- to 4-foot plant. 7.2

'PRISTINE'.   Warriner, 1978, W. True to its name, 'Pristine' has flowers that are pure white edged in delicate tones of pink. Blooms have 30 to 35 petals, measure 4 to 5 inches across, and are set off by very large, dark green leaves. Plants grow about 4 to 5 feet high and have almost thornless canes, but sometimes do not grow vigorously. 8.7 ROY

'RED LION'.   McGredy, 1964, MR. The high-centered 5-inch flowers are bright cherry red and have excellent substance. As the flower's 35 to 40 petals open, they turn back into a quill form that gives the plant a starry outline. Plants grow 5 to 6 feet tall and have oversized, leathery foliage. 7.1

'ROYAL HIGHNESS'.   Swim and Weeks, 1962, LP. A delicate, stately, pale pink rose with slender buds and narrow, high-centered flowers, 'Royal Highness' has 40 to 45 petals and is 4 to

'Pristine'

'Princesse de Monaco'

'Precious Platinum'

'Sheer Bliss'

'Sunbright'

'Sutter's Gold'

5 inches across when fully open. The wonderfully fragrant flowers grow on plants 4 to 5 feet high. 'Royal Highness' has reigned supreme for many years even though it is very tender in cold winters. 8.3 AARS

'SHEER BLISS'. Warriner, 1987, W. Although it is classified as a white rose, 'Sheer Bliss' is more of a pale pink, with creamy white petals that radiate a soft pink tone. Excellent for cutting, 'Sheer Bliss' has good substance, long stems, and strong fragrance. Its 4- to 5-inch flowers have 35 petals. The compact plants grow 3 to 4 feet high and have excellent disease resistance. They also have better than average hardiness, especially for a rose in this color range. 7.6 AARS

'SHEER ELEGANCE'. Twomey, 1989, PB. Pointed, oval buds open into 3- to 4-inch flowers with 35 to 40 petals and the classic high-centered hybrid tea form that is bound to be a winner on the show table. Blooms are soft pink to pale salmon with a deeper pink edge, and are borne on long, stiff stems. Flowers are set off by dark green, disease-resistant foliage that covers 4- to 5-foot plants. + AARS

'SUMMER DREAM'. Warriner, 1987, AB. The peach-colored buds of 'Summer Dream' open to reveal shades of pink and orange on the insides of the petals, blending to yellow on the outsides. The flowers, which have 30 to 35 petals and are 4 to 5 inches across, bloom in sprays and repeat their bloom very quickly. Plants grow 4 to 5 feet tall and are clothed in dark green, glossy foliage. 'Summer Dream' is more winter hardy than most other apricot-colored roses. 7.6 ROY

'SUMMER SUNSHINE'. Swim, 1962, DY. More of a golden yellow than other yellow roses, 'Summer Sunshine' is also more vigorous and disease resistant than other yellow roses, although it is not very winter hardy. The 3½- to 5-inch blooms with 25 to 30 petals repeat quickly all summer. Plants grow 4 to 5 feet tall and have gray-green, leathery foliage. 6.9

'SUNBRIGHT'. Warriner, 1984, MY. The name aptly describes the brilliant yellow flowers of this hybrid tea. Repeating their bloom quickly, the flowers are 4 inches across and have 24 to 30 petals. Plants grow 4 to 5 feet high with dark green, glossy foliage. Resistance to fungal diseases is very good for a yellow rose. 7.4 ROY

'SUTTER'S GOLD'. 1950, OB. Named for the 1948 centennial of the discovery of gold in California, 'Sutter's Gold' is one of the most fragrant hybrid teas. The flowers are golden yellow, overlaid with tones of orange and tipped in red. The flowers are tall, slender, and urn shaped, with 30 to 35 petals. When fully open, the blooms are 4 to 6 inches across. Plants grow 4 to 5 feet tall with dark green, leathery, semiglossy foliage on thorny canes. 6.5 AARS, JAGFM

'SWARTHMORE'.   Meilland, 1963, PB. Rose-red blooms, tending to medium deep pink, are 4 to 5 inches across and have 45 to 55 petals. They are high centered and slender, with a slight fragrance. Petal edges usually turn smoky dark red or black, especially in bright sunlight. The long, straight stems are clothed in dark green, leathery foliage on a 4- to 6-foot plant that is quite winter hardy. 8.3

'TIFFANY'.   Lindquist, 1954, PB. A highly fragrant rose, 'Tiffany' has medium pink, satiny flowers blending into yellow at the bases of the petals. The 4- to 5-inch flowers have 25 to 30 petals and a classic hybrid tea form atop long stems good for cutting. Plants grow 4 to 5 feet tall with medium to dark green glossy foliage, and are moderately thorny. 8.4 AARS, JAGFM

'Tiffany'

'TOUCH OF CLASS'.   Le Clerc, 1984, PB. 'Touch of Class' is the top-rated exhibition rose, according to results of ARS rose shows, and with good reason. Flowers have a classic, high-centered shape, and produce their perfectly spiraled form repeatedly all summer on exceptionally long cutting stems. The color is warm pink, shading to coral at the edges, and the broad petals show a hint of a ruffle. Blooms can be 4½ to 5½ inches across and have 30 to 35 petals. Plants grow 4 to 5 feet high. 8.3 AARS

'TROPICANA'.   Tantau, 1962, OR. A color breakthrough at the time of its introduction, 'Tropicana' was the first orange-red hybrid tea. Called 'Super Star' in Europe, it has 30 to 35 petals and a moderate fruity scent. High centered when it first opens, 'Tropicana' becomes cup shaped and 4 to 5 inches wide as the blooms mature. Plants grow 4 to 6 feet high and have dark green, glossy, leathery foliage. 'Tropicana' has better-than-average disease resistance and is very winter hardy. 8.3 AARS, ROY

'Touch of Class'

'UNCLE JOE'.   Kern, 1971, DR. For many years there was controversy as to whether 'Uncle Joe' and 'Toro' were the same rose. It has been decided that they are, and that the correct name is 'Uncle Joe'. Flowers are dark red and high centered, opening to 6 inches across from very large buds. Flowers need hot weather to open; often the flower fails to open completely in cool weather, since it has so many petals (60 or more) and fades before the petals open. Leaves are large, dark green and leathery on long cutting stems. Plants grow 5 to 6 feet tall. 7.7

'WHITE DELIGHT'.   Warriner, 1989, W. Despite its name, 'White Delight' is not a pure white rose. Rather, it is an ivory rose that blends to a soft pink at the center, with pink-tinged outer petals. The blooms, which have 35 to 40 petals, are 4½ inches wide and are set off by dark green, leathery foliage. Plants grow about 4 to 5½ feet tall and produce long cutting stems. + ROY

'Tropicana'

'Anabell'

'Apricot Nectar'

'Betty Prior'

FLORIBUNDAS

*W*ith a name that reflects their profusion of flowers, floribundas are the product of a cross between a hybrid tea and a polyantha. They are generally hardier, lower growing, and bushier than hybrid teas, making them a perfect choice for landscaping. They're at their best when used in hedges, borders, or mass plantings, since they are floriferous and fast to repeat their bloom. Some have flowers with high-centered, hybrid tea form, while others have decorative, flatter or cup-shaped blooms. Although some produce flowers one to a stem, most floribundas bloom in sprays. Most flowers are single (5 to 12 petals) or semidouble (13 to 25 petals), with a few double (25 to 45 petals) and very double (over 45 petals) varieties. The following varieties are good choices for the garden.

'ANABELL'. Kordes, 1972, OB. The fragrant, showy, 3- to 4-inch blooms of 'Anabell' are rich orange-salmon blended with silver; flowers have 30 petals and a classic hybrid tea shape. They bloom all summer in large sprays, on neat and tidy plants that grow 2 to 3 feet high. Plants are disease resistant and winter hardy. 8.6

'ANGEL FACE'. Swim and Weeks, 1968, MB. 'Angel Face' is deep mauve, and like most mauve roses it is extremely fragrant. The 3½- to 4-inch flowers have 35 to 40 curvy petals and usually bloom in sprays. The blooms are informal, flat to slightly cupped, and accented with ruffled petals and bright yellow stamens. Plants grow 2½ to 3 feet tall in a mounded, spreading shape, and are covered by leathery, semiglossy foliage in dark coppery green. 8.2 AARS

'APRICOT NECTAR'. Boerner, 1965, AB. The crowded sprays of 'Apricot Nectar' have 3- to 4½-inch flowers of soft apricot to pink, with shadings of yellow at the bases of the petals. The 35-petaled blooms can be either high centered or cup shaped, and have a strong fruity fragrance. The bushy plants, excellent for mass plantings, are 3 to 5 feet tall, with smooth, almost thornless canes and medium green, semiglossy foliage. 'Apricot Nectar' is fairly winter hardy—something unusual for an apricot rose—but has a tendency to mildew. 8.0 AARS

'BETTY PRIOR'. Prior, 1935, MP. One of the earliest floribundas, 'Betty Prior' remains an excellent choice for a hedge or for planting singly, as its bloom is prolific. The sprays of fragrant flowers are medium to deep pink with five petals, and somewhat resemble dogwood blossoms. Flowers are 2 to 3½ inches across and repeat quickly. Plants can grow 5 or more feet tall and are very bushy, with medium green, semiglossy foliage. They are quite winter hardy, but likely to mildew. 8.0

'Brown Velvet'. McGredy, 1982, R. This is one of the few roses that the American Rose Society has classified as russet. This unique color results from an orange base with a purplish cast that therefore appears to be brown. Flowers 2½ to 3 inches across have 35 petals and a slight fragrance, and appear in small sprays. The decorative blooms consist of a rounded mass of ruffled petals. The disease-resistant foliage is dark green, on 4-foot plants. 6.8

'Cathedral'. McGredy, 1975, AB. Dedicated as a fund-raiser for the tenth anniversary of the rebuilding of England's war-torn Coventry Cathedral, this rose has high-centered flowers of dark apricot to orange, blending into a touch of yellow. The slightly fragrant blooms are waxy, with 18 to 24 petals, and open to 3 to 4 inches across. Plants are bushy and 3½ to 4 feet tall, with shiny olive to dark green foliage. 7.0 AARS

'Cherish'. Warriner, 1980, MP. The floribunda member of the 'Love', 'Honor', and 'Cherish' trio (the first two are a grandiflora and a hybrid tea, respectively), 'Cherish' has hybrid tea–type flowers that bloom in the profusion one would expect of a floribunda. The slightly spice-scented blooms are a soft, warm coral-pink with 28 petals; they open 2 to 3 inches across. Leaves are large and glossy dark green, resistant to disease, and borne on 3- to 3½-foot plants. Unfortunately, the plants are quite tender in zones 7 and colder. 7.8 AARS

'Class Act'. Warriner, 1989, W. The long, pointed buds of 'Class Act' open into informal flowers of pure, bright white. The blooms, which have 20 to 25 petals and are 3 to 4 inches across, have a light fruity fragrance and may appear singly or in sprays. The 3- to 5-foot plants are naturally bushy and rounded, filled with dark green leaves that have excellent disease resistance. 'Class Act' is quite winter hardy as well. (7.8) AARS

'Escapade'. Harkness, 1967, MB. Although classified as a mauve blend, 'Escapade' is really more of a pink blend. The flowers are single, with 12 petals that open flat into saucer-shaped disks. The fragrant 2- to 3-inch blooms have white centers and pinkish edges, and repeat quickly in sprays all summer. Compact plants grow 2½ to 3 feet tall with light to medium green foliage. 'Escapade' has good disease resistance and is fairly winter hardy. 8.2

'Europeana'. De Ruiter, 1968, DR. 'Europeana' produces huge sprays of velvety red blossoms that virtually hide the bronzy dark green foliage when the plant is in full bloom. The double flowers, which are 3 inches across, are slightly fragrant and very decorative. The plant is 2 to 3 feet tall with a spreading habit, making it perfect for mass plantings. It is particularly effective when planted with 'Iceberg', a fellow floribunda. 'Europeana' is both winter hardy and disease resistant. 9.0 AARS

'Fashion'. Boerner, 1949, PB. Oval, deep peach buds open into lively coral-peachy pink flowers with 20 to 25 petals and a

'Cherish'

'Europeana'

'First Edition'

'Gene Boerner'

'Gingersnap'

sweet fragrance. The 3½-inch blooms appear in large sprays on vigorous, 3-foot plants. This variety has found its way into the parentage of many of today's floribundas. 7.2 AARS

'FIRE KING'. Meilland, 1959, OR. Oval buds open into sprays of fiery scarlet to orange-red very double flowers with 50 petals. High centered when they first open, the flowers finish flat and 2½ inches across. Blooms have a musky fragrance, and the foliage is dark green and leathery. Plants are bushy and 4 to 5 feet high. It has good winter hardiness but is somewhat mildew prone. 7.2 AARS

'FIRST EDITION'. Delbard, 1976, OB. Long, pointed buds open into flowers with hybrid tea form that are a luminous coral color shading into orange. Flowers usually bloom in large sprays. This variety is one of the most reliable repeaters among the floribundas, making it an excellent variety for hedging. However, it is quite tender. The 2½- to 3-inch blooms have 28 petals and a slight fragrance. Spreading plants grow 3 to 4 feet tall with large, medium green, glossy leaves. 8.5 AARS

'FRENCH LACE'. Warriner, 1981, W. Dainty and refined, 'French Lace' has pointed buds of creamy ivory splashed with pale apricot that open into 3-inch flowers of ivory to white with peachy tones. The blooms have 30 petals and perfect hybrid tea form, and appear in small sprays. The small, dark green leaves are fairly disease resistant, but the plants are very tender in zones colder than Zone 7. They grow about 3 feet tall. 7.6 AARS

'GENE BOERNER'. Boerner, 1968, MP. Named for one of the twentieth century's best hybridizers of floribundas, who died in 1966, this rose has flowers with a hybrid tea shape and a clear, medium pink color that is faintly luminescent. Blooming in sprays, the slightly fragrant flowers have 35 petals and are 2 to 3 inches across; they repeat dependably all summer. Plants grow 3 to 4 feet high with medium green, semiglossy foliage and are quite winter hardy. 8.6 AARS

'GINGERSNAP'. Delbard-Chabert, 1978, OB. The pointed buds of this French hybrid open into mildly fragrant 4-inch flowers with 35 broad and ruffled petals. Colors are brilliant pure orange to tangerine. The foliage is dark green on bushy, 2-to 3-foot plants. 7.7

'ICEBERG'. Kordes, 1958, W. Flowers of 'Iceberg' are pure white and highly fragrant, with 30 petals. The decorative 2- to 3-inch, cup-shaped blooms appear in large sprays all summer. Plants grow 4 to 5 feet tall and are slightly spreading, making 'Iceberg' an excellent hedge rose. The light green, narrow, glossy leaves need extra protection from black spot, although they are highly resistant to mildew. The plant is very winter hardy. 'Iceberg' is particularly effective when combined with bright red floribundas. 8.7

'IMPATIENT'. Warriner, 1984, OR. This variety's name was intended to imply that the plant was impatient to rebloom, but gardeners have found that they grow impatient waiting for it, as its repeat interval is long. The high-centered, slightly fragrant flowers are bright orange with a yellow base. The 3-inch blooms with 20 to 30 petals appear singly or in small sprays. Very thorny canes are covered with semiglossy dark green to mahogany leaves that resist disease. Plants grow 2 to 3½ feet tall. 7.8 AARS

'INTRIGUE'. Warriner, 1984, MB. Intriguing it is, for there are few roses with this medium purple to plum color overcast with gray. The strongly fragrant blooms start out high centered, then open into decorative ruffled flowers 3 inches across that have 20 petals. Shiny medium to dark green foliage covers thorny canes. The compact plants grow only 1 to 2 feet tall, making this variety good for edging. Blooming does not repeat very quickly, however, and the plants are quite tender in areas colder than Zone 7. 7.1 AARS

'IVORY FASHION'. Boerner, 1958, W. The long-lasting, creamy white flowers of 'Ivory Fashion' begin as rounded buds suffused with yellow and peach. These open into flat, fragrant 3½- to 4-inch flowers with 15 to 18 petals that bloom in sprays all summer. Plants grow 3½ to 4 feet tall, with leathery, medium green, semiglossy foliage on almost thornless canes. 8.3 AARS

'LITTLE DARLING'. Duehrsen, 1956, YB. A blend of yellow and salmon-pink, the flowers of this rose are both little and darling, although the plant can grow quite large and spreading. Blooms are a perfect hybrid tea form when they first unfold, finishing in an open, cupped form 2 to 2½ inches across. They have 24 to 30 petals and appear in small sprays on arching stems. Plants grow 3 to 4 feet tall; pruning to an inward-facing bud will help keep the plant compact. Leaves are dark green, leathery and glossy, and have better-than-average disease resistance. 'Little Darling' is also very winter hardy. 9.0

'LIVERPOOL ECHO'. McGredy, 1971, OB. Named for an English newspaper, 'Liverpool Echo' has soft salmon, slightly fragrant flowers with 23 petals that open into a high-centered form. The reverse sides of the petals have a hint of pale yellow. As the blooms continue to mature, they open into 4-inch flowers. The disease-resistant, light green leaves cover a 5-foot plant. Sprays can be quite large, but after the first bloom the plant tends to produce 6- to 8-foot canes that do not flower. 8.0

'MARINA'. Kordes, 1974, OB. Long, pointed buds open into 3-inch, high-centered flowers of bright orange-red with a yellow base. The flowers, which have 35 to 40 petals, are delicately fragrant and bloom in sprays on long stems good for cutting. The leathery leaves are dark green and glossy. 'Marina' is one of the few roses that grows as well in a greenhouse as it does in the garden. However, it is somewhat winter tender. 7.5 AARS

'Impatient'

'Intrigue'

'Marina'

'Matador'

'Playgirl'

'Pleasure'

'MATADOR'. Van Rossem, 1972, OB. Evoking the excitement of a bullfight, the flowers of 'Matador' are flashing scarlet and orange with a golden yellow reverse. The flower is called 'Esther O'Farim' in Europe for a German singer who was a favorite of the introducer. 'Matador' has high-centered, slightly fragrant blooms with 25 to 30 petals that open to 2 to 3½ inches across. Ideal for containers and mass plantings, 'Matador' has dark green, leathery foliage on a 2- to 3-foot plant. 7.5

'NICOLE'. Kordes, 1984, PB. White-centered blooms with pink edges contrast attractively with large, dark green, semiglossy leaves. The slightly fragrant flowers have 35 petals and are 3 to 4 inches across. Plants are upright and grow 3 to 4 feet tall. Although the plant is listed as 'Nicole' in catalogs, you'll have to label it as 'Koricole', its registered name, if you want to show it in rose shows. 8.1

'ORANGEADE'. McGredy, 1959, OR. The slightly fragrant, 2½-inch flowers of 'Orangeade' have 12 to 15 petals of pure, clear, bright orange accented by bright yellow stamens. The sprays are large, airy, and long lasting. The rounded, 3-foot plants have sparse, dark green foliage that needs extra protection from mildew. 8.0

'PERMANENT WAVE'. Leenders, 1935, MR. This variety is a sport of 'Else Poulsen', the first floribunda, which has single flowers of bright rose-pink. 'Permanent Wave', so named because its petals are highly ruffled (unlike those of 'Else Poulsen'), is also single, with about 10 petals, but its flowers are a bright deep pink to carmine-red. The 2- to 2½-inch flowers bloom in small sprays and have a slight fragrance. This plant is so vigorous and prolific that when in bloom it appears to be covered with flowers. The foliage is dark green and shiny; the bushy plant is 4 to 5 feet high and winter hardy, but susceptible to mildew. 7.5

'PLAYBOY'. Cocker, 1976, RB. The 7- to 10-petaled blooms of this variety have deep yellow centers with bright orange to scarlet edges. Flowers are 3½ inches across with a slight apple fragrance. They bloom in large sprays above very glossy, dark green foliage on 3- to 4-foot plants. (8.2)

'PLAYGIRL'. Moore, 1986, MP. The counterpart of 'Playboy' shows off an endless display of 5- to 7-petaled, hot pink, 3½-inch flowers that appear in large sprays and have a light fragrance. The abundant blooms are set off by dark green leaves. Plants are rounded, growing 3 to 4 feet high. (8.0)

'PLEASURE'. Warriner, 1988, MP. Two- to 4-inch, ruffled, well-formed flowers are coral-pink flushed with salmon. Sprays have slightly fragrant flowers and are good for cutting because they have long stems and long-lasting flowers. Don't hold back—they quickly bloom again. Foliage is medium green and very disease resistant on 2- to 4-foot plants. (7.8) AARS

'REGENSBERG'. McGredy, 1979, PB. White at the base, each petal of 'Regensberg' is brushed with hot to dusty pink in various intensities. The 3-inch flowers have 20 to 25 petals and a sweet apple fragrance. Perfect for borders or containers, 'Regensberg' grows only about 2 feet tall and is very compact. It is one of the so-called Hand-Painted series of Sam McGredy IV, because each flower on the plant has slightly different shading. 8.0

'SARABANDE'. Meilland, 1959, OR. Named for a stately antique court dance, this lightly fragrant rose has enormous flat sprays of luminous, 3- to 4-inch flowers with 8 to 14 petals. The color is a bright to burnt orange, punctuated by bright yellow stamens. Plants are rounded and 2 to 3 feet high. 6.9 AARS

'SARATOGA'. Boerner, 1963 W. This rose was named in honor of the New York State race track, and early advertisements pictured it with a glass horse. Its white blooms may be either slightly high centered or decorative, and appear in large sprays. Strongly sweet scented, the flowers have 30 to 35 petals and open to 4 inches across. Hardy, spreading plants grow 2 to 3½ feet tall, with leathery, glossy light green foliage. 7.5 AARS

'Sea Pearl'

'SEA PEARL'. Dickson, 1964, PB. Buds of pastel pink open into 4½-inch, 24-petaled flowers of pearly pink diffused with peach and yellow. Bushy plants are about 5 feet tall, usually producing one bloom per stem instead of the typical floribunda spray. The foliage is dark green and disease resistant. 8.6

'SEXY REXY'. McGredy, 1984, MP. 'Sexy Rexy' is the nickname of a friend of the hybridizer, Sam McGredy IV. Light to medium pink, 3-inch flowers with more than 40 petals are ruffled and have a slight fragrance. Blooms are produced in very large sprays over light green, glossy small-leafed foliage. The bushy plants stay under 3 feet in height. 8.1

'Showbiz'

'SHOWBIZ'. Tantau, 1981, MR. An excellent edging rose, 'Showbiz' grows only 2 feet tall. Its exuberantly ruffled, bright scarlet flowers open very quickly to reveal brilliant yellow stamens. Flowers are about 2 inches across, with 20 petals. Large sprays of flowers cover the compact plants, which have dark green, glossy, disease-resistant foliage. 7.9 AARS

'SIMPLICITY'. Warriner, 1979, MP. 'Simplicity' is often marketed as a "living fence" because it forms an excellent tall hedge. Its showy, medium pink flowers are cup shaped to flat and 3 to 4 inches across. The slightly fragrant blooms with 18 to 20 petals appear in small sprays on long stems. Unfortunately, cut flowers do not last long. The 3- to 6-foot plants have medium green, semiglossy foliage that is hardy but prone to black spot. 8.0

'SPARTAN'. Boerner, 1955, OR. Pointed burnt orange buds open into high-centered flowers colored orange-red to reddish coral. The highly fragrant blooms, which are borne singly or in

'Simplicity'

'Spartan'

'Sun Flare'

'Sweet Vivien'

sprays, have 30 petals and are 3½ inches across. Stems are long and good for cutting, and the vigorous 3- to 4-foot plants are covered with shiny, leathery, dark green leaves. 7.1

'SUMMER FASHION'. Warriner, 1985, YB. This variety could as well have been a hybrid tea, for its flowers have perfect high-centered form and appear singly or in small sprays. Petals are light yellow edged in pink, with the pink spreading and darkening as the bloom matures. The sweetly fragrant, 3- to 5-inch flowers have 35 petals. Foliage is large, medium green and semiglossy, on 2½- to 3-foot plants. 7.8

'SUMMER SNOW'. Perkins, 1938, W. 'Summer Snow' represents the unique case in which a bush rose sported from a climber ('Climbing Summer Snow') rather than vice versa. The 2½- to 3-foot plants produce large sprays of creamy pointed buds and snowy white blossoms. Flowers repeat quickly against light green leaves, making this variety good for mass plantings. The 2½- to 3-inch flowers have 20 to 25 petals and a slight tea fragrance. 7.8

'SUN FLARE'. Warriner, 1983, MY. This descendant of 'Sunsprite' is a bright, nonfading lemon yellow with an unusual licorice scent. Its 2- to 3-inch flowers have 27 to 30 petals and bloom singly or in sprays. They are high centered when they open, becoming cup shaped as they mature. Leaves are light green and glossy on spreading, 2- to 3-foot plants with very good disease resistance and hardiness. 7.7 AARS

'SUNSPRITE'. Kordes, 1977, DY. One of the most disease-resistant floribundas, especially for a yellow, 'Sunsprite' has deep golden yellow flowers whose color does not fade in the heat. The very fragrant, 3-inch flowers have 28 petals and open flat. Plants are compact and 2 to 3 feet high. In addition to its disease resistance, 'Sunsprite' is also quite winter hardy. 8.8 JAGFM

'SWEET VIVIEN', Raffel, 1961, PB. Oval buds open into slightly fragrant, 3-inch flowers with 17 petals. Flowers are pink with light yellow centers, and bloom in sprays on medium-length stems. The disease-resistant foliage is small leafed, dark green, and glossy on compact, slightly spreading 2-foot plants. 8.0

'TRUMPETER'. McGredy, 1977, OR. 'Trumpeter' has brilliant, long-lasting orange to scarlet flowers with 35 to 40 ruffled petals and a mild fragrance. The glossy green foliage is quite disease resistant, covering bushy, compact, 2- to 3-foot plants. This is an excellent variety for mass plantings and landscape color. 7.8

'VOGUE'. Boerner, 1951, PB. Still popular after many years, 'Vogue' has high-centered flowers of medium to deep coral-pink. The slightly fragrant blooms have 25 petals and open to 2½ to 3½ inches wide, in very large sprays. Medium green, semiglossy leaves cover bushy, 4- to 5-foot plants that are prone to black spot but very winter hardy. 7.5 AARS

POLYANTHAS

Typical polyanthas are low-growing, compact, continually blooming plants with extreme winter hardiness. The small, informal flowers cover the plants in large sprays. Use polyanthas for bedding, low hedges, and foregrounds. Although now largely surpassed by their bigger and showier relatives the floribundas, several polyanthas are still worth growing.

'CÉCILE BRÜNNER'. Ducher, 1881, LP. Sometimes called the 'Sweetheart Rose', 'Cécile Brünner' has tiny, perfectly formed buds of pastel pink that bloom in airy sprays. The diminutive and sweetly fragrant high-centered double flowers are no more than 1 inch across and are set off by dark green leaves. Plants are 2 to 3 feet tall, and bushy and rounded in shape. Use this rose for boutonnieres. 8.0

'CHINA DOLL'. Lammerts, 1946, MP. This variety is perfect for containers or for low edges or borders, as it grows only 1 to 2 feet high. The large sprays of small (1- to 2-inch), fluffy, pure pink blooms with 24 petals can literally cover the mounded plant and bright green foliage. 8.1

'MARGO KOSTER'. Koster, 1931, OB. This sport of the polyantha 'Dick Koster', which is similar but red flowered, has 1-inch salmon flowers that look somewhat like a ranunculus—small, rounded, and cupped, with concentric rings of 20 petals in all. Blooms appear in large sprays on a low, compact plant that usually does not exceed 1 foot in height. 'Margo Koster' is often sold by florists as a potted plant for the holidays. 7.6

'THE FAIRY'. Bemtail, 1932, LP. Tiny, 1-inch, ruffled double flowers of pale pink bloom in dome-shaped sprays whose flowering period begins later than that of almost any other rose. Tiny, light green foliage is resistant to disease, and plants can survive a great deal of neglect. The 2- to 4-foot plants are best used as a ground cover, hedge, or massed planting. The stems of larger specimens tend to grow in an arching manner. 8.7

'Cécile Brünner'

'China Doll'

'Margo Koster'

'Aquarius'

'Gold Medal'

'Love'

GRANDIFLORAS

*C*reated in 1954 with the introduction of the rose 'Queen Elizabeth', the grandiflora class represents the first true melding of hybrid tea and floribunda characteristics. From its hybrid tea parent the grandiflora inherits flower form and long cutting stems; from the floribunda side come increased hardiness and prolific, clustered blooms. Most grandifloras, although not all, are taller than either hybrid teas or floribundas.

'AQUARIUS'. Armstrong, 1971, PB. A blend of cream with light and medium pink colorings, the flowers of 'Aquarius' are long lasting when cut. Long, tight buds open into high-centered, slightly fragrant, 3½- to 4½-inch flowers with 35 to 40 petals. The bushy plants grow 4½ to 5 feet tall and have large, leathery leaves of dull medium green. 'Aquarius' is fairly disease resistant and is quite winter hardy. 7.2 AARS

'ARIZONA'. Weeks, 1975, OB. Like the colors of a desert sunset, the flowers of 'Arizona' are a warm blend of bronzy orange and golden yellow. The high-centered blooms have 25 to 30 petals, are 2 to 4 inches across, and have a strong, sweet fragrance. Tall, upright plants grow 5 to 6 feet high and have glossy, bright green, leathery leaves that contrast nicely with the flowers. However, they are stingy bloomers and are somewhat winter tender. 6.0 AARS

'CAMELOT'. Swim and Weeks, 1964, MP. 'Camelot' is long lasting both in the garden and as a cut flower. The cup-shaped flowers are 3½ to 5 inches across with 40 to 55 petals. Blooms are coral to salmon-pink with a spicy fragrance, and appear in sprays. The bushy plants grow 5 to 6 feet tall, with large and glossy, dark green, leathery leaves that have good disease resistance. Plants are also fairly winter hardy. 7.5 AARS

'GOLD MEDAL'. Christensen, 1982, DY. A near-perfect exemplar of the grandiflora class, 'Gold Medal' has large, classically shaped flowers that bloom in sprays on long stems. The blooms are rich gold, with the petal edges tinged in red or orange, especially during cool weather. However, the flowers fade almost to white as they age. Double flowers have 35 to 40 petals, are 4 to 5 inches across, are long lasting when cut, and have a slightly fruity or tealike fragrance. Bushy plants have dark green, semi-glossy leaves and grow 5 to 7 feet tall. Unfortunately, they are slightly prone to black spot and moderately tender in cold climates. 8.0

'LOVE'. Warriner, 1980, RB. The grandiflora member of the wedding trio of 'Love', 'Honor', and 'Cherish' (the others are a hybrid tea and a floribunda, respectively), 'Love' has 3- to 4-inch, slightly fragrant flowers of bright red with a pure white reverse.

The blooms have 35 petals and a high-centered form, and are produced singly early in the season and in sprays when temperatures climb. Plants, which grow about 4 feet tall, have dark green, disease-resistant foliage and are fairly winter hardy. 7.1 AARS

'MONTEZUMA'.   Swim, 1955, OR. Urn-shaped buds of this rose open into high-centered, 3½- to 4-inch, slightly fragrant flowers that are a reddened coral-orange. Blooms have 30 to 35 petals and a slight tea fragrance. Bushy, compact, slightly spreading plants are 4 to 5 feet tall and clothed in abundant dark green, leathery, semiglossy foliage. 7.0

'NEW YEAR'.   McGredy, 1982, OB. The 20-petaled flowers of 'New Year' are a blend of gold and terra-cotta. Individual blooms, which have a slight fruity fragrance, are 2 to 3 inches across and are produced in sprays on compact, 3-foot plants. The leaves are large, dark green, and glossy with fair disease resistance. As with many grandifloras, winter hardiness is better than average. 7.7 AARS

'New Year'

'OLÉ'.   Armstrong, 1964, OR. Large, long-lived, ruffled flowers with luminous hues are bright orange-red, an exciting color reminiscent of a bullfight. Blooms have 40 to 50 petals, are 3½ inches across, are high centered or cupped, and have a slight fruity scent. Bushy, 4-foot plants are covered in shiny foliage. 7.5

'PINK PARFAIT'.   Swim, 1960, PB. This prolific bloomer is a blend of light and medium pink, with the petal edges darker than the bases. The 2- to 3-inch flowers with 20 to 25 petals have a slender, high-centered form. Slightly fragrant, the blooms are produced singly or in sprays on long, slender cutting stems. The bushy plants, which are disease resistant and very winter hardy, grow 3½ to 5 feet tall and have leathery, semiglossy foliage of medium green. 8.6 AARS

'Pink Parfait'

'PRIMA DONNA'.   Shirakawa, 1983, DP. Long, slender buds open into high-centered blooms of deep fuchsia pink shaded in lavender. The 3- to 4-inch flowers have 25 to 30 petals and a slight fragrance. They are produced singly early in the season and in small sprays later on. Plants are long stemmed and have medium to dark green, shiny leaves that stay disease free. Bushy, spreading plants grow 4 to 5 feet tall. Despite its name, 'Prima Donna' is not fussy and grows as well in a greenhouse as it does in a garden. 7.7 AARS

'PROMINENT'.   Kordes, 1971, OR. Known as 'Korp' in Europe, 'Prominent' has fluorescent orange-red flowers. The blooms are a small 2½ to 3 inches wide, with a classic high-centered form. The slightly fragrant flowers with 30 to 35 petals may appear singly or in sprays. Plants reach heights of 3 to 4 feet and have dull, leathery, dark green leaves. 7.0 AARS

'QUEEN ELIZABETH'.   Lammerts, 1954, MP. Named in honor of the queen's accession to the throne in 1952, this rose

'Prominent'

'Shining Hour'

'Shreveport'

'Sonia'

was the founding member of the grandiflora class. Its flowers, which have 40 petals, are light to medium pink, with darker pink at the edges. Fragrant individual 3½- to 4-inch blooms may be high centered or cupped, and are produced in sprays on long cutting stems. The plants are very tall (5 to 7 feet), with dark green, leathery, glossy leaves on almost thornless canes. Plants are characterized by both good disease resistance and good winter hardiness. 9.2 AARS

'SHINING HOUR'. Warriner, 1989, DY. One of the few yellow grandifloras, this one is a gleaming yellow that does not fade in the heat. The 4-inch blooms, which have 25 to 30 petals, are high centered or decorative in shape, with a moderate fruity fragrance. The shiny, disease-resistant leaves cover rounded, 3- to 4-foot plants. + AARS

'SHREVEPORT'. Kordes, 1981, OB. Named for the Shreveport, Louisiana, home of the American Rose Society, this variety has oval, pointed buds that open into high-centered flowers borne on small sprays. The very double, 4-inch flowers (with 50 petals) are a blend of amber and orange, with a slight tea fragrance. They are long lasting and therefore excellent as cut flowers. The leaves are large, dark green and shiny, and the canes are covered with small, downward-facing thorns. The vigorous 5-foot plants are disease resistant and winter hardy. 7.3 AARS

'SONIA'. Meilland, 1974, PB. 'Sonia' has well-formed, shrimp pink flowers that are 3 to 4 inches across and have excellent substance, making them long lasting when cut. Blooms have 30 petals and a very fruity fragrance. The foliage is dark green, shiny, and leathery, covering compact, 3- to 4-foot plants. 'Sonia' will grow equally well in a greenhouse or a garden. 8.0

'TOURNAMENT OF ROSES'. Warriner, 1988, MP. Named for the hundredth anniversary of the Tournament of Roses, this variety has pink flowers overlaid with warm orange. The high-centered 4-inch blooms have 35 to 40 petals each. They appear in small sprays and are fairly fragrant. Winter hardy plants are 4 to 5 feet tall and are clothed in crisp, dark green leaves that resist disease. (7.8) AARS

'WHITE LIGHTNIN''. Swim and Christensen, 1980, W. This variety has medium-sized, 3½- to 4-inch flowers that usually appear in sprays. The blooms have 26 to 32 petals of pure, clear white. Flowers are cup shaped, with a lively lemony fragrance. The bushy plants grow 3 to 4 feet tall and have dark green, glossy foliage. 7.2 AARS

MINIATURES

*W*ith their elfin scale and ever-widening range of colors and forms, miniature roses appeal to gardeners of all ages. Their small size makes it possible to grow an extensive rose garden in a tiny space, either indoors in containers or outdoors in beds and borders. Most will bloom all year under indoor lighting, and most are winter hardy outdoors.

Everything about a miniature rose is small, from its flowers and leaves to the length of its canes. The tiniest miniatures, called micro-minis, grow as small as 3 inches high. Larger types range in height from 10 to 30 inches, depending on variety. Some have tiny, high-centered flowers resembling those of hybrid teas; others have decorative flowers produced in sprays like small floribundas. The following are the best miniatures as of this writing, but the list is growing rapidly.

Although some garden centers sell miniature roses, the largest selection is found in mail-order catalogs. See pages 340 and 341 for names and addresses.

'AVANDEL'.   Moore, 1977, YB. Pointed pink buds open into double yellow flowers blended with peach and pink. Blooms have 20 to 25 petals and measure 1 to 1½ inches across, with open flowers being flat to cup shaped. They repeat well all summer and have a strong, fruity fragrance. Bushy plants grow 12 inches high and are extremely winter hardy. The disease-resistant leathery foliage is medium to dark green. 7.3 AOE

'BEAUTY SECRET'.   Moore, 1965, MR. Medium red flowers with 24 to 30 petals are 1 to 1½ inches wide and have a heavy fragrance. They repeat quickly throughout the growing season. Semiglossy medium to dark green foliage clothes the bushy plant, which grows 10 to 18 inches tall. 9.3 AOE

'BLACK JADE'.   Benardella, 1985, DR. The darkest red of any rose, 'Black Jade' is so dark it is almost black. High-centered, velvety, ¾-inch flowers have 30 petals and long cutting stems. Rounded 18- to 24-inch plants have glossy, dark green, disease-resistant foliage. 6.5 AOE

'BRASS RING'.   Dickson, 1981, OB. Pointed buds open into flat blooms that appear in large sprays. The very prolific 1- to 1¼-inch flowers have 21 petals, and are coppery orange fading to rose-pink as they age. Leaves are small, pointed, and glossy on upright, 18-inch plants with arching stems. 8.0

'CENTER GOLD'.   Saville, 1981, DY. Originally introduced as a fund-raiser for the American Rose Center, the American Rose Society's headquarters, 'Center Gold' has high-centered, deep

'Beauty Secret'

'Black Jade'

'Center Gold'

'Debut'

'Dee Bennett'

'Dreamglo'

yellow, very double 1-inch flowers with 60 petals and a spicy fragrance. It occasionally produces white flowers. Blooms appear one to a stem or in large sprays on 14- to 18-inch plants with glossy, textured leaves. 7.2 AOE

'CENTERPIECE'. Saville, 1985, MR. High-centered, velvety, 1- to 1¼-inch flowers with 35 petals have a slight fragrance and excellent substance, making them long lasting in the garden or as a cut flower. Flowers are deep to medium red; disease-resistant leaves are small, dark green, and semiglossy. Plants grow 12 to 16 inches tall. 7.1 AOE

'CINDERELLA'. De Vink, 1953, W. A long-time favorite, this micromini has ½- to 1-inch flowers of satiny white tinged in pale flesh pink. Blooms have 55 tiny petals and a spicy fragrance and appear on plants that grow 8 to 10 inches high. 8.8

'CORNSILK'. Saville, 1983, MY. Fragrant, pastel yellow, 1-inch flowers the color of corn silk have 40 petals and hybrid tea form. Flower color is often pinker in cool weather and whiter in hot weather. Vigorous, bushy 15- to 18-inch plants have medium green, semiglossy leaves. 7.0 AOE

'CUDDLES'. Schwartz, 1978, DP. Oval buds open into deep coral-pink, very double, flowers with 55 to 60 petals. The flowers are high centered, 1 to 1½ inches across, and slightly fragrant. Excellent substance makes this a long-lasting flower. Compact plants grow 14 to 16 inches high. 8.4 AOE

'CUPCAKE'. Spies, 1981, MP. As pure pink as the icing on a cupcake, this variety has double, 1½-inch, high-centered, mildly fragrant flowers with 45 to 50 petals. The 12- to 18-inch plants are neat, rounded, and compact with abundant shiny foliage, and good for containers. 8.5 AOE

'DEBUT'. Meilland, 1988, RB. Named because it was one of the first three miniatures to win an AARS award (the others were 'New Beginning' and 'Pride 'n' Joy'), 'Debut' has pointed buds and high-centered flowers that bloom prolifically on spreading, 12- to 18-inch plants with dark green, disease-resistant foliage. Flowers are 1 to 2 inches across, have 15 to 22 petals, and are ivory to pale yellow with a broad red edging. (7.7) AARS

'DEE BENNETT'. Saville, 1988, OB. This brilliant apricot variety was named for the late Dee Bennett, a hybridizer of fine miniatures. Its 1-inch flowers are double, with excellent substance, making this a long-lasting flower in the garden or in a vase. Dark green foliage covers a mounded, 14- to 18-inch plant. (7.8) AOE

'DREAMGLO'. Williams, 1978, RB. White flowers edged in red are very double (with 50 petals), and measure 1 to 1½ inches across. The blooms open from pointed buds into high-centered flowers with a light fragrance; the color does not fade in the heat.

Cutting stems are long on this 18- to 24-inch plant with dark green, semiglossy foliage. 8.6

'HOLY TOLEDO'. Christensen, 1978, AB. Double, slightly fragrant flowers have 28 petals and measure 1½ to 2 inches across. The outstanding characteristic of this mini is its unusual color, a bright orange to deep apricot with a yellow base. Vigorous, bushy plants grow 18 to 24 inches tall and have shiny, dark green, disease-resistant leaves. Unfortunately, 'Holy Toledo' is tender where winters are cold. 8.3 AOE

'HOMBRE'. Jolly, 1982, PB. High-centered flowers of light apricot-pink have petals with a light pink reverse. The 1-inch blooms, with over 40 petals, open out flat. Compact plants are 12 to 14 inches high with small, medium green, semiglossy leaves. 7.0 AOE

'HUMDINGER'. Schwartz, 1976, OR. 'Humdinger' is a micro-mini and therefore a good choice for containers. The very double, 1-inch flowers have 50 petals and good repeat bloom. Blooms are orange-red and high centered. Plants grow only 8 to 10 inches high and have dark green, shiny leaves. 7.0 AOE

'JEAN KENNEALLY'. Bennett, 1984, AB. Pale apricot in color and high centered in form, the flowers are 1½ inches wide and have 22 petals. They have a slight fragrance and excellent repeat-blooming ability. The bushy plant is 10 to 16 inches tall and has medium green, semiglossy foliage. 8.7 AOE

'JEANNE LAJOIE'. Sima, 1975, MP. This climbing miniature can grow as tall as 4 to 8 feet. Young plants look outstanding when allowed to trail from hanging baskets. Beautiful, well-formed, 1-inch double flowers with 40 petals are medium pink with a darker pink reverse. The leaves are small, shiny, dark green, and textured. 8.3 AOE

'JENNIFER'. Benardella, 1985, PB. Delicate light pink 1½-inch flowers with a white reverse have 35 petals, hybrid tea form, and a heavy fragrance. Dark green, semiglossy foliage covers bushy, spreading, 18- to 24-inch plants. 7.7 AOE

'JIM DANDY'. Benardella, 1988, RB. A successful product of amateur hybridizing, 'Jim Dandy' is a bright orange-red with a yellow base. Blooms are high centered, double, and 1 inch across. Medium green foliage covers the 18- to 20-inch plant. (7.5) AOE

'JULIE ANN'. Saville, 1984, OR. High centered, vermilion to orange-red 1-inch flowers have 20 petals and a pleasing fragrance. Leaves are small, medium green, semiglossy, and disease resistant, and cover bushy, 12- to 14-inch plants. 7.4 AOE

'LAVENDER JEWEL'. Moore, 1978, MB. Pointed buds open into high-centered, 1-inch, slightly fragrant, clear soft lavender

'Holy Toledo'

'Jean Kenneally'

'Lavender Jewel'

'Loving Touch'

'Magic Carrousel'

'Mary Marshall'

flowers with 35 to 40 petals. As the flowers mature, they open flat. Sometimes petals are edged in magenta. Leaves are dark green, on compact, bushy plants that grow 10 to 15 inches high and wide. 8.0

'LITTLE JACKIE'. Saville, 1982, OB. Light, orange-red, high-centered ¾- to 1-inch flowers with a yellow reverse have 20 petals and are very fragrant. As the blooms open, the petals reflex back to form points. Plants grow 18 to 24 inches tall and have medium green, semiglossy foliage. 8.0 AOE

'LITTLEST ANGEL'. Schwartz, 1976, MY. One of the finest of the microminis, 'Littlest Angel' has medium to deep yellow, ½-inch, high-centered flowers with 28 petals. The low, compact, bushy growth reaches heights of only 4 to 8 inches. 'Littlest Angel' is best grown in partial shade if grown outdoors, especially in hot climates. 7.0

'LOVING TOUCH'. Jolly, 1982, AB. Large brandy-colored buds spiral open into high-centered, creamy apricot blossoms with 20 to 25 petals. Flowers can be 2 inches across in cool weather and 1 inch across in hot weather, are usually borne one to a stem, and have a mild tea fragrance. Abundant medium green, semiglossy foliage covers the compact, 12- to 18-inch plant. 7.5 AOE

'MAGIC CARROUSEL'. Moore, 1972, RB. Flowers are 1¾ to 2 inches across and double, with 30 to 35 petals. The blooms are white with red edges and have a very slight fragrance. They open in a rounded to flat shape. One of the tallest of the miniature roses, 'Magic Carrousel' can reach 30 inches in height. Shiny leaves are medium green to bronze and very disease resistant. Plants are quite winter hardy. 9.1 AOE

'MARY MARSHALL'. Moore, 1970, OB. Named for an avid amateur miniature rose grower, 'Mary Marshall' has 1½-inch flowers of deep coral with pink, yellow, and orange overtones. Long lasting on the plant or as cut flowers, the slightly fragrant blooms have 24 to 30 petals and a high-centered form. The bushy, winter-hardy plant grows 14 inches tall; there is also a climbing form that can reach 5 feet in height. Medium green, semiglossy leaves have better-than-average disease resistance. 8.8 AOE

'MINNIE PEARL'. Saville, 1982, PB. Named for the country music performer, 'Minnie Pearl' has high-centered flowers of light pink with a salmon blush and a darker pink reverse that bloom one to a stem. Color may deepen in hot sun. The flowers are 1 inch across, and have 35 to 40 petals and a slight fragrance. Plants are rounded, 14 to 20 inches high, and dressed in small, medium green, semiglossy foliage. This variety is not as winter hardy as most miniatures. 8.3

'NEW BEGINNING'. Saville, 1988, OB. One of the first three miniatures to win an AARS award (the others were 'Debut' and 'Pride 'n' Joy'), 'New Beginning' has hot orange blooms with a yellow reverse. Its 1½-inch very double flowers have 45 to 50 petals. Rounded plants grow 14 to 20 inches high and have disease-resistant, dark green leaves. (7.7) AARS, AOE

'NIGHT HAWK'.   Hardgrove, 1989, MR. Long lasting when cut, this variety's 1-inch flowers have 25 petals and are high centered in form and velvety crimson in color. Plants grow 18 to 24 inches high with deep green foliage that is bronzy green when new. (7.2) AOE

'OLD GLORY'.   Benardella, 1988, MR. Double flowers with 30 to 35 petals are 1 to 1½ inches across and colored medium red with a touch of yellow at the base of the petals. The high-centered flowers are long lasting when cut and bloom prolifically over dark green leaves on 16- to 20-inch plants. (7.8) AOE

'Over the Rainbow'

'OVER THE RAINBOW'.   Moore, 1972, RB. Vigorous, bushy plants grow 14 to 18 inches high and have flowers that are red on the insides of the petals and yellow-orange on the reverse. Double blooms are high centered, slightly fragrant, and 1 to 1¾ inches across, appearing above medium green, leathery leaves. 8.3 AOE

'PACESETTER'.   Schwartz, 1979, W. Elegant pointed buds open into pure white, very double flowers with 45 to 50 petals and long cutting stems. The fragrant, high-centered flowers are 1 to 1½ inches across. Disease-resistant, dark green foliage clothes this compact 18- to 24-inch bush. 7.7 AOE

'PARTY GIRL'.   Saville, 1979, YB. Long, pointed buds open into high-centered, 1-inch flowers with 20 to 25 petals and a spicy fragrance. This variety is a frequent winner at rose shows, thanks to its exhibition-quality form and long-keeping abilities. Blooms are soft apricot-yellow flushed in salmon-pink; compact, bushy growth is 12 to 15 inches high. 8.3 AOE

'Pacesetter'

'PEACH FUZZ'.   Carruth, 1990, AB. This variety is one of the "mossed" miniatures; as with moss roses, its buds and stems are covered with soft hairs. Buds are peachy apricot-pink and open into 1½-inch fragrant flowers of the same color that have 25 to 30 petals. Rounded plants grow 14 to 20 inches tall and have glossy, disease-resistant foliage. +

'PEACHES 'N' CREAM'.   Woolcock, 1976, PB. Very double blooms have 50 petals and measure 1½ inches across. The flowers are a blend of peachy pink and creamy white and are slightly fragrant. The form is high centered, and the flowers repeat quickly all summer. Bushy plants grow 15 to 18 inches high, have dark green, semiglossy foliage, and are very winter hardy. 8.7 AOE

'POPCORN'.   Morey, 1973, W. This plant's sprays of tiny, pure white buds and flowers do indeed look like popped corn. The honey-scented, 1-inch semidouble flowers have 13 petals set off

'Popcorn'

309

'Rainbow's End'

'Razzmatazz'

'Rise 'n' Shine'

by bright yellow stamens. Winter-hardy plants grow 10 to 14 inches high and have medium green, shiny foliage. 8.3

'PUPPY LOVE'. Schwartz, 1978, OB. Pointed buds open in a melange of pink, coral, and orange on 1½-inch flowers. The slightly fragrant blooms have 23 petals and are almost always borne one to a stem. The leaves are dull green and disease resistant, covering compact, 15- to 18-inch plants. 8.6 AOE

'RAINBOW'S END'. Saville, 1984, YB. Like the proverbial pot of gold, this miniature is golden yellow, shading to deep pink and red at the edges of the petals. When grown indoors, the pink-and-red coloration does not appear. Blooms have high centers, 30 to 35 petals, and are 1½ inches wide. Dark green, glossy foliage covers the bushy, 10- to 14-inch plant. 8.0 AOE

'RAZZMATAZZ'. Warriner, 1981, OR. High-centered, 1- to 1½-inch blooms of smoky orange-red to coral have 25 to 30 petals and appear in sprays above semiglossy foliage on 18- to 24-inch plants. 7.1

'RED CASCADE'. Moore, 1976, DR. The cascading habit of this variety suits it best for use in a hanging basket, as a ground cover, or as a climber. The decorative and slightly fragrant deep red flowers are 1 inch across, with 40 petals. Leaves are small and leathery and grow along canes that can reach several feet in length. 7.5 AOE

'RED FLUSH'. Schwartz, 1978, MR. Oval buds open into cupped, very double flowers in light to medium red; blooms are 1½ inches across with 50 to 55 petals. Dull green, disease-resistant foliage covers the compact, 16- to 20-inch plant. 7.7 AOE

'REGINE'. Hefner, 1989, PB. Hybridized by an amateur, 'Regine' is a high-centered miniature of soft pink blended with light pink to cream on the reverses of the petals. The 1-inch flowers with 25 petals grow on rounded 14- to 20-inch plants. + AOE

'RING OF FIRE'. Moore, 1987, YB. Disease-resistant, 16- to 20-inch plants have 1- to 1½-inch flowers of glowing yellow edged with fiery red, making the plants appear orange from a distance. Flowers are high centered and long lasting when cut. 7.7 AOE

'RISE 'N' SHINE'. Moore, 1977, MY. One of the best yellow miniatures, 'Rise 'n' Shine' has pure butter yellow, high-centered, 1½-inch flowers with 30 to 35 petals and a fruity fragrance. Bushy, 14- to 20-inch plants have dark green leaves. 9.1 AOE

'SEQUOIA GOLD'. Moore, 1987, MY. Named in honor of the fiftieth anniversary of Ralph Moore's nursery, Sequoia Nursery, 'Sequoia Gold' blooms profusely with 1½- to 2-inch fragrant, medium yellow flowers that do not fade in the heat. Plants grow 14 to 18 inches high. 7.8 AOE

'S IMPLEX'. Moore, 1961, W. Pure and simple as the name implies, 'Simplex' is a single-flowered miniature with five white petals set off by showy yellow stamens. When grown indoors or in cool, cloudy weather, the flowers have either a yellow or a pink hue. Blooms are 1½ inches across on a 15- to 18-inch plant that has light green, semiglossy foliage. 8.5

'S NOW B RIDE'. Betty Jolly, 1982, W. High-centered, 1½-inch flowers with 20 petals are white with a hint of yellow inside, and have a slight fragrance. Blooms are long lasting and usually appear one to a stem. Medium to dark green, semiglossy foliage covers bushy plants that grow 15 to 18 inches high. 8.0 AOE

'S TARGLO'. Williams, 1973, W. Double, off-white flowers that often develop a yellowish green tinge have 35 petals and are 1¾ inches across. The flowers are high centered, with a slight fragrance. Plants grow 10 to 14 inches high and tend to sprawl along the ground, clothed in medium green foliage. 8.5 AOE

'S TARINA'. Meilland, 1965, OR. Long considered the perfect miniature because of its high-centered, hybrid tea form and abundant flowering, 'Starina' has bright orange-red flowers with 35 petals that are 1½ inches across. Long-lasting blooms have a touch of yellow at the base. Bushy plants grow 12 to 16 inches high, with good disease resistance and fair winter hardiness. 9.4

'T IPPER'. Jolly, 1987, MP. Named for Tipper Gore, wife of Senator Albert Gore, Jr., of Tennessee, 'Tipper' has 1½-inch, high-centered flowers of medium pink with 20 to 25 petals. Blooms usually appear one to a stem, although occasionally they will cluster. Plants grow 22 to 30 inches high. (7.4) AOE

'T OY C LOWN'. Moore, 1966, RB. 1½-inch flowers with 12 to 20 petals are white with red edges. Pointed buds open into high-centered flowers that spread out flat. Spreading 10- to 14-inch plants have dark green, red-tinged leaves. 8.4 AOE

'V ALERIE J EANNE'. Saville, 1980, DP. Round buds open into deep magenta-pink, very double, 1½-inch flowers with 55 to 60 petals. The high-centered blooms open flat and appear one to a stem or in large sprays. The 15- to 18-inch stems are covered with shiny foliage and long, straight, thin thorns. 7.9 AOE

'W INSOME'. Saville, 1985, MB. Deep magenta blooms are high centered, 1½ to 2 inches across, with 35 to 40 petals and excellent substance. Medium to dark green, semiglossy, disease-resistant leaves clothe vigorous 16- to 22-inch plants. 8.0 AOE

'Z INGER'. Schwartz, 1978, MR. Actually a semidouble rose with 11 petals, 'Zinger' opens so flat that it appears single. Its bright red, slightly fragrant petals are set off by yellow stamens on 1½-inch blooms. Plants grow 12 to 18 inches high, with medium to dark green, glossy leaves. 7.4 AOE

'Snow Bride'

'Valerie Jeanne'

'Winsome'

'Altissimo'

'America'

'American Pillar'

CLIMBERS & RAMBLERS

C limbing roses are not climbers in the sense that many vines are, since they do not send out tendrils or other growths to attach them to their supports. Instead, climbers have long canes that are usually tied to a support to keep them from arching to the ground. Some climbers have more pliable canes than others; the stiffer types are best trained upright to a pillar or a trellis, while the more pliable ones can be trained horizontally on a fence, which also induces plants to increase their blooming. Most climbers produce loose clusters of flowers that bloom on old (last year's) wood, and most are fairly winter hardy. Many climbers, though not all, repeat their bloom throughout the season.

Ramblers are the predecessors of climbers. Although many have disappeared from the marketplace in favor of the larger-flowered climbers, some are still available and worth growing. Ramblers are generally much larger plants than climbers, with small flowers that are borne in large clusters on new wood. Most ramblers bloom only once a year, and most are very winter hardy. Although they can be allowed to sprawl, they produce tidier plants if they are tied to a pillar, a fence, or some other support. Except where designated as ramblers, all plants in the list below are large-flowered climbers.

In addition to these, many popular bush roses—particularly hybrid teas—have produced climbing sports. In most cases the flowers of these sports have the same color and form as those of their bush siblings, but are much larger. Bush roses with climbing sports include 'Angel Face', 'Cécile Brünner', 'Charlotte Armstrong', 'Chrysler Imperial', 'Crimson Glory', 'Dainty Bess', 'Double Delight', 'First Prize', 'Granada', 'Paradise', 'Peace', 'Queen Elizabeth', 'Summer Sunshine', 'Sutter's Gold', 'Tiffany', and 'Tropicana'.

'ALOHA'.   Boerner, 1949, MP. Long-stemmed clusters of 3½-inch, fragrant, medium rose-pink flowers with a deeper pink reverse have 58 petals, a cupped shape, and recurrent bloom. The foliage is leathery and dark green on a climber best grown on an 8- to 10-foot pillar. 7.0

'ALTISSIMO'.   Delbard-Chabert, 1966, MR. Scarlet to blood red, velvety, 4- to 5-inch, slightly fragrant, recurrent flowers are single but have 7 to 10 petals instead of the usual 5. The stamens are deep gold and the plant is covered with dark green, serrated, disease-resistant foliage. Plants will grow quite large (12 feet) or can be pruned to keep them smaller and more shrublike. 8.7

'AMERICA'.   Warriner, 1976, OB. Slow growing to about 8 feet, 'America' has salmon buds that open into coral-pink, high-centered flowers with a lighter reverse. The blooms are 3½ to 4½ inches across, have 45 petals, exhibit recurring bloom, and are strongly spice scented. 'America' is very tender where winters are harsh. 8.9 AARS

'AMERICAN PILLAR'.   Van Fleet, 1902, PB. The single, 2-inch flowers of this rambler are carmine-pink with a white eye and golden yellow stamens. They bloom in large clusters once each year over shiny, leathery leaves. Growth is vigorous and plants can grow 15 to 20 feet high. %

'BLAZE'.   Kallay, 1932, MR. Large clusters of bright scarlet, semidouble, cupped, slightly fragrant, 2- to 3-inch decorative flowers with about 25 petals bloom heavily in early summer and fairly regularly for the rest of the season. Plants are vigorous and easy to train, will grow to 15 feet, have dark green, leathery foliage, and are very winter hardy. 7.3

'BUTTERSCOTCH'.   Warriner, 1986, R. Hybridizer William Warriner originally wanted to name this rose 'Coffee and Cream', a name that closely evokes its unusual tannish to golden brown color that fades as the flowers mature. Perhaps he should have, since the name 'Butterscotch' still technically belongs to a hybrid tea introduced in 1942. (Thus if you ever exhibit this rose at an ARS show, you must show it under its code name, 'Jactan'.) The slightly fragrant, 4½- to 5½-inch flowers have 25 loosely cupped petals and bloom in small clusters all season. Plants are slow growing to 8 to 10 feet and have medium green, semiglossy foliage. 7.6

'CHEVY CHASE'.   Hansen, 1939, DR. This rambler has masses of small (1- to 2-inch), dark crimson-red, fragrant flowers with 65 petals that bloom in large clusters, once per season. Plants are vigorous, attaining heights of about 15 feet, and have soft, light green, wrinkled leaves. 8.0

'CITY OF YORK'.   Tantau, 1945, W. Creamy white, semidouble, fragrant flowers with 15 petals are 3 to 4 inches across and cup shaped. Flowers appear in clusters of up to a dozen but bloom only once a year. Plants are vigorous and will quickly clothe an arbor with their shiny, leathery leaves. In fact, 'City of York' is worth growing for the beauty of its foliage alone. %

'DON JUAN'.   Malandrone, 1958, DR. Slightly stiff stems make 'Don Juan' a good rose for an 8- to 10-foot pillar. Flowers are dark velvety red, very fragrant, and have hybrid tea form on long cutting stems. The 4- to 5-inch blooms have 35 petals and flower throughout the season above dark green, glossy, leathery leaves that are resistant to black spot. 'Don Juan' suffers from frost damage during cold winters, but will snap back fairly quickly. 8.3

'DOROTHY PERKINS'.   Jackson and Perkins, 1901, LP. Pale rose-pink, 2- to 3-inch flowers are fragrant, fully double and decorative, blooming over dark green, shiny leaves. This rambler is vigorous, growing 10 to 20 feet high, but it blooms only once per season. %

'Chevy Chase'

'City of York'

'Don Juan'

'Excelsa'

'Handel'

'Joseph's Coat'

'DR. J. H. NICOLAS'. Nicolas, 1940, MP. Globular, 4- to 5-inch flowers of medium rose-pink are borne in small sprays that give the plant an airy look. The fragrant flowers, with 50 petals, bloom repeatedly against dark green, leathery foliage. This variety grows best upright on a 10-foot pillar or trellis. 7.0

'DR. W. VAN FLEET'. Van Fleet, 1910, LP. Cameo pink flowers fade to flesh white as they mature. They are 2 to 3 inches across and bloom only once a year. The fragrant double flowers are high centered at first but open quickly into flat, decorative blooms. Dark green, small, glossy foliage clothes this vigorous climber that can grow 15 to 20 feet high. 7.5

'ETAIN'. Cant, 1953, OB. This rambler has slightly fragrant, salmon-pink, 3-inch double flowers borne in large clusters. The leaves are glossy, reddish brown, and almost evergreen in milder climates. The open plant is vigorous, growing 10 to 12 feet high, and quickly covers slopes or fences. This is one of the few ramblers that repeats its bloom and grows best in light shade. 7.0

'EXCELSA'. Walsh, 1909, MR. Sometimes called 'Red Dorothy Perkins', this rambler has medium red, double, cupped, ruffled, 2-inch flowers that are borne in large, heavy clusters. Rich green, glossy leaves cover 12- to 18-foot plants that bloom only once per season. %

'GOLDEN SHOWERS'. Lammerts, 1956, MY. Stems of this climber are so strong it can stand unsupported as a shrub. It can also be trained on a 6- to 10-foot pillar, although it is hard to train horizontally along a fence. The 4-inch daffodil yellow flowers, which have 25 to 30 loosely arranged petals, are ruffled and sweetly fragrant, and are among the first roses to bloom in the garden. They appear singly or in clusters and have frequent recurrent bloom. Leaves are dark green and glossy. 7.1 AARS

'HANDEL'. McGredy, 1965, RB. Clusters of wavy, frilled, 3½-inch, double flowers with 22 petals are ivory edged in deep rose-pink to red. Blooms are slightly fragrant. Plants, which have olive green, disease-resistant leaves, grow quickly to 15 feet and are fast to repeat their bloom. They can be trained to a fence or trellis. 8.0

'JOSEPH'S COAT'. Armstrong and Swim, 1964, RB. Like the biblical garb for which it was named, 'Joseph's Coat' is multi-colored, with buds of orange and red opening into yellow flowers that change to orange and scarlet as they mature. The 3-inch fluffy, slightly fragrant flowers with 25 petals bloom in clusters all season. This rose is best trained on a pillar and has dark green, glossy foliage. 'Joseph's Coat' grows to 12 feet and is tender in cold climates. 7.6

'MAY QUEEN'. Manda, 1898, MP. This rambler has a profusion of very double, quartered, 2-inch pink flowers with a fruity fragrance that open fairly flat. Plants occasionally repeat their bloom, an unusual ability for a rambler, and can grow to 25 feet. They can be allowed to climb or can be grown as a shrub. 7.5

'MINNEHAHA'.   Walsh, 1905, LP. This rambler has small (1- to 2-inch), semidouble, slightly fragrant, flat flowers of light pink that fade to white and bloom in large clusters once a year. Plants grow 15 to 20 feet high and have small, shiny, dark green leaves. %

'NEW DAWN'.   Somerset Rose Nursery, 1930, LP. This sport of 'Dr. W. Van Fleet' is identical to it in all respects except that it is repeat blooming. This was the first plant of any type to be patented. 7.1

'PAUL'S SCARLET CLIMBER'.   Paul, 1916, MR. 'Paul's Scarlet Climber' looks very similar to 'Blaze', its offspring, except that it rarely has recurrent bloom. Its large clusters of bright scarlet 2- to 3-inch flowers are semidouble, decorative, and slightly fragrant. Plants are very vigorous, growing 15 to 20 feet high, are quite winter hardy, and have dark green, glossy, disease-resistant foliage. 7.7

'PELÉ'.   Benardella, 1979, W. Technically a climbing hybrid tea (for which there is no bush counterpart), 'Pelé' has 4-inch, double white flowers with 35 petals that are borne in small sprays all season and have a fruity fragrance. Upright canes grow to 10 feet in height and are clothed in medium green, triangular foliage and hooked thorns. This variety was named for the famous soccer player. 7.0 ARSTG

'PINK PILLAR'.   Brownell, 1940, PB. This rambler has a very distinct citrus fragrance. The long-lasting 2-inch flowers, which bloom repeatedly after opening from dark pink buds, have 16 to 20 petals and are a blend of pale pink, coral, and orange. The petals have scalloped edges and the flowers bloom in small clusters. Plants grow 7 to 8 feet high and are very winter hardy. Unfortunately, the hybridizer of this plant never registered any of his roses with the American Rose Society, so this variety cannot be exhibited in rose shows and has no rating.

'PIÑATA'.   Suzuki, 1978, YB. Flowers are similar to 'Joseph's Coat'—yellow diffused with orange and red—but are somewhat larger (3 to 4 inches). The blooms, which are slightly fragrant, have 28 petals and open with a high center. Plants repeat bloom dependably and are strong enough to stand alone as a shrub. Canes are too stiff for training to a fence, but the plant may be grown on an 8-foot pillar. 7.5

'RED FOUNTAIN'.   J. Benjamin Williams, 1975, DR. Arching canes are filled with clusters of velvety dark red, very fragrant, ruffled and cupped 3-inch blooms with 20 to 25 petals that bloom all season. Plants are strong and vigorous, growing 12 to 14 feet high, making this a good pillar or trellis rose. Foliage is dark green and leathery. 7.4

'New Dawn'

'Paul's Scarlet Climber'

'Piñata'

'Royal Sunset'

'Tausendschön'

'Veilchenblau'

'RHONDA'. Lissemore, 1968, MP. Hybridized by an amateur, 'Rhonda' has clusters of double, slightly fragrant, salmon-pink, 4-inch flowers that bloom repeatedly on vigorous, 8-foot plants over dark green, glossy foliage. 7.5

'ROYAL GOLD'. Morey, 1957, MY. Deep golden yellow, nonfading flowers are moderately fragrant, blooming heavily at the start of the season and then repeating sporadically. The 4-inch, cup-shaped flowers have 35 petals and bloom singly or in small clusters. Stiff, compact plants grow 5 to 10 feet high. 7.4

'ROYAL SUNSET'. Morey, 1960, AB. High-centered or cup-shaped, 4½- to 5-inch flowers are fragrant and deep apricot, fading to light peach in summer heat. Repeat-blooming flowers have 20 petals. Leathery foliage is coppery green, disease resistant, and somewhat tender. Stiff plants grow about 6 feet high. %

'TAUSENDSCHÖN'. Schmidt, 1906, PB. This is technically a hybrid multiflora (an old garden rose), but since many ramblers were hybridized from *Rosa multiflora,* it is usually included with ramblers. The 3-inch flowers are deep rose-pink, with a number of white petals in the center. Double, cupped, slightly fragrant blooms appear once a year in medium-sized clusters on slender, 8- to 10-foot thornless canes. 6.7

'TEMPO'. Warriner, 1975, DR. An early bloomer, this is one of the first climbers to come into flower in the garden. Its deep red, high-centered, very double flowers are 3 to 4 inches across and bloom in clusters all summer on tidy, 8-foot plants. Flowers are long lasting and slightly fragrant. Dark green leaves are large, glossy, and very disease resistant. 7.0

'VEILCHENBLAU'. Schmidt, 1909, MB. Like 'Tausend-schön', this is technically a hybrid multiflora but is normally listed as a rambler in deference to its *Rosa multiflora* forebear. It is commonly known as 'Blue Rambler', because its violet flowers (accented with white) are among the very few roses that approach true blue. The fragrant 1-inch flowers are semidouble, cupped, and decorative, and bloom once in large clusters. The 10- to 15-foot plants have light green, large, shiny leaves. 7.0

'WHITE DAWN'. Longley, 1949, W. This was the first and is still the best white-flowered climber. Its fragrant, clustered, snow white, 3-inch flowers are gardenia shaped, double (35 petals), and repeat blooming. Foliage is glossy, and the plants are vigorous, growing to 15 feet, and winter hardy. 7.3

'YELLOW BLAZE'. Burks, 1989, MY. This sport of the floribunda 'Sun Flare' has clusters of 3-inch, double, showy bright yellow flowers with 25 to 30 petals and a light licorice fragrance. Repeat-blooming plants grow 12 to 14 feet high with glossy, disease-resistant leaves. If you exhibit this rose in an ARS show, you must label it 'Climbing Sun Flare'. (7.5)

SHRUB ROSES

'Alba Meidiland'

his class of modern rose was created by the American Rose Society to include plants with a large and bushy growth habit that eluded other categories. Almost without exception, shrub roses are tough, winter-hardy plants that can tolerate neglect and poor growing conditions. In most cases you can count on a shrub rose to be hardy to Zone 6. A few (listed as "hardy" in the following descriptions) will survive to Zone 5, and several (designated "very hardy") will endure to Zone 4.

Use shrub roses as landscape plants, mass plantings, hedges, ground covers, or shrub borders. For the most part they are large plants whose decorative flowers bloom in clusters all summer, followed in many cases by showy hips. Exceptions to these generalizations are noted below.

The shrub class has many subclasses, including hybrid blanda, hybrid hugonis, hybrid laevigata, hybrid macounii, hybrid macrantha, hybrid moyesii, hybrid musk, hybrid nitida, hybrid nutkana, hybrid rugosa, hybrid suffulta, and kordesii. However, many of these subclasses are obscure and have no members that are commonly grown or sold. Roses that don't fit into any subclass are called simply shrub.

The most commonly grown shrub roses come from the hybrid moyesii, hybrid rugosa, kordesii, hybrid musk, and shrub categories. Hybrid moyesii are large, stiff, winter-hardy plants that usually grow to 6 feet in height. All have uniquely attractive red hips following the bloom, and most are very disease resistant. Hybrid rugosas are hardy, disease resistant, easy to care for, and tolerant of salt air. They have wrinkled foliage, dense growth, and attractive hips.

Kordesii are modern shrubs and low-growing climbers that are very hardy and offer a variety of flower forms and colors. Hybrid musk roses have large clusters of flowers that have a heavy fragrance. Most, although not all, have single flowers. Hybrid musks are tall, disease resistant, and winter hardy. Members of the catchall shrub category have varied backgrounds but are generally large, winter-hardy, and disease-resistant plants.

Many shrub roses hail from the turn of the century, but in recent years there have been many new introductions as growers rediscover their beauty, charm, and value as landscape plants. The most satisfying shrub roses, old and new, are described in the entries that follow.

'Alchymist'

'ALBA MEIDILAND'. Meilland, 1989, W. Shrub. White with a hint of pink, the continually flowering 2-inch double blooms of 'Alba Meidiland' appear in small clusters on plants that grow 2 feet high and spread 6 feet wide. Useful as a ground cover or in a massed planting, this shrub rose has small, dark green foliage. +

'Belinda'

'Blanc Double de Coubert'

'Bloomfield Dainty'

'Bonica '82'

'ALCHYMIST'. Kordes, 1956, AB. Shrub. Very double, fragrant, 3- to 4-inch flowers are yellow shaded with orange, pink, and red. Blooms appear only once a year. Glossy, bronzy foliage covers vigorous, 6- to 10-foot plants that tolerate shade. 8.1

'ALL THAT JAZZ'. Twomey, 1990, PB. Shrub. 'All That Jazz' has an outstanding and prolific flowering effect against glossy, dark green foliage that is very disease resistant. The open flowers have 12 petals and are 5 to 6 inches across. They are a coral-salmon blend with a moderate damask fragrance. Plants grow upright to 5 feet in height. + AARS

'AUTUMN DELIGHT'. Bentall, 1933, W. Hybrid musk. Single, fragrant, white, 3-inch flowers have red stamens and are borne in large clusters all summer on 4- to 5-foot plants. 7.5

'BELINDA'. Bentall, 1936, MP. Hybrid musk. Wavy petals of soft medium pink grace small, semidouble, white-centered, fragrant 2-inch flowers that bloom in large, erect clusters. Roses flower repeatedly on 4- to 6-foot plants. 8.5

'BISHOP DARLINGTON'. Thomas, 1926, AB. Hybrid musk. Oval buds appear all summer, opening into cream-colored to flesh pink flowers with a yellow glow. The 3-inch blooms are semidouble (with 17 petals), cupped, and have a fruity fragrance. Foliage is soft and bronzy on a plant that grows 4 to 7 feet tall and can be used as a freestanding shrub or low-growing climber. 7.2

'BLANC DOUBLE DE COUBERT'. Cochet-Cochet, 1892, W. Hybrid rugosa. Double, sweetly fragrant, snow white, 2- to 4-inch flowers appear all summer on spreading plants that grow 5 to 7 feet high and have wrinkled foliage. Attractive red hips appear in the fall. 7.8

'BLOOMFIELD DAINTY'. Thomas, 1924, MY. Hybrid musk. Long, pointed, deep coral to orange buds open into canary yellow, single, 2-inch, fragrant flowers that appear in clusters all season. The bright yellow fades to soft creamy pink with deeper pink at the edges of the petals. Glossy leaves cover the 5- to 7-foot plant. 7.2

'BLOOMIN' EASY'. Christensen, 1988, MR. Shrub. Bright red, double, 3-inch flowers bloom in small clusters all season on bushy plants that grow 4 to 6 feet high and have dark green, disease-resistant foliage. This variety is a dense grower ideally suited for a hedge. (7.9)

'BONICA '82'. Meilland, 1981, MP. Shrub. This shrub is so named to distinguish it from another rose called 'Bonica', although it is often listed in catalogs simply as 'Bonica'. If you want to exhibit it in an ARS rose show, you must call it 'Meidomonac', its official registered name. Warm pink, 1- to 2-inch flowers with light pink on the edges and the outsides of the petals appear in profusion on spreading, arching, 3- to 6-foot plants. Each flower has 40 or more petals. The tiny foliage is dark green, glossy, and very disease resistant. This was the first shrub rose to win an AARS award. 8.0 AARS

'BUFF BEAUTY'. Bentall, 1939, AB. Hybrid musk. Flowers of pale apricot-yellow bloom repeatedly in clusters of a dozen on 6-foot plants. Blooms are fully double, with 50 petals, and are 3 to 4 inches across. Foliage is large, medium green, and semiglossy. 7.5

'CAREFREE BEAUTY'. Buck, 1977, MP. Shrub. Semidouble (15 to 20 petals), coral-pink, 4½-inch fragrant flowers bloom freely all summer on this excellent hedge rose. Plants grow 6 feet tall and have olive green, disease-resistant foliage. Orange-red hips add interest in the fall. 7.4 AARS

'Buff Beauty'

'CAREFREE WONDER'. Meilland, 1989, PB. Shrub. The semidouble flowers with 20 petals are bold pink on the inside of the petal and creamy white to creamy pink on the reverse, and have a white eye. Blooms are 4 to 5 inches wide and appear in clusters all summer over medium green, disease-resistant foliage. Well-rounded plants grow 4 to 5 feet in height and are very winter hardy. + AARS

'CONSTANCE SPRY'. Austin, 1961, LP. Shrub. Light pink, double, cupped, 3½- to 5-inch flowers bloom in clusters and have a myrrh fragrance. The blooms occasionally, but not dependably, repeat their flowering. The leaves are dark green on 5- to 8-foot arching plants. %

'CORNELIA'. Pemberton, 1925, PB. Hybrid musk. Coral-pink to strawberry-colored 3-inch flowers are flushed with yellow and are slightly double, fragrant, and fluffy. Blooms appear all summer in flat clusters on vigorous 8-foot plants. The leaves are dark bronze, leathery, and glossy. 8.9

'Constance Spry'

'DELICATA'. Cooling, 1898, LP. Hybrid rugosa. This shrub is anything but delicate, as it will survive winters as cold as those in Zone 2. The 3-inch, semidouble flowers are soft lilac pink and appear repeatedly; hips are the size and color of crab apples. Vigorous plants grow to 8 feet high. 7.7

'DORTMUND'. Kordes, 1955, MR. Kordesii. This bushy plant that can grow 8 to 15 feet and be used as a freestanding shrub or a climber has single, fragrant, striking crimson-red 3-inch flowers with white eyes. The blooms appear in clusters and repeat profusely. Bright orange hips appear in fall after all the flowers have faded. Foliage is dark green, very glossy, and very disease resistant. 9.1

'ERFURT'. Kordes, 1939, PB. Hybrid musk. Long, pointed buds open into medium pink, semidouble 3- to 4-inch flowers with 10 petals that have yellow bases and cherry rose edges. The

'Dortmund'

'F. J. Grootendorst'

'Frau Dagmar Hartopp'

'Golden Wings'

blooms are very fragrant, and appear in small clusters throughout the summer. The bronze foliage is leathery and wrinkled. Plants have trailing, bushy growth and reach heights of 5 to 6 feet. 7.0

'FAIR BIANCA'. Austin, 1983, W. Shrub. Double blooms of pure white are cupped at first, opening into flat, saucer-shaped flowers with reflexed outer petals. The large, satiny flowers have a pleasing, spicy fragrance and appear several times a season on bushy, 3- to 5-foot plants. %

'F. J. GROOTENDORST'. De Goey, 1918, MR. Hybrid rugosa. Tiny (1- to 1½-inch), double, slightly fragrant, bright red flowers are frilled like carnations and bloom in large clusters throughout the summer on upright, 3-foot, very hardy plants. The leaves are small, leathery, wrinkled, and dark green. 8.0

'FRAU DAGMAR HARTOPP'. Hybridizer unknown, 1914, MP. Hybrid rugosa. Also called 'Frau Dagmar Hastrup', this variety has 3-inch, very fragrant flowers with five silvery pink petals that bloom repeatedly over rich green, crinkled foliage. Plants grow 2½ to 4 feet tall and have large red hips in the fall. 8.7

'GOLDEN WINGS'. Shepherd, 1956, MY. Shrub. Large, single, 4- to 5-inch blooms of sulfur yellow are graceful and slightly fragrant, with prominent and attractive stamens. They flower throughout the summer. Vigorous, bushy plants can reach heights of 6 to 8 feet and are very winter hardy. 8.5

'GRAHAM THOMAS'. Austin, 1983. DY. Shrub. Double flowers have 35 cupped petals of pure deep yellow and a strong tea fragrance. Blooms appear in sprays and repeat moderately. The leaves are small and shiny, on 4- to 6-foot plants that can be allowed to grow bushy or trained as climbers. 8.0

'GROOTENDORST SUPREME'. Grootendorst, 1936, DR. Hybrid rugosa. This sport of 'F. J. Grootendorst' is identical to it in all respects except that its flowers are a deeper and brighter crimson-red. 7.7

'HANSA'. Schaum and Van Tol, 1905, MR. Hybrid rugosa. The red, 30-petaled 3- to 4-inch flowers are flushed with mauve and have the fragrance of cloves. Blooms are double, and bloom all summer on short, weak stems. Large red hips form in the fall on plants that grow 4 feet high and are winter hardy. 8.5

'HANSEAT'. Tantau, 1961, MP. Shrub. Single, five-petaled flowers are bright rose-pink with a lighter pink center surrounding bright red stamens. The blooms are cupped, 3 inches across, and fragrant, appearing all summer on 6-foot plants. 7.8

'HEIDELBERG'. Kordes, 1959, MR. Kordesii. Clusters of 4-inch, bright crimson-red flowers with a lighter red reverse bloom on bushy, 7- to 15-foot plants that can be used as shrubs or trained as climbers to a pillar or a trellis. Blooms are high centered, have 32 petals, and appear atop glossy, leathery foliage. 7.5

'HERITAGE'. Austin, 1984, LP. Shrub. This variety is the favorite of its creator, David Austin, a champion and premier hybridizer of English shrub roses. Its medium-sized double flowers are clear shell pink with a cupped form and a heavy fragrance that has a trace of lemon. Blooms appear in sprays, on and off all season, on spreading 4-foot plants. 8.3

'KATHLEEN'. Pemberton, 1922, LP. Hybrid musk. Single, richly fragrant blush pink flowers are small (1 to 1½ inches), but bloom in large clusters all summer. The prominent stamens give the blooms the appearance of apple blossoms. Vigorous plants grow 6 to 12 feet tall and have disease-resistant foliage. Orange hips form in the fall. 7.0

'LAVENDER DREAM'. Interplant, 1984, MB. Shrub. Masses of 2- to 3-inch, semidouble (16 petals), medium lavender-pink flowers that bloom in sprays all season cover long, arching canes that grow 5 feet high and more than 5 feet wide. (8.1)

'MALAGUENA'. Buck, 1976, MP. Shrub. Double flowers with 28 petals are 4 inches wide, shallowly cupped, slightly fragrant, and pale to medium geranium pink. Spots like freckles appear on the inner petals. Blooms appear heavily early in the season and intermittently the rest of the season. Foliage is large, dark green, and leathery, and covers an erect, bushy, 3- to 4-foot, very hardy plant. %

'MARY ROSE'. Austin, 1983, MP. Shrub. This neat shrub has sprays of rich pink, 4- to 5-inch double rosette-shaped flowers with a strong damask fragrance and moderate repeat bloom. Plants grow 4 to 6 feet tall. %

'MAX GRAF'. Bowditch, 1919, PB. Hybrid rugosa. This variety is valuable as a ground cover, growing 1 to 2 feet high with a trailing growth habit. It has single, bright pink 3-inch flowers with golden centers. Bloom is profuse and fragrant but appears only once a year. Foliage is shiny and wrinkled and appears on trailing stems. 7.2

'MAYTIME'. Buck, 1975, PB. Shrub. Carmine-rose to soft coral flowers with yellow bases are single (with 6 to 10 petals), shallowly cupped, fragrant, and 3½ to 4 inches across. Long-lasting flowers appear all summer on bushy, 3- to 4-foot, very hardy plants with dark bronzy green, leathery foliage. %

'MUSIC MAKER'. Buck, 1973, LP. Shrub. Double, high-centered, light pink flowers are 3 to 4 inches across and fragrant. They bloom repeatedly in clusters of six to eight. The light green, leathery, glossy, disease-free foliage covers bushy, 2- to 3-foot very hardy plants. 7.2

'Kathleen'

'Lavender Dream'

'Mary Rose'

'Penelope'

'Pink Grootendorst'

'Red Meidiland'

'NEVADA'.   Dot, 1927, W. Hybrid moyesii. Pink or apricot buds open into creamy white, 4- to 5-inch flowers that are often splashed with red and bloom on short stems. Each bloom has prominent, attractive, golden stamens. Plants are vigorous, grow 5 to 7 feet tall, and have good repeat bloom. 8.2

'OTHELLO'.   Austin, 1990, DR. Shrub. Also known as 'Auslo', this rose has fully double, cupped, 4- to 5-inch flowers that are rich crimson to burgundy with a heavy old-rose fragrance. As the flowers fade, they turn mauve to purple. There is moderate repeat bloom. Vigorous, thorny, spreading plants grow 5 to 6 feet tall and are highly disease resistant. +

'PEARL MEIDILAND'.   Meilland, 1989, LP. Shrub. Iridescent, dainty pastel pink, semidouble 2- to 3-inch flowers bloom in clusters all summer on vigorous, spreading plants that grow 2 feet high and 6 feet wide and have deep green foliage. +

'PENELOPE'.   Pemberton, 1924, LP. Hybrid musk. Flowers are shell pink fading to creamy white and have a lemon yellow center. In cool weather, the flowers do not fade. The 2½- to 3-inch, semidouble blooms appear in large clusters all summer, and have a heavy fragrance. Dark green, glossy leaves cover shrubby plants that grow 5 to 8 feet high. The hips are pale apple green changing to coral-pink. 7.5

'PINK GROOTENDORST'.   Grootendorst, 1923, MP. Hybrid rugosa. This sport of 'F. J. Grootendorst' is identical to it in all ways except the flowers are a clean medium pink fading to dusty pink as the blooms age. 8.6

'PINK MEIDILAND'.   Meilland, 1985, PB. Shrub. Upright, repeat-blooming plants grow 4 feet high and have single, deep pink, 3- to 4-inch flowers with white eyes. The leaves are small, medium green, and glossy. (8.1)

'PRAIRIE FLOWER'.   Buck, 1975, RB. Shrub. Cardinal red flowers have white centers and seven petals that open flat into 2- to 3-inch blooms. Flowers have a slight fragrance and appear singly or in clusters all summer above dark green, leathery foliage on bushy, 4-foot plants. 'Prairie Flower' is one of 11 roses (whose names all begin with "Prairie") hybridized by Professor Griffith Buck of Iowa State University. All are very winter hardy. %

'RALPH'S CREEPER'.   Moore, 1987, RB. Shrub. Single, bright red 2-inch flowers have a white to yellow eye and a cluster of prominent golden stamens. They bloom repeatedly all summer. Best used as a ground cover, this plant grows 1½ feet high and spreads to 6 feet or more. The foliage is small and glossy and the fragrance is that of apple blossoms. (7.6)

'RED MEIDILAND'.   Meilland, 1989, RB. Shrub. Deep red, single 1- to 2-inch flowers with white centers bloom continually

'Sparrieshoop'

in heavy clusters on plants that grow 1½ feet high and 5 feet wide—dimensions that make them useful as a ground cover. Abundant orange-red hips appear in the fall. +

'RUGOSA MAGNIFICA'. Van Fleet, 1905, MB. Hybrid rugosa. Reddish lavender 3-inch flowers with golden stamens are fragrant and double. Orange-red hips appear in the fall on vigorous, spreading, 4- to 5-foot, very hardy plants with glossy, ribbed foliage. %

'SCARLET MEIDILAND'. Meilland, 1987, MR. Shrub. This mounding ground cover grows 3 feet high and spreads to 6 feet across. Rich, deep scarlet, double 1- to 2-inch flowers bloom abundantly in clusters in early summer and intermittently until frost. (7.8)

'SEA FOAM'. Schwartz, 1964, W. Shrub. A sea of double (30 to 35 petals), slightly fragrant, creamy white 2-inch flowers borne in clusters envelop this trailing plant all summer. The flexible, normally arching canes can be trained up a trellis or allowed to grow as a ground cover 1 to 2 feet high. The leaves are small, glossy, and leathery. 7.5

'SPARRIESHOOP'. Kordes, 1953, LP. Shrub. Large (4-inch), single, very fragrant, light pink flowers have five broad, wavy petals and prominent golden stamens. They bloom all summer on upright, bushy plants that can grow 5 to 10 feet high. 8.0

'SUNNY JUNE'. Lammerts, 1952, DY. Shrub. Deep canary yellow flowers have five petals, are 3½ inches across, and are slightly cupped to flat. Blooms have deep red stamens and a spicy fragrance, and appear in large clusters all summer. Dark and glossy black spot–resistant foliage covers an upright, 8-foot, hardy plant best grown as a pillar rose. 7.5

'Thérèse Bugnet'

'THÉRÈSE BUGNET'. Bugnet, 1950, MP. Hybrid rugosa. Square-tipped, lilac pink buds open into double (35 petals), 4-inch, fragrant flowers of pinkish lilac that age to pale pink and bloom in small clusters all summer. The blooms are veined and crinkled. Vigorous 4- to 6-foot plants are very hardy and covered with textured grayish blue-green leaves that may be prone to mildew. 7.8

'WHITE MEIDILAND'. Meilland, 1987, W. Shrub. Vigorous, horizontal branches form a plant 2 feet high and 5 feet wide. The very double, sparkling white flowers are 4 inches across and bloom continually all summer. Large, leathery foliage covers thick canes. +

'WILL SCARLET'. Hiling, 1948, MR. Hybrid musk. Semi-double, fragrant 2-inch flowers of scarlet bloom repeatedly throughout the season and have colorful orange hips in the fall. Flowers are borne in clusters of up to 50 blooms on 6- to 8-foot plants that have large, glossy, leathery leaves. 8.8

'Will Scarlet'

'Baronne Prévost' (Hybrid Perpetual)

'Charles de Mills' (Gallica)

'Honorine de Brabant' (Bourbon)

OLD GARDEN ROSES

*B*y definition, an old garden rose is one belonging to any class that existed before 1867, the year the first hybrid tea was introduced. Even if the rose was hybridized or discovered after 1867, it is considered "old" if it belongs to one of these classes.

It is more than nostalgia or historical significance that makes old garden roses popular. They have virtues of their own—beauty, charm, fragrance, low maintenance, long life, and sometimes hardiness. Plants vary in size from dwarf to giant, with flowers of all colors that range in form from delicate singles to the fullest of very doubles.

The old-rose category is made up of a large number of subclasses. The most common of these are the alba, hybrid alba, Bourbon, centifolia, China, damask, eglanteria, gallica, hybrid foetida, hybrid perpetual, hybrid spinosissima, moss, noisette, Portland, species, and tea roses. Chapter 2 describes their distinctive characteristics.

Teas, Chinas, and noisettes are reliably hardy only to Zone 8. Most others, unless noted otherwise in plant descriptions, are hardy to at least Zone 6; centifolias and damasks are hardy to Zone 5.

There are also a number of relatively obscure classes: Ayrshire, Boursault, hybrid bracteata, hybrid Bourbon, hybrid canina, hybrid China, hybrid multiflora, hybrid sempervirens, and hybrid setigera. Since most of these are rare both in gardens and in commerce, none is included in the listings that follow.

Some old garden roses are known by both their English and Latin names. The usage of these names in the following descriptions conforms with that in Modern Roses, the standard reference for rose growers. If a rose commonly goes by more than one name, this is so noted.

Because many old garden roses were discovered growing in the wild or in gardens, some as far away as the Orient, the name of the hybridizer may not be known. In these cases the date of introduction refers to the year the rose was first discovered or named. (Those noted "prior to" may actually be far more ancient than their dates indicate.) If the hybridizer's name is known, the date refers to the year of introduction.

The following list of old garden roses represents the best that are currently available for purchase. There are nurseries that specialize in old garden roses, which are otherwise difficult to buy; these sources are listed on pages 340 and 341. Many forgotten old roses still survive in waysides, cemeteries, and old gardens, waiting to be rediscovered. If you're interested in learning more about these, or in helping to perpetuate languishing varieties, you may wish to join the Heritage Rose Foundation or the Heritage Roses Group. See page 339 for addresses.

'ALFRED DE DALMAS'.   Laffay, 1855, LP. Moss. Sometimes incorrectly confused with a similar rose called 'Mousseline', this variety has double, pale pink, fragrant 1- to 2-inch flowers that bleach to white in the hot sun and bloom in clusters. Compact, sprawling plants grow 2 to 3 feet tall, have a multitude of thorns, and show some, but not prolific, repeat bloom. 7.1

'APOTHECARY'S ROSE'.   Prior to 1600, DP. Gallica. Botanically, this rose is *R. gallica officinalis*. It was used by medieval apothecaries and was also the Red Rose of Lancaster made famous during the Wars of the Roses. The semidouble 2- to 3-inch flowers are deep pink, fragrant, and open to reveal yellow stamens. The branching plants grow 3 to 4 feet high, with dark green leaves and few thorns. 9.2

'AUTUMN DAMASK'.   Ancient, MP. Damask. This is probably the same rose grown and loved by the Romans for its then-remarkable ability to bloom more than once a year. The 3½-inch very double flowers bloom in late spring and again in the fall. They appear in fragrant clusters of soft, clear pink on plants that grow about 3 to 4 feet tall. This rose is known botanically as *R. damascena bifera* or *R. damascena semperflorens*. %

'BARONESS ROTHSCHILD'.   Pernet Père, 1868, LP. Hybrid perpetual. These stiff, erect plants are graced with large, fully double (40 petals), cupped, very fragrant 3- to 4-inch flowers of soft rose-pink overlaid with white. They bloom singly or in small clusters. Flowers are darker pink toward the center and appear profusely in spring and again in fall on 4- to 5-foot plants. 6.0

'BARONNE PRÉVOST'.   Desprez, 1842, MP. Hybrid perpetual. Rose-pink flowers with lighter pink shadings are fully double, flat, 4 inches across, and richly fragrant. They bloom throughout the summer. The blooms have a large number of tightly packed petals that are silvery on the reverse sides. Plants are upright and vigorous, growing 4 to 5 feet high. 'Baronne Prévost' is one of the first hybrid perpetuals to come into bloom in the spring. 7.5

'BELLE DE CRÉCY'.   Roesner, prior to 1829, MB. Gallica. Very fragrant cerise and purple flowers with green buttonlike centers turn lavender-gray to blue-violet as they mature. Blooms 3 to 4 inches across are fully double and flat, with the innermost petals curving toward the center of the flower. Plants bloom once a year and grow 4 to 5 feet high. Because the stems are weak, the weight of the flowers makes it necessary to support the plant. 7.5

'BOULE DE NEIGE'.   Lacharme, 1867, W. Bourbon. French for "snowball," the name aptly describes these rounded, fully double, and intensely fragrant pure white 2- to 3-inch flowers. These sometimes rebloom on the compact, erect, 4- to 5-foot plants with dark green foliage. %

'Baroness Rothschild'

'Belle de Crécy'

'Boule de Neige'

'Celsiana'

'Communis'

'Crested Moss'

'CAMAIEUX'.   1830, MB. Gallica. Low-growing, 3-foot plants have crisp, double, 3-inch flowers of white striped with rose-purple. The spice-scented blooms appear only once a year. 7.5

'CARDINAL DE RICHELIEU'.   Laffay, 1840, MB. Gallica. Double, dark wine red to dark purple flowers appear once a year on large, bushy, 4- to 5-foot plants. The flowers are 3 to 4 inches across and fragrant, taking on a metallic sheen as they mature. 7.0

'CATHERINE MERMET'.   Guillot Fils, 1869, LP. Tea. Long grown as a florist's rose in greenhouses, this variety has long stems and flesh pink, high-centered flowers with petal edges tinted in lilac. The large, double, fragrant 3-inch flowers show dependable repeat bloom. Plants grow 3 to 4 feet tall and like most tea roses, are tender. 7.5

'CELESTIAL'.   Prior to 1848, LP. Alba. Light blush pink 3½-inch flowers are double and fragrant, and bloom once a year above bluish green leaves that cover vigorous, 6-foot plants. 7.5

'CELSIANA'.   Prior to 1750, LP. Damask. A graceful, slender, 4- to 5-foot plant with gray-toned fragrant foliage bears 4-inch, semidouble, loose, flat, fragrant blooms of pale pink that fade to a warm blush. The petals are crinkled, with golden stamens that set off the center of the flower. Flowers appear in small clusters only once a year. 9.2

'CHARLES DE MILLS'.   Date unknown, MB. Gallica. Rounded, cup-shaped, quartered, 4½-inch blooms are packed with petals that look very much like crepe paper. Strongly perfumed flowers are deep red with purple overtones and a silvery lavender reverse. They bloom once a year on bushy, 4- to 5-foot, almost thornless plants. 8.5

'COMMUNIS'.   About 1696, MP. Moss. Also called 'Common Moss', this variety has pale rose-pink, very double, globular, 2½- to 3-inch flowers that are very fragrant. These open flat to reveal a buttonlike center. Plants grow 4 to 5 feet high and bloom once a year. 8.5

'CRESTED MOSS'.   1827, MP. Moss. Sometimes called 'Chapeau de Napoléon' (Napoleon's hat), this variety has tricornered buds. It is similar in appearance to 'Communis', to which it is closely related, but its moss is confined to the edges of the sepals. Plants grow 4 to 5 feet high and bloom once a year. The heavily scented, clear pink, 2- to 3-inch flowers have a long period of bloom. 8.7

'DUCHESSE DE BRABANT'.   Bernède, 1857, LP. Tea. Soft pearly rose-pink flowers have 45 petals and are 2 to 3 inches across, cup shaped, and very fragrant. This is one of the first roses to bloom in spring, and it blooms consistently all summer. Vigorous, spreading growth reaches heights of 3 to 5 feet. 7.7

'FANTIN-LATOUR'. Origin and date unknown, LP. Centifolia. Flowers are 2 to 3 inches across, blush pink, very fragrant, and have about 100 petals that open into a flat shape. Dark green, broad foliage covers a vigorous, bushy plant that grows 4 to 5 feet high and blooms once a year. 7.6

'FÉLICITÉ PARMENTIER'. 1834, LP. Alba. Very double, very fragrant flowers are soft flesh pink and bloom once a year in clusters of three to five. They open flat, then the petals curl under the flower to form a 2½-inch ball with a green center. Gray-green foliage covers compact, 4- to 5-foot growth. 7.8

'Félicité Parmentier'

'FERDINAND PICHARD'. Tanne, 1921, RB. Hybrid perpetual. Flowers are 2½ to 4 inches across, fragrant, cup shaped, streaked in pink and red, and have 25 crisp petals. Vigorous plants with bright green leaves reach a height of 5 to 6 feet and bloom repeatedly throughout the season. 7.7

'FRAU KARL DRUSCHKI'. Lambert, 1901, W. Hybrid perpetual. Pointed buds tinged with pink open into snow white flowers with 35 petals. Flowers are 3 to 4 inches across, and have a high center and sometimes a blush pink middle. Plants grow to 6 feet in height and flower repeatedly all summer. This variety is sometimes called 'Snow Queen'. 7.5

'FRÜHLINGSGOLD'. Kordes, 1937, MY. Hybrid spinosissima. "Spring gold" in German, this variety has very fragrant pure golden yellow flowers that bloom once a year. The single flowers (with 5 to 10 petals) measuring 3½ to 5 inches across appear on vigorous, arching 6- to 8-foot canes. The large, light green leaves are soft and wrinkled. %

'Frau Karl Druschki'

'FRÜHLINGSMORGEN'. Kordes, 1942, PB. Hybrid spinosissima. The single 3-inch flowers are cherry pink with a soft yellow center and maroon stamens. Plants grow 6 feet high, producing dark green foliage and large red hips. There is intermittent repeat bloom on this variety whose name means "spring morning". 8.5

'GÉNÉRAL JACQUEMINOT'. Roussel, 1853, RB. Hybrid perpetual. Long cutting stems made this an early florist's rose. Blooms are 2½ to 4 inches across, cupped, bright, clear red, and extremely fragrant. They have 25 to 30 petals, whose reverse side is overtoned in white. Often considered the prototype of the hybrid perpetual class, this variety blooms repeatedly on bushy, 4- to 5-foot plants with rich green foliage. Rose growers have dubbed this variety "General Jack." 6.7

'GLOIRE DES MOUSSEUSES'. Laffay, 1852, MP. Moss. Heavily mossed buds open into clear, bright pink, double flowers with a deeper pink center. The petals overlay each other on 4-inch flowers that appear in clusters once a year above large, light green leaves. Plants grow 3 to 4 feet high. 7.6

'Général Jacqueminot'

'Harison's Yellow'

'Henry Nevard'

'Hermosa'

'GREEN ROSE'. Prior to 1845, green. China. Known botanically as *R. chinensis viridiflora,* this rose is unique in that it is truly green—and therefore fits none of the standard color classifications. Its 1½- to 2-inch blooms with narrow, leaflike medium bright green petals appear singly or in clusters throughout the summer. Plants grow 3 to 5 feet high. 7.0

'HARISON'S YELLOW'. About 1830, DY. Hybrid foetida. Early American settlers took this rose with them as they crossed the country. It has multitudes of 2- to 3-inch, semidouble, open, very fragrant, bright yellow flowers that almost hide its diminutive, rich green, ferny leaves. It is extremely disease resistant. Botanically, this rose is *R. foetida harisonii.* 7.6

'HENRI MARTIN'. Laffay, 1863, MR. Moss. Sometimes called 'Red Moss', this variety has shining crimson-red, semi-double, 2½-inch flowers that bloom once a year in clusters of three to eight. Blooms have a rich perfume and are long lasting as cut flowers. Arching, thorny plants grow 5 to 6 feet tall and have medium green, finely textured leaves. %

'HENRY NEVARD'. Cant, 1924, DR. Hybrid perpetual. Double flowers of crimson to scarlet have 30 petals and are cupped, 4 inches or more across, and very fragrant. They appear throughout the summer on bushy, 4- to 5-foot plants with dark green, leathery leaves. Plants are susceptible to mildew. 6.1

'HERMOSA'. Marcheseau, 1840, LP. China. *Hermosa* means "beautiful" in Spanish, and aptly describes these fragrant, high-centered, blush pink double 1- to 3-inch flowers (with 35 petals) that bloom repeatedly in clusters. Foliage is blue-green on 4-foot plants. 7.5

'HONORINE DE BRABANT'. Unknown, PB. Bourbon. Pale lilac pink flowers are spotted and striped in mauve and crimson. The coloration is darker and bolder in warm, dry climates than it is in cool, damp places. The 3½- to 4-inch flowers are fragrant, double, loosely cupped, and quartered, appearing repeatedly on vigorous, 4- to 6-foot plants with light green leaves. 7.7

'ISPAHAN'. Prior to 1832, MP. Damask. Bright pink 2- to 3-inch flowers are double, loose, and very fragrant. As the blooms mature, they fade to a soft pink. There is one long blooming season on these plants that grow 5 to 6 feet high in an arching habit with small leaves. %

'JACQUES CARTIER'. Moreau-Robert, 1868, LP. Portland. Pearly rose flowers with darker pink, buttonlike centers are very full, highly fragrant, and often quartered. The 3-inch blooms appear all summer on 2½- to 3½-foot plants with closely spaced, light green leaves. This rare variety is one of the few Portlands that are still available. Some old-rose enthusiasts believe it is in fact an older variety correctly known as 'Marquise Boccella'. 7.6

'KÖNIGIN VON DÄNEMARK'.   1826, MP. Alba. Also
called 'Belle Courtisanne' and 'Queen of Denmark', this rose has
2½- to 3-inch, flesh pink, very double, quartered, fragrant flowers
with darker centers. They open from peachy buds, appearing once
a year on 4- to 5-foot plants with blue-green foliage. 7.9

'LA REINE VICTORIA'.   Schwartz, 1872, MP. Bourbon.
Introduced in the thirty-fifth year of Queen Victoria's reign, these
slender, upright plants have cup-shaped, rich pink, double,
1½- to 4½-inch flowers that deepen in tone as they age. The repeat-blooming flowers are highly fragrant and long lasting. Plants
grow 4 to 6 feet high and have soft green foliage. 7.5

'LADY PENZANCE'.   Penzance, 1894, PB. Eglanteria. Small,
1- to 2-inch single flowers of coppery pink with yellow centers
look scarlet from a distance and bloom on 8-foot, arching plants.
Foliage and flowers are fragrant, but plants are susceptible to
black spot. 7.8

'LOUISE ODIER'.   Margottin, 1851, DP. Bourbon. Full,
bright rose-pink, 2½- to 3½-inch flowers are very double and cup
shaped. The strongly fragrant blooms open wide and flat, and are
long lasting when cut. They appear all summer on 5-foot plants
with fine, light green leaves set closely together. 7.8

'MADAME ALFRED CARRIÈRE'.   Schwartz, 1879, W.
Noisette. Pale pinkish white flowers are fully double, globular, 3½
inches across, and very fragrant. The centers of the flowers have
tightly curved petals. Plants bloom recurrently and have a climbing habit, reaching heights of 12 to 20 feet. This variety has more
winter hardiness than most noisettes. 6.5

'MADAME HARDY'.   Hardy, 1832, W. Damask. The very
double, very fragrant, cup-shaped, white 2½- to 3½-inch flower
opens flat to reveal an erect green center (called a pip). A tinge of
pink sometimes appears on the flowers, which bloom in clusters
and only once a year. Plants grow 4 to 6 feet tall. 8.8

'MADAME ISAAC PEREIRE'.   Garcon, 1881, DP. Bour-
bon. Large, fully double, very fragrant flowers are deep rose-pink
shaded with purple. The 3- to 4-inch blooms are quartered and
open into a saucer shape. They bloom all summer on 4- to 6-foot
plants with large, bold foliage. 7.2

'MADAME PIERRE OGER'.   Oger, 1878, PB. Bourbon.
This sport of 'La Reine Victoria' is identical to it in all respects
except that its flowers are blush pink, developing a rosy cast as
they open. 7.4

'MAIDEN'S BLUSH'.   Kew, 1797, W. Hybrid alba. Pale
blush pink, double, globular, fragrant 2- to 3-inch flowers fade
to white and bloom once a year on long, arching canes with
blue-green leaves. Plants grow 4 to 8 feet high. This variety is

'La Reine Victoria'

'Lady Penzance'

'Madame Alfred Carrière'

'Marie Louise'

'Mrs. John Laing'

'Mutabilis'

sometimes called 'Small Maiden's Blush' to distinguish it from a second similar variety called 'Great Maiden's Blush'. 7.9

'MAMAN COCHET'. S. Cochet, 1893, PB. Tea. Very double, 4-inch flowers have classic form and petals of soft pink with a deeper pink center and a yellow base. Scented blooms appear all summer; as they mature, the outer petals darken. Plants grow 3 to 4 feet tall and have dark green, leathery foliage. There is also a climbing form of 'Maman Cochet'. 7.0

'MARCHIONESS OF LONDONDERRY'. Dickson, 1893, LP. Hybrid perpetual. High-centered and fragrant pale pink flowers have 50 petals and measure 4 to 5 inches across. They bloom repeatedly on very vigorous 5- to 7-foot plants. 7.4

'MARÉCHAL NIEL'. Pradel, 1864, MY. Noisette. Long, pointed buds open into double 3- to 4-inch flowers of golden yellow that bloom profusely and repeatedly, strongly fragrant of a mixture of violets and tea. The flower stems have weak necks, making the blooms tend to droop. The very vigorous, climbing growth produces plants 10 feet high. Like most noisettes, it is very tender where winters are cold. 7.8

'MARIE LOUISE'. Prior to 1813, MP. Damask. Very double, highly fragrant 4- to 5-inch flowers are pink tinged with mauve, revealing buttonlike centers as they open. They bloom once a year. If not supported, the bushy 4-foot plants will arch to the ground under the weight of the copious flowers. 8.0

'MRS. JOHN LAING'. Bennett, 1887, MP. Hybrid perpetual. Low growing for a hybrid perpetual, this 3- to 4-foot variety has soft pink flowers that are strongly fragrant. Blooms are 3½ to 4 inches across, have 45 petals, and bloom recurrently during the summer. 8.0

'MUTABILIS'. Prior to 1894, YB. China. As they mature, these sulfur yellow flowers change to orange, copper, red, and finally crimson. Single and 2 inches wide, they bloom repeatedly in clusters on 3- to 6-foot plants with reddish leaves and stems. This rose is sometimes confused with a centifolia by the same name that was painted by Redouté. 8.7

'OLD BLUSH'. Prior to 1752, MP. China. This was the first China rose introduced into the Western world. Two-tone pink, semidouble, 2½-inch flowers appear in large, loose clusters on upright, 3- to 5-foot plants. The flowers have a very slight fragrance and are reliable repeat bloomers. 7.9

'PAUL NEYRON'. Levet, 1869, MP. Hybrid perpetual. Cupped flowers of clear to rose-pink are tinted with lilac and bloom over large, rich green foliage on 5- to 6-foot plants. The very large (5-inch), fragrant blooms have 50 petals; some plants may exhibit repeat flowering. 7.9

'PETITE DE HOLLANDE'. Prior to 1838, MP. Centifolia. Small, double, rose-pink, fragrant 2-inch flowers bloom in clusters once a year on a 3-foot, bushy plant. This rose is known botanically as *R. centifolia minor*. 8.5

'REINE DES VIOLETTES'. Millet-Malet, 1860, MB. Hybrid perpetual. Violet-red, 3½- to 4-inch flowers tinged with pink, lilac, and blue have 75 petals and are very fragrant. Sparse, glossy leaves cover thornless 6- to 8-foot plants that bloom throughout the season. 7.1

'ROGER LAMBELIN'. Schwartz, 1890, RB. Hybrid perpetual. This distinctive variety has wavy petals of bright crimson fading to maroon and edged in white, creating an effect that looks something like shredded red cabbage. The slightly fragrant 4-inch blooms, which appear throughout the summer, have 30 petals and a rounded, decorative form. Plants grow 4 to 5 feet high. 7.0

Rosa eglanteria

ROSA EGLANTERIA. Prior to 1551, LP. Species. Known as the eglantine or the 'Sweet Brier Rose', this variety has single, 2-inch, pink flowers that bloom individually or in small clusters. Curiously, the foliage smells like apples, especially after a rain. The very vigorous plants have many thorns and grow 8 to 10 feet in height. 7.7

ROSA FOETIDA. Prior to 1542, MY. Species. Single, bright yellow flowers are 2 to 2½ inches across and bloom once a year on 10-foot plants. The blooms have an almost sickening sweet odor. This rose was the basis of yellow coloring in modern roses, and unfortunately is very prone to black spot. %

ROSA FOETIDA BICOLOR. Prior to 1590, RB. Species. Known as 'Austrian Copper', this sport of *R. foetida* has petals that are orange-scarlet on the inside and yellow on the reverse. The single blooms are 1½ to 2½ inches across and appear once a year on 5- to 10-foot plants with arching canes. Like *R. foetida*, it is prone to black spot. 8.1

Rosa foetida bicolor

ROSA FOETIDA PERSIANA. Prior to 1837, MY. Species. This rose is similar in all respects to *R. foetida* except that its flowers are double. It is often called the Persian rose. 7.7

ROSA GLAUCA. Prior to 1830, MP. Species. Sometimes called *R. rubrifolia* in reference to its reddish leaves, this rose has 1½-inch pink flowers that are borne singly or in small clusters once a year. Leaves are narrow, and appear on plants that grow 4 to 6 feet tall. 8.8

ROSA HUGONIS. 1899, MY. Species. Also called 'Father Hugo's Rose', this rose is one of the first to bloom in late spring. Its masses of single, 2½-inch flowers are sunny yellow, blooming on drooping branches over small, dark green leaves. Because of its 6- to 10-foot height, this rose is best grown as a climber. 9.1

Rosa glauca

Rosa multiflora

'Rosa Mundi'

'Rose de Rescht'

ROSA MACRANTHA. Prior to 1832, LP. Species. Single, 2-to 3-inch, blush pink flowers bloom once a year and are followed by ¾-inch, round, dull red hips. Plants grow to 10 feet in height and have upright arching canes as well as canes that grow along the ground; both are thickly covered with blue-green leaves. 7.8

ROSA MOYESII. 1894, MR. Species. Single flowers vary in color from light pink to deep rose and deep blood red. They are 1½ to 2½ inches across and are borne singly or in pairs. Flowers bloom once a year, followed by oblong hips that are 2 to 2½ inches long and deep orange-red. The 10-foot-high, arching plants have fine, fernlike foliage. Although this rose was discovered in 1894, it is believed to be of ancient origin. %

ROSA MULTIFLORA. Prior to 1810, W. Species. Although usually grown as an understock, this rose is sometimes cultivated for its dense, hedgelike growth. Indeed, its growth is so rampant that the planting of this rose is outlawed in some areas. The ¾-inch white flowers bloom once a year in pyramidal clusters. 6.2

'ROSA MUNDI'. Possibly prior to 1581, PB. Gallica. The oldest striped rose on record, this sport of the 'Apothecary's Rose' has semidouble 4-inch white flowers striped with red and pink, accented by bright yellow stamens. Two petals are rarely alike. Flowers bloom once a year on sprawling 3-foot plants. Known botanically as *Rosa gallica versicolor,* this rose is often confused with 'York and Lancaster'. 9.1

ROSA PENDULINA. Prior to 1683, DP. Species. Also known as the 'Alpine Rose', this rose has single, 2-inch, pink flowers that bloom singly or in small clusters once a year. The red hips are oblong or oval and have an elongated neck. Plants grow 3 feet tall. %

ROSA ROXBURGHII. Prior to 1814, MP. Species. Known also as the 'Chestnut Rose', this rose has gray branches with shredding bark, and prickly flower buds that look like a chestnut burr. The double, flat flowers are medium lilac pink and 2 to 2½ inches across. Hips are rounded and 1 to 1½ inches across. Plants grow to 6 feet tall, and bloom recurrently throughout the summer. %

'ROSE DE MEAUX'. Prior to 1789, MP. Centifolia. Sometimes called simply 'De Meaux', this variety has 1- to 1½-inch, double, very fragrant, light to medium pink flowers that look like pompoms. These give a charming, airy grace to the dwarfish 2- to 3-foot plant. Blooms appear once a year, in huge clusters. Leaves are susceptible to black spot. 8.3

'ROSE DE RESCHT'. Prior to 1940, DP. Damask. Bright fuchsia red, very fragrant, 2- to 2½-inch flowers fade with lilac tints and have a full, crowded, circular rosette form. Foliage is closely spaced on compact, 2- to 3-foot plants that have a long season of bloom. 8.6

'ROSE DU ROI'.   Lelieur, 1815, MR. Portland. A parent of the first hybrid perpetual, this rose has large, very fragrant, double flowers of bright red shaded with violet. The central petals fold and curl to show lighter tones on the reverse sides of the petals. The leaves are bright green and slightly ruffled. Blooms are 3 inches across and appear throughout the summer on 3- to 4-foot plants. 7.0

'SALET'.   Lacharme, 1854, MP. Moss. Very large, full, flat, 2- to 3½-inch flowers are rose-pink and bloom intermittently throughout the summer after the first flush of bloom. Vigorous plants grow 4 to 5 feet high. 8.3

'SOUVENIR DE LA MALMAISON'.   Béluze, 1843, LP. Bourbon. Named for the estate where Empress Josephine maintained her famous rose garden, this variety has 3- to 4-inch, flat, double, quartered blooms of flesh pink with a rosy center. Flowers have a very spicy fragrance and appear freely and repeatedly on a compact, 2- to 4-foot plant. Unfortunately, this variety is not winter hardy in cold climates. 8.2

'Souvenir de la Malmaison'

'STANWELL PERPETUAL'.   Lee, 1838, W. Hybrid spinosissima. The 3- to 4-inch double flowers are white to blush pink and have a slight sweet fragrance. Plants bloom off and on after the first flush of bloom on this graceful, 6- to 8-foot plant with very small leaves and a multitude of thorns. 8.0

'VARIEGATA DI BOLOGNA'.   Bonfiglioli, 1909, RB. Bourbon. One of the finest striped roses, this variety has very double, globular, highly fragrant, white flowers that are striped in purplish red. Blooms are 3 to 4 inches across, appear in small clusters, and occasionally repeat in the fall. Vigorous plants grow 6 to 8 feet high. 7.5

'Variegata di Bologna'

'WHITE ROSE OF YORK'.   Prior to 1597, W. Alba. Sometimes called 'Bonnie Prince Charlie's Rose' or the 'Jacobite Rose', this rose is believed to be the original *R. alba,* symbol of the Yorkists during the Wars of the Roses. (The opposing Lancastrians chose the red 'Apothecary's Rose', *R. gallica officinalis,* as their emblem.) The fragrant 3-inch flowers are white, loosely semi-double to double, and usually borne in small clusters all along the canes. They bloom once a year, followed by oval scarlet hips. Plants grow 6 to 12 feet high. %

'YORK AND LANCASTER'.   Prior to 1629, PB. Damask. Loosely double 1½- to 2½-inch flowers have white and light pink petals, sometimes all one color or the other, and sometimes mixed in variegated splotches. Blooms appear once a year in clusters. Leaves are light gray-green, on arching plants that grow 5 or more feet high. This rose, which has been confused with 'Rosa Mundi', was named to commemorate the end of the Wars of the Roses (1455–1485), although it is not the same rose whose discovery supposedly inspired the truce. 8.1

'White Rose of York'

PUBLIC AND PRIVATE ROSE GARDENS

The following list of rose gardens was compiled from listings by the Public Gardens Committee of the American Rose Society, All-America Rose Selections (an association of U.S. rose producers), and other sources. Some are in public places; others are on the grounds of private homes. Only the largest and most beautiful gardens are listed (listings for a state are alphabetical by city); there are many more locations where roses are grown for public viewing. Before visiting one of these gardens, phone for information about hours, admission fees, and travel directions. Those marked with an asterisk (*) require that you phone ahead for reservations.

ALABAMA

David A. Hemphill Park of Roses
Springdale Mall, Airport Boulevard
Mobile, AL 36606
205-479-3775

Bellingrath Gardens Rose Garden
12401 Bellingrath Gardens Road
Theodore, AL 36582
205-973-2217

ARIZONA

Sahauro Historical Ranch Rose
  Garden
9802 North Fifty-ninth Avenue
Glendale, AZ 85302
602-931-5321

Valley Garden Center
1809 North Fifteenth Avenue
Phoenix, AZ 85007
602-461-7055 or 602-967-7001

Gene C. Reid Park
900 South Randolph Way
Tucson, AZ 85716
602-791-4873

ARKANSAS

Kirkland Rose Garden*
8102 Westwood
Little Rock, AR 72204
501-565-9168

State Capitol Rose Garden
State Capitol Building
Little Rock, AR 72201
501-371-5176

Clark Smith
2001 Strait Place
Stuttgart, AR 72160
501-673-3122

CALIFORNIA

William S. Hillman, Jr.*
1124 Story Place
Alhambra, CA 91801
818-570-1124

Berkeley Rose Garden
1201 Euclid Avenue
Berkeley, CA 94708
510-644-6530

Fountain Square
7115 Greenback Lane
Citrus Heights, CA 95621
916-969-6666

Rose Acres*
6641 Crystal Boulevard
Diamond Springs, CA 95619
916-626-1722

Mr. and Mrs. Richard Streeper*
1333 Wenatchee Avenue
El Cajon, CA 92021
619-448-0321

Empire Mine State Historic Park
10791 East Empire Street
Grass Valley, CA 95945
916-273-8522

Descanso Gardens
1418 Descanso Drive
La Cañada Flintridge, CA 91011
818-952-4400

Exposition Park Rose Garden
Exposition Boulevard and Figueroa
Los Angeles, CA 90037
213-748-4772 or 213-485-5529

Morcom Amphitheater of Roses
700 Jean Street
Oakland, CA 94610
510-658-0731

Tournament of Roses Wrigley
  Garden
391 South Orange Grove
  Boulevard
Pasadena, CA 91184
818-449-4100

Fairmont Park Rose Garden
2225 Market Street
Riverside, CA 92521
714-782-5301

Capitol Park Rose Garden
1300 L Street
Sacramento, CA 95814
916-445-3658

Inez Parker Memorial Garden
Balboa Park
Park Boulevard
San Diego, CA 92112
619-525-8200

Golden Gate Park Rose Garden
Golden Gate Park
San Francisco, CA 94117
415-666-7200

San Jose Municipal Rose Garden
Naglee and Dana Avenues
San Jose, CA 95126
408-287-0698 or 408-277-4661

Huntington Botanical Gardens
1151 Oxford Road
San Marino, CA 91108
818-405-2100

Mission Historical Park Rose
  Garden
Upper Laguna and Los Olivos
  Streets
Santa Barbara, CA 93103
805-564-5433

Windsor Lodge*
(Dr. Tommy Cairns)
3053 Laurel Canyon Boulevard
Studio City, CA 91604
213-654-0626

CALIFORNIA (continued)

Wasco Community Garden
Barker Park
11th at Birch
Wasco, CA 93280

Roses of Yesterday and Today
803 Brown's Valley Road
Watsonville, CA 95076-0398
408-724-3537 or 408-724-2775

Westminster Civic Center
8200 Westminster Boulevard
Westminster, CA 92683
714-895-2860

Rose Hills Memorial Park
3900 South Workman Mill Road
Whittier, CA 90601
213-699-0921

Filoli House and Gardens*
Filoli Center
Cañada Road
Woodside, CA 94062
415-366-4640 or 415-364-2880

COLORADO

Four Corners Rose Garden
East Second Avenue and Twelfth
  Street
Durango, CO 81302

Joe Longseth
1089 South Coffman
Longmont, CO 80501
303-776-4371

CONNECTICUT

June and David Berg*
11 Oxbow Lane
Bloomfield, CT 06002
203-242-8760

Norwich Memorial Rose Garden
Rockwell Street and Judd Road
Norwich, CT 06360
203-886-2381, Ext. 210

Elizabeth Park Rose Garden
150 Walbridge Road
West Hartford, CT 06119
203-722-6543

FLORIDA

Florida Cypress Gardens
Box 1
Cypress Gardens, FL 33884
813-324-2111, Ext. 217

Walt Disney World
Box 10000
Lake Buena Vista, FL 32830
407-824-6987

Sturgeon Memorial Rose Garden
Serenity Gardens Memorial Park
13401 Indian Rocks Road
Largo, FL 34644
813-595-2914

Giles Rose Nursery
2966 State Road 710
Okeechobee, FL 34974
813-763-6611

GEORGIA

The State Botanical Garden
2450 South Milledge Avenue
Athens, GA 30605
404-542-1244

Atlanta Botanical Garden—
  Rose Garden
Piedmont Park at the Prado
Atlanta, GA 30309
404-876-5859

Rose Test Garden
Thomasville Nurseries, Inc.
1840 Smith Avenue
Thomasville, GA 31792
912-226-5568

HAWAII

University of Hawaii
Maui Cty Research Station
Mauna Place
Kula, Maui
HI 96790
808-878-1213

IDAHO

Boise Park System
Julia Davis Park Memorial
  Rose Garden
The Boise River and Capitol
  Boulevard
Boise, ID 83706
208-384-4240

ILLINOIS

Nan Elliott Memorial Rose Garden
4550 College Avenue
Alton, IL 62002
618-463-3580

Chicago Botanic Garden
Lake Cook Road
Glencoe, IL 60022
708-835-5440

George L. Luthy Memorial
  Botanical Garden
2218 North Prospect Road
Peoria, IL 61603
309-686-3362

Rockford Park District
1300 North Second Street and
  Route 251
Rockford, IL 61107
815-987-8800

Washington Park Botanical
  Garden
Box 5052
Corner of Fayette and Chatham
  Roads
Springfield, IL 62705
217-787-2540

Cantigny Gardens
1 South 151 Winfield Road
Wheaton, IL 60187
708-668-5161

INDIANA

Lakeside Park Rose Garden
1500 Lake Avenue
Fort Wayne, IN 46805
219-427-1253

IOWA

Iowa State University Horticulture
 Garden*
Haber Road and Pammel Drive
Ames, IA 50011
515-294-0042

Bettendorf Municipal Garden
2204 Grant Street
Bettendorf, IA 52722
319-359-0913

Noelridge Park Garden
4900 Council Street NE
Cedar Rapids, IA 52402
319-398-5101

Vander Veer Park Municipal
 Rose Garden
215 West Central Park Avenue
Davenport, IA 52803
319-326-7818

Greenwood Park Rose Garden
Forty-eighth Street and
 Grand Avenue
Des Moines, IA 50317
515-271-4708

Dubuque Arboretum and Botanical
 Gardens
3125 West Thirty-second Street
Dubuque, IA 52001
319-556-2100

Weed Park Memorial Rose Garden
Muscatine, IA 52761
319-263-0241

KANSAS

City Park of Manhattan
1100 Poyntz Street
Manhattan, KS 66502
913-587-2757

Reinisch Rose Garden
Tenth and Gage Streets
Topeka, KS 66604
913-272-6150

KENTUCKY

Bill and Dot McMahon
1133 Nutwood Street
Bowling Green, KY 42103
502-842-7532

Kentucky Memorial Rose Garden*
Kentucky Fair and Exposition
 Center
Louisville, KY 40232
502-366-9592

LOUISIANA

L.S.U. Rose Variety Test Garden
4560 Essen Lane
Baton Rouge, LA 70809
504-766-3471

Hodges Gardens
Box 900, Highway 171 South
Many, LA 71449
318-586-3523

David Davidson
4440 Kawanee Avenue
Metairie, LA 70006
504-888-6825

American Rose Center
8877 Jefferson-Paige Road
Shreveport, LA 71119
318-938-5402

Harold and Ida Hayden*
3912 Sunset Drive
Shreveport, LA 71109
318-635-8579

MARYLAND

Brookside Gardens
1500 Glenallan Avenue
Wheaton, MD 20902
301-949-8230

MASSACHUSETTS

Memories Are Made of This*
4 Bandera Drive
Bedford, MA 01730
617-275-2343

Cornelius Kelly*
48 Bright Road
Belmont, MA 02178
617-484-8481

Harry and Estelle Pugatch*
293 Hartman Road
Newton Center, MA 02159
617-332-4433

Gene O'Leary
6 Kittredge Street
South Peabody, MA 01960

Stanley Park
400 Western Avenue
Westfield, MA 01085
413-568-9312

MICHIGAN

Michigan State University
Horticultural Demonstration
 Gardens
Horticulture Department
Plant and Soil Sciences Building
East Lansing, MI 48823
517-355-0348

Frances Park Memorial Garden
2600 Moores River Drive
Lansing, MI 48910
517-483-4227

MINNESOTA

Chuck and Charlotte Bock*
13212 Girard Avenue South
Burnsville, MN 55337
612-890-6752

Lyndale Park Municipal Rose
 Garden
4125 East Lake Harriet Parkway
Minneapolis, MN 55409
612-348-4448

MISSISSIPPI

Hattiesburg Area Rose Society
 Garden*
University of Southern Mississippi
Hattiesburg, MS 39401
601-583-8848

MISSOURI

Kight Rose Garden*
County Road 262
Advance, MO 63730
314-794-2659

Bob and Doris House
330 Loma Linda Drive
Joplin, MO 65608
417-781-1835

MISSOURI (*continued*)

Jacob L. Loose Memorial Park
Fifty-second Street and
  Pennsylvania Avenue
Kansas City, MO 64112
816-333-6706

Sandie Morris
11 Elmwood Road
St. Joseph, MO 64505
816-232-1162

Missouri Botanical Garden
4344 Shaw Boulevard
St. Louis, MO 63110
314-577-5100

NEBRASKA

Father Flanagan's Boys' Town
  Constitution Rose Garden
Boys Town, NE 68010
402-498-1104

Hanscom Park Greenhouse
1500 South Thirty-second Street
Omaha, NE 68105
402-444-5497

Memorial Park Rose Garden
Fifty-seventh and Underwood
Omaha, NE 68132

NEVADA

Reno Municipal Rose Garden
2055 Idlewild Drive
Reno, NV 89509
702-334-2270

NEW HAMPSHIRE

Fuller Gardens
10 Willow Avenue
North Hampton, NH 03862
603-964-5414

NEW JERSEY

Lambertus C. Bobbink Memorial
  Rose Garden
Thompson Park
Newman Springs Road
Lincroft, NJ 07738
908-842-4000

Laurence Toole*
19 Azalea Court
Little Silver, NJ 07739
201-741-3304

Frank Benardella*
266 Orangeburgh Road
Old Tappan, NJ 07675
201-768-0158

Rudolf W. van der Goot Rose
  Garden
Colonial Park
RD# 1, Mettler's Road
Somerset, NJ 08873
908-234-2677

Jack D. Lissemore Garden
Davis Johnson Park
137 Engle Street
Tenafly, NJ 07670
201-569-PARK

NEW MEXICO

Prospect Park Rose Garden
8205 Apache Avenue NE
Albuquerque, NM 87111

The Garden of David and Claudia
  Bonnett*
3816 Moon Street NE
Albuquerque, NM 87111

NEW YORK

The Peggy Rockefeller Rose Garden
The New York Botanical Garden
Southern Boulevard
Bronx, NY 10458
212-220-8700

The Cranford Rose Garden
Brooklyn Botanic Garden
1000 Washington Avenue
Brooklyn, NY 11225
718-622-4433

Sonenberg Gardens
151 Charlotte Street
Canandaigua, NY 14424
716-394-4922

Queens Botanical Garden
43–50 Main Street
Flushing, NY 11355
718-886-3800

Roseview*
(Mr. and Mrs. Robert Pearles)
743 Wayneport Road South
Macedon, NY 14502
315-986-5838

United Nations Rose Garden
Forty-second Street at the East
  River
New York, NY 10017
212-963-6145

Central Park Rose Garden
Central Parkway
Schenectady, NY 12309
518-382-5152

Edmund Mills Memorial Rose
  Garden
Thornden Park
Syracuse, NY 13220
315-473-4336

Esther Jasik*
711 Oxford Street
Westbury, NY 11590
516-334-5146

NORTH CAROLINA

Biltmore Estate
One North Pack Square
Asheville, NC 28801
704-255-1776

Tanglewood Park Rose Garden
Route 158, Box 1040
Clemmons, NC 27012
919-766-0591

Fayetteville Tech Community
  College
Fayetteville Rose Garden
Box 35236
Fayetteville, NC 28303
919-323-1961

Raleigh Municipal Rose Garden
301 Pogue Street
Raleigh, NC 29607
919-821-4579

Baxter and Doris Morgan
Route 3, Box 177
Rickwell, NC 28138
704-279-5646

NORTH CAROLINA (*continued*)

Wake Forest University
Reynolda Rose Garden
100 Reynolda Village
Winston-Salem, NC 27106
919-759-5593

OHIO

Stan Hywet Hall and Gardens
714 North Portage Path
Akron, OH 44303
216-836-0576

Columbus Park of Roses
3923 North High Street
Columbus, OH 43214
612-445-3350

Peter J. Zimmerman*
4141 West 217th Street
Fairview Park, OH 44126
216-331-6479

Home Garden
(Paul Jerabek)
10763 Beechwood Drive
Kirtland, OH 44026
216-256-1634

Ohio State University
Secrest Arboretum
1680 Madison Avenue
Wooster, OH 44691
216-263-3761

OKLAHOMA

J. E. Conard Municipal Rose
 Garden
Honor Heights Park
Forty-second Street and West
 Okmulgee Avenue
Muskogee, OK 74401
918-684-6302

Charles E. Sparks Garden
Will Rogers Park
3500 Northwest Thirty-sixth
 Street
Oklahoma City, OK 73112
405-495-6911

Tulsa Municipal Rose Garden
Woodward Park
Twenty-first Street and Peoria
 Avenue
Tulsa, OK 74114
918-747-2709

OREGON

Shore Acres State Park
13030 Cape Arago Highway
Coos Bay, OR 97420
503-888-3732

Avery Park Rose Garden
Avery Park Drive
Corvallis, OR 97333
503-757-6918

Owen Memorial Rose Garden
300 North Jefferson Street
Eugene, OR 97401
503-687-5334

International Rose Test Garden*
400 Southwest Kingston Avenue
Portland, OR 97201
503-823-3636

PENNSYLVANIA

Malcolm Gross Memorial Garden
2700 Parkway Boulevard
Allentown, PA 18104
215-437-7628

Hershey Gardens
Hotel Road
Hershey, PA 17033
717-534-3492

Longwood Gardens
Route 1, Box 501
Kennett Square, PA 19348
215-388-6741

Morris Arboretum
9414 Meadowbrook Avenue
Philadelphia, PA 19118
215-247-5777

Robert Pyle Memorial Rose
 Garden
Routes 1 and 796
West Grove, PA 19390
215-869-2426

SOUTH CAROLINA

Bynum Manor Roses
(Charles and Lephon Jeremias)*
2103 Johnstone Street
Newberry, SC 29108
803-276-8540

Edisto Memorial Gardens
200 Riverside Drive
Orangeburg, SC 29115
803-533-5870

SOUTH DAKOTA

Rapid City Memorial Rose Garden
444 Mount Rushmore Road
Rapid City, SD 57702
605-394-4175

TENNESSEE

Warner Park
1254 East Third Street
Chattanooga, TN 37404
615-757-5056

Memphis Botanic Garden
Audubon Park
750 Cherry Road
Memphis, TN 38117
901-685-1566

Robert and Glenda Whitaker Rose
 Garden*
1129 Overton Lea Road
Nashville, TN 37220
615-373-2835

TEXAS

Mabel Davis Rose Garden
Zilker Botanical Garden
2220 Barton Springs Road
Austin, TX 78746
512-477-8672

K. O. and Enola Collins
6980 Plant Road
Beaumont, TX 77708
409-898-0205

L. O. (Gator) Dollinger
3255 Blackmen Lane
Beaumont, TX 77703
409-892-4220

TEXAS (*continued*)

E. H. (Slats) Wathen
4780 Elmherst
Beaumont, TX 77706
409-892-2720

Samuell-Grand Municipal Rose
 Garden
6200 East Grand Boulevard
Dallas, TX 75223
214-670-8281

El Paso Municipal Rose Garden
1702 North Copia
(Copia and Aurora Streets)
El Paso, TX 79904
915-598-0771

Fort Worth Botanic Garden
3220 Botanic Garden Boulevard
Fort Worth, TX 76107
817-870-7686

Houston Municipal Rose Garden
1500 Hermann Drive
Houston, TX 77044
713-529-3960

A. J. Warner
3802 South Highlander
Orange, TX 77630
409-735-2130

Tyler Municipal Rose Garden
420 South Rose Park
Tyler, TX 75702
903-531-1213

Victoria Rose Garden
480 McCright Drive
Victoria, TX 77901
512-572-2767

UTAH

Utah Botanical Gardens
1817 North Main
Farmington, UT 84025
801-451-3204

Territorial Statehouse, State Park
50 West Capitol Avenue
Fillmore, UT 84631
801-743-5316

Nephi Federated Women's
 Rose Garden
100 East 100 North
Nephi, UT 84648
801-623-2003

House Park
Municipal Rose Garden
1602 East 2100 South Sugarhouse
 Park
Salt Lake City, UT 84106
801-467-0461

VIRGINIA

Bon Air Park
Bon Air Memorial Rose Garden
850 North Lexington Street
Arlington, VA 22205
703-358-3317

Lt. Col. and Mrs. William Soltis*
311 Gaines Mill Lane
Hampton, VA 23669
804-851-2535

Norfolk Botanical Garden
Airport Road
Norfolk, VA 23518
804-441-5831

WASHINGTON

Fairhaven Rose Garden
Chuckanut Drive
Bellingham, WA 98226
206-676-6801

Woodland Park Rose Garden
5500 Phinney Avenue North
Seattle, WA 98103
206-684-4803

Rose Hill
Manito Park
4 West Twenty-first Avenue
Spokane, WA 99203
509-456-4331

WEST VIRGINIA

The Palace Rose Garden
RD 1, Box 319
Moundsville, WV 26041
304-843-1812

Mr. and Mrs. Paul E. Sullivan
811 Echo Road
South Charleston, WV 25303
304-744-1486

WISCONSIN

Boerner Botanical Gardens
5879 South Ninety-second Street
Hales Corners, WI 53130
414-425-1130

FOR MORE INFORMATION

The world of rose growing is
continually expanding. The
following organizations keep their
members informed about new rose
varieties and the latest development in rose culture. They can also
put members in touch with local
groups and experts.

American Rose Society
Box 30,000
Shreveport, LA 71130
318-938-5402
*America's largest association of
amateur rose gardeners*

Heritage Rose Foundation
c/o Charles A. Walker, Jr.
1512 Gorman Street
Raleigh, NC 27606
*Information for growers and
fanciers of old garden roses*

Heritage Roses Group
c/o Miriam Wilkins
925 Galvin Drive
El Cerrito, CA 94530
*The original old-roses group,
founded in 1974*

MAIL-ORDER ROSE SOURCES

The following is a list of the leading mail-order rose nurseries in the United States and Canada. Most issue annual catalogs, which are available anytime from fall through early winter; order as soon as possible for the best selection for late winter or early spring delivery. In many cases there is no charge for the catalog, and once on a company's mailing list, you will remain on it as long as you continue to buy. Other nurseries charge a small fee for their catalogs. Most of the companies listed below are general nurseries, selling many different types of roses. Those that specialize are so indicated.

In addition to the major nurseries listed here, a number of small or specialty nurseries ship roses; and some wholesale nurseries are willing to ship large orders to private groups such as rose society chapters. A complete roster of U.S. and Canadian rose nurseries is compiled in a booklet called the *Combined Rose List,* which also contains an annotated listing of all rose varieties available for sale in the United States, Canada, and abroad; each annotation tells where the rose can be purchased. Revised annually, it is an invaluable guide for anyone with a serious interest in rose growing. The *Combined Rose List* is available from Beverly Dobson, 215 Harriman Road, Irvington, NY 10533.

NURSERIES

The Antique Rose Emporium
Route 5, Box 143
Brenham, TX 77833
Old garden roses

W. Atlee Burpee Company
300 Park Avenue
Warminster, PA 18974

Carroll Gardens, Inc.
Box 310
444 East Main Street
Westminster, MD 21157

Country Bloomers Nursery
Rural Route 2, Box 34A
Udall, KS 67146

Donovan's Roses
Box 37800
Shreveport, LA 71133-7800

Henry Field's Heritage Gardens
1 Meadow Ridge Road
Shenandoah, IA 51601

Gloria Dei Nursery
36 East Road
High Falls, NY 12240
Miniatures

Gurney Seed and Nursery
  Company
110 Capital Street
Yankton, SD 57079

Heirloom Old Garden Roses
24062 Riverside Drive NE
St. Paul, OR 97137
Old garden roses

Hortico, Inc.
723 Robson Road
Rural Route 1
Waterdown, Ontario L0R 2H1
Canada
Understock for budding; modern and old garden roses

Inter-State Nurseries
Catalog Division
Box 10
Department BN114L
Louisiana, MO 63353

Jackson and Perkins Company
One Rose Lane
Medford, OR 97501

J. W. Jung Seeds and Nursery
335 South High Street
Randolph, WI 53956

Justice Miniature Roses
5947 Southwest Kahle Road
Wilsonville, OR 97070
Miniatures

Kimbrew-Walter Roses
Route 2, Box 172
Grand Saline, TX 75140

Lowe's Own Root Roses
6 Sheffield Road
Nashua, NH 03062
Old garden roses

Milaeger's Gardens
4838 Douglas Avenue
Racine, WI 53402

Mini Roses of Texas
Box 267
Denton, TX 76202
Miniatures

Nor'East Miniature Roses
58 Hammond Street
Rowley, MA 01969
Miniatures

Carl Pallek and Sons Nurseries
Box 137
Virgil, Ontario L0S 1T0
Canada
Mail orders in Canada only; no shipments to the United States

Pickering Nurseries, Inc.
670 Kingston Road
Highway 2
Pickering, Ontario L1V 1A6
Canada

Pixie Treasures Miniature Rose
  Nursery
4121 Prospect Avenue
Yorba Linda, CA 92686
Miniatures

NURSERIES (*continued*)

The Rose Garden and Mini Rose
    Nursery
Box 203
Cross Hill, SC 29332

Rosehill Farm
Gregg Neck Road
Galena, MD 21635
Miniatures

Roses by Fred Edmunds, Inc.
6235 Southwest Kahle Road
Wilsonville, OR 97070

Roses of Yesterday and Today
803 Brown's Valley Road
Watsonville, CA 95076-0398
Old garden roses

Sequoia Nursery, Moore Miniature
    Roses
2519 East Noble Avenue
Visalia, CA 93277-3249
Miniatures

Spring Hill Nurseries
110 West Elm Street
Tipp City, OH 45371

Thomasville Nurseries, Inc.
Box 7
Thomasville, GA 31799

Tiny Petals Nursery
489 Minot Avenue
Chula Vista, CA 91910
Miniatures

Wayside Gardens
1 Garden Lane
Hodges, SC 29695

MISCELLANEOUS SUPPLIERS

Mitchells'
Box 521
Holmdel, NJ 07733
Potpourri supplies

Natural Gardening Research
    Center
Highway 48, Box 149
Sunman, IN 47041
Natural insect and disease controls

U.S. Measure and Metric Measure Conversion Chart

		Formulas for Exact Measures			Rounded Measures for Quick Reference		
	Symbol	When you know:	Multiply by:	To find:			
Mass	oz	ounces	28.35	grams	I oz		= 30 g
(Weight)	lb	pounds	0.45	kilograms	4 oz		= 115 g
	g	grams	0.035	ounces	8 oz		= 225 g
	kg	kilograms	2.2	pounds	16 oz	= I lb	= 450 g
					32 oz	= 2 lb	= 900 g
					36 oz	= 2¼ lb	= 1000g (1kg)
Volume	pt	pints	0.47	liters	I c	= 8 oz	= 250 ml
	qt	quarts	0.95	liters	2 c (I pt)	= 16 oz	= 500 ml
	gal	gallons	3.785	liters	4 c (I qt)	= 32 oz	= I liter
	ml	milliliters	0.034	fluid ounces	4 qt (I gal)	= 128 oz	= 3¾ liter
Length	in.	inches	2.54	centimeters	⅜ in.	= I cm	
	ft	feet	30.48	centimeters	I in.	= 2.5 cm	
	yd	yards	0.9144	meters	2 in.	= 5 cm	
	mi	miles	1.609	kilometers	2½ in.	= 6.5 cm	
	km	kilometers	0.621	miles	12 in. (I ft)	= 30 cm	
	m	meters	1.094	yards	I yd	= 90 cm	
	cm	centimeters	0.39	inches	100 ft	= 30 m	
					I mi	= 1.6 km	
Temperature	° F	Fahrenheit	⅝ (after subtracting 32)	Celsius	32° F	= 0° C	
	° C	Celsius	⅘ (then add 32)	Fahrenheit	212° F	= 100° C	
Area	in.²	square inches	6.452	square centimeters	I in.²	= 6.5 cm²	
	ft²	square feet	929.0	square centimeters	I ft²	= 930 cm²	
	yd²	square yards	8361.0	square centimeters	I yd²	= 8360 cm²	
	a.	acres	0.4047	hectares	I a.	= 4050 m²	